HUMANITIES, CULTURE, AND INTERDISCIPLINARITY

HUMANITIES, CULTURE, AND INTERDISCIPLINARITY

The Changing American Academy

JULIE THOMPSON KLEIN

STATE UNIVERSITY OF NEW YORK PRESS

Published by
State University of New York Press, Albany

© 2005 State University of New York

Printed in the United States of America

For information, address State University of New York Press,
194 Washington Avenue, Suite 305, Albany, NY 12210-2365

Production by Kelli Williams
Marketing by Susan Petrie

Library of Congress Cataloging-in-Publication Data

Klein, Julie Thompson.
Humanities, culture, and interdisciplinarity : the changing American academy / Julie Thompson Klein.
    p. cm.
Includes bibliographical references and index.
ISBN 0-7914-6577-2 (hardcover : alk. paper) — ISBN 0-7914-6578-0 (pbk. : alk. paper)
1. Humanities—Study and teaching (Higher)—United States. 2. Humanities—Philosophy. 3. Culture—Study and teaching—United States. 4. Education, Humanistic—United States. 5. Interdisciplinary approach to knowledge. 6. Learning and scholarship—United States. 7. Learned institutions and societies—United States. I. Title.
AZ183.U5K57 2005
001.3'071'173–dc22   2005001021

10 9 8 7 6 5 4 3 2 1

For George Klein

who embodies the vitality of humanities in public life

through his commitment to music and American culture

CONTENTS

ACKNOWLEDGMENTS

I am grateful for the conversations and resources that nurtured this book. Barbara Ashbrook and the recently departed Enayet Rahim hosted me on several trips to the National Endowment for the Humanities, affording access to the Endowment's library and in-house materials. Fred Schroeder of the University of Minnesota at Duluth supplied the entire backlist of the journal of the National Association for Humanities Education, providing a rare glimpse of sustained deliberation on the nature of interdisciplinary humanities. In conferring on me the post of Senior Fellow in 1997–98, the Association of American Colleges and Universities gave unparalleled access to leading thinkers on higher education. I especially thank the president, Carol Geary Schneider, and senior scholar and former vice president, Jerry Gaff.

For offering valuable suggestions on parts of an earlier draft, I thank William Newell of Miami University, Fran Shor of Wayne State University, and the anonymous reviewers. Beth Babini provided welcome secretarial help in preparing the manuscript, and Wayne State University granted me the most precious resources: time to complete the project, in the form of a sabbatical leave, and a rare academic home. The opportunity to incubate the ideas in this book with the Interdisciplinary Studies program's diverse adult student population has been vital to its development. They continue to teach me about the meaning and value of humanities in American life.

Finally, I am grateful to Kelli Williams, for valuable help as production editor, and James Peltz, for his generous and steadfast support of the book as Editor-in-chief of the Press.

Parts of chapters 3, 4, 7, and 8 are adapted from my previous book, *Crossing Boundaries: Knowledge, Disciplinarities, and Interdisciplinarities*. Grateful acknowledgment is made to the original publisher, the University of Virginia Press.

INTRODUCTION
Humanities, Culture, and Interdisciplinarity

This book investigates the relationship of three ideas in the American academy—humanities, culture, and interdisciplinarity. Of the three keywords, "humanities" and "culture" have a longer history. The English word "humanities" derives from an educational program introduced in ancient Rome under the heading of *humanitas*. The ancient Greeks did not speak of humanities per se, but devices for dealing with the accomplishments of humans were developed in the dialogues of Plato; Aristotle's treatises on logic, rhetoric, and poetics; and other writers' pronouncements on grammar, music, and higher learning. The Romans gave us the Latin root of the word, the subject as a distinct object and body of content, and a framework of terms and distinctions for discussing related issues (Crane 26–27). Italian humanists, who were the first to actually be called humanists, aligned the subject with works of classical antiquity in the curriculum of the *studia humanitatis*. During the sixteenth and seventeenth centuries, the discovery of new civilizations and rise of modern empirical science added to the general body of knowledge and, by the eighteenth and nineteenth centuries, the scope of humanities was expanding with scholarly interest in English and other languages, the new fields of comparative philosophy and folk- ?philology
lore, and recovery of the vernacular literatures of the Middle Ages.

As a result of this history, the word humanities carries many connotations. It stands for a tradition of knowledge and aesthetic expression that is vested in a canon of works and ideas. It invokes values of wisdom and normative qualities required for humane conduct, ethical decision-making, and civic responsibility. It designates skills of inquiry, communication, and reflection. It distinguishes particular objects, such as novels, paintings, musical compositions, philosophical and religious treatises, and historical documents. It labels specific subjects, especially literature, languages, the arts, music, philosophy, history, and religion. And, over the course of the twentieth century, it took on new meanings as disciplinary practices changed, new interdisciplinary fields arose, and the boundaries of humanities and social sciences were crossed.

"Culture," Raymond Williams commented when defining keywords in the vocabulary of culture and society, is one of the most complicated words in English. The Latin root *colere* had several connotations, ranging from inhabit and cultivate to honor with worship. The primary meaning of cultivation or tending passed into English and during the sixteenth century extended metaphorically from natural to human development. In the eighteenth century, the notion of culture as an abstract process or product of such a process took on class associations when it was aligned with"civilization," fostering the notion of becoming cultured or civilized. In the late eighteenth century, Johann Gottfried Herder objected to the universal histories of civilization or culture established by Enlightenment historians. Herder advocated "cultures" in the plural, including specific and variable cultures of different nations and periods as well as social and economic groups within a single nation. In the nineteenth century, this connotation was used in the Romantic movement to emphasize national and traditional cultures, including the new concept of "folk culture" (87–89).

Three categories of meaning emerged from this history: a general process of intellectual, spiritual, and aesthetic development; the way of life of a people, period, group, or humanity in general; and works and practices of intellectual and artistic activity. The latter connotation, which gained currency in the twentieth century, aligned culture with literature, painting and sculpture, music, theater and film, philosophy, history, and scholarship (Williams 90). Elite forms of Western history were initially privileged, though in the latter half of the century a broader social and anthropological meaning fostered interdisciplinary redefinition of the idea of culture in humanities.

The final word has a shorter etymology. The actual term "interdisciplinary" did not appear until the opening decades of the twentieth century. Roberta Frank argues the idea was born in the 1920s at the corner of 42nd and Madison Avenue, where the Social Science Research Council was located. The term was shorthand for research that crossed more than one of the Council's divisions (91). This is not the only origin story, however. Some date the beginning of interdisciplinarity to the general education and core curriculum movements that arose in the United States in the early twentieth century. Others point to the rise of area studies and American studies in the 1930s and 1940s. Some highlight problem-focused work in science and technology, beginning with agricultural and defense-related research in the 1940s. Others cite educational experiments in the 1960s and 1970s. Nowhere, though, is the genealogical reach of interdisciplinarity longer than it is in humanities. The underlying ideas of synthesis, holism, connectedness, and general knowledge developed in ancient Greek philosophy were transmitted throughout the history of liberal education. Along with the Renaissance tradition of *studia humanitatis,* these ideas were accorded central place in the first American college.

The ideas of humanities, culture, and interdisciplinarity converge with particular force in the concept of "American cultural studies." The term is enjoying currency in the field of American studies, driven by changes in the definition of culture and the burgeoning field of cultural studies. John Hartley highlights the thematics of identity, power, and culture in stimulating new practices that interrogate older notions of "America" using the critical, theoretical, and analytical tools of cultural studies (8). I talk about this development, at length. However, the study of culture in the American academy is not confined to a single field. It is a broad-based set of interests located within and across disciplines and interdisciplinary fields. Moreover, while this project requires examining changes in the way that *American* culture in particular is being studied, the current interdisciplinary reconfiguration of the idea of culture cannot be understood without also factoring in new understandings of European tradition and the global arena in the work of U.S. scholars and educators.

Why is a book on the triangulation of these three ideas needed? At a time when the phrase "increasingly interdisciplinary" has become commonplace, studies of interdisciplinary formations take on heightened importance. They are crucial to understanding the changing American academy, especially new scholarly activities and communities that redefine intellectual and institutional structures. Higher education has changed fundamentally. Yet, to echo Stephen Graubard's introduction to a recent collection of reports on the transformation of American academic culture, the changes are still insufficiently understood (vii). In the latter half of the twentieth century, humanists in this country also had a lot to say about interdisciplinarity and about culture. However, their commentaries are dispersed across disciplines, interdisciplinary fields, and writings on higher education and the nature of contemporary knowledge. Consequently, definition is an archaeological task, requiring a genealogical search for intersections of the three ideas and, in the course of that search, identifying both commonalities and conflicts in theory and in practice.

The Book

Part I establishes a framework for two subsequent sets of case studies. It begins when the American academy began, with the founding of Harvard College in 1636. The curriculum was a common prescribed core based on the Bible, the classical *trivium* of language-oriented arts, and the *quadrivium* of mathematical or scientific arts. The structural principles of this curriculum and accompanying philosophical principle of unitary knowledge shaped the programs of the other colonial colleges and, more generally, influenced thinking about higher education in this country for nearly two and a half centuries (Levine and Niddifer 54, 66–67; Hutcheson 105). In the late nineteenth and early twentieth centuries, humanities underwent a profound transformation. They assumed modern disciplinary form. Even as ancient subjects were becoming specialized domains, however, a group Lawrence Veysey called the "culture camp" of humanities asserted a competing vision. Its members upheld a model of spiritual idealism and social and moral education with deep roots in European intellectual history and English models of higher education ("Plural Organized Worlds" 53–54). In order to understand the view of knowledge and culture they endorsed, as well as competing models in the past and the present, chapter 1 traces precedents for the generalist model from the colonial college to the *studia humanitatis* of the Renaissance, the *humanitas* and *artes liberales* of ancient Rome, and the *paideia* of ancient Greece.

When the modern system of disciplinarity displaced the generalist model from the center of American academic experience, it found a new home in the general education movement that arose in the early twentieth century. From the beginning, though, two constructions of interdisciplinarity were apparent: one hearkening back to the colonial college and heritage of *studia humanitatis,* and the other engaging the present in a historically situated problem focus. New forms of interdisciplinarity also began to appear. Chapter 2 traces their emergence in a series of new developments that unfolded over the latter half of the century. This history extends from the importation of European philosophy and literary theories in the 1950s to social and political movements in the 1960s, structuralism and the language-based psychoanalysis of Jacques Lacan, newer kinds of Marxist criticism and deconstruction, and, in the 1970s and 1980s, widening interest in feminism and semiotics. Further into the 1980s, an array of practices lumped under the umbrella label of "poststructuralism" took root, including new historicism, Foucauldian studies of knowledge, and cultural and post-colonial critique. By the 1990s, multiculturalism had become a major thematic in research and education, and many proclaimed that humanities was evolving into cultural studies.

Interdisciplinarity was implicated at every turn. Each movement differed in some way, but together they fostered a new generalism that countered both the modern system of disciplinarity and the culture camp's vision of humanities. The new generalism was not a unified paradigm. It was a cross-fertilizing synergism in the form of shared conceptions of language, culture, and history. A new rhetoric of interdisciplinarity developed in turn. "Plurality" and "heterogeneity" replaced "unity" and "universality." "Interrogation" and "intervention" supplanted "synthesis" and "holism." And, older forms of "interdisciplinarity" were challenged by "anti," "post," "non," and "de-disciplinary" formulations. The keywords of the new rhetoric signaled the evolution of a general form of "critical interdisciplinarity" that challenged the existing structure of knowledge and education. Critical interdisciplinarity gained a certain orthodoxy in humanities. However, it is not the only formulation. Chapter 3 completes the foundation for the case studies by sorting out similarities and differences in theory, practice, and patterns of institutionalization.

Parts II and III explore the trajectories of interdisciplinarity in specific disciplines and fields. In Part II, the choice of literary studies (chapter 4), art history (chapter 5), and music (chapter 6) is deliberate, inviting comparison of the verbal, visual, and aural aspects of humanities and culture. Interdisciplinarity did not assume identical form in each domain. Nonetheless, there are significant parallels. At the dawn of the twentieth century, the historical warrants for interdisciplinarity in humanities were the generalist model of culture, a synoptic view of subjects, and the methodology of interart comparison. Period style was the most powerful basis for synchronic relation, grounded in common motifs, themes, and genres within historical eras. As disciplines moved away from older paradigms of historical empiricism and positivist philology, increasing attention was paid to the contexts of aesthetic works and the responses of readers, viewers, and listeners to those works. The concept of culture expanded from a narrow focus on elite forms to a broader anthropological notion, and once discrete objects were reimagined as forces that circulate within a network of forms and actions. The disciplinary categories of literature, art, and music have not been abandoned. Yet, their meaning has broadened to encompass more subject matter, conditions of production, and previously marginalized groups and other cultures. Interdisciplinarity also broadened in kind. Today, it spans a range of forms, from borrowing and interart comparison to "radical" and "de-disciplinary" critiques and the formation of new fields such as visual culture and jazz studies. Practices are often hybrid as well. Close reading of a novel or technical analysis of a painting or a musical composition may be combined with psychoanalytic, sociological, semiotic, deconstructionist, or feminist approaches.

Part III examines the trajectories of change in three fields that center on American cultural experience. The meaning of interdisciplinarity in American studies (chapter 7) has shifted since the field's institutional beginnings in the 1930s and 1940s. The current plurality of practices that were shaped by the new developments traced in chapter 2 have made American studies a crossroads of interests and approaches. Traditional humanistic methods are being combined with cultural anthropology and new ethnography, oral history, social history and the study of material culture, reader-response criticism, and new transnational perspectives on the concept of "America." American studies was an early home for scholars and teachers with interests in race and gender. In order to develop their interests fully, however, they had to forge new fields. Both African American and women's studies (chapter 8) were conceived as multipurpose. Interdisciplinarity connoted breaking down disciplinary boundaries, forging a self-defined epistemology, developing alternative structures and pedagogies, borrowing disciplinary methodologies, and performing political work and community service. Despite the pejorative taint that unity, holism, and disciplinarity have among proponents of critical interdisciplinarity, those concepts have had a strong resonance in African American and women's studies. These fields also reveal the current complexity of American cultural studies. Individuals who study American culture call themselves literary critics, historians, art historians, musicologists, and film and media critics, as well as Americanists, feminists, African Americanists, and members of other identity fields. In addition, many consider themselves involved in some way in cultural studies.

The conclusion returns full circle to the origin of humanities. Not only did many of the earliest writings center on education, the original curriculum of the American college was an undergraduate core that was deeply rooted in humanities. So, it is appropriate to ask in closing what impact new scholarly practices have had on humanities education and, in particular, on general education cores. National trendlines indicate that humanities education is becoming more collaborative across departments and programs, more comparative in the study of culture, and more inclusive of new materials, interdisciplinary scholarship, and women, minorities, and ethnic groups. Yet, the state of humanities is often dichotomized as a contest between a preservationist campaign to restore a traditional model of liberal education and a reformist campaign to forge a critical alternative. The actual practice of humanities education is far more variegated across the roughly 4,000 postsecondary institutions in the United States. Significant shifts in the representation of cultural history are occurring, but they not sweeping across the country as quickly or uniformly as either opponents or proponents claim. Contrary to allegations by opponents of reforms, Western tradition has not been jettisoned either. The content of traditional humanities remains central to core curricula organized around topic-based surveys of Western or world civilization. Nonetheless, in the 1980s and 1990s a new relational pluralism emerged, fostering interdisciplinary configurations that have expanded the nature of cultural study in the American academy.

Three themes cut across this book. The first is the disputed meaning of interdisciplinarity. In sorting out definitions and practices, I also address the second theme, the tendency of one discipline—literary studies—to generalize about humanities. I discuss literature and literary studies but also include a wider range of disciplines and fields. Only a comparative study can speak for "the other humanities." The third theme is the persistence of exaggerated claims and outright errors in discussions of interdisciplinarity. I counter totalizing statements about the homogeneity of disciplines that ignore the heterogeneity of practices, the dichotomizing of disciplinarity and interdisciplinarity at the expense of seeing one in the other, the naïve premise that interdisciplinary work entails an integration of entire disciplines, the outdated supposition that interdisciplinarity is a fad or fashion, and the tendency to hover at the level of theory with little or no attention to what is happening on the ground of practice. In defining the nature of practice, I also take up one of the most neglected topics in the literature—How does one actually *do* interdisciplinary work?

A single book cannot account for all the phenomena that define the complex relationship of humanities, culture, and interdisciplinarity. An entire volume could be written about one discipline, field, or an area of increased interest, the relationship between humanities and science and technology. I make choices, establishing a framework for others to use and adapt in their own projects. To the extent that another sphere is engaged, I consider the changing relationship between humanities and its nearest intellectual rival for the study of human culture and behavior, the social sciences (Wilson 59–60). Even with this narrowed scope, though, the book is intended for a wide audience. It will be of interest to scholars, educators, and students who study the nature of interdisciplinarity, humanities, and the individual disciplines and fields I discuss, as well as cultural studies and general, liberal, and humanities education. It will also be of interest to the staff of institutions that support humanities, including funding agencies, libraries and archives, publishing houses, and museums.

This breadth of audience creates a particular obligation in a book that aims to present an ethnography of current humanistic thought and the organization of knowledge in the American academy. To echo June Howard's introduction to her exemplary interdisciplinary study of the collaborative novel *The Whole Family*, any work that calls on a wide range of scholarship in multiple disciplines and fields requires conceptual maps of key issues and thick descriptions of historical periods, in order to synthesize what is known and to innovate. Matters that are well known in one discipline or field but not in others must be explained in a language that is accessible to nonspecialists in the family of humanities but also engages the expertise of the specialist (4, 11). Some readers will be familiar with parts of the early and contemporary histories brought together in this book. However, the links with interdisciplinarity have never been fully traced. Fragments and selected precedents, no matter how well informed, do not substitute for a shared syncretic understanding of the complementarities and tensions that constitute humanities, culture, and their interdisciplinary dynamics.

Part I

HISTORICAL WARRANTS

Chapter 1

FORMING HUMANITIES

This story begins in 1636. When the first institution of higher education opened in this country, humanities played a central role. Harvard College was a Puritan-based institution with a prescribed curriculum based on the Bible, the classical *trivium* of language-oriented arts, and the *quadrivium* of mathematical or scientific arts. Students learned Greek, Aramaic, Hebrew, and Syriac, along with logic and rhetoric, history and politics, astronomy and botany, ethics, and catechism. The philosophical complement to this common curriculum was the idea of unitary knowledge. Together, these structural and philosophical principles shaped the educational programs of the other colonial colleges and, more generally, influenced thinking about higher education in the United States for nearly two and a half centuries. The central mission of the American college was teaching in the European and English tradition. The students, who came primarily from the elite of colonial society, were trained to take their place in prestigious vocations. The faculty, who came primarily from the clergy, placed classical learning in a religious framework. Individuals offered recitations and lectures in specific subjects. However, they were not divided into separate schools or departments. A returning missionary might teach biology or a teacher of rhetoric do double duty in history, logic, or metaphysics (Levine and Niddifer 54, 66–67; Hutcheson 105; D. Bennett 132–33; Bogue and Aper 19–20; Kuklick, "Professionalization" 43).

Even though common principles would have a long-lasting impact, differences were already evident by the founding of the second colonial college in 1692. Modeled on the Scottish tradition of higher education, William and Mary placed greater emphasis on mathematics, history, and science. In the eighteenth century, new utilitarian curricula and chairs in the professions were introduced and, by the nineteenth century, new technical and vocational schools were being founded. Scientific investigation was also making inroads into the curriculum, modern and pragmatic courses were proliferating, and interest in vernacular languages was increasing. These changes prompted a prominent defense of tradition by Yale College faculty. The purpose of college according to the Yale Report of 1828 was to prepare students in "the disciplines and furniture of the mind." The term "disciplines" connoted expanding the powers of mental faculties and "furniture" filling the mind with knowledge. Since the founding of the colonial colleges, exercises in grammar and mathematics had been regarded as the best means of disciplining mental and moral faculties. The most important subject was the classics. Patient study of the grammar, syntax, and etymology of classical texts was considered the key to the spiritual essence of ancient Greece and Rome. Yale faculty rebuked critics of this tradition, faulted technical or partial courses of study, and dismissed popular studies, modern languages, and professional subjects (Levine and Niddifer 67–69; Hutcheson 106; Kuklick, "Professionalization"49; Kuklick, "Emergence" 202–05, 210; J. H. Miller, "Theory" 121).

Yet another change was on the horizon as well, one so profound that Laurence Veysey called it the first genuine academic revolution in the United States. Between 1870 and 1910, higher education was reorganized around twenty to twenty-five disciplines, each with its own department, major, and set of courses (D. Bennett 137). Even as disciplinarity was transforming American higher education, though, a group Veysey dubbed the "culture camp" of humanities upheld the values of the older American college. They extolled the Renaissance ideal of *litterae humaniores,* the social and moral purpose of education, spiritual idealism, and a conception of culture as process rather than research product. Some professors from social and natural sciences shared their views, but the culture camp was composed primarily of classicists and individuals from English literature and art history along with some philosophical idealists and college presidents. They preached a gospel of "civilization" and "cultivated generalism" that was also advanced by editors of literary monthlies, organizers of the fine arts in major cities, and an assortment of schoolmasters, authors, lawyers, clergy, artists, and performers (Vesey, "Plural Worlds" 53–54; Graff 85).

Gerald Graff dates the emergence of generalists as a distinct academic type to the 1870s. In adapting the old college ideal of liberal or general culture to modern times, they formed a dissenting tradition that fostered a kind of humanist myth. The divide between generalists and specialists was not absolute. They shared the same genteel social code. Specialists were expected to fulfill responsibilities for general education, and many of them held generalist views of literature, culture, and teaching. Theoretically, professional research was even a vehicle for general humanistic culture. The disciplinary "investigators" saw themselves as heirs of Matthew Arnold, who espoused a broad humanistic view of literature and culture. Few individuals or departments, however, successfully integrated the two. The gap between traditional ideals and professional practices would continue to widen and generalization lose favor (4, 55–56, 85).

Understanding the tension between the new disciplinary model of humanities and the culture camp's traditional view of knowledge and culture is a necessary first step in this study. The opening chapter addresses a series of related questions. What were the historical precedents for the generalist model? How were evolving constructions of humanities and liberal education linked with precedents for interdisciplinarity? What were the defining tensions in the emergence of interdisciplinarity as an explicit problem of knowledge? What subjects and methods dominated in the early history of humanities? How were humanities "disciplined" in America, and what impact did the new system of knowledge production have on traditional values of unity, holism, synthesis, connectedness, and general knowledge? When the general education movement arose in the early twentieth century, what principles of humanistic knowledge and culture were prominent in the first interdisciplinary models?

The Generalist Model

Warrants for the generalist model lie in a genealogy that extends from Matthew Arnold in the nineteenth century to the tradition of the American college, the *studia humanitatis* of the Renaissance, the *humanitas* and *artes liberales* of ancient Rome, and the *paideia* of ancient Greece. In speaking of a Greek contribution to modern thinking about humanities and interdisciplinarity, it is important to remember that neither concept existed in the ancient world. Archaeological salvaging of the past to anchor claims in the present sometimes borders on historical anachronism. Greek philosophers, though, developed a view of knowledge that promoted a broad synoptic outlook, harmonious unity of divisions, a holistic approach, and the value of general knowledge. Humanists today trace precedents for interdisciplinarity to these ideas in the roots of Western philosophy and writings about education. The Greek program of education evolved in the course of a gradual conversion of Greek culture from oral to written form. The core was epic poetry and drama, which had been the focus for ritual community activity and the formal oratory on which public debate and negotiations depended. Even after the concept of history replaced myth, Homer and Hesiod were still treated as repositories of ancient lore and moral wisdom, conferring on them the stature of precedent and a corresponding belief that knowledge resides within certain works (Grafton and Jardine 4–6).

The concept of *paideia* was central to the Greek program. Prior to Aristotle, there was only a general division between *paideia,* the studies forming part of a young gentleman's education, and more specialized higher studies for ages seventeen and older. The *paideia* included some forms of physical training; some study of music, poetry, dance, and, as Martha Nussbaum speculates, probably some form of political and social history as well. In this respect, it included part of what we now regard as humanities. The curriculum of the *enkuklios paideia* was neither utilitarian nor vocational. Nor did it include technical study of language or exacting varieties of historical inquiry, systematic and theoretical study of ethical and political questions, or the metaphysical, epistemological, and natural-scientific inquiries that lie at the heart of Greek philosophy. *Paideia* connoted human wisdom and its application for living a virtuous life, an idea that has been traced back to the fifth century B.C. Both meanings would become central to the ideas of humanities and liberal education. Humanists today also hearken back to another precedent. Founded in 387 B.C., Plato's Academy is often invoked as the first interdisciplinary school on the premise that it lacked subject boundaries. Plato did distinguish subjects when outlining a curriculum in *The Republic,* and his academy offered instruction in gymnastics, music, poetry, literature, mathematics, and philosophy. Yet, the experience promoted physical, moral, and social development of the "whole person." This concept became part of the legacy of integrative values in humanities, liberal education, general education, and many programs of interdisciplinary studies (Levine and Nidiffer 59; Nussbaum, "Historical Conceptions" 6–7; Hirst 30–31; Mayville 20; Mehl, "Why Define?" 4).

Even with these precedents, tension between unity and differentiation was apparent from the beginning. In the first century B.C., Dionysius of Halicarnassus complained that Greek higher education fostered premature specialization in rhetoric before students had completed the *enkuklios paideia.* In the Roman era, Cicero would also express concern about early overemphasis on rhetoric. Aristotle is usually associated with the beginnings of specialization. Aristotle distinguished two broad groups of inquiries: studies that were not systematized (ethical and political theory) and scientific studies in the sense of being systematized in a hierarchical deductive structure starting from first principles (encompassing natural sciences, metaphysics, general philosophy of nature, and, perhaps, general study of life or the soul). Aristotle further distinguished studies with a theoretical or a practical aim and in his own school, the Lyceum, sought a broader and more empirical basis for education than Plato. He also advocated the study of nature with a search for verification through evidence and observation. As a result, the study of objects and physical evidence became part of the notion of good education (Boudreau 34; Nussbaum, "Historical Conceptions" 6–7, 21; Levine and Niddifer 59).

Roman Adaptations

The ancient Romans did not make explicit contributions to the idea of interdisciplinarity, but their influence on our conceptualization of humanities was profound. They gave us the Latin root of the word, the subject as a distinct object and body of content, and a framework of terms and distinctions in which issues related to the subject are treated to this day. During the late Republic and early Empire, Romans formulated the discussion of arts in terms of which specific arts, studies, or disciplines are best suited to expressing and serving the needs of *humanitas* (humanity). Humanistic inquiry became associated with exploring the meaning and purpose of human existence expressed in particular symbolic modes. In his later writings, Cicero designated poetry, geometry, music, and dialectic as the arts that pupils should study to ensure that they achieve full humanity. These subjects were the basis for *artes liberales*. In the second century, the grammarian Aulus Gellius further stipulated that those who used Latin correctly, especially Cicero and Marcus Varro, did not give *humanitas* the meaning it was commonly thought to have—the Greek notion of *philanthropia,* connoting a friendly spirit and good feeling. They gave it the force of the Greek *paideia,* connoting education and training in the good arts. The goodness of the *bonas artes* lies in their adaptation to serving moral and practical ends, a purpose that became a cornerstone of humanities as well as liberal education and general education (Crane 23, 156; R. McKeon 162; Mehl, "Postmodern Humanism" 5).

The version of humanities that the Romans constructed drew on the Greek tradition, but it also met their needs and interests. When Romans became interested in Greek culture during the middle of the third century B.C., they adapted a program of education recommended by the teachers they consulted. They shared the Greek notion that certain texts provided insight into the *res magnae*—the great issues of truth, goodness, beauty, and justice that gave human existence its meaning and significance. They believed that careful study of texts conveyed a kind of normative and well-rounded general education. However, Roman teachers changed the emphasis. They simplified and restated in Latin portions of the Greek tradition that were most suited to their aims, accentuating a rhetorical, public, practical, prescriptive, and literary education over logic and mathematics. They also introduced indigenous Latin works into schools. Greek language and literature were still endorsed as the proper foundation for general wisdom. Yet, by the time of Quintilian, the emphasis was on the art of speaking correctly and literary interpretation of poets. Romans conceived of the liberal arts as a pre-professional form of education and compendia of information, not as methods of systematizing philosophy or organizing erudition. Cicero and Quintilian's primary goal was educating the role model of the public man—the orator. A command of oral and written communication was considered essential preparation for influencing public opinion and policy and for serving the state (R. McKeon 162–64; Crane 157; Grafton and Jardine 4–7; Mehl, "Why Define?" 4).

The Roman formulation of the Greek *enkuklios paideia* was the *disciplinae liberae,* and the foundation of the Roman *artes liberales* was grammar, understood as study of literature and language. Varro listed nine liberal arts: the *trivium* of grammar, rhetoric, and dialectic; and the *quadrivium* of arithmetic, music, geometry, and astronomy; plus medicine and architecture. Arithmetic, geometry, and astronomy were not formal or theoretical disciplines in the manner of Plato and Aristotle. Romans treated them as bodies of facts that supplied the orator with useful words and matter. Comparably, music was sometimes studied as practical training for the ear and voice and as an aid to appreciating poetry, but not as a formal and theoretical science. Logic, or dialectic, provided skeletal arguments for speeches, but rhetoric was the primary art because it supplied methods of constructing persuasive arguments and eloquent discourse on any topic (Levine and Niddifer 61; Mehl, "Postmodern Humanism" 5; Crane 26, 156–57; Kimball 4–5).

The word *liberalis* had two connotations. The older meaning, dominant in Seneca's Rome, connoted "fitted for freedom" in the sense of initiating freeborn gentlemen of propertied classes into the traditions of their society. This connotation discouraged critical reflection. The second and new meaning, favored by Seneca, differed. Education would only be truly fitted for freedom if it produced citizens who could call their minds their own. This capacity was to be gained through study of the subjects and methods best suited for enlightened decision-making, whether individuals were slave or freeborn, rich or poor, male or female. The second connotation would be modified to accommodate new forms of knowledge, such as Christian doctrine and modern science. It would be redirected, in the Renaissance equation of liberal education with classical learning. It would be opposed on philosophical grounds, by Dewey and the pragmatists. Yet, it has reappeared throughout the history of humanities, liberal education, and general education (Nussbaum, *Cultivating* 293; Hirst 31–32).

Recovery and Revival

Italian humanists were the first to actually be called humanists. The word *umanista* was Latin slang for scholars and teachers of *studia humanitatis* in Italian universities of the late fifteenth century. Like the members of American culture camp, Italian humanists looked to tradition. The Italian *humanitatis* countered the technical practice of scholasticism in the late medieval period. In the early Middle Ages, Augustine and other Christian writers adapted the Greek program of education to the ideas of Christianity in an effort to create a harmonious unity. During the twelfth and thirteenth centuries, dialecticians at the Cathedral Schools of Reims and Chartres and in the newly emerging institution of the university shifted the focus of liberal arts education toward rational analysis of texts. Rhetoric faded in importance, and grammar was transmuted into a narrow *scientiae speculativae* that privileged logic. They also redirected mathematics and music toward abstract number. The *Summae* of Thomas Aquinas exemplified the scholastic method. Questions of faith and reason were systematically addressed in summaries of theology and secular learning that were incorporated within theological treatises. The distinguishing trait of the Christian synthesis was not the broad *sapientia* of human wisdom. Syllogistic use of dialectical arguing in disputations, accompanied by reading sacred scriptures and biblical commentaries, became the norm (Roberts and Turner 75; Kimball 5–7;

Mehl, "Liberal Arts" 38; Mehl, "Postmodern Humanism" 4; Levine and Nidiffer 64; Levin 8; Kuklick, "Professionalization" 43; Kuklick, "Emergence" 202; Kockelmans, "Science and Discipline" 32, 34).

In contrast, Italian humanists emphasized ideals of liberal culture and education, reviving the notion of humanities suggested by Cicero. When the poet Petrarch hearkened back to ancient writers and the architectural ruins of classical Rome in the mid-fourteenth century, he found personal solace and a model for cultural and political renewal that later writers would dub the "Renaissance." Italian humanists did not use the term. Familiarity with ancient Roman culture and eloquence in Latin became preferred preparation for public affairs among the elite patricians who controlled most North and Central Italian states. By the mid-fifteenth century, humanistic courses were part of the curriculum in Italian universities and spread subsequently to northern Europe, where Erasmus became humanism's most prominent representative. From the Renaissance forward, humanities were increasingly institutionalized as a subject and a discipline. Italian teachers of grammar and rhetoric shifted the focus from the ideal product of classical education to classroom aids codified in textbooks, manuals, and instructional drills. Many were also in religious orders and worked on ecclesiastical reform, theological *aggiornamento,* and canonical texts. Yet, they distinguished *studia humanitatis* from *studia divinitatis.* Since the Renaissance, the word "humanity" has delimited certain subjects or arts from theology or divine studies. Humanities became imbued with secular import and the idea of humanism aligned with classical antiquity in general and intellectual and artistic life in particular. Noble ideals were not necessarily matched in practice, however. The most perceptible result was the growing number of individuals fluent in ancient languages and, in the classroom, grammatical issues and textual detail (Mehl, "Postmodern Humanism" 4–6; Crane 155; Levin 8; Grafton and Jardine 62, 122–25; Kockelmans, "Science and Discipline" 32).

Like its Roman counterpart, the Renaissance humanities was a literary education. Since ancient times, literature has been a vehicle for moral education. Until the late nineteenth century, the study of literature in American colleges and elsewhere was ancillary to the study of something else—especially Greek and Latin languages and rhetoric, oratory, and forensics. The word "literature" encompassed a broad range of meanings, from polite letters and poetry to any writings. The narrower connotation of imaginative writing did not emerge until the late eighteenth century. In the fifteenth century, the program of *humaniora* was a well-defined cycle of disciplines that included grammar, rhetoric, poetry, history, and moral philosophy based on careful reading in Latin of Roman and to a lesser extent Greek authors. The impulse toward interdisciplinarity in this era has been attributed in large part to an education that cultivates breadth of learning. The role model of a humanist was an *uomo universale*, polymath, *cortegiano*, *bonnete homme*, and scholar-gentleman adept at arms and well read in a wide range of subjects. During the medieval era, the classical model of rhetorical and literary learning was amplified with Christian ethics and a social etiquette of courtesy inherited from the tradition of knighthood. These three traditions coalesced to produce an ideal of Christian gentility that became the archetype of a liberally educated person in sixteenth- and seventeenth-century England and in the American colonies. Interdisciplinarity has also been linked with a new institutional formation. Lectureships and chairs for eloquence and poetry were established bearing the titles *literrae humanae, literrae humanitatis, studia de humanita, lectras de humanidad,* and *humanity.* These chairs, though, were more "pre-disciplinary" than "interdisciplinary" in the modern sense (Graff 19; Kockelmans, "Science and Discipline" 32; Mehl, "Liberal Arts" 38; Kernan, *Literature* 13).

The Terms of Modern Relation

The emergence of interdisciplinarity as an explicit problem of knowledge is linked with the rise of modernity. The beginning of the modern era is disputed, but it is conventionally associated with the ascendancy of science and technology, secularization and urbanization, emergence of the nation-state and capitalist world market, the study of contemporary languages and works, and the growing autonomy of disciplines. The latter development had an especially powerful impact. When the unity found in the classical and humanistic tradition could no longer be assumed, Wilhelm Vosskamp explains, interdisciplinarity emerged as a modern problem of *Wissenschaft.* From the sixteenth century forward, a series of attempts at producing or bringing out unification appeared in the work of Comenius, Leibnitz, d'Alembert, Kant, Hegel, and Wilhelm von Humboldt. The most direct expression of the wish for unity was the early Romantic notion of *Symphilosophie,* which attempted to produce unity in *mythos.* Philosophical and mythological concepts were not phrased explicitly in terms of interdisciplinarity. Yet, their subject was put forward as a theory capable of unifying all *Wissenschaft* and *Wissenschaften* ("Scientific" 20, "Crossing" 45). In the seventeenth century, discussion of the ages of learning also promoted cultural history as a general framework of differentiated periods with defining characteristics or conditions. Periodization became a master narrative for the cultural coherence of an era and the interdisciplinary practice of interart comparison (Mitchell, *Picture Theory* 85–86).

Michael McKeon dates the origin of interdisciplinary studies to the eighteenth century. At the time, subjects were assuming increasingly distinct identities. The relationship between the divine and the human was being secularized. The subjective act of knowing was being separated from its objects. The sphere of aesthetic judgment was being delimited from contingencies of social, political, and economic interests. The material and institutional conditions that gave modern divisions of knowledge a sociopolitical foundation were being put into place, including curricular reform and professionalization. And, efforts were being made to historicize knowledge as a modern inheritance of ancient practice and to map it as a logical and genealogical system. At the same time, a synthesizing countermovement was apparent, aimed at providing a foundation for a unified scheme based on analogy, continuity, casual interconnections, and contextual relations. Even as the "aesthetic" and "free enterprise" were becoming distinct categories, artistic expression and economic behavior were embedded in a network of social, political, and ethical concerns. The satirist Jonathan Swift connected madness and the theory of sublimation to realms of empire, philosophy, religion, poetic convention, female beauty, and human pride. Alexander Pope explored a theory of ideology that situated poetry in its socioeconomic context as a coordination of aesthetic value and exchange. The force of Pope's insight into the commodity status of poetry depended on the premise that economy and poetry were divergent spheres. These discourses, McKeon cautions, were only rudimentary exercises in interdisciplinarity. Bodies of knowledge were not sufficiently detached to permit bringing the expertise of one discipline methodologically to bear on the matter of another. Nevertheless, the basic structure of interdisciplinary operation was already visible as an inseparable implication of disciplinary thought.

Two other responses to the problem of differentiation, Vosskamp adds, were at work. A pragmatic attitude developed toward reciprocal borrowing between neighboring disciplines, and interdisciplinary cooperation was increasingly institutionalized. The founding of scientific academies in the seventeenth century was a decisive event in the formation of modern knowledge. At first, no formal internal differentiation between fields was attempted. In the second phase, differentiation was made for the sake of discussion and research in specific fields. In the third phase, groups began to form in a retraction of differentiation, although the philosophical problem of unity was usually subordinate to the progress of knowledge achieved by applying *Wissenschaft* and technology. Disintegration of the given and the philosophically grounded unity of knowledge offered opportunities for new combinations that proved productive. The search for interdisciplinarity, however, would be framed increasingly as a limited endeavor. Both theoretically and practically, the problem of unity was no longer readily solvable ("Scientific" 21).

Science and Modern Works

The changing prospects for disciplinary relations were further evident in a project that marks the contrast between the medieval and the modern eras—Diderot's *Encyclopédie*. The goal of this quintessential Enlightenment project was to gather all of the learning available to arts and sciences. However, the French Encyclopedists criticized the classical conception of humanities and, while unity remained an ideal, they were mindful of the pragmatic difficulties of realizing it. The "encyclopedia" was just that, a compendium that aligned varied parts of knowledge. Francis Bacon invoked the image of a common source. He even considered science and humanistic arts to be parts of an organic whole that reflected the unity of the human mind. Yet, Bacon acknowledged that individual fields were no longer nourished by a single force. The *Encyclopédie* also asserted a new priority. The Greek *paideia* encompassed virtually everything known scientifically at the time, at least to the degree thought relevant to educating citizens. From classical antiquity through the Middle Ages, everything that could be known scientifically was considered part of a harmonious unity of the *kosmos* that could be discovered and made explicit in systematic fashion. In the Middle Ages, art and science continued to be roughly interchangeable concepts and, even in the Renaissance, science was viewed as a means to ends that were not strictly scientific. For Diderot and Bacon, though, empirical science was the new basis of universality. The common fountain was natural philosophy and the science of nature the most basic discipline (Crane 56, 59, 67; Kockelmans, "Science and Discipline" 33; Durbin 127–28).

Scientists continued to embody the generalist model. Joseph Priestly, best known for his contributions to chemistry and electricity, also wrote on philosophy, theology, government and politics, history, linguistics, and literature. Yet, the terms of relation had undergone a seismic shift. Renaissance conceptions of humanities came increasingly into conflict with doctrines of science and learning oriented to principles and methods of natural philosophy. The study of languages and literature was pitted against "real," "solid," and "useful" knowledge acquired by direct inspection. Elegance and correctness of style, along with improved taste in poetry, were no match for principles of child rearing and the laws of health. Humanities were deemed useless, unprogressive, and, in the young United States, poorly suited to the needs of democracy. After Immanuel Kant, unity of science was largely given up. During the twentieth century, the Unity of Science movement made a truncated effort to unify the rational and empirical domains through logical positivism, and the search for unifying principles in science continues to this day. Yet, these and other efforts are framed by limits. In the seventeenth and eighteenth centuries, the realm of science was becoming broader and more complex than the classical *kosmos*. Even if they believed God created the cosmos as a rational unity, influential thinkers conceded they could only know what was accessible through scientific study of the way things appeared (Crane 73, 123; Kockelmans, "Why Interdisciplinarity" 152).

Wilhelm Dilthey's distinction between natural or scientific knowledge (*Naturwissenschaften*) and human or cultural knowledge (*Geisteswissenschaften*) was a benchmark of the growing divide. The latter "human studies" or "human sciences" included history, psychology, economics, anthropology, sociology, and politics. In contrast to the nomothetic purpose of natural sciences, formulated as a systematic search for general laws, cultural sciences were deemed idiographic, focused on understanding (*verstehen*) of unique and particular events, situations, and personalities. Dilthey's approach to history and humanistic studies, Marjorie Garber suggests, is vital to our modern notion of interdisciplinarity. The time had passed, Dilthey reflected in 1903, when there could be an independent philosophy of art, religion, law, or the state. Garber considers his reflection a "predisciplinary interdisciplinary moment" (Mehl, "Liberal Arts" 39–40; Garber 94–95, 166n67).

The pressing weight of modern works was an added benchmark of change. During the eighteenth and nineteenth centuries, classical studies remained the basis of liberal education in Europe and America. As late as

1850, the term "humanities" still indicated principally the study of Greek and Latin, with close attention to grammar. Yet, modern writings and vernacular languages, along with the discovery of new continents and civilizations and the development of science and technology, broadened the scope of knowledge and heightened awareness of changing historical circumstances. By 1870, a further distinction between classical study and "literary culture" or "liberal culture" was becoming apparent even in traditional colleges in the U.S. and, in turn, the notion of "humanities" in plural form became attached to the broadening idea of "liberal culture." By 1990, "humanities" meant a range of culture studies that included literature, philosophy, art history, and often general history. Greek and Latin also took on the label of "classics" in the mid-nineteenth century, along with a new literary orientation and cultivating aim (Roberts and Turner 75).

At first, modern works were admitted begrudgingly into the curriculum, with the exception of textbooks on grammar or rhetoric and handbooks in logic and philosophy. By the eighteenth century, a palpable tension was apparent. The fervor of debate was signified by the Battle of the Books, also known as the Quarrel of the Ancients and the Moderns. By the late nineteenth century, modern works were gaining status as new classics, and humanities remained by and large text-based. Since the eighteenth century, the writing of poetry has been distinguished from rhetoric and classified as a "fine art." So have music, painting, sculpture, and drama. This transformation of meaning appears in Kant's writings and systems derived from it. Kant deemed humanities "purposive," intended to persuade. The fine arts were "nonpurposive," intended to edify or entertain. As a result, rhetoric remained humanistic, while poetry became a fine art. Following Dilthy, Otto Bird also distinguished language arts (the old *trivium*) from subjects dealing primarily with the great concerns of human life (Cicero's *res magnae*), especially literature, history and philosophy (Mehl, "Why Define?" 4–5; Kockelmans, "Science and Discipline" 33; R. McKeon 160).

The practical goal of how disciplines could be utilized as guides to individual and social action did not disappear. It became subordinate, though, to the question of how the particularity of material could be illuminated. The characteristic effort, R. S. Crane explains, was a kind of organic unification of principles and methods thought common to humanities. The new unity that emerged took two main forms, depending on whether emphasis fell on materials and devices of the arts or on natural characteristics of the mind to which all arts are addressed and from which they draw materials to produce their effects. In one form of unification, rhetoric tended to assume the role of an architectonic art with respect to other arts that borrowed its devices or assimilated its ends. In the other form, philosophers tried to infuse a generalizing and abstract philosophical spirit and universal principles into disciplines (72–89, 102–11).

The Disciplining of American Humanities

The disciplining of knowledge was not a new phenomenon. Between the mid-seventeenth and late–eighteenth centuries, physics, biology, and chemistry began assuming separate identities. By the mid-nineteenth century, social sciences were segmenting into anthropology and economics, followed by psychology, sociology, history, and political science. Ironically, though, since they include the oldest subjects, humanities were the last to assume modern disciplinary form (Easton 11). Our present conception of humanities, Veysey and Bruce Kuklick found in tracing their early history in America, did not emerge until late—according to Veysey, not until after World War I. Use of the term humanities for a particular set of disciplines came about slowly. It was not widely employed as an intellectual or academic category before 1900. It did not enjoy strong resonance as an organic division of knowledge. From the 1560s to 1860s, there is little or no evidence that students thought consciously about whether they were studying humanities per se, and between 1870 and 1940 few book titles bore the name. More often, the terms "culture" and "liberal education" were used. The disciplines that bonded together in order to defend themselves intellectually and bureaucratically against the encroaching natural and social sciences were the "least worldly leavings" in the university, with the exception of the portion located in divinity schools. Interests in personality and society once explained by myth, theology, and philosophy were relocated to social sciences. Humanities assumed responsibility for "eternal truths" and an aestheticized study of civilization legitimated by the intrinsic purity of scholarship for its own sake (Veysey, "Plural Worlds" 55–57, 94n16, 96n40; Kuklick, "Professionalization" 51–53; Kuklick, "Emergence" 209–10; Putzell 197–98; Wilson 60–61).

The breakup of moral philosophy was a major event in the formation of modern humanities. When social sciences branched off from the broad field of moral philosophy, the remaining part, known as "intellectual philosophy," was composed of logic, epistemology, and metaphysics. Philosophy and psychology developed out of this branch. Philosophy was not new. It was taught in some form in the early colonial colleges, but it was transformed with the introduction of Scottish moral philosophy in the late eighteenth century and its later entry into the disciplinary humanities. By the start of the twentieth century, English literature had replaced Latin and Greek as "the backbone" of humanities in the American academy. History, which played a minor belletristic role in the nineteenth-century college, grew rapidly as an independent discipline that absorbed aspects of politics and economics with a past dimension. History's ambiguous identity as a social science or a member of humanities stems from its association with moral philosophy and literary inquiry. After the Civil War, history spread quickly throughout American higher education, though with more of a utilitarian bent than the model of liberal culture. Belles lettres ("fine letters" or "literary studies") were admitted late into the academy as electives, and introduced the subject of vernacular literature into universities for the first time. They were equivalent to beaux arts ("fine arts") and, in the eighteenth century, connoted literature or even the whole of humanities. Ancient languages were still regarded as a prerequisite to any learned endeavor, but their hegemony eroded in the nineteenth century, with Greek and Latin acquiring the new label "classics." Art and music lagged behind in the transformation into separate departments, though by 1920 they were well established at most better universities and colleges. Like literature, art history took on connotations of "culture" and "humanities." Music as a member of humanities and comparative literature made appearances in the late nineteenth century but did not emerge fully into the academy of disciplines until decades later (Garber 15; Kuklick, "Professionalization" 50–51; R. McKeon 169; Veysey, "Plural Worlds" 58, 64; Roberts and Turner x–xi, 21, 76–79, 86; Guillory 20).

The disciplining of humanities was reinforced by professionalization. Early learned societies patronized a general form of civic humanism that fused Christian principles and classical ideals, including the Platonic notion of striving toward humanity in a unified view of natural, human, and divine forms of knowledge. With the exception of groups devoted to particular professions, these organizations continued to reflect a wide range of interests until the early nineteenth century. The membership of the American Philosophical Society (APS), for instance, included political and civic leaders, academicians, physicians, lawyers, clergy, artisans, merchants, and "gentlemen scientists." During the eighteenth and nineteenth centuries, a cluster of other institutions in cities also nurtured intellectual interests, including philosophical and historical societies, libraries and museums, the Chautauqua lecture circuit, women's clubs, and publication and performance networks. The academy, though, became the sanctioned site of humanistic endeavor. As basic science gained favor over practical improvement, literary and philosophical components of organizations such as the APS diminished, and older learned societies were soon outnumbered by new organizations identified with specialized subjects. By the mid-twentieth century, fewer private individuals were engaged in humanistic scholarship, amateur intellectuals lessened in number, and even creative artists were gravitating toward academic institutions. The growing bureaucracy of the academy echoed the larger division of labor in society, marked by general bureaucratic characteristics such as self-maintenance, inertia, and orientation to rules (McCorison 249, 251–55; T. Bender, "Erosion" 85–86, 88; Kuklick, "Professionalization" 48; Veysey, "Plural Worlds" 65–66; Stone 16; Swoboda 79).

Faculty, in turn, distinguished themselves increasingly from the heterogeneous world of amateurs and popularizers. Their annual meetings became the locus for presenting research in a language that differed from popular and general learned discourse (Swoboda 72). The terms "amateur" and "professional," Garber cautions, are never fully equal. They are always "in each other's pockets," producing and defining each other by mutual affinities and exclusions. The word "amateur," though, was increasingly juxtaposed to academic endeavors (5). Even in history, where the tradition of amateur scholar continues, a member of the clergy or a lawyer did not hold the same status as a graduate-school trained historian (Kuklick,"Emergence" 208). Professional distinction was reinforced by a new prototype based on the German research university. It offered advanced training in research and scholarship supported by a comprehensive system of libraries, material resources, and specialized programs. Americans studying in Germany brought back the model of a research university, although the German academic environment differed. The broad, contemplative concept of German *Wissenschaft* connoted a connected search for truth and all-encompassing idealism and sense of unity. Returning Americans interpreted the concept more narrowly, emphasizing "pure research" over "pure learning," scientific aims, and the production of new knowledge. Founded in 1876, Johns Hopkins University was the prototype for the American version, complete with laboratories and technical studies kept outside the historical college, plus such defining genres of scholarship as the thesis and dissertation, scholarly article, and graduate seminar (Flexner 103; Graff 57; Swoboda 59; Oleson and Voss xvii–xviii; Russell 47).

The disciplining of humanities was further reinforced by the growing scientification of knowledge. The attempt to orient humanities toward a science of things began in the early nineteenth century, initially in Germany and in linguistics. Philology was the first dominant paradigm in the newly disciplined humanities. Dating to Plato, the term was revived in 1777 by Friedrich Wolf at the University of Göttingen. Philology embodied a different rationale for studying vernacular literature than the generalist goal of cultivating gentlemen. Introduced into the American university at the same time departments of vernacular languages were being established, it became a precondition for work in the American learned tradition. Language was central to understanding the nature of human culture and reality, and philology was the most powerful approach to studying language. The prevailing practice was a form of grammatical study that differed from the normative and philosophical grammar of the eighteenth century. Scholars aimed to construct a comparative history of languages classified into families of Indo-European, Germanic, and other branches. Like the tenets of classical study, the tradition of philology implied a larger cultural vision, an *Altertumwissenschaft* aspiring to a total view of civilization and a method capable of integrating the "humane" disciplines. Modern language scholars, who promoted their subjects as an updated form of mental discipline, invoked the names of nineteenth-century scholars who viewed philology as "the whole study of the history of cultures" entered through the study of texts and background contexts of a period style. However, the new specialists emphasized philological science over a comprehensive and speculative view. Academic theologians also took up philology as a professional method for understanding the Bible, with mastery of Greek, Latin, and Hebrew considered the key to comprehending sacred texts (Crane 139; Graff 69, 72; J. H. Miller, "Theory" 123; Kuklick, "Professionalization" 51; Kuklick, "Emergence" 209; Roberts and Turner 97).

Adding to the sum of knowledge became the professional business of humanists and, James Stone summarizes, four characteristics of scholarship that were prominent in the late nineteenth century became canonical in the twentieth century. Discovery became the primary purpose. Scholarship underwent secularization and professionalization. A system of analytic abstraction was developed, and the presumption of neutrality with respect to the value of humanistic objects was cultivated. The tendency toward painstaking research and minute methodology became as evident in historiography as in science. The humanist's equivalent of the laboratory was analytic abstraction, reinforced by description, classification, comparison, and compilation. Like laboratory specimens, humanistic objects could be manipulated, dissected, and embalmed; measured, counted, and calibrated; and subjected to precise methodologies. A credo, a comedy, a portrait, an idea, or a hero could be subdivided by analysis and abstraction into the propositions of philosophers, the techniques of literary and art historians, and the events of historians. The contents of teaching, especially at entry level, were not necessarily connected with products of advanced research. Nevertheless, scholars in growing numbers embraced ideals of scientific objectivity, precision, and specialization. Humanism remained a stated goal. The heightening of professional tasks, though, marginalized general knowledge. As experts developed increasingly esoteric investigations, the notion of a shared culture diminished. Decentralization and fragmentation of education hastened. Older unified fields of inquiry began decomposing under centrifugal forces of differentiation. Older unitary principles of the university eroded, and new unifying hypotheses were foreshortened (15).

A New Home for the Generalist Model

By the end of the 1880s, academic humanists were split into two camps. One advocated advanced research and specialization, while the other identified with culture (Veysey, "Plural Worlds" 53). In England, the most prominent defenders of liberal humanism and the generalist model were William Whewell, Cardinal Newman, John Stuart Mill, and Matthew Arnold. Arnold's ideas about the social function of literary studies, in particular, were widely diffused during the nineteenth century. Reasserting the organic wholeness of human nature, Arnold countered narrow sectarianism in religion, excess practicality and provincialism, the "anarchy" of individualism, and the distrust of standards among middle-class "Philistines." His canon of "the best that has been thought and said in the world" was neither systematic philosophy nor narrow grammatical or literary study. It was a general education encompassing polite literature, Greek science, mathematics, and poetry, and the writings of Copernicus, Galileo, Newton, Darwin, Shakespeare, and Goethe. Arnold located human powers of intellect and knowledge, beauty, social life, conduct, and manners in the interrelations of those powers and the generality of the species. This belief was institutionalized in the teachings and writings of distinguished Americans who advocated broad study of documents and writers (Crane 45, 141–47, 150–53).

Even so, literature and history asserted dominance in the cause of liberal education and as the core subjects of "liberal culture." In North America, classics were never rooted as deeply as they were at Oxford and Cambridge. Philosophy was not in a strong position either. To this day, in fact, departments of history and of literature make up a sizable proportion of humanities faculty. The conceptual category of humanities, W. B. Carnochan found in reviewing the period from 1884 to 1909, gave literature a kind of "protective cover" and a "halo of the sacred." The underlying premises were evident in Irving Babbitt's 1908 book *Literature and the American College: Essays in the Defense of the Humanities*. A teacher of French, Babbitt promoted a view that became known as new humanism, despite his personal objection to the term. Babbitt opposed Rousseau, Spencer, Darwin, and the elective system introduced by Harvard President Charles Eliot to allow students greater freedom of choice. The proper model of humanities, Babbitt contended, was Harvard's *Honors in Literature* course. Classical and modern literatures were combined, knowledge of one ancient and one modern language besides English required, and literature and appreciation privileged over research, philology, and history. When Babbitt and Paul Elmer promoted new humanism during the 1920s, one of their objectives in invoking the humane universal truths embodied in literature was to guard against intrusions of historical scholarship and the narrow interests of practical reform (Carnochan 55–56, 59, 63–69; Roberts and Turner 93).

The need for a broad basis of studies, Roberts and Turner also found in studying this period, became a "talisman" of humanities. Breadth alone did not provide coherence in the cause of cultivating humanistic "sympathies." The notion of continuity linked the broadly conceived "poetry" of one era to succeeding periods. This notion evolved from the idea of "universal civilization." The cultural distinctiveness and continuity of Europe, in particular, were reinforced by a pedagogical concept of civilization that reasserted the primacy of culture over nature. Together, the notions of civilization and culture filled a vacuum left by the disintegration of moral philosophy. Traceable from Greece through the present, the historical line was not static, since the principle of development inferred maturation of ideas. Yet, enduring basic human characteristics played a central role in historically based educational programs. The notion of humanities, in turn, provided a kind of integration or at least a broad understanding that counteracted specialized studies. It was not a mere copy of precedents, however. The classical curriculum emphasized discipline of mind. The new model of "culture" valued development of imagination and broadening humanistic sympathies. It differed from moral philosophy as well. Moral philosophy acquainted students with a range of human and natural sciences in a scheme linking all knowledge. The new generalist model was vested in a "poetic" tradition constructed from literary, artistic, religious, and philosophical works. Individual programs might develop in different forms. Still, they shared the same cultural and culturing agenda of humanities by broadening sympathies, deepening understanding of the human condition, infusing ideals, and performing the role of the older course in moral philosophy. With the academic displacement of religion, humanities also became the principal bearer of the spiritual and moral meanings of higher learning (102–08).

On the heels of the growing displacement of liberal humanism from the center of American higher education, the generalist model found a new home in the general education movement that arose in the early twentieth century. The movement responded to several problems of culture and education, including a declining sense of national unity, proliferating vocational and individual interests, the negative consequences of specialization, and the eroding cohesiveness of undergraduate education (Boyer 4–5). General education, Richard McKeon recalled, promised a new effectiveness and content for liberal education. It was intended to rediscover the arts that make humans free, the arts needed to understand the problems they face, and the values they might achieve. Four aspects of generality, McKeon added, had emerged over the history of humanities. They are general in the sense of applying to all subject matters, providing an approach to any subject placed in the context of other parts of information or knowledge. They embrace all fundamental skills, providing a basis for particular skills that supplement or advance other processes of thought and action. They bear on the formation of the whole person, providing a model or ruling principle for any specific notion of excellence in the pursuit of a good life. And, they are the arts of all humans, providing guidance for individuals and their responses to cultures (159, 171–72).

The grandparent of modern general education was a required course on *Contemporary Civilization* (CC) introduced in 1919 at Columbia University for all first-year students. CC evolved from the "war-aims" course introduced in 1914 and a successor "peace-aims" course. In 1937, "Masterpieces" of Western literature and philosophy were added and, in 1947, counterpart courses in Western art and music. CC was built on a historical spine of significant texts that inspired other institutions to build general education cores, including Dartmouth, Reed, and the University of Chicago. In the 1930s, Chicago embarked on a more radical experiment centered on a four-year required sequence, comprehensive examinations, and a prescribed canon. The concept of a canon originated among scholars in the Alexandrian library during third and second centuries B.C. The Greek word *kanon* means a straight rod or a ruler, connoting a standard. The word *kanna* refers to a reed, a measuring stick or a physical model that embodies a standard of measure. Canons, Charles Altieri explains, have two functions. One is curatorial, preserving frameworks that create a cultural grammar for interpreting experience. It is not simply a semantic function, though. Canons also involve values, making their other function normative. The collective ideals of culture were presumed to lie in texts that provided the connective synthesis of universality. This view was embodied in Erskine and Hutchins's Great Books programs, Charles Eliot's five-foot shelf of classics, and Meiklejohn's belief that books are the basis of intelligence (Altieri 51; Hutcheson 109–10; Kennedy 225; Mayville 25–26; Bogue and Aper 70–71; Flexner 110).

There is no hard etymological proof of the first use of the word "interdisciplinary" in humanities. Other terms were used more often, including "integration," "synthesis," "unity," and "holism." Furthermore, two differing conceptions of interdisciplinarity were apparent in the early general education movement: one hearkening back to the *studia humanitatis* and the other engaging the present in study of historically situated problems of society. Cardinal Newman and Robert Maynard Hutchins defined general education as the place where all the parts would add up to a cohesive whole (Hutcheson 109–10). For Hutchins, a common core of great books and ideas was the best hope for restoring metaphysics to the center of higher education. Placing the Great Conversation at the center of education also promised to stem the threatening forces of materialism, vocationalism, empiricism, relativism, specialism, and departmentalization (Graff 162). Hutchins's model and like-minded programs were grounded in a conception of knowledge that located the coherence and integration of all fields in an epistemological realism. In this respect, Charles Anderson maintains, one of the first motivations for interdisciplinary studies in this country was to demonstrate unity of knowledge and to teach that Truth is one (456–57). Yet, W. B. Carnochan points out, the great books approach amounted to a "textual takeover" of history that reasserted literature and the "Great Conversation" as the foundation of Western intellectual tradition and universal truths of liberal culture (86).

Columbia's CC represented a different form of interdisciplinarity than the great books model. In the early 1900s, Columbia began shifting from the tradition of unitary knowledge to a historically situated notion of shared knowledge. The great books approach eventually made its way to Columbia. It was introduced in 1920 as an honors course. However, in contrast to Chicago's emphasis on modes of thought and inquiry, CC emphasized the process of knowing and contemporary problems. The intellectual, economic, social, and political life of the day were considered in relation to the past with a heightened problem focus and international consciousness in the postwar era. CC made an effort to involve other departments and disciplines as well, bringing economics, government, philosophy, and history into the dialogue about civilization. Other institutions followed suit, including Stanford and Dartmouth. These and similar curricula constituted a form of civics education that attempted to marry the agendas of liberal education and civic education (Hutcheson 110; Rudolph 71; Carnochan 70–72, 76, 79).

A second general education reform followed in the World War II era. It was signified most prominently by a 1945 Harvard report *General Education in a Free Society*. The Harvard report called for a new core curriculum based on science and texts of the European humanist tradition. Framed against the backdrop of fascism and communism, Thomas Bender recounts, the report preserved a role for history and historical disciplines in an education oriented to contemporary concerns and aligned with ideals of freedom and democracy ("Politics" 20–21). For James Conant, who sponsored the report while president, the truths of the core were not timeless. Their significance was a function of their historical role. For Hutchins, Louis Menand notes in comparison, general education upheld the permanency of classics whose truths were permanent and "timeless," making them "contemporary" in any age for anyone. *General Education in a Free Society* also endorsed a meritocratic vision. All citizens needed a common fund of knowledge, beliefs, and values—a cultural lingua franca capable of preventing class divisions. In this respect, Menand and Bender concur, general education was a "benign substitute" for a national ideology opposed to communism in the Cold War era. Great books were to be read not because they articulate truths that transcend historical circumstances. The writers in the canon were "touchstones" for contemporary culture and debate, supplying a "fund of allusion" that constituted a common heritage bonding all citizens to each other in an increasingly diverse world ("Re-imagining" 5–6).

This introductory history furnishes two important insights for the remainder of this book. First, the ideas of humanities and liberal arts have been marked by tension since their inception (Kimball 136). The story of humanities is an ongoing narrative of tradition pitted against change. The "timeless" and the "permanent" were neither timeless nor permanent. The aura of classical antiquity perpetuated in Greco-Roman classics was changed more than once to meet the needs of Romans, medieval scholastics, Italian humanists, and subsequent generations. The past was not lost in the process, but it was refigured. The kind of scholarship we now regard as traditionally humanistic, Graff also reminds us, was considered a subversive innovation by traditionalists of a previous era (4).

Second, even though interdisciplinarity has a philosophical grounding in ancient ideas, it arose as a response to a new and pathological condition. The challenges of the modern world and the proliferation of specialization required alternatives. Some were imported from the tradition of liberal humanism, perpetuating the generalizing and integrative principles of humanities. Those principles, though, were adapted for a changing world. New role models of the humanist arose in keeping with adaptations. The synoptic philosopher of ancient Greece was supplanted by the orator of Rome, the polymath of the Renaissance, the gentleman-scholar of the eighteenth century, the new specialists and the cultural generalists of the late nineteenth and early twentieth centuries, and, in the latter half of the twentieth century, Richard Carp's notion of a "boundary rider" skilled at walking the borders of disciplinarity and interdisciplinarity in a more complex terrain. The old college ideal did not die. It survives strongly in many small liberal arts colleges, in general education, and in generalist values in humanities disciplines. Those disciplines, though, were about to undergo tremendous change, knowledge and culture become more diverse, and new interdisciplinary approaches to studying them emerge within and across disciplines.

Chapter 2

CHANGING HUMANITIES

Over the course of the twentieth century, higher education in the United States underwent a profound transformation. The numbers alone are staggering. In 1910, 355,000 students were enrolled. After World War II, the count rose to 2 million and by 2000 had reached 15.3 million. The institutional profile changed as well. In 1900, there were 977 postsecondary institutions. By 1950, the tally was 1,900. By 1994, it had risen to 3,595 and at the dawn of the twenty-first century was pegged at roughly 4,000. In addition to liberal arts colleges and major research universities, American higher education now encompasses research facilities, land-grant colleges and universities, trade and business schools, community colleges, colleges for women and for minority groups, and online institutions. The professorate changed too. In the 1950s, there were fewer than 250,000 faculty. By 1988, the count was 670,000 and in 1999 had risen to roughly 1,028,000 (Hunt 18–20; Hawthorne 42; Oakley, "Elusive" 65; Bogue and Aper vii; 5, 9–10; http://nces.ed.gov/fastfacts; for 2001, http://nces.ed.gov/programs/digest/).

The biggest changes since 1945, Thomas Bender emphasizes, are demographic. The faces of the student body changed, with women making the most substantial enrollment gains and the number of minorities increasing. The composition of humanities faculty changed in kind. Women and African American scholars assumed greater roles in setting intellectual agendas, both generally and in the domains of race and gender. The generation now in mid- to late-career also came from a wider social and economic background than their predecessors. They entered the profession in an era marked by demands for social change and educational reform, postcolonial political movements, and mounting critique of traditional authorities. They played instrumental roles in developing interdisciplinary approaches, and they were part of the first academic generation to embark on extensive studies of media and popular culture (Bender, "Politics" 43–45; Brantlinger ix; Oakley, "Elusive" 47).

Demographic change was matched by intellectual change. A gradual importation of European philosophy and literary theories began in the 1950s, beginning with existentialism and phenomenology. In the 1960s, as social and political movements were bringing cultural and minority issues into American public life, structuralism, the language-based psychoanalysis of Jacques Lacan, new kinds of Marxist criticism, and deconstruction made inroads into academic culture. During the late 1970s and early 1980s, interest in feminism and semiotics widened, and further into the 1980s a number of practices lumped under the label "poststructuralism." In addition to deconstruction, feminism and Lacanian analysis, they included a form of French poststructuralist theory that was moving toward postmodern theory, new historicism, Foucauldian-style studies of knowledge and power, and cultural and postcolonial critique. By the 1990s, many discourses were positioning themselves under the rubric "multiculturalism," heightening awareness of difference and propelling the notion that humanities was evolving into cultural studies. One of the added effects of change, Bender notes, has been the de-Europeanization of academic culture. The arrival of French theoretical influences coincided with accelerating humanistic study of American culture. European ideas, models, and traditions are still predominant, but they are no longer transparent. They are being interrogated and contextualized (Bender, "Politics" 43–45; J. H. Miller, "Theory" 129–30; Bender and Schorske, "Introduction" 9; Kellner, *Media Culture* 20–24).

Interdisciplinarity was implicated at every turn. Proponents took pains to distinguish their goals, but the cumulative force of the various discourses fostered a new generalism that countered both the culture camp's vision of humanities and the modern system of disciplinarity. The new generalism was not a unified paradigm. It was a cross-fertilizing synergism in the form of common methods, concepts, theories, and a metalanguage. This chapter traces the host of developments that made "increasingly interdisciplinary" a new mantra in humanities by the end of the century. In turning to this part of the history, the chapter addresses several related questions. What developments are most closely associated with interdisciplinarity in humanities? What shared imperatives constituted the new generalism? How did the conception and practice of interdisciplinarity differ in particular developments? How has the relationship between disciplinarity and interdisciplinarity changed as a result? How has the meaning of culture shifted, and what role does interdisciplinarity play in American cultural studies?

The Contemporary Humanities

The increasing importance of interdisciplinarity was signaled by two presidents of the American Council of Learned Societies (ACLS), an umbrella organization for professional organizations representing humanities and social sciences. In 1985, ACLS presented reports from its twenty-eight members. Introducing the reports, John William Ward compared the growing pessimism about humanities to a greater sense of optimism and self-confidence in a 1964 *Report of the Commission on the Humanities*. Enrollments were declining, and job opportunities for recent PhDs were limited. Ironically, though, intellectual horizons had widened. Ward described learning and scholarship as vigorous, lively, and so various that the official definition of the National Endowment for Humanities (NEH) no longer seemed adequate. Two themes stood out. The first was heightened concern about the meaning of a field of study. A broader and more generous sense of subject was accompanied by a more inclusive sense of materials and techniques. The second theme emerged from the first. ACLS members reported pervasive movement toward interdisciplinary work and, in stark contrast to 1964, reassessment of the relationship between humanities and social sciences. As materials had become more inclusive and methodologies more various, an "inevitable" interest in interdisciplinarity had developed, especially among contiguous disciplines.

These trends continued unabated. In 1996, Ward's successor, Stanley Katz, highlighted two mounting pressures on academic organizations: the weakening of disciplinary boundaries and the emergence of alternative structures of knowledge. Together, he declared, they have the potential to transform the paradigm of the disciplinary department. Since the mid-1960s, the counter pressure of new fields has led to the creation of such departments as African American studies, women's studies, and ethnic studies. The political economy of the academy forces them to play the traditional power game of seeking resources and securing institutional space. Yet, they mark the possibility of a more flexible design. The radicalism of the 1960s, new definitions of culture and politics, and challenges to the existing structure of higher education encouraged methodological creativity and experiments with new approaches. Many academics today, Katz added, are by inclination or training "multi," "inter," or "non"disciplinary. As a result, they find the departmental structure confining and academic taxonomies inadequate to reflect the profusion, confusion, and richness of current categories. Broadly speaking, Catherine Gallagher also observed elsewhere, in the late twentieth century, faculty cultures in general began leaning toward synthetic projects such as Marxism, humanism, structuralism, feminism, semiotics, and cultural history (163–64).

The changes Ward and Katz identified cannot be encompassed under a single label. The rhetorical trope of a turn, though, is a common characterization. The second half of the twentieth century was a time of turns—linguistic and rhetorical, hermeneutic and interpretive, sociological and political, historical and cultural, poststructuralist and postmodern. These turns lie at the heart of the new generalism in humanities.

The New Generalism

Bender groups a number of trends in humanities and social sciences under the label of a "cultural turn." Despite differences, the discourses associated with this turn share a tendency to view culture from a wider and more critical perspective ("Politics" 41–42). David Hollinger highlights four intellectual movements that had an impact across disciplines. The first—Kuhn—is shorthand for a broad-based challenge to positivist and analytical strategies of the 1950s. In his 1962 book, *The Structure of Scientific Revolutions,* Thomas Kuhn presented an interpretation of scientific knowledge that incorporated sociological insights into the ways contingent and historically specific communities of inquiry authorize knowledge. Anthropologist Clifford Geertz and philosopher Richard Rorty also advanced antifoundationalist thinking and historical self-awareness. The second—antiracism—fostered expansion of affirmative action programs, inspired ethnic and minority studies, and deepened sensitivity to ethnoracial exclusions. The third—feminism—expanded in the wake of the feminist movement. The debate on gender also overlapped to an extent with discussion of ethno-racial distinctions and, later, poststructuralist discussion of the "subject." The fourth—Foucault—refers to the poststructuralist ideas developed by French theorists. The work of Michel Foucault and others accelerated the shift Kuhn had stimulated from objectivist to constructivist theories of knowledge. Foucault's focus on the matrix of power codified in subjects, objects, and categories of knowledge led to intensified scrutiny of the humanist tradition as well (359–65).

Inevitably, talk of "posthumanism" arose. In his 1993 presidential address to the National Association for Humanities Education, James Mehl spoke of a postmodern turn in humanities. Mehl dated its emergence to the 1960s and 1970s, citing popular manifestations such as the civil rights movement and antiwar protests, novel forms of art and expression in the 1980s and 1990s that rejected modernist aesthetics while combining earlier styles, new theories of linguistics and approaches to literary interpretation, the impact of new technologies on communication and the organization of knowledge, and the rise of international corporations that led to a restructuring of the global economy. Together these developments contributed to the broad cultural shift known as postmodernism. The possibility of posthumanism followed, although Mehl cautioned his audience against cultural amnesia. He urged bringing traditional humanities into a new dialogue with the challenges of the present and future by reintroducing classical texts while incorporating previously neglected texts and promoting more historical study, ethics education, and greater interdisciplinarity in scholarship and teaching ("Postmodern Humanism").

Postmodernism is one of four "posts" that have transformed modern thought. Postpositivism, poststructuralism, postmodernism, and postcolonialism all worked to unsettle previous ideas about knowledge (Vickers 14). The keywords and names of influential thinkers became shared icons in a new generalism of knowledge and culture. Postmodernism is closely associated with humanities because the movement began in fields of culture. In the 1930s, the term was a descriptive label for a minor reaction to modernism. It became popular in the 1960s when artists, writers, and critics used it to describe movement beyond exhausted modes. The concept crystallized around the mid-1970s then widened in the later 1970s and 1980s when claims for a postmodern social and cultural phenomenon began hardening in and across cultural areas and academic disciplines. In architecture, modernist aesthetics were rejected, and classical and popular styles were blended in the same building. In art, literature, film, music, theater, and dance, genres and styles were mixed in novel intertextual and intermedia forms, the boundaries of art and everyday life were crossed, the divide between elite and popular culture eroded, the phenomena considered "art" expanded, and criteria of judgment and quality broadened. In intellectual work, the presumed fixity of a text or artwork, absolute correspondence between language and reality, and the objectivity of all practitioners were called into question. Ultimately, critiques of modern theory and alternative practices also emerged in philosophy, social theory, politics, economics, anthropology, geography, psychoanalysis, theology, and historiography (Kellner, *Media Culture* 46, 48; Kellner, "Postmodernism" 239–42; Featherstone 203: Connor 6).

The New Humanities

New ways of thinking prompted alternative forms of scholarship and teaching. In a 1993 report on the state of humanities, Alberta Arthurs highlighted two particular and parallel developments. The first, "specializations of difference," is embodied in the examples Katz highlighted—ethnic, minority, and women's studies. The second is signified by anthropologist Clifford Geertz's phrase "blurring of the genres." The two developments became visible in different ways. Specializations of difference built canons of contemporary or neglected works and findings. Even as they opposed essentialism, though, they exhibited a strong foundational imperative and perennialist intention to preserve, to perpetuate, and to transmit a particular tradition and culture (Ratcliff 155). Genre blurring broke down established lines of intellectual inquiry, suggesting intersections, overlays, juxtapositions, and fresh formulations. The cumulative effect of both developments altered thinking about knowledge while facilitating new uses and openings for humanities in society at large. It may even have changed the disciplines permanently, Arthurs suggested. The disaggregation of disciplines brought humanities into new importance as they broke away, bled, or blurred into other disciplines and sectors. Scholars moved out of their usual spaces into new and shared territories.

Of the two developments, genre blurring is more amorphous. In 1980, Geertz identified a cultural shift within intellectual life in general and social sciences in particular. The model of physical sciences and a laws-and-instances ideal of explanation, Geertz argued, was being supplanted by a case-and-interpretation model and symbolic form analogies. Social scientists were increasingly representing society as a game, drama, or text, not as a machine or quasi-organism. They were also borrowing methods of speech-act analysis, discourse models, and cognitive aesthetics. Borrowing from humanities crossed the traditional boundary of explanation and interpretation, replacing former keywords of "cause," "variable," "force," or "function" with a vocabulary of "rules," "representation," "attitude," and "intention." The jumbling of varieties of discourses is not limited to a few isolated events, Geertz contended. It is a general phenomenon in "a vast, almost continuous field of variously intended and diversely constructed work." Conventional rubrics remain, but they are often jerry-built to accommodate a situation that has become "fluid, plural, uncentered, and ineradicably untidy." Geertz rejected "interdisciplinary brotherhood" or "highbrow eclecticism." Yet, he acknowledged that principles of mapping knowledge were changing. A borders-and-territories view of knowledge, a Linnean catalogue of scholarly species, and conventional rubrics block from view the "culture shift" that was well under way in the early 1980s.

Not all social scientists took the turn toward humanities Geertz described. Economists were and still are the most resistant. Yet, the stress on empirical research and logical positivism that characterized the behavioral revolution of the 1950s and 1960s eased with growing interest in the ways that people make and communicate meaning. The social sciences were not immune, either, from existentialism and phenomenology, structuralism, deconstruction, poststructuralism, neo-Marxism, and comparative cultural studies. Meanwhile, on the other side of the fence humanists were moving. As social scientists were taking interpretive, linguistic, and literary turns, Geertz reported, humanists were taking anthropological, sociological, political, and historical turns. As social scientists were talking of "actors," "scenes," "plots," "performance," and "personae," humanists were talking of "motives," "authority," "persuasion," "exchange," and "hierarchy."

Affirming an earlier prediction by Gerald Graff, Arthurs declared that a significant proportion of research in the 1990s would not have been regarded as research or scholarship in previous decades. It was bolder, more relevant to contemporary events, and less tidily derived from traditional disciplines. Echoing Ward, Arthurs deemed the NEH definition inadequate to account for the many inchoate, complicated, and uncategorizable ideas afloat in contemporary humanities. It does not acknowledge the growth of new specialties and subfields, the extensive shifting of disciplinary boundaries, and the expanding functions and effects of humanities. In calling for another taxonomy, she highlighted eight major points of definition:

1. *Advancing learning:* the classical function of humanities research through preservation and interpretation of the past in dialogue with discovery of new knowledge and reformulation of ideas;
2. *Enhancing quality of life and providing public service:* arts appreciation, non-scholarly travel, language use, historical study, the making of social and artistic institutions, and civic contributions;
3. *Aiding individual growth:* transmission of information and ideas from a "learned" to a "learning" generation;
4. *Articulating ideals for society:* the study of societal ideals as subjects;
5. *Adjusting the contexts of authority:* the wider impact of interdisciplinary identity fields and new and changing specialties such as urban studies, social history, and film studies;

6. *Inspiring social change and activist concerns about justice:* extension of traditional discussion of these subjects, e.g., in reevaluations of the roles of women and minorities and other issues of access and diversity;

7. *Mediating across sectors of society:* contributions to issues in medical ethics, science and technology, environment and culture;

8. *Mediating across cultures:* the study of other cultures.

(Arthurs 265–67)

Interdisciplinarity is implicit throughout the taxonomy, but it is explicit in categories 5, 7, and 8. In addition to urban studies, social history, and film studies, category 5 includes women's and feminist studies, gender theory, and Black studies. Hispanic American, Asian American, and Native American studies emerged as well, and the older field of American studies is changing. Category 7 is a relatively recent function that marks the limits of the term "interdisciplinary studies" and even "genre blurring." The participation of philosophers in medical ethics, the emergence of STS (science, technology and society studies), and the inclusion of contemporary Hispanic American and Latin American literature in Spanish language departments did not simply extend academic inquiry. They mediated a middle ground across sectors. The growth of cultural studies also pressed all sectors of humanities to consider questions that were traditionally located elsewhere. Category 8 is an added form of mediation. The study of other cultures and interactions between cultures and nations was once considered the province of language departments and disciplines such as history and literature. Less familiar cultures were located in area studies, international relations, and anthropology. Today, more interactive definitions of culture and cultural relationships appear across humanities and social sciences.

Given the plurality of developments, it is hardly surprising that new forms of interdisciplinarity arose. Their differences and similarities are evident in the shift from structuralism to Theory; subsequent historical, sociological, and political turns; and the more recent turn toward cultural studies.

The New Interdisciplinarity

Structuralism was the first major exemplar of a "new interdisciplinarity." It was a "loose interdisciplinarity," in the sense that Jonathan Culler described the chameleon-like shapes of Theory (205). It was not a discrete field so much as a sprawling set of methods and approaches. Most varieties of structuralism and semiotics, Vincent Leitch recounts, exhibited a common interest in formulations and concepts derived from Ferdinand de Saussure. During the 1960s, linguistic and stylistic analysis of a formalist kind dominated. Cast in opposition to historicist and hermeneutical modes, structuralism sought deep structures of meaning. *Langue* was privileged over the *parole* of speech, social or collective dimensions over individual events, grammar over usage, rules and competence over expressions and performance, and models over data. Roman Jakobson and Claude Levi-Strauss also disregarded biography, literary and cultural history, and readers' and viewers' responses to works.

When structuralism and semiotics arrived in the American academy, Leitch recalls, their appearance was heralded as an interdisciplinary event. American literary critics, art historians, historiographers, musicologists, philosophers, theologians, and other specialists began exploring the possibilities of applying their methods and models. Saussure envisioned a discipline or a general science of signs and sign systems. A general theory did not take root, but structuralism expanded into a global field of interests with commitments to linguistic modeling and investigations of sign systems, codes, and conventions of many kinds (239, 241, 245, 260–61). By the late 1970s, the boundaries of structuralism were loosening, scientific claims were softening, methodological skepticism was increasing, and semiotics was replacing structuralism as a common framework. Yet, even in the midst of common vocabulary and shared interests, local disciplinary economies continued to operate. In literary studies, for example, structuralism challenged the determining categories of the discipline—an author and a canonical literary text. Emphasis on "intertextuality" opened up boundaries with other texts. Analysis, however, often remained within the sphere of language and discourse (Moran 84).

Theory emerged in France during the 1960s as poststructuralist discourses were circulating. Theory added to the new generalism by stimulating widening reflection on problems of language and representation, the role of gender and sexuality, a historically oriented cultural criticism, and categories of critical thought undertaken by deconstruction (Moran 82). New syntheses of Marxism, psychoanalysis, semiotics, and feminism also emerged as proponents tested their relationship to other practices. Both structuralism and poststructuralism, Catherine Gallagher remembers, were inspired by a synthetic zeal that was sustained by corroborating work in text-based and interpretive fields such as philosophy, psychoanalysis, linguistics, and anthropology. Jonathan Culler calls Theory an "unbounded corpus of writings" that placed literary and philosophical texts, psychoanalytic case histories, and historical documents in a wider dialogue. Students in law, anthropology, art history, music, classics, and sometimes history and psychoanalysis began incorporating new developments as well. The most notable approaches were deconstruction, poststructuralist Marxism, critiques of colonial discourse, theories of popular culture, and the discourses of identity fields and gay and lesbian studies (Culler 202–06; Kellner, *Media Culture* 20, 22).

Despite Theory's expanding presence, the reception was not uniform. Literature departments, Dominick LaCapra explains, were the "busiest academic ports of entry" for European developments because they already had a cosmopolitan outlook that encouraged comparative literature, world literature, and literature-in-translation courses. Theory also proved more compelling in continental philosophy, interpretive social theory, and intellectual history than in literary history, analytic philosophy, positivistic social science, and traditional historiography. Even when accommodated in the mainstream, it was more profound in already marginalized areas. The American critics, historians, and theorists who responded earliest were located in French and comparative literature departments. New approaches had a sporadic role in intellectual history, gaining attention where exceptional voices and counterdiscourses were already of interest before affecting social historians interested in representative discourses and collective mentalities (236).

New approaches also met resistance in philosophy. Jean Paul Sartre was read in English departments more than philosophy departments, where Anglo-American analytic philosophy dominated. Moreover, the discipline did not experience the same generational, political, and ideological split or the dramatic shifts that occurred in English. In this sense, Gallagher argues, literature departments often took responsibility for contemporary thought because other disciplines defaulted as critical approaches were making their way into the American academy. In England and the United States, literary studies came to play the central cultural role that philosophy once enjoyed. After the 1960s, and especially the 1980s, philosophy's horizon broadened with renewed discussion of metaphysics, revival of American pragmatism, dialogue with Continental philosophers, integration of science with philosophy of science, and feminist perspectives. Artificial intelligence

made cognitive science one of the discipline's most active areas, with coop-
erative research conducted in the philosophy of mind and psychology, linguistics, and neurobiology. In addition, philosophy reentered the public
and normative arena, addressing new ethical and sociopolitical questions.
Yet, limits persist. The concerns of continental philosophers for problems
of culture, history, art, and affective values are still taught largely outside of
philosophy departments in the United States (APA; Nehamas 235–37; Put-
nam 219; Bender, "Politics" 45; Hollinger 368).

Theory, Vivek Dhareshwar suggests, illustrates what Pierre Bourdieu
meant when he likened the intellectual field to a magnetic field of power
lines. The intellectual field cannot be reduced to a simple aggregate of isolated agents or the sum of juxtaposed elements. Like a magnetic field, it is
made up of a system of power lines. By their very existence, opposition,
and combination, multiple forces determine its structure at a given moment. Extending Bourdieu's analogy, Dhareshwar highlighted three issues
in the institutionalization of Theory that illustrate the changing character
of interdisciplinarity in humanities. It accommodated a heterogeneous set
of impulses and stances. It allowed seeing the institutional space of Theory
as another field of social representation where intellectuals from different
histories, cultures, and positions attempted to impose their views. And, it
illuminated the ways that heterogeneous trends exist in active tension, not
a simple or static coexistence. Differences were not resolved in a synthesis,
grand theory, orthodoxy, or discipline, even though all of those claims were
advanced at times. Theory also indicates the changing relationship of the
general and the particular. Theory with a "long view" was an expansive
problem surveyed panoramically from a plurality of critical perspectives.
Embodying the force of generalism, Theory operated in horizontal fashion,
moving above and between texts and disciplinary formations. At the same
time, it took the form of a "close view," operating in vertical fashion
through intensive textual proddings in particular domains (6–8).

Finally, Theory illustrates the complicated institutional dynamics of critique. Even as it deconstructed the metanarrative of Western humanities
and the accompanying discourse of universality, LaCapra recalls, Theory
bred its own essentialism. It became a norm with the power to determine
research and to set agendas. Yet, Theory had an uneasy relation to its own
institutionalization. It was a "discursive agitation" moving across disciplines, seeking out "threshold" positions that could not securely locate
their own theoretical grounds and running the risk of hybridized discourses

that breed fruitful but ultimately sterile variants. As a "transgressive" strategy, Theory demanded a "generalized displacement and rearticulation" of established discourses and disciplines, not a quarantined place in their margins. By breaking down conventional barriers, liminal criticisms invent alternative modes of social and individual behavior. As new practices become located in the very structures that legitimated older claims of humanism and culture, they risk being reduced to one more specialty in a crowded field (236). Once oppositional voices are grouped, categorized, named, and their position systematized, Joseph Buttigieg adds, they can be managed within an institutional order (19).

The Historical, Sociological, and Political Turns

Delivering the 1986 presidential address to the Modern Language Association, J. Hillis Miller announced a sudden and almost universal turn away from Theory in the direction of history, politics, culture, and society (qtd. in Montrose 15). The academic world rarely moves that fast. However, with the waning of Theory humanists have been paying greater attention to history, sociology, and politics. Like Theory, these developments exhibit both a long view and a close view. The long view takes the form of a general trend toward historicizing, sociologizing, and politicizing of all subjects and objects. The close view is situated within local disciplinary economies.

The reengagement with history stands in stark contrast to disciplinary relations at mid-century. In the 1950s, the cutting of ties with history was so widespread that Carl Schorske called it a generalized paradigm shift in academic culture. Social sciences turned to behaviorism and natural-scientific modes, while humanities turned to self-referential formalistic criticism. In the 1960s and 1970s, a variety of "new histories" opened space for interdisciplinary contextualization and partnerships. In characterizing practices in the period spanning the 1960s through early 1990s, Peter Burke called the pace of change "dizzying." Burke identified six points of comparison between the Old and the New in the discipline of history that also had an impact on historical perspectives in other disciplines and interdisciplinary fields.

The first distinction lies in subject and object. The traditional paradigm accentuated politics of the state in national and international contexts. The new history embraces virtually all human activities. The second distinction is method and approach. The traditional paradigm privileged narration of events while focusing on regimes and administrations, legislation and politics, diplomacy and foreign policy, wars and revolutions. Today's practices tend to be analytic and thematic, and some of the most influential work is emanating from efforts to recast intellectual history as cultural history. The third distinction lies in the difference between "history from above" and a "history from below" that takes into account the everyday experience of ordinary people. The fourth distinction follows from the third. Instead of prioritizing archival documents, records, and treatises, new scholarship draws on a greater variety of evidence, making use of statistics, oral history, visual images, material culture, sociological models, and psychological theories. Official records are also being read in new ways. The fifth and sixth distinctions accentuate interpretative differences. In contrast to earlier emphasis on key actors in events, questions are being raised about collective movements and individual actions and trends. Variations over time and culture are being recognized as well, and the single "objective" voice being replaced by a heteroglossia of voices.

The attraction to historical, sociological, and political explanation was enhanced by several factors. Historical, political, and economic issues were central to Marxist interpretations of texts and the production of art, culture, and ideas (Moran 123). Young scholars in all disciplines also carried political and social interests kindled in the 1960s and 1970s into their professional work. In this respect, part of the impetus was demographic. Moreover, Ralph Cohen recalls, historical interventions into disciplinary discourses were often perceived as broadening their scope whether the context was literature, cultural studies, or the discourse of sexuality. The development of some new interests—such as film studies and performance—required historical justification of their origin and development as well. So did efforts to enlarge the concept of culture. The impetus for change was not a simple matter of intervention. It was linked with the growing realization that disciplinary discourses are multigeneric. Generic writing has always been latently combinatory but, Cohen emphasizes, what is distinctly contemporary is overt insistence on the interdisciplinarity of disciplinary discourses in a deliberate effort to restructure texts and institutions (396–98).

The reengagement with sociology and politics differed. It is linked more closely to the 1960s and 1970s, especially social movements that challenged established forms of society and culture, produced countercultures, and stimulated interest in all social classes. Even so, Douglas Kellner stresses, the renewal of social and political interests was more than simple nostalgia. The subfield of social history fostered greater space for popular histories and popular culture in multiple disciplines and fields. The momentum created by postmodern discourses in the 1970s and 1980s also reinvigorated sociological and political scholarship. The problems of the contemporary world and new technological and economic systems called for new theoretical and political modes of understanding linked with struggles for human rights, the civil liberties of oppressed people, peace and justice, ecology, and the search for a more humane organization of society on a global scale (*Media Culture* 1, 17, 19).

The cumulative force of change produced such a widespread rhetoric of crisis that talk of crisis, Buttigieg suggested, appears to have become a permanent feature of the humanist's repertoire (4). A conjunction of crises with roots in the late 1960s continues to frame discussions of the state of humanities and higher education. During the early 1990s, the flashpoint was political correctness. By the mid-1990s, it had shifted to attacks on faculty for abandoning education in favor of research (Nelson and Bérubé 6), and multiculturalism and kindred discourses became prominent targets. Ironically, new developments generated an opposite tendency. In introducing the 1985 ACLS report, Ward remarked that the ferment of openness and variety was generating an opposite quest for order and unity, laced with anxiety about identity (xi). Ten years later, Joan Scott reported a renewed consensus and codification. The more the university community diversified, Scott observed, the more relentless attempts to enforce community became. The more opponents of institutionalizing diversity extolled individualism, the more advocates invoked it. The greater the need for open-ended research, reflection, and criticism, the more instrumental the justification for taking new directions. The greater the need for theorizing, the more rapid the turn to moralism and a therapeutics of the personal (294)

Opponents faulted new developments for distorting humanities by grounding it in ideology, but proponents countered that traditional claims of disinterestedness carried unacknowledged ideologies. Representing the defense of tradition, John Searle took direct aim at institutionalization of some of the "more offensive" features of the cultural wars in certain departments, most notably comparative literature, English, French, and identity fields. Searle blamed critical theory for eroding the cultural mission of studying literature and other humanities and for abandoning the distinction between high and popular culture. Lost in the process was the Arnoldian view of humanities and liberal education's mandate to help students overcome the limits of their backgrounds. Universal human civilization, Searle charged, has been sacrificed to individual identity, "great" works supplanted by "representative" works, and objective or intersubjective standards replaced with relativism. In some departments, he added, pervasive dissatisfaction with American society, official institutions, and traditional academic subjects is rampant, producing a Nietzchean "resentiment" anchored by leftwing orthodoxy. The United States is a multicultural society, Searle acknowledged, but an ideology of multiculturalism trounces the notion of mainstream or dominant culture.

Questions of disciplinarity also became questions of politics and institutional structure. In a volume that promotes the "new interdisciplinarity," Ann Kaplan and George Levine reminded readers that the transformation of humanities centered on not only the canon and curriculum but the organization of knowledge and hierarchies that govern intellectual and political lives (3–4). Debate on the social and political significance of intellectuals gave reinvigorated meaning to the notion of a genuinely "public humanities" capable of crossing the boundaries of academic disciplines and institutional sectors by inviting partnerships and organizational networks. Throughout their history, humanities have been closely involved with areas of paramount concern to society, such as moral conduct and civic duty (Chodorow 15). However, Richard Lyman cautions, interdisciplinarity is not a panacea. Merely blurring genres or collaborating with neighboring disciplines will not bring humanities into effective contact with the rest of the world and its problems (qtd. in Ward xiii–xiv). Nor will a nostalgic call for a return to an eighteenth-century model of a cultural commentator or a 1920s-style integration of the university into the local community.

The Cultural Turn

Scholars in several disciplines have historically studied the same topics now being claimed as the province of cultural studies. Today, though, their control over the domains of mass communications, social problems, the family, and cultural texts is being challenged. New areas are also being studied—such as popular film and music, pulp fiction, and pornography—and the label "cultural studies" is associated with a variety of revitalized inter-ests—such as neo-Marxism, social history, ethnomethodology, and textual-ism. The history of the field has been constructed on several grounds, in-cluding labor politics and left scholarship in England during the late 1950s and early 1960s; the precedents of the Frankfurt School and the Birming-ham Center; deconstruction of cultural texts in the manner of Derrida and critical readings of postmodern society in the manner of Baudrillard, Lyo-tard, and Jameson; feminist cultural studies; neo-Marxism; and a cultural and pragmatic approach to communication studies in the United States. The biographical ground of the British movement looms large. For found-ing figures Richard Hoggart and Raymond Williams, the major site was lit-erary criticism; for E. P. Thompson, it was orthodox political and economic history; and, for all three Marxism. Hoggart and Williams, who came from working-class families, were also among the first to make their heritage part of the formal study of culture (Denzin 74–75; Bathrick 251; Nelson, Treichler, and Grossberg 12; Brantlinger 36–37, 64; Fiske)

Initial work retained literary inclinations. However, the meaning of cul-ture shifted from discipline-specific notions of text and artifact into a broader anthropological definition, followed by a historical approach that questioned anthropological meaning and its presumed universality. As re-searchers began grappling with material, social, and historical conditions, a break into Marxism occurred, fostering new questions about the politics of culture and theorizations around the problem of ideology. Subsequent inter-ventions focused on questions of feminism and race, and in later years cul-tural studies became a set of projects with its own object, themes and issues, and problematic. Former director Stuart Hall recalled the different method-ological emphases that emerged at the Birmingham Center. Some projects relied on ethnographic fieldwork and interviewing, some on analysis of texts and discursive practices, others on historical methods of working with ar-chival, documentary, and additional sources. Even so, methods were com-bined and recombined across projects, fostering a certain kind of "regional-ism." Each region maintained responsibility for its area while remaining open to others, stimulating cultural studies as a whole through collective combinations of regional and general emphases. The whole was not homo-geneous, however. Reflecting the changed conditions of holism, the knowl-edge that was produced was characterized by divergencies and conflicts. Projects and knowledge fields, Hall concluded, are discursive formations in a Foucauldian sense. They do not have simple origins. They are composed of multiple discourses with different histories, trajectories, methodologies, and theoretical positions ("The Center," "Theoretical Legacies").

The changing character of disciplines, Hall adds, is an important part of the story of cultural studies. As humanists were becoming more sociological, sociologists began appropriating sociology from within. At the time, sociology was dominated by the structuralist-functionalist paradigm. Researchers familiarized themselves with other traditions that dealt with social action and institutions as objectivated structures of meaning. As concrete historical work developed, the dichotomy of literature versus sociology dissolved into an emphasis on lived practices, belief systems, and institutions. Reactions followed in both disciplines. Traditional sociologists faulted new work for not being proper sociology, while traditional humanists reasserted the definition of culture in liberal humanism. The break into a complex Marxism was made possible by changes within the mainstream of sociology, including a phenomenological reprise associated with Berger and Luckmann's social construction of reality and ethnomethodology's focus on language and conversational analysis as a paradigm for social action. Interest in narrative, textuality, and communication also fostered a rehabilitation of social interactionism and greater use of qualitative methodology. The ethnographical tradition, in turn, linked cultural studies with descriptive emphases of some kinds of social anthropology and a history-from-below being promoted by new social history.

An American Cultural Studies

The American version of cultural studies both differs from and was influenced by the British version. In Britain and the United States, debates over mass culture and mass media's place in cultural life promoted a heterogeneous field of interests. In Britain, though, the question of ideology emerged sooner and more sharply. The notion of the popular also occupied a different position within the dominant culture of the United States, and discussions of countercultural movements in the 1960s tended to be identified with the middle-class and mostly white male college students. At the Birmingham Center, discussions were oriented toward working-class subcultures. The influence of cultural studies was first felt in communications departments specializing in media studies and popular culture. By the mid-1980s, American studies scholars with an interest in neighboring fields began adapting some of their methods. Feminism and the cultural epistemologies of other groups were added influences in shaping cultural studies that became located primarily in humanities (Denzin 75; Brantlinger 117-19; Shank, "Culture" 447; Seidman 41).

Like Theory, cultural studies illustrates the complex spatial dynamics of interdisciplinarity. It is located within disciplines, on their margins, in subfields and alternative practices, and in interdisciplinary enclaves. More broadly, it constitutes a network of overlapping projects and a general problematizing force. The field is counterdisciplinary in stance, multidisciplinary in scope, sometimes collaborative in work patterns, and transdisciplinary in its broad-based reformulation of the category of culture. Disciplinary economies register in local practices, but they have a relational character born of shared interests. In the American academy, David Bathrick found, three areas have provided direction for a programmatic understanding of what the field might mean within the framework of existing disciplines:

1. Critique of ethnocentrism of scholarship and curriculum within ethnic studies, African American, Third World, and Latin American programs;
2. Critique of essentialism and universalism in feminism;
3. Questioning of separations of culture, race, and gender in popular and mass culture.

(Bathrick 328–29)

Pluralism is invoked, but the word "plural" is both a descriptor and a problematic. Pluralism is often indicted as an inclusive politics that results in accommodation of practices without rethinking the raison d'etre of the academy. In a tamed liberal pluralism, existing power structures remain intact (J. H. Miller, *Illustration* 51). At the same time, the immense variety of subjects, topics, and methods constitute an indisputable plurality of practices. Hall called the label cultural studies a "terminological mutant" and an "uneasy marker" for a diverse and contentious set of competing but related discourses. No single subject metonymically represents the field, although the suggested groupings of Grossberg, Nelson, and Treichler's 1992 anthology of scholarship worldwide indicate prominent subjects and topics:

history of cultural studies	politics of aesthetics
gender and sexuality	culture and its institutions
nationhood and national identity	ethnography and cultural studies
colonialism and postcolonialism	the politics of disciplinarity
race and ethnicity	discourse and textuality
popular culture and its audiences	science, culture, and the ecosystem
rereading history	identity politics
pedagogy	global culture in a postmodern age

(Nelson, Treichler, and Grossberg 2–3)

The most common methods are familiar from the account of new developments in this chapter—Marxism, feminism, deconstruction, psychoanalysis, ethnography, race and gender theory, semiotics, and textual analysis. Methods usually reflect original disciplinary training, amplified by situational borrowings. Most self-identified members of the field work simultaneously at disciplinary sites and in the trading zone of cultural studies. Hence, methods are sometimes combined, meshing survey research with ethnography, information from marketing research with utopian conceptions of empowered consumers, and textual or ethnographic analysis with social, political, and cultural commentary. The publishing boom and rapid institutionalization of the field in the United States have resulted in a climbing on the interdisciplinary bandwagon, with existing humanities departments, programs, and centers renamed "cultural studies," "cultural theory," and variations on the field's keywords (Nelson, Treichler, and Grossberg 2–3, 10–11). With its "'big tent' inclusivity, Ellen Messer-Davidow finds, U.S. cultural studies now functions as a "cross-discipline" with permeable boundaries, divergent practitioners, and a non-uniform intellectual core. It is a small enterprise in the larger economy of knowledge production, but it is a prominent enterprise for producing and circulating knowledge in humanities and its relations with social sciences ("Cultural Studies" 494).

Given the diversity of practices, cultural studies will continue to be elastic. Bathrick calls it a "gravitational field" or magnet that gathers coalescing practices into a problematic and perhaps impossible synthesis. The holism of culture is not *unified* in a totalizing sense but *unifying* in the sense of Theory with a long view, generating shared values and objectives. It enacts partial integrations that leave unresolved tensions. There is a sense, Joe Moran observes, in which cultural studies can be said to be synonymous with interdisciplinarity and, others claim, with "new humanities." Yet, proponents of cultural studies have been critical of interdisciplinary programs that merely adopt an inclusive approach to studying culture without engaging the politics of knowledge and representation (50–51). As a cross-disciplinary and multimedia enterprise, J. Hillis Miller agrees, cultural studies presupposes questioning the presumption of an agreed-upon canon that constitutes the center of humanistic studies. It also has an uneasy relation to Theory, although the term "critical theory" is sometimes used synonymously with cultural studies (*Illustration* 13–19).

The recent closing of the department of cultural studies at Birmingham sent shock waves across humanities. The immediate basis for the decision was a decline in research quality measured by a national assessment exercise. Paul Gilroy, though, links the closing to larger problems in British higher education, including prioritizing a small number of institutions that conduct disciplinary and interdisciplinary research in areas of international economic competition. The university maintains that closure does not mean the demise of cultural studies. However, the argument that faculty in other departments and disciplines are now "doing cultural studies" ignores the threat to the field's long-term integrity. At the same time, Gilroy points to the global network of cultural studies spawned by the Birmingham school. Its worldwide popularity marks a deeper realignment in the constellation of disciplines and scholarly interests (B20).

The claim that humanities have been transformed into cultural studies is also checked by the limits of individual competence. Goodwin and Woolf call them "the weak link in the chain of cross-disciplinary reasoning." Many undergraduate cultural studies programs in North America come together in a haphazard manner, depending on which colleagues a coordinator can round up. The arrangements have produced worthwhile combinations of literary studies, visual studies, media studies, musicology, anthropology, sociology, and gender and ethnic studies. Yet, several problems occur, especially at the graduate level. As first and second generations of students in the field move beyond coursework to dissertations, the problem of expert advice arises. For all the antidisciplinary talk of dismantling specializations, in the absence of pertinent expertise charges of dilettantism haunt the work of graduate students, faculty, and individuals in disciplines and other fields who want to widen their study of cultural objects and subjects. The lack of self-reflexivity within traditional disciplines, which cultural studies is in part motivated by, also renders disciplines subject to critical analysis along historical, ideological, and institutional lines. In the end, Goodwin and Woolf admonish, "There are no short cuts to knowledge." An interdisciplinary cultural studies requires continued close work with colleagues within the disciplines, even as their domains are changing (138–40).

In an April 2005 interview and earlier comments in the MLA journal *Profession* and his book *Theory Matters*, Vincent Leitch reflected on the current nature and status of interdisciplinarity. In the 1970s, the rise of new interdisciplines and Theory displaced the modernist formalism that dominated in the U.S. from the 1930s to the 1960s. New interdisciplines proliferated, including fields that challenge modern humanistic objectivity and have activist roots, such as black, women's, media, cultural, postcolonial, science, disability, body, and queer studies. Despite wide dissemination, though, theoretically inflected interdisciplinary cultural studies are still limited and constrained by the departmental structure of the American academy. They are generally housed in underfunded and nomadic programs or institutes, and they submit to modern disciplinarity's requirements, standards, certifications, and methods. The university finesses difference and interdisciplines by shoring up traditional departmentalization, occasionally softened by a humanities center and volunteer-staffed programs. At the same time, Leitch adds, the autonomy of many disciplines has imploded: "Hybridity has trumped purity." In contrast to the dream in "modern interdisciplinarity" of an end of disciplines, "postmodern interdisciplinarity" respects difference and heterogeneity in a new mixed institutional reality of disciplines and interdisciplines (Ruiz).

Humanists responded to new developments by moving in two directions. Some, Bender recalls, worked to expand the domain of humanities. Others assumed an increasingly defensive posture. The culture wars continue, but the unstable balance between responsibility for custody of traditional European humanism and cultivation of a critical intellect did not survive the 1980s. The two positions became competing academic ideologies. At present, Bender sees two major directions in humanities. One eschews essentialism, emphasizing the contingent and treating even conventional categories of identity as cultural and historical constructs. At the same time, much of current scholarship points in the opposite direction of restoring essentialism by advancing particular interests, especially around race or gender. A new ideology has emerged in forms of cultural studies that envision a postdisciplinary academy. New practices bespeak cosmopolitanism. Yet, fractionality has increased. Departments also continue to be the basic organizational unit of the academy, but though they no longer clearly or fully denote the intellectual work that is sustained within traditional structures ("Politics" 35, 44–47; "Locality and Worldliness" 3). New practices are transforming the character of disciplinary work and in their interaction with interdisciplinary fields have shifted the metaphor of knowledge from unity to a complex and dynamic web of relations.

Chapter 3

FORGING THEORY, PRACTICE, AND INSTITUTIONAL PRESENCE

Any nomenclature, Kenneth Burke taught us, acts as a terministic screen that filters, directs, and redirects attention along some paths rather than others. Terminology is not only a reflection of reality. It is also a selection and a deflection. Much of what we take to be observations about reality may well be the playing out of possibilities implicit in our choice of terms (45–46, 49). The most commonly used terminology for interdisciplinarity dates from the first international conference on the subject, sponsored by the Organization for Economic Cooperation and Development (OECD) in France in the year 1970. The OECD typology distinguished multi, pluri, inter, and transdisciplinary forms of interaction (25–26). Most humanists are unaware of the origin of the typology, but several terms passed into wide use. The difference between "multi" and "interdisciplinarity" is the most basic distinction. Multidisciplinary approaches juxtapose disciplinary perspectives, adding breadth and available knowledge, information, and methods. They speak as separate voices in an encyclopedic alignment. The status quo is not interrogated, and disciplinary elements retain their original identity. In contrast, interdisciplinarity integrates separate disciplinary data, methods, tools, concepts, and theories in order to create a holistic view or common understanding of a complex issue, question, or problem (Klein and Newell 393).

Not all interdisciplinarities are the same, however. Disagreements about definition reflect differing views of the purpose of research and education, the role of disciplines, and the role of critique. The developments traced in chapter 2 fostered a new rhetoric of interdisciplinarity in humanities. "Plurality" and "heterogeneity" replaced "unity" and "universality." "Interrogation" and "intervention" supplanted "resolution" and "harmony."

"Synthesis," "holism," and "integration" became pejorative notions, and even "interdisciplinarity" was challenged by new "anti," " post," "non," and "de-disciplinary" stances. Taken together, the keywords of the new rhetoric signaled the evolution of a form of "critical interdisciplinarity" that aims to transform existing structures of knowledge and education. It highlights the difference between what Joe Moran calls a "retrospectively interdisciplinary" model of an organic society of the past, when culture and society were presumably joined, and a "prospectively interdisciplinary" vision of a future society, when divisions between culture and history would no longer exist (132).

Chapter 3 completes the foundation for the case studies by introducing three sets of questions that will recur throughout the remainder of the book. How is interdisciplinarity theorized, and what are the tenets of the "new interdisciplinarity" in humanities? What are the major factors shaping practice, what role does disciplinarity play, and what are the interdisciplinary work practices of humanists? And, how are practices institutionalized?

Theory

Three pronouncements mark the tenets of critical interdisciplinarity. In a 1983 essay on "The Principle of Reason," Jacques Derrida critiqued the rational calculus of programmed research on "applied" and "oriented" problems of technology, the economy, medicine, psychosociology, and military defense. Much of this research, he observed, is interdisciplinary (11–12). Jean-Francois Lyotard presented a similar conclusion in *La Condition Postmoderne,* which appeared in this country in English translation in1984. Lyotard critiqued metanarratives for attempting to totalize knowledge around a new paradigm and called the interdisciplinary approach specific to the age of delegitimation and its hurried empiricism. The relationship to knowledge, Lyotard argued, is not articulated in terms of the life of the spirit or the emancipation of humanity. It serves the users of a complex conceptual and material machine. Lacking an emancipatory metalanguage or metanarrative in which to formulate the final goal and correct use of that machine, they practice performative techniques of brainstorming and teamwork to accomplish designated tasks. Even imagination is channeled into instrumental production, implicating humanists in the production of "excellence" and training workers (52). In 1996, Bill Readings extended these earlier critiques in *The University in Ruins*. Readings linked interdisciplinarity with the transformation of the Western university into a "transnational bureaucratic corporation" in the service of the marketplace and an empty notion of "excellence" that is replacing the older appeal to "culture."

The swift embrace of Lyotard, Derrida, and Readings in American humanities signaled an expanding backlash against older forms of interdisciplinarity. The first objection was directed at research and problem solving that produce technologies of information and application for "instrumental," "strategic," "pragmatic," or "opportunistic" purposes. During the 1980s interdisciplinarity gained heightened visibility in science-based areas of intense international economic competition, especially computers, biotechnology, manufacturing, and high technology. In this instance, interdisciplinarity serves the political economy of the market and national needs. "Critical" and "reflexive" forms differ. They interrogate the existing structure of knowledge and education, raising questions of value and purpose that are silent in instrumentalist forms. They seek to transform, rather than to build bridges across existing units for utilitarian purposes. (For overviews of definitions, see Klein, *Interdisciplinarity* 55–73; Klein, *Crossing Boundaries* 173–208.)

The second objection was aimed at forms of interdisciplinary study that combine existing approaches without transforming them, including the generalist model of culture. In a 1996 collection of research stories from the Canadian academy, Salter and Hearn called interdisciplinarity the necessary "churn in the system," aligning the concept with a dynamic striving for change. The momentum for an alternative interdisciplinarity mounted over the latter half of the twentieth century. In 1977, David Marcell called for a "critical interdisciplinarity" in American studies. Marcell faulted "mere interdisciplinary" attempts at synthesizing disciplinary perspectives on two counts: failing to do justice to the pluralism of American culture and failing to create a genuine synthesis of humanities and social sciences. In a 1980 essay on Canadian Studies, Arthur Kroker distinguished the mechanically normalized modes of thought in "vacant interdisciplinarity" from a critical strategy of inquiry that develops knowledge of the whole of Canada, including the silent prairie discourse, lived history of the Maritimes, social economy of Quebec, mythology of the North, and reality of First Nations people. Only a genuinely "critical interdisciplinarity," Kroker admonished, can regenerate method and epistemology. By 1984, Henry Giroux, David Shumway, and James Sosnoski were pushing for a full-fledged "counterdisciplinary praxis" of cultural studies that would do what they claimed American studies and other interdisciplinary programs had failed to do—dismantle the boundary between the literary and the political, treat cultural objects relationally, be inclusive of low culture, and question the premises of dominant practices.

The distinction between "instrumental" and "critical" interdisciplinarities is not absolute. Research on problems of the environment and on health often combine critique and problem solving. Conventional and critical discourses are not airtight categories either. Over time, critical interdisciplinarities have influenced the way that research and teaching is conducted in established disciplines, older interdisciplinary fields, and general education. In the rush to accentuate critique, proponents of critical interdisciplinarity are often quick to dismiss other practices. Nascent fields are chided for not moving fast enough or being radical enough, even though cultural critique and anti-essentialist theories are not without their own contradictions. The interdisciplinary question, Melville and Readings caution, may seek to prevent crisis or exacerbate it. New synthetic discourses make the case for alternatives, but they do not escape the dangers of totalizing themselves ("Introduction" 6).

Douglas Kellner offers two glosses on the question of definition that contribute to a more nuanced understanding. Kellner contrasts Lyotard's generalized critique of "master narratives" that attempt to subsume every particular viewpoint into one totalizing theory—such as science, liberal humanism, some versions of Marxism, or feminism—with "grand narratives" that attempt to tell a particular Big Story—such as the rise of capitalism, patriarchy, or the colonial subject. Within grand narratives, metanarratives that tell a story about the foundation of knowledge can also be distinguished from macro social theory that attempts to conceptualize and interpret a complex diversity of phenomena. Synchronic narratives that tell a story about a given society at a given point in history are further distinct from diachronic narratives that analyze historical change, accounting for discontinuities and ruptures. Lumping all grand narratives together, Kellner advises, ignores the diversity of theoretical narratives that operate in culture and under the name of interdisciplinarity ("Postmodernism" 252–53).

Ultimately, W. J. T. Mitchell argues, everything depends on what sort of interdisciplinarity is being practiced. Mitchell distinguished three major types:

1. *top-down:* comparative, structural formations that aim to know an overarching system or conceptual totality within which all disciplines are related;
2. *bottom-up:* a compulsive and compulsory interdisciplinarity that is dictated by a specific problem or event;
3. *inside-out:* the indisciplined or anarchist moment, a site of convergence and turbulence.

("Interdisciplinarity" 541)

The top-down model hearkens back to a Kantian architectonic of learning, in a pyramidal or corporate organization of knowledge production capable of regulating flows of information from one part of the structure to another. It appears in philosophy and in critical theory, in claims for a utopian convergence of theory and practice, and in promotion of semiotics as a universal metalanguage for studying culture. The bottom-up model emerges "on the shop floor," in response to emergencies and opportunities. Cultural studies is a general form of the bottom-up model. The inside-out form is the "indiscipline" of breakage or rupture. It disturbs continuity and practice, though ruptures can become routinized, as the rapid transformation of deconstruction into an institutionalized method of interpretation demonstrated. The "anarchist" moment, Mitchell maintains, may well be the most important event. Like Salter and Hearn's "churn in the system," it is the time before routine or ritual is reasserted. The act may be public or esoteric and professional. Edward Said went public, addressing a readership that was not confined to a single discipline. Jacques Lacan penetrated so deeply into his particular discipline that he imploded its boundaries, sending shock waves into other disciplines and forms of public life ("Interdisciplinarity" 541).

Trans, Post, and Antiinterdisciplinarity

Use of the terms "trans," "post," and "antidisciplinarity" marked a new phase of definition in humanities. In the OECD typology, transdisciplinarity was defined as a comprehensive framework that transcends the narrow scope of disciplinary worldviews through an overarching synthesis (*Interdisciplinarity* 26). General systems, structuralism, Marxism, policy sciences, feminism, and sociobiology have been leading examples. New connotations emerged in the 1980s and 1990s as well. In 1987, Basarab Nicolescu called for a new kind of transdisciplinarity in an open structure of unity informed by the new worldview of complexity in science. In place of reduction, Nicolescu envisioned a principle of relativity that is both transcultural and transnational. In 1994, Michael Gibbons and colleagues proposed that a new mode of knowledge production is fostering synthetic reconfiguration and recontextualization of available knowledge by drawing on expertise from a wider range of organizations and stakeholders. In the realm of sustainability, transdisciplinarity has also become a label for collaborative research and problem solving that cross both disciplinary boundaries and sectors of society (Klein "Unity of Knowledge").

In the past, "transdisciplinarity" was not commonly used in humanities, but in the 1990s it began appearing more often as a label for knowledge formations that are imbued with a critical imperative. Michael Peters associated the term with new theoretical paradigms, questions, and knowledge that could not be addressed within the boundaries of existing disciplines (xn3). Ronald Schleifer linked the notion of a new interdisciplinarity with transdisciplinary Theory or cultural study of large social and intellectual formations that breach canons of wholeness and the Kantian architecture of knowledge and art (180). In media studies, Keller wrote, the transdisciplinary operation of cultural studies draws on a range of fields to theorize the complexity and contradictions of media/culture/communications. It moves from text to contexts, pushing boundaries of class, gender, race, ethnicity, and other identities (*Media Culture* 27–28). In women's and gender studies, Dölling and Hark associated transdisciplinarity with critical evaluation of terms, concepts, and methods that transgress disciplinary boundaries (1196–97), and in Canadian studies Jill Vickers aligned trans- and antidisciplinarity with movements that reject disciplinarity in whole or in part while raising questions of sociopolitical justice (41).

The term "postdisciplinary" is an inevitable by-product of a transformation in thinking about knowledge and culture. The dissociation of academic work from traditional departments, Louis Menand observed in an essay in *The Wilson Quarterly*, has become a widely held assumption in humanities. The question of collapse is usually accompanied by promotion of interdisciplinary teaching and scholarship. Yet, he contends, interdisciplinarity is completely consistent with disciplinarity. Each field develops its own distinctive program of inquiry, resulting in increases in interdisciplinary classes and even new majors. Increased interdisciplinarity, though, is neither new nor the cause of current confusion. Menand attributes that to "postdisciplinarity," a phenomenon driven in part by demographic shifts that coincided with the culture wars of the late 1980s and early 1990s. Many nonwhite and female students and faculty considered disciplines to be rigid, exclusionary abstractions. They brought a spirit of transgressiveness and play into the academy, creating demands for new subject matter and reinforcing the notion that the disciplines were collapsing or at least in a process of profound redefinition. When departments were slow to respond, a backlash occurred, resulting in a kind of "antidisciplinarity." Women's studies departments, for instance, emerged not only because female academics wanted separate domains. English, history, and sociology departments did not initially welcome gender-based courses.

Even so, the arrival of new populations alone is not enough to explain why adding new areas does not threaten the integrity of a discipline. Postdisciplinarity, Menand continues, is a different phenomenon with a distinct etiology. Most early influential theorists were white males, and the seeds of undoing old disciplinary models were already present. The people most closely associated with the initial demise of faith in disciplinary autonomy were working within traditions in which they had been trained. In the late 1970s, Clifford Geertz, Paul De Man, Hayden White, Stanley Fish, Richard Rorty, and others criticized the failures and omissions of their disciplines. Rorty's landmark *Philosophy and the Mirror of Nature,* for example, constructed its attack on the claims of analytic philosophy from within the discipline, from arguments advanced by mainstream philosophers. Today, Menand contends, the era of antidisciplinarity is over because most traditional disciplines have been "co-opted." Still, he warns, there is a risk of sliding into an aimless eclecticism. Doctoral education is a major obstacle. Of all spheres of American education, it is the most resistant to reform. The curriculum of the liberal arts college, the demographic composition of student bodies, and the status of knowledge in the global economy have all moved on. Yet, for all the talk about sex and gender studies, cultural studies, American studies, and postcolonial studies, credentialing goes on in English, history, sociology, philosophy, and other liberal arts fields ("Undisciplined").

Menand is right to argue that demographic factors alone do not account for the postdisciplinary condition of knowledge. However, interdisciplinarity is not completely consistent with disciplinarity. Fields develop individual programs, but their nature and impact differ dramatically.

Furthermore, impediments to inter and postdisciplinarity remain, even in liberal arts colleges. Across the variegated terrain of American higher education, there are also significant differences in the status of interdisciplinarity, antidisciplinarity is not dead, and the co-option of disciplines is not universal. Finally, even with the cache that critical interdisciplinarity currently enjoys in humanities, it is not the only sanctioned form, and there is plenty of skepticism about trans, anti, and postdisciplinarity. Generalizing about "its history," art historian Thomas Reese warns, is dangerous. A closer look at the relative permeabilities of boundaries in different settings is required. If disciplinary structures are strong and boundaries fixed, strategies for interdisciplinarity require force and are considered trangresssive. If structures are weak, they are assumed to be natural and permit excursions (544). The assumption that interdisciplinarity has an inherent political agenda is no less problematic. An activist agenda requires interdisciplinarity from the beginning, Jeff Konz remarked in a discussion of ideology on the Association for Integrative Studies listserv. Any attempt by definition confronts the hegemonic assumptions of disciplines. Yet, interdisciplinarity does not imply an inherent or a particular kind of social consciousness or ideological agenda (10.8.2002 <INTERDIS@Listerv.muohio.edu>).

The contest of definition is neither surprising nor limited to humanities. In an analysis of forms of interdisciplinary explanation, Mark Kann identified three political positions. Conservative elites want to solve social and economic problems without concern for epistemological questions. Liberal academics demand accommodation, but maintain a base in the existing structure, in the middle ground of harmonious interaction. Radical dissidents challenge the existing structure of knowledge, demanding that interdisciplinarity respond to the needs and problems of oppressed and marginalized groups in order to achieve greater equality (197–98). Within humanities, Giles Gunn adds, the radical response calls for a revolt against not only disciplinary boundaries but all institutional hierarchies. The left interdisciplinary project is more militant than the liberal one, which preserves the distinction between the academy and the world with the aim of reforming how knowledge is produced within the academy. The radical project exposes the political nature of the distinction, with the aim of transforming not only academic structure but the larger structure of social articulations (*Thinking* 187–88).

Practice

Interdisciplinarity, in short, has no inherent meaning. Patterns of practice reveal shared definitions. Yet, Stephen Turner cautions, "practices-talk" gets into trouble over the notion of sharing. Shared practices enable audiences to be persuaded, conduct joint work, and establish new facts. Practices are learned in heterogeneous ways, however, and they differ in nature (11, 23, 33, 110). In the case of interdisciplinarity, scope is one factor. "Narrow interdisciplinarity" occurs between disciplines with compatible methods, paradigms, and epistemologies, such as history and literature. It has a different dynamic than "broad interdisciplinarity" between disciplines with little or no compatibility, such as sciences and humanities (J. Kelly; Paxson; van Dusseldorp and Wigboldus).

Local institutional culture is an added factor. Most of the thirty-eight humanities and social science faculty Lisa Lattuca interviewed for her book on *Creating Interdisciplinarity* were influenced by the developments surveyed in chapter 2. Yet, contexts vary. One historian called his approach "inherently interdisciplinary." For him, using a history text in a survey course or a novel or an anthropology text comes "naturally." A professor of Romance languages who believes students need to understand the political context of what they are reading considers her work more akin to cultural studies and has taught in women's studies. Comparably, an English professor believes her interpretation of literature was enhanced by exposure to cultural studies and her experience in women's studies made her look critically at her discipline. Another individual with a joint appointment in history and sociology reported that postmodernism is on the fringes at her campus. An English professor also encountered resistance, even though her shift from a linguistic-based to a more context-historical approach is a general trend within her discipline. She likened her version of interdisciplinarity to cultural studies, where the move beyond texts has been more radical. In contrast, an art historian placed his position at the forefront of a major movement in his discipline defined by new questions about methodology and objects (85–86, 203–04, 220–22).

Doing Interdisciplinary Work

The topic of practices raises the least understood aspect of all. How does one actually *do* interdisciplinary work? Put another way, Kenneth Wissoker asked, "How interdisciplinary is interdisciplinarity?" Does a literary critic who analyzes five novels and a film to understand the rise of consumer culture count? Or, an environmental scientist borrowing a model from game theory? Or, are they simply expanding the tool kits of their own disciplines? (1). The definition of interdisciplinarity in the OECD typology suggests that the answer is yes. It encompassed a broad range of practices, from simple communication of ideas to mutual integration of ideas and approaches (*Interdisciplinarity* 25). Many definitions, however, assume a more substantial outcome. A widespread sense of disappointment also appears, for good reason.

The hazards of interdisciplinary work are well known. It has been likened to straying from the beaten path, mucking around in uncharted swamps, and standing on the edge of a cliff. An old joke even comes to mind. What do an interdisciplinarian and a grave robber have in common? In both cases, the goal is to get in, steal something, and get out fast before being detected. George Levine called failure to check on the accuracy and current validity of borrowed material and ideas "the quiet scandal of interdisciplinarity" (pers. comment, 27 April 1991). Old chestnuts may be overused and contradictory evidence and explanations disregarded (Klein, *Interdisciplinarity* 88; Vickers 17). Even if a borrowing is used correctly, the result may be a jumble. "To steal random parts of different engines," Charles Bazerman cautioned, "leaves one with a junkpile, even if one can create the appearance of a coordinated assembly" (9). Or, Steve Fuller warned, the fallacy of eclecticism rears its head. Partial methods do not add up to a complete picture of the phenomena being studied (42).

The terms integration, synthesis, and holism also continue to raise hackles. Readings, for example, critiqued my "automatic privileging" of unity and synthesis while claiming I regard teamwork as the only "truly" interdisciplinary form of work, a form that is "entirely mortgaged to assumptions of communicational transparency" ("Cultural Politics" 186n6). In doing so, he ignored my discussions of the historical decline of unity of knowledge, the role of conflict in interdisciplinary communication, disputed definitions, and multiple outcomes. Vickers also faulted my assertion that interdisciplinarity is "essentially" a process for achieving an integrative synthesis. Using this term, she charged, ignores issues raised by the "four posts" and advocates a hierarchical progression toward a reorganized knowledge enterprise or master synthesis (20–21, 35). Yet, Vickers conflated ordinary-language use of "essential" for necessary steps in a process with an ideological doctrine or motive. In some way, all interdisciplinary activities integrate different perspectives in a new whole that is greater than the sum of the parts, whether the goal is solving a particular disciplinary problem or building a new critical paradigm. The root of the English word "integrate" is the Latin *integer,* meaning whole (Kuczynski 143). Crafting a holistic perspective, however, does not necessarily involve restoring a lost wholeness or imposing a new unity.

Disciplines also loom large in discussions of practice. "A good interdisciplinary conversation," Lynn Hunt maintains, "depends on a serious commitment to other disciplines as disciplines." They are sources of new evidence and approaches, and they provide necessary vantage points. In her book on *The Family Romance of the French Revolution,* Hunt used art historical and literary sources alongside more conventional historical documents. Hunt treated paintings, engravings, and novels as "grist for my historical mill," though she tried not to reduce them to just another form of historical expression. Eighteenth-century paintings and novels had separate codes of representation, requiring her to reconstruct how specialists worked with them and to resist the temptation to make them simply illustrations of historical premises. Hunt, though, stopped short of a more general historical and cultural transformation in the mode of the *Annales* school.

"Good" interdisciplinary work, Hunt allows, entails an intensive encounter of two or more disciplines. Yet, she draws the line at creating a completely new interstitial space. Interdisciplinarity, she fears, may be in danger of losing meaning if humanities dissolves into an "undifferentiated pool of cultural studies" (74). Hunt also stops short of Fuller's requirement that "interpenetration" occur, to the point that disciplines begin to see each other involved in a common enterprise and their boundaries are renegotiated. Interdisciplinary work is most successful, Fuller contends, when borders are constantly engaged. Hunt's view and that of like-minded humanists depends on a view of the relationship between disciplinarity and interdisciplinarity that is undergoing a dramatic shift. As late as the 1970s, disciplines were not associated with interdisciplinarity. New research on everything from the mind and the body to the earth and the solar system has altered the relationship. Interdisciplinarity, Moran adds, assumes both the existence and the relative resilience of disciplines as models of thought and institutional practices (17). Hunt acknowledges that change is occurring and that interdisciplinary work produces effects back in the disciplines.

These changing conditions make it all the more important to invest time in learning about what is being borrowed and its context. Yet, her primary dialogue remains with historians. She does not veer too far from "home," lest she risk "excommunication."

Admitting disciplines into the discussion does not blunt the force of critique. It moves beyond the simplistic dichotomy of disciplinarity versus interdisciplinarity to a closer inspection of situated practices. It also raises the question of quality. Interdisciplinary quality does not lie in the imposition of an epistemically superior discipline or a neutral repository of cognitive criteria (Fuller xx, 37). Its dynamics are determined by the particularities of the task, the participants, the resources that are available, and the ultimate goals. That said, even in the absence of a universal paradigm there are common patterns. In an overview of definitions of integration and synthesis, William Newell identified three generic approaches: a conceptual framework, a comprehensive perspective, and a locus of activity (547–58). Within humanities in particular, Nancy Anne Cluck identified four integrative frameworks—historical periods, ideas, aesthetic themes, and structures. Cluck built on R. S. Crane's scheme of four arts or groups of skills that constitute common methodological dimensions in humanities. Linguistics, analysis of ideas, literary and artistic criticism, and historiography are pertinent in varying degree to all subject matters. Their convergence on any one of them, Crane argued, makes it humanistic in a complete degree comparable to the scientific method. As we will see in the case studies, periodization and cultural analysis have been particularly powerful syntheses. Yet, their definition and practice have changed over time, and the four approaches Cluck identified do not account fully for the visuality and aurality of humanities or, given that she was writing in 1980, the new developments surveyed in chapter 2. Those developments produced new integrative frameworks and loci of activity.

Not surprisingly, the word *bricolage* pops up a lot in humanities. It is a trendy term for taking bits and pieces from various disciplines and fields. The positive connotation is the free play of creativity. Interdisciplinarity, however, requires more than an eclectic mix of concepts, methods, and terminology. It entails conscious triangulation of depth, breadth, and synthesis. Disciplinarity is usually signified as depth, lying along a vertical axis, and interdisciplinarity as breadth, lying along a horizontal axis. The depth/breadth dichotomy, however, fails to acknowledge a third element—the synthesis that occurs in putting together different parts. Breadth opens up multiple perspectives. Depth ensures competence in pertinent disciplinary, professional, and interdisciplinary approaches. Synthesis moves across the vertical and horizontal planes, patterning and testing the relatedness of materials, ideas, and methods to a given task (Klein, *Crossing Boundaries* 212). "The days of the jigsaw puzzle metaphor," as Newell put it, are over (548). Interdisciplinary work in any form requires more than aligning pieces into a predetermined order, producing at best a multidisciplinary construct.

Discussions of how to do interdisciplinary work are hampered by the near paucity of studies of the actual work practices of humanists. Most of the discussion has focused on education and on scientific and technological research, with emphasis on collaboration in teams. Carole Palmer and Laura Neumann's interviews of twenty-five individuals at a humanities research center contribute new insights. Research questions and mixes of information sources were highly individualized, but respondents had common ways of conducting and managing interdisciplinary research. Each had a select core of resources that led to centrifugal activities. Two general types of boundary crossing also occurred: exploration and translation. Exploration fosters breadth by extending one's knowledge base (by scanning and receiving new information) and priming (by retooling, eclectic reading, and anchoring new knowledge). Interdisciplinary work inevitably confronts the problem of scatter. In low-scatter fields, underlying principles are well developed, and a literature and width of a subject area are well defined. In high-scatter fields, the number of subjects is greater and the organization of the literature may be almost nonexistent (Bates 156). Digests of scholarship on a particular topic and multiple-discipline bibliographies and review essays were vital aids to Palmer and Neumann's informants, of the kind published in the journals *Signs* and *American Quarterly*. They also used textbooks, handbooks, canonical works, journals in new specializations or unfamiliar fields, "push sources," and other mechanisms that route information directly, such as mailings and listservs.

Priming plays a crucial role. In a study of the link between interdisciplinarity and creativity, David Sill highlighted the role of ripeness, an active imagination, preinventive structures, and the subconscious. Preinventive structures in the subconscious—such as ideas, images, or concepts—provide raw material for inventive combinations. As scholars moved into foreign disciplines and work with unfamiliar languages, Palmer and Neumann found that they begin making connections and engage in translation, considering a word (or object or entity) in association with something else rather than as an isolated phenomenon. Translation entails Learning (through consulting, apprenticing, and schooling) and Crafting (through contextualizing and converting). Translation reflects the thought process that leads to interdisciplinary thinking, since it is a form of situational thinking and a problem-solving activity. Palmer and Neumann highlight the role of Anchoring. Information becomes more concentrated as ideas are assimilated, integrated, written down, and revised. Consulting with others and working directly with objects aids in defining, interpreting, and redefining new information. Essential elements of original context are retained but revised and reapplied for the task at hand. Reconsideration, reformulation, and restating are vital activities for constructing higher-order comprehensive meanings or metaperspectives. Fuller likens the process to moving from lower-level translation of disciplinary perspectives by "bootstrapping" up to higher levels of conceptual synthesis (45).

Even though studies of integrative process are small in number, authors agree on several points. Borrowing from another discipline requires assuming what Janice Lauer called the "burden of comprehension." A minimal understanding of its cognitive map is needed, including basic concepts, modes of inquiry, terms, observational categories, representational techniques, standards of proof, and types of explanation. Learning a discipline in order to practice it, though, is different than using it for an interdisciplinary purpose. Disciplinary mastery connotes complete knowledge. Interdisciplinary work requires adequacy. Borrowers do not claim expertise in all areas. They identify information, concepts or theories, methods, or tools relevant to understanding a particular problem, process, or phenomenon. Furthermore, there is no interdisciplinary *Esperanto*. Even a powerful metalanguage must be grounded in the particularities of a project. Nor is the popular metaphor of bilingualism an accurate description of what happens. Interdisciplinary language typically evolves through development of a trade language that becomes a pidgin—defined in linguistics as an interim tongue—or a creole—a new first language of a community (Klein, *Interdisciplinarity* 41–42, 85–94; Klein, *Crossing Boundaries* 43–44, 61–70; Sarah Van den Berg in "Forum" 276; Vickers 16–18).

A Lesson from "North" America

Vickers's reflection on teaching graduate students how to do interdisciplinary work provides a powerful lesson in practice. The context is Canadian studies, but all culture-based studies are confronted by the same changing conditions of practice. Interdisciplinarity was once regarded as a single kind of activity framed against a stable system. That is no longer the case. Multiple kinds of fields, Vickers explains, are now "in the mix." Some have "congealed" to the point that they have a recognized canon or foundational theory. They effect a partial closure, acting like disciplines because they have a shared epistemological base, journals, learned societies, and in some cases separate departments. In contrast, "open or cross-roads interdisciplinary fields" do not have a paradigm, canon, foundation, or epistemology, although they have attained influence in some disciplines. Other fields remain open to new ideas and movements, especially identity fields centered on "self-studies." Combining and comparing insights crossculturally creates an added complication. So does combining the insights of one or two disciplines with a "congealed interdisciplinarity," such as political economy, or the insights of two or more disciplines.

When Vickers first began working in Canadian studies, students practiced a discipline-dependent form of interdisciplinarity. Knowledge from one or several other disciplines was added to a discipline-based methodological spine. Correspondingly, most faculty were trained in disciplines. They had moved into interdisciplinary work primarily because of a national interest in "things Canadian" that were either neglected or suspect in their disciplines and fields. As new inter- and transdisciplinary fields developed, the context changed. Some fields were problem driven, such as environmental studies. Others were linked with a broad societal movement for change, such as the women's movement and Quebec and First Nations's movements for self-determination. The most important transdisciplinary fields for Canadian studies were women's, native/aboriginal, cultural communications, regional, northern (or circumpolar), urban, and environmental studies. In addition, heritage conversation studies played a role. The first three examples involved some degree of rejecting the disciplines. The others were primarily emerging fields that were discipline-dependent.

Graduate students excited by new scholarship entered Canadian studies. However, the lack of interdisciplinary PhD programs meant moving back into the disciplines. At the time, Vickers taught master's-level students the principle of borrowing from disciplines "respectfully and respectably" in order to avoid distortions and lend credibility to work that would be evaluated by disciplinary faculty. Alternative understandings of how to practice interdisciplinarity or how to teach that practice within particular fields were lacking. The students most likely to resist this principle were in women's studies and native/aboriginal studies. Asserting "antidisciplinary" positions, they tended to use materials in ways dictated by their own trans-disciplinary theories, cultural traditions, and lived experience. Vickers labels this intermediate phase in the history of Canadian studies "multidisci-plinary," since disciplinary insights were used without attempting to reconcile contradictions in units and levels of analysis, concepts, or standards of evidence. Students were also expected to perform "solo interdisci-plinarity." They were not taught to be part of an interdisciplinary team or, in transdisciplinary cross-cultural projects, a team of academic and community-based knowers. Faculty teaching teams, in turn, were usually assortments of disciplinary scholars who offered a smorgasbord of insights and made conflicting demands on students.

In the third and most recent phase, the context has changed again. New fields have gained a firmer reality anchored by undergraduate and some graduate programs, learned societies, and journals. More than half the students in Vickers's graduate interdisciplinary courses in the late 1990s had completed interdisciplinary undergraduate degrees and, increasingly, junior instructors and teaching assistants in Canadian studies have most of their experience in inter- or transdisciplinary fields or a combination of interdisciplines (such as art, history, political economy) mixed with trans-disciplinary fields (such as women's or native/aboriginal studies). Multidis-ciplinarity persists. Books and conferences still tend to be organized around thematic issues, not a systematic building of a field. Moreover, Canadian studies is still dominated by people whose training was discipline-based. Yet, a familiar generational dynamic is apparent. The faculty pushing openly for greater legitimation of interdisciplinarity tend to be younger.

When interdisciplinarity in Canadian studies was simpler, a "respect-able" account of a borrowing meant understanding it well enough in its original context that a disciplinary practitioner would be satisfied. At present, more students are entering interdisciplinary programs with no training in a disciplinary method. Some also contend that knowledge of a "donor discipline" is unnecessary when its cognitive map is being read "against the grain." In open cross-roads fields, two forces may be at work: an "integrative" tendency—evident in Canadian studies as area studies—and a self-asserting "disintegrating tendency" that draws the focus away from the center of existing knowledge systems—evident in critical, opposi-tional, or self-studies. Students and faculty choosing projects with conflicting understandings of evidence encounter several problems. They may prioritize one discipline or field. They may have difficulty integrating knowledge from an epistemologically "softer" field into a "harder" one. In transdisciplinary or antidisciplinary movements, they may reject epistemological claims of disciplines altogether, preferring alternative understandings of "knowledge" and "evidence." Yet, they may be uncertain how to make knowledge claims, other than on the ground of life experience. Complications arise even in recognized disciplines. Literature and history, for example, have undergone so much change that characterizing them as "stable" disciplinary matrices is problematic. Bridging certain practices of a discipline or even two disciplines with compatible epistemologies can be as difficult as bridging disparate fields. In some disciplines, evidentiary protocols are also in dispute.

Danielle Boutet's notion of artistry, Vickers suggests, provides a model of how to teach interdisciplinarity in an open field. Boutet conceives of interdisciplinarity as a process that begins with knowledgeable borrowing from different disciplines. During the generative process, an artist unbinds tools, techniques, methods, theories, and materials from disciplinary packages. The working context is not supplied by the disciplines, but instead the goals and frameworks an artist creates to mediate the interaction of components. Students in an open field that is not dictated by disciplines are in a similar position. Their research should be evaluated in its own right, on the ground of the generative process and explanation/legitimation processes for the new conceptual frame that mediates interaction of the elements. At the same time, the burden of comprehension remains. Artists are not usually required to weigh evidence and proof for a particular piece of creative work. In academic work, though, it is still necessary to become familiar with the languages of the disciplines and fields in question. The crucial skills, Vickers emphasizes, are *knowing how to select* among pertinent tools, mediums, and theories within disciplinary packages, and *knowing how to design* one's own goals and the tools needed to communicate in their working contexts.

Institutionalization

The question of institutionalization is hotly contested in humanities. The radical response is that institutionalization is the death knell of innovation, blunting its oppositional force and reducing a new field to "just another discipline." Yet, Janet Wolff submits, the question of becoming a department is less important than determining the best strategy for institutional survival. Setting up departments and centers is not in and of itself counterproductive if the critical spirit is protected and fields are not ghettoized. The argument that interdisciplinary fields need to exist in marginal spaces sidesteps the question of how they can have a lasting impact. If they become self-contained, traditional disciplines are left to their old practices ("Excess and Inhibition" 714).

In contrast to their counterparts in science and even in social science, humanists tend to be solo scholars and teachers, despite noteworthy exceptions such as the *Utopieforschung* project at the University of Bielefeld's Center for Interdisciplinary Research, the *Reallexikon fur Antike und Christentum,* and humanities labs at Stanford University and the University of Illinois. Solitary though they may tend to be, however, there is still a social dimension to the work of individuals. Their affiliations often constitute the home of interdisciplinary work, especially at the outset. A Marxian economist, for example, may share more concepts, approaches, and methods with a Marxian literary theorist, art historian, or ethnomusicologist than a neoclassical economic theorist (Amariglio, Resnick, and Wolff 151). A historian may be teaching a departmental survey course while collaborating with a feminist art historian on representations of women in American painting and participating in the visual culture interest group of the American Studies Association. A member of an English department specializing in American literature may be coordinating a program in media studies while working within a network of film scholars. A member of the music department may teach traditional composition courses while working on an electronic music program and coordinating a national listserv. And so on. . . .

In reviewing the track record of experiments in the 1960s and 1970s, Keith Clayton concluded that the "concealed reality of interdisciplinarity" was greater than "overt interdisciplinarity" (195–96). Clayton was talking about geography, medicine, veterinary science, agriculture, and oceanography. Yet, his observation is no less true of humanities. J Hillis Miller calls the combined formation of new developments a "hidden university" that crosses departmental, disciplinary, and institutional boundaries ("Theory" 130). Faculty study groups are an underappreciated site. In the 1980s, voluntary groups formed on a number of campuses as individuals sought to acquaint themselves with new developments. At Bryn Mawr College, a group of faculty from literature, philosophy, anthropology, and art history met to talk about European thinkers and the ways other disciplines interpret language, knowledge, and culture. At the University of California at Berkeley, an informal cross-departmental study group led to the founding of the journal *Representations,* a defining event in the rise of new historicism (C. Campbell A18–19). At Rice University, the Rice Circle brought together members of anthropology and several humanities disciplines. Their discussions led to establishment of a center that served as a Rockefeller-funded site for boundary-crossing work (Fischer 126).

The dissemination of structuralism and poststructuralism illustrates how multiple elements combine to legitimate projects on a wider scale. A 1966 symposium sponsored by the Humanities Center at Johns Hopkins University, on "The Languages of Criticism and the 'Sciences of Man,'" drew worldwide attention to structuralism. A two-year series of colloquia and seminars followed, building a broad base for introducing French theory into the U.S. Pioneer programs on Theory were founded at major research universities and new forums of exchange emerged, including the School of Criticism and Theory, the Division on Literary Criticism within the Modern Language Association, the Society for Critical Exchange, and the International Summer Institute for Semiotic and Structural Studies. Founded in 1980, the Institute attracted individuals from anthropology, history, linguistics, literary studies, mathematics, philosophy, and religious studies (Leitch 260).

Despite their gatekeeping powers, established professional organizations are key sites, though relations with disciplinary hosts vary. Some, such as the Modern Language Association's (MLA) literature and science group, maintain a presence in the parent body after establishing their own organization, typically anchored by a professional society, annual meeting, newsletter, and journal. Over time, the MLA has hosted interdisciplinary interest groups in women's studies, ethnic studies, and gay studies; popular culture; children's literature; literature's relations with other arts and sciences; and anthropological, linguistic, philosophical, psychological, religious, and sociological approaches to literature. Special sessions at annual meetings are often catalysts for further work. A session on "Representing Jazz" at the 1990 MLA led to the first major book on jazz to adopt critical theory (Gabbard vii). The May 1992 issue of *PMLA* focused on the topic of performance, and a 1993 conference included a session on "Disciplining

Performance." Performance was traditionally the subject of theater departments and, to a lesser degree, theater interests in English departments and
performance-related topics in speech and communication departments. Contemporary inquiry into performative aspects of the arts and social life has extended the study of drama, theater, and performance beyond older modes of
literary and theatrical formalism. Performance-related topics now appear in
the literatures of ethnography, performance studies, cultural studies, and literary theory ("Special Topic"; see also "Theatre and Interdisciplinarity").

   The academic system of publication plays a role as well. In new fields
and subdisciplines, dedicated interdisciplinary journals are a pivotal site of
communication (*Humanities* 100–01). Some are large and prestigious,
such as *Science* and *Nature,* Most, however, are small with loyal follow-
ings, but limited circulation. Interdisciplinary journals serve several functions. Some bridge traditional disciplines, among them *Comparative Studies in Society and History, Philosophy and Public Affairs,* and *Les Annales.*
Some cover interdisciplinary problem-focused fields, such as the *Journal of
Peace Research* and the *Journal of Conflict Resolution.* Others advance hybrid fields, such as the *Journal of Historical Geography* and the *Journal of
Psycholinguistic Research* (Dogan and Pahre 162–63). The disciplinary innovative journal belongs in the latter category. *New Literary History,* for
example, was a key site for work on Theory and cultural studies. So were
boundary 2 and *Diacritics* (Arac 120).

   The proliferation of a new kind of transdisciplinary professional journal, David Hollinger adds, documents the weakening of disciplinary boundaries and loyalties. In the 1950s, this kind of journal was rare. By the
1980s, well-regarded scholars were publishing in them. The fervor of debate on Theory and identity was particularly intense in journals in which
scholars from different disciplines confronted each other. Transdisciplinary
journals as a group exhibit a blend of *wissenschaftliche* and essayistic styles
that differ from disciplinary journals and journalistic periodicals read by
the wider public. *Critical Inquiry* is a primary example. Literary scholars
have dominated, but philosophers, historians, art historians, musicologists,
and film critics also contribute. *American Quarterly, Public Culture, Dias-
pora,* and *Modernism/Modernity* have topical specialties, and a number of
other journals reach across the boundaries of humanities and social sciences. *Raritan,* for example, has editorial advisors and contributors from
political science and anthropology as well as humanists. *October, Common Knowledge, Representations,* and *Salmagundi* appeal to humanistic

elements within political science, anthropology, sociology, history, and geography. A certain "tilt" toward humanities is also evident in *Social Text* and *Theory and Society* (353–56).

Special occasion publications are important sites as well, especially issues of disciplinary journals that examine interdisciplinary practices and books from interdisciplinary conferences. By and large, though, this genre of scholarship is more multi- than interdisciplinary. Editorial prefaces and introductions carry the weight of integration while individual contributions exhibit a disciplinary orientation. Interdisciplinary books occupy a tenuous niche. Marjorie Garber cites the back covers of books listing multiple suggestions for advertising as evidence of the popularity of interdisciplinarity: Pierre Bourdieu's book *On Television* is labeled for "Sociology/ Media Studies," James Elkin's *The Poetics of Perspective* for "Art History/ Aesthetics," and Foucault's *Discipline and Punish* for "Philosophy/Criminology" (75–76). Yet, editor William Germano cautions, all publishing is market-driven, and scholarly publishing, in particular, has been discipline-driven. New fields take their place, but scholarship written against the grain often makes publishers nervous. Crossover titles do not automatically guarantee two audiences, and work that ranges across fields requires more resources to be "published well" (328–30, 332).

Centering Interdisciplinarity

During the 1980s, humanities institutes were established on many campuses on the model of scientific research institutes (Herbert 549n32). In the late 1980s, the University of California at Irvine compiled a list of nearly 300 centers throughout the country (Levine et al. 30), and the current website of the Consortium of Humanities Centers and Institutes lists 130 members in the U.S. and abroad (http://www.fas.harvard.edu/~chci). Some centers carry broad titles such as "humanities," "theory," or "culture." Specialized foci, though, are common in international studies (e.g., Slavic, Japanese), regional studies (e.g., Appalachia, the West), period studies and other interdisciplinary fields (e.g., medieval studies, comparative literature), gender or race (e.g., women's, African American, Asian American, and Latino studies), and a range of topic areas (e.g., ethics, folklife, and Baudelaire).

Humanities centers serve several functions. They are catalysts for cross-campus dialogue and new programs. They sponsor local and national conferences. And, they provide research support, fellowships, and lecture series. Some are prestigious. Most, though, tend to be modest in size and exist on soft money or the largess of their hosts. Founded in 1959, the Center for the Humanities at Wesleyan University is the oldest model in the U.S. and the National Humanities Center in North Carolina is the country's only independent institute for advanced study in humanities. At the University of Utah, forming a center was a means of moving beyond empty rhetoric to formal support for interdisciplinarity. One of the purposes in founding a center at Yale was to facilitate a new doctoral program in American studies. Like counterpart institutes and centers at the University of California at Irvine, Stanford, and the University of Iowa, Yale's Whitney Center also supports cutting-edge scholarship. Their counterpart at the University of Wisconsin at Madison has hosted a series on the boundary-crossing scholarship of leading scholars, and the University of New Hampshire's center oversees the *Encyclopedia of New England Culture* while providing ongoing support for innovative research, teaching, and service. Michigan State University's center works with faculty and departments to offer the arts and humanities portion of the University's Integrative Studies Program while supporting interdisciplinary arts and humanities research on campus.

Two well-known centers illustrate one of the central premises of this book—that interdisciplinary initiatives are not isolated to one site, even on a single campus. The Humanities Institute at Stony Brook has three missions: to stimulate new modes of interdisciplinary research in humanities and social sciences; to build bridges with medical, technical, and natural sciences; and to reach out to the local community. In addition to fellowships, symposia, and conferences, the Institute designs programs of broader interest with the community and theme-based graduate and faculty courses. Regular collaborations also occur with departments and the medical school, and the Center works closely with women's studies, Africana studies, the Latin American and Caribbean Center, and the Center for Science Studies. The University of California (UC) Humanities Research Institute serves all nine campuses of the UC system. On the Irvine campus, the Institute promotes collaborative work aimed at bridging gaps between disciplines across humanities and overcoming barriers that isolate humanities from social and natural sciences, technology, and medicine. By articulating the cultural dimensions of social issues, individual projects build frameworks for policy decisions. In addition, the Institute administers fellowships and promotes collaborations with the Universidad Complutense de Madrid.

The word "center" is ironic, since many are not central to the mission of an institution. They are peripheral enclaves. Moreover, the emphasis has been on individual research and paper reading rather than collaborative work. Jonathan Arac lamented that there is "too much shop window, too little laboratory." In comparison to sciences and social sciences, humanities centers also receive less financial support (120, 122). Yet, they have played a crucial role in the intellectual development of humanities. At an April 1991 meeting of the national consortium at Yale, directors of centers were highly conscious of managing a "space in between," an "other" or "shadow" structure characterized by organizational flexibility and intellectual experiment. Disciplinary boundaries on many campuses remain firm, and departments retain power. Nonetheless, dialogue has changed, existing curricula have been enriched and reformulated, and humanities and interdisciplinarity have become more visible. On their own, as Thad Tate of the College of William and Mary remarked at the Yale meeting, centers are not changing disciplinary maps, but they are often in the forefront. Most are not antidisciplinary. They do not attempt to devise a new interdisciplinary core, either, rather a context that allows contemporary thinking to be brought to bear on classical texts and issues while interrogating underyling premises of centrality, universality, and authority.

Interdisciplinary Studies

The rise of interdisciplinary fields is a major episode in the history of knowledge. They constitute one of the frontiers of innovation in higher education and have been a primary locus for new scholarship and teaching (D. Bennett 144). Their emergence is often dated to the 1960s and 1970s. Their history began earlier, though, in the 1930s and 1940s, with the development of area studies, American studies, and expansion of comparative literature. By the early twenty-first century, a host of examples populated the academic landscape: from molecular biology, cognitive science, and materials science to criminology, gerontology, and policy studies to gender studies, media studies, and cultural studies.

Raymond Miller identified two major impetuses for new fields: crosscutting topics and life experience. Interdisciplinary topics often emerge from problem areas such as crime and the environment. Area studies was another topical focus as well as labor studies, gerontology, and future studies. During the 1960s and 1970s, life experience became a major category with the emergence of black studies, women's studies, and ethnic studies (13–15). Today, the rise of new disciplines, interdisciplines, and paradisciplines is no longer regarded an unusual event. In the wake of anti, cross-, and interdisciplinary studies, Marjorie Garber adds, some traditional disciplines have been renamed, becoming English studies, literary studies, and romance studies. Clearly, interdisciplinary studies serve a need that is not going away (78). Yet, Wissoker reminds us, it is easier to produce disciplinary versions of purportedly interdisciplinary spaces such as literary cultural studies and sociological cultural studies than to construct and maintain full-fledged interdisciplinary spaces (4).

The concept of critical mass is helpful in thinking about how interdisciplinary spaces are constructed and sustained. Derived from physics, "critical mass" means the minimum quantity of nuclear fuel required for a chain reaction to start. The elements of critical mass in interdisciplinary fields are grouped roughly by kind (composite of Rich and Warren 56, 59; Caldwell 255; Klein, *Crossing Boundaries* 34–35):

- An adequate number of individuals sharing common interests
- An adequate number and scale of programs

- An infrastructure for communication
- A network of hybrid communities and mediating structures
- Adequate economic and symbolic capital
- Formal conducting/contracting of research

- Full-time appointments in an interdisciplinary program, center, or department
- A secure location in the organizational hierarchy of a campus
- Autonomy in curriculum and budget decisions
- Control of staffing, including recruitment, retention, and rewards

- The rise of a scholarly body of knowledge
- The capacity for generating new knowledge and synthesis.

Interdisciplinary fields are often heralded as the prototype of the future. However, there is a pronounced gap between the rhetoric of transformation and the realities of critical mass. Their structures range widely, from an augmented form of specialization to a center or program to an autonomous department, school, or college. More programs carry the name than grant a degree, few offer all undergraduate and graduate degrees, and many turn out to be multidisciplinary combinations of departmental courses coordinated by a faculty member and housed in a traditional department or other program. Fields also have a different character from campus to campus. Their intellectual development at the national level is a powerful factor in their legitimation, but the local political economy of academic power, administrative fit, economic incentives, and community pressures are strong determinants. On one campus faculty enjoy the freedom to pursue their interests and all the perks. On another, a program struggles to survive, and interdisciplinary work is discounted in the reward system. The balance of education and research differs as well, and academic values come into conflict with problem solving, activism, and vocational service. The fusion of critique and problem solving in fields that sprang from social movements puts political and intellectual work theoretically on the same level. They are not valued equally, however (Klein, *Crossing Boundaries* 87–132).

Categories of knowledge are institutions, not in the conventional sense of buildings and organizations but a set of marks constructed and maintained in cultural space. They enable collectivities to tell their members where they are and how to conduct themselves (after Shapin 355). The boundary work of interdisciplinary studies is threefold. They detach a category as subject and object from existing disciplinary frameworks, loosening boundaries and stimulating trading zones. They fill gaps in knowledge from lack of attention to a category, creating new pidgins and creoles. If they attain critical mass, they constitute new social and cognitive formations. Even then, however, both centers and interdisciplinary studies wind up caught in the balancing act of being institutional and extra-institutional at the same time. They have tended to reside in the shadow structure of the academy. Yet, they are the surface structure of the categories of knowledge they develop. Many also have multiple identities. "Creolized disciplines," Cornwall and Stoddard observe, can be alternative, resistant, or emergent. Women's studies, for instance, may be viewed as an emergent discipline with its own canons, methods, and issues. At the same time, it is an alternative or is resistant to traditional discursive practices of disciplines ("Epistemology" 162).

The emergence of interdisciplinary fields raises a question that ultimately applies to all interdisciplinary activities—"Where do they fit?" Lynton Caldwell originally posed the question about environmental studies. The metaphor of fit, Caldwell answered, prejudges the epistemological problem at stake in their emergence. Many fields arose because of a perceived misfit among need, experience, information, and the structuring of knowledge and curriculum embodied in disciplinary organization. If the structure of the academy must be changed to accommodate them, then perhaps the structure itself is part of the problem. Interdisciplinary studies represent a latent and fundamental restructuring of knowledge and education (247–49). Interdisciplinary practices arise from different motivations and have different trajectories. Yet, their cumulative force has made boundary crossing a major factor in shaping contemporary knowledge.

The conventional notion of a boundary is implicated as well. Multiple boundaries are now at stake—not only disciplinary and interdisciplinary demarcations but national and geographical, historical and generational, racial and ethnic, social and political, ethical and religious lines. Boundaries, Stephen Greenblatt and Giles Gunn observed, "can be crossed, confused, consolidated, and collapsed; they can also be revised, reconceived, redesigned, and replaced." They cannot, however, be entirely abolished. Furthermore, they differ. Boundary lines are drawn in bold, unbroken strokes and as a series of intermittent, irregular dashes. They have multiple functions and are accepted or redrawn from multiple stances. They cross, overlap, or converge at different places and in different degrees ("Introduction" 4). Only by mapping situated practices can we fully understand the dynamics of boundary crossing and interdisciplinarity.

Part II

INTER/DISCIPLINING HUMANITIES

Chapter 4

REWRITING THE LITERARY

The dominant trend in higher education for much of the twentieth century was the growth of specialization, but in the latter half of the century a historical reversal of this trend began (Gaff and Ratcliff, "Preface" xiv). Since the 1950s, many disciplines have become more porous and multi or interdisciplinary in character, to the point that Dölling and Hark now describe them as "shot through with cross-disciplinary pathways" (Bender and Schorske, "Introduction" 12; Dölling and Hark 1196–97). Interdisciplinary developments are often described in the metaphors of the "frontier" or "cutting edge." Popular metaphors, though, are misleading. The center and the periphery are neither uniform nor stable, and the dichotomy may have outlived its usefulness in some areas, especially literary studies (Gates, "'Ethnic'" 293; Gates, "African" 310). Likening disciplines to biological cultures, Tony Becher portrayed individual cells in a state of constant flux. They subdivide and recombine, changing shape and disposition. Some even exhibit an anarchic tendency to appear more closely allied with counterparts in other disciplines (333–36, 343–44). Mapping the results is not an easy task. Interdisciplinary interests, Giles Gunn suggested, are more akin to fractals than straight geometric lines ("Interdisciplinary Studies" 249).

The next three chapters trace the changing relationship of disciplinarity and interdisciplinarity in literary studies, art history, and music. Why start with literary studies in a book that aims to speak for other disciplines as well? Literature assumed early prominence in the history of humanities, it was a primary site for importing new developments, and it has been a major locus of interdisciplinary theorizing. In a previous study, I examined shifting configurations of interdisciplinarity in guides to practice published by the Modern Language Association. Over the course of the twentieth century, multiple forms emerged from the interplay of mainstream and alternative practices, framed by the shifting balance of "text" and "context"

(*Crossing Boundaries* 139–41). This chapter extends that study in an updated overview that addresses a series of related questions. What were the
early warrants for interdisciplinarity in the discipline? How did the conception of disciplinary relations change, and what practices promoted a sense
of greater interdisciplinarity and the notion of a "new interdisciplinarity"?
What similarities and differences appear in theory and in practice? What
are the key points of debate on interdisciplinarity in the discipline, and how
do they figure in discussions of its current status and future trendlines?

Beginnings

The subject of literature appeared in English academies during the late seventeenth century and by the mid-eighteenth century was a recognized subject in Scottish universities. In the American colonial college, the bulk of literary education occurred in Greek and Latin courses intended to inspire
students with the nobility of cultural heritage (Graff 1). The discipline had
a threefold origin in this country:

- as an outgrowth of training students in composition, oratory, and forensic
  rhetoric for writing and speaking well in their professional and personal lives;
- as an adaptation to study of vernacular literature in the tradition of scientific
  philology;
- as a development of humanism, especially the version associated with Matthew Arnold with its emphasis on study of literature as an acculturating power
  in education that would make students better persons and citizens.

(J. H. Miller, "Theory" 119–20)

From roughly 1860 to 1915, philology and literary history were the dominant practices. The new science of literary study emphasized editing and an-
notating texts; compiling bibliographies, dictionaries, and concordances;
conducting source and etymology studies; discovering facts; and writing bi-
ographies and literary and intellectual histories (J. H. Miller, "Theory" 119–
20). In the 1930s and 1940s, criticism became the dominant practice. It was
not a monolithic practice. The strain led by the New Critics emphasized aesthetic formalism through close readings of poems treated as organically unified objects. The strain led by the Chicago Critics emphasized theory and
argued for a pluralist approach and humanist moralism concentrated on the
qualities literature shares with philosophy, ethics, and general ideas. Both
groups, though, believed the integrity of the discipline was threatened. R. S.

Crane of the Chicago Critics warned against treating literature as psychology, history, sociology, ethics, or autobiography. New Critic Allen Tate chided critics for being "obsessed by politics" and faulted the historical approach for undermining the unique nature of literature. John Crowe Ransom announced that the English department might as well proclaim itself a branch of history or ethics. The New Critics did not reject the moral and social functions of literature, but they placed them within the internal structure of a text. This move affirmed the timeless universality that Aristotle attributed to literature and established a bulwark against threats to tradition. The problem of historical and cultural change became extrinsic to the business of literary scholarship, history one more discipline, and sociology and politics intrusions. The idea of academic seriousness also increasingly excluded reflection on the relations of one field to another (Leitch 62; Shumway and Dionne, "Introduction," 8–9; Graff 148; Weber 32).

Interdisciplinary "Interference"

Even though New Criticism was the dominant practice, it did not establish complete hegemony in the discipline (Greenblatt and Gunn, "Introduction" 8). In the 1930s, teaching English as a second language was professionalized as a branch of applied linguistics, and in the 1940s, creative writing gained a place. Many younger critics with generalist inclinations moved toward literary journalism, and some adapted generalist interests to the mold of New Criticism. Others dissociated themselves from the generalists' moral and social interests, though a group known as the New York Intellectuals conceived of literature as a cultural phenomenon open to multiple points of view. One of their leading members, Alfred Kazin, spoke to general anxieties and hopes, engaging not only artistic and critical interests but economic, social, ethical and moral, religious, and political concerns. Marxist and sociological analysis also fueled cultural criticism, though political bias against Marxism in the United States impeded fuller sociopolitical analysis. At mid-century, Marxism and other interdisciplinary interests were in what Gunn called "a state of noticeable arrest." Even when not arrested, they were "seriously eclipsed" by formalistic methodologies (Russell 54–55; Robbins, "Introduction" xiii; Bender, "Public" M1; W. Cohen 330–33; Gunn, "Interdisciplinary Studies" 252).

Over the next several decades, interdisciplinary interests expanded. In Europe, interdisciplinary research was promoted as the model for a regenerated study of literature opposed to strict formalism and open to historical awareness. By the mid-1950s, similar voices were being heard in the U.S. in the name of "multiple interpretation," "multiple parallelism," and "multiple causation" (Hermand and Beck 150). This kind of "interference," Gerald Graff contends, was so substantial that the direction of postwar literary studies was as much interdisciplinary as it was intrinsic. In 1948, Stanley Edgar Hyman described criticism as "the organized use of non-literary techniques and bodies of knowledge to obtain insights into literature." Hyman's model critics borrowed from linguistics and psychology (I. A. Richards), anthropology (Maud Bodkin), sociology and rhetoric (Kenneth Burke), Marxism (Christopher Caudwell), and linguistics and psychology (Richards and William Empson) (209–10).

Polymaths such as Burke and Northrup Frye also developed influential synoptic frameworks. Initially, Burke privileged linguistic and literary forms, but his approach widened to include biography, psychology, sociology, philosophy, politics, aesthetics, ethics, religion, anthropology, and subsequently a Marxist perspective. Burke employed the New Critical method of close reading of texts, though he used a set of protocols linked to social sciences. Frye objected to the proliferating determinisms that threatened to reduce literature to manifestations of the "nonliterary." Yet, his 1957 book *Anatomy of Criticism* presented a system of myths, modes, and genres that extended into literature, religion, philosophy, political theory, and aspects of history. In addition, it drew on categories of interpretation from psychology and anthropology. The book's wide reception is attributable to serving the needs of both pioneering and traditional critics. Frye's mythopoetic structure accommodated allegorical and genealogical modes of inquiry as well as sociological, religious, historical, and formalist approaches. It proved compatible with the fields of American studies and comparative literature as well. Ultimately, though, moral and social significance were made a function of the formal properties of the text "itself." Frye shifted the work of civilization to the inside of literature (Graff 210; Leitch 42–45, 136).

Disciplinary Relations

The logic of intrinsic criticism is conspicuous throughout the first MLA report on disciplinary relations, the 1967 *Relations of Literary Study*. By 1967, New Criticism was waning. Editor James Thorpe announced a series of new vantage points promised a more "stereoscopic view." Yet, in treating round—the fifth player chosen in that round—by scout Dick Bowie.

Arizona State third baseman Bob Horner was the first selection in the 1978 draft. Selecting 22nd, Baltimore made Bob Boyce their first choice. In round two Baltimore chose outfielder Larry Sheets and pitcher Ed Hook as compensation for losing free agents, and then, in their own pick, the O's chose Cal Ripken, Jr., the 42nd selection in the 1978 draft.

Branzell and Bowie were friends and rival managers, the former of the Washington Boys Club, the latter of the nationally known Johnny's team. Branzell was pained in later years that he let Cal slip through. The scout saw Cal pitch but ignored him as a shortstop. Branzell jested that his friend Dick Bowie "hid" Cal's fielding and hitting talents. "Dick and I were good friends," he said, "but we never talked about Cal. . . . I think Dick might have hid him a little bit."

Conceded Branzell in a *Baltimore Evening Sun* interview, "I never saw Cal junior play the infield. Looking back now, you realized that he pitched every big game.

"The fact that he was also playing shortstop when he wasn't pitching probably took something away from his arm in both positions. That's something that might not have been taken into consideration at the time."

For this reason, Branzell's scouting report of May 1978 totally ignored the Non-Pitchers section that describes offensive potential.

On the 10th anniversary of Cal's Major League debut, the *Baltimore Evening Sun* ran a feature on Cal's being scouted and signed. Branzell lamented to John Henneman how he let Cal get away. Branzell came to Aberdeen High to watch Cal pitch in May 1978.

He described the observee as having a "strong, raw-boned, rangy-live body. Built like and has Jim Palmer actions." In the Additional Comments section, the scout notes that Cal "mixes his pitches well . . . has an idea [about pitching] . . . good competitor . . . bat pretty good . . . good loose, long arms . . . good poise and savvy . . . only 17 should get faster."

All this, according to Branzell, merited $20,000. "I put down $20,000 as a bonus," he recalled, "and that was good money in those days, so I must have liked him." (Cal signed for $20,000 with the O's.)

Although the scout commented that Cal was a "little short on baseball velocity," Branzell told Henneman, "he threw about average for me, but his fastball and slider were close to the same speed, which is good; he had a good curve and change-up. I don't remember him being that big (Branzell recorded Cal as six foot three, 195 pounds, which was about one inch and 15 pounds more than the actual measurements), but you had to figure he'd get faster.

"But you had to be crazy not to like his makeup. I don't turn in reports unless I think a kid is a prospect, and I'm a conservative."

Cal senior insists that he spoke to no scouts before the draft. "When the Orioles drafted Cal, it was only then that Tom Giordano [director of scouting for the Orioles] approached me about Cal's future plans."

Cal was drafted in the first week of June while the Aberdeen Eagles were fighting for the state championship. After winning the state title, coach Connolly expressed confidence Cal would succeed because of "his enthusiasm and desire to play good ball." Teammate David Easter recalled that Cal "never spoke about his being drafted until it became public knowledge and the local press questioned him. He was never the boastful type."

Naturally, Cal was delighted: "I have always wanted to play for the Orioles and now I'm getting the chance to at least try and make it. I don't guess the full impact of what it means to be drafted so high has hit me yet. I haven't heard anything from the Orioles about where I will be sent or anything about a contract. I was happy the Orioles drafted me, especially because of all the teams that expressed interest in me." The *Aegis* spoke of 18 teams, while Vi Ripken spoke of 26.

As for holding off till he graduated college, Cal said, "I have a chance to play professional baseball, so I'm going to do it. I may never get a chance to do so again." Cal made it clear that his father's position in the Baltimore organization had no influence on his being drafted. "In fact," said Cal, "Dad has been trying to find out what the Orioles were going to do in the draft, and he wasn't able to learn anything." Cal's selection meant that Aberdeen High could now boast two grads in pro baseball. Mike Gustave, Eagles hurler class of '74, was toiling for the Minnesota Twins Class A farm team in Wisconsin Rapids.

With Cal now in the Orioles fold, the pressing question became: Where would he play—at shortstop or on the mound? Giordano told the *Record*, "We're still not sure where Cal Ripken will fit in for us. We're going to wait and see before saying anything definite."

In Cal's eyes the Orioles were favoring him as an infielder, and that suited him fine. As he told the *Record*, "The Orioles were the ones looking at me more as an infielder than as a pitcher. I would like definitely to have a chance to play the infield."

Surprisingly, Baltimore was the only team that had looked at Cal as a position player. Credit Dick Bowie, a foresighted and persistent scout. Bowie knew of Cal's desire to play every day, so he scouted him on days that he didn't pitch.

Jim Gilbert was then a part-time Orioles scout assisting Bowie. "About a week before the draft," related Gilbert, "Dick took Cal to Memorial Stadium for a private workout. Dick, his son, Randy, Paul McNeil, Bill Timberlake [associate scouts], and myself were the only ones there.

"We had seen enough of him as a pitcher, and Dick liked his bat and wanted to see his arm from shortstop. We were satisfied." Fifteen years later, Cal senior recounted the signing during an interview in his Aberdeen home. "As a lifelong Oriole," said

Senior, "I was very happy that the Orioles drafted him. Because he paid attention and he watched as a youngster, Cal knew all the cutoffs and relays, all the bunt relays that we use in our system. . . .

"After the Orioles drafted Junior, Tom Giordano asked me, 'What do you want to do? I've got to ask you something as a father, and what you say will have a bearing on what we do. Tell me if you have anything to do with the decision of where he has to play. I know Cal wants to play every day.'

"I told Tom that it wasn't what I wanted to do that mattered. It was what Cal junior wanted to do. He wanted to play every day. Had he been drafted by another team, that would have been a stipulation before he signed. The Orioles thinking was that if something happened, he could always go back to pitching before he was 20 or 21 years old. But if he started out pitching and didn't hit or field for three or four years, it would be difficult to go back to hitting and fielding every day."

Cal had continued to grow and was six foot two when he signed. The profile of the shortstop throughout baseball history has been slight and speedy. Cal junior was neither. When people think of shortstops, they cite Rabbit Maranville, Phil "the Scooter" Rizzuto, Luis Aparicio. There are 15 shortstops in the Hall of Fame: not a one is six feet or more; nine are five-nine or less.

And did Cal junior have the range of a shortstop? "I get irritated," said Vi Ripken, "when I recall that scout Scarborough [Ray Scarborough pitched in the American League from 1942 to 1951], who said that Cal would never make it at short because he didn't have the range. Wasn't he wrong!"

Cal and his family had little time to reflect about the future. Junior became a baseball player on June 13, 1978, and joined the Bluefield Orioles of West Virginia for "practice." Cal made his professional baseball debut on June 20 in an intrasquad game between the Al Lewises and the Ralph Rowes, named for the two coaches.

Cal had first-day butterflies. "I was a little bit shaky with all this competition," he said. Dick Bowie kept an eye on his newly signed prodigy and hurried to Bluefield. Soon "everything kind of loosened up" for the youngster. Cal poled a 370-foot homer and added two hits to help the Lewises rally for a 7–6 victory. The nervousness was gone. "As soon as I hit it, I knew it was gone," said an elated Cal, "and I believe everyone else did, too. The outfielders didn't move much. It was a fastball that was up. It felt good."

On the eve of the Appalachian League opener, Cal was very eager and confident. "I'm excited about it," he said. "I'm really up. I know that I'll be able to play in this league." Junior Miner was also eager to do well in his managerial debut at Bluefield. The Baby Birds already had a set mound staff that included Tim Norris, Bill Purdy, and two future Major Leaguers Don Welchel, an all-American at Sam Houston State, and Mike Boddicker from the University of Iowa. Miner needed an everyday infielder, so despite Cal's heralded pitching accomplishments, the manager designated Junior as his shortstop. The third baseman was the O's top 1978 draft choice, Bob Boyce.

Cal made a quick, favorable impression on Miner. "He's a good student, a dedicated kid," said the skipper. "He's dedicated to professional baseball. He's a workhouse and a hustler. He can outwork any one boy in a week's time. As for on-field strengths, Cal has a very good arm and quickness. He shows me a little bit of power—home run power. His fluid is not all there yet, but that's our job to rectify. But for a kid that's not developed yet, the power is kind of remarkable."

The opening day crowd of 1,500 at Bluefield's Bowen Field left delighted, as did Miner and visiting Clyde Kluttz, Baltimore's farm director. The Orioles whipped the Paintsville Highlanders 4–1, getting a solid seven frames from Don Welchel, three RBIs, including a homer from John Shelby, and three double plays in the late innings.

"It may be the best opening-night game I've ever seen for a bunch of kids," raved Miner. "I don't want to blow them up too much, but now we know that they're fundamentally sound. I'm proud of them. We instructed, they absorbed, and they executed. The defense executed well all night long. We showed we can play some defense."

Defense was Kluttz's theme. "I can never remember a rookie team making three double plays the opening night of the season," he beamed. Cal was involved in all three twin killings, having started two. Although he had no hits, he did smack a long shot to deep center that Roy Dixon chased down for the defensive play of the game.

Cal provided the heroics at a home game during the first week of July against the Kingsport Braves. The Orioles climbed out of the cellar, as Cal had three hits and scored the winning run in the 12th. But the clutch hit was a two-out single into center in the bottom of the ninth that prevented a Bluefield defeat.

Buoyed by the win, the Baby Birds reeled off a seven-game winning streak and moved to a 12–11 mark. The pitching improved, but equally significant was a more solid infield defense. Cal received high grades as an improved gloveman. "Cal Ripken was having trouble making the plays at shortstop and piled up a bunch of errors," said Miner. "I talked to Cal about his arm. The problem was that he wasn't putting enough confidence in it. He was charging the ball, taking the in-between hops, and was being handcuffed. Now he's got confidence in that arm and is playing deeper and can go into the hole and make that tough play.

"We have one of the younger teams in the six-team circuit. Cal is 17; our third baseman Bob Boyce is 18; and second baseman Eddie Rodriguez is 19. Their first taste of professional baseball was bound to produce mistakes, and it did. Cal is young and is bound to make mistakes. But what pleases me is that when he has made a mistake, he hasn't repeated it. He's learning and having fun, and that's what baseball is all about."

General manager George Fanning was also having fun. Attendance was good and the fans supportive even while Bluefield was losing. Now, a winning team meant rising attendance. As Bluefield

GM for more than three decades, Fanning has seen many go from the Rookie League to the bigs: Boog Powell, Don Baylor, Dean Chance, Bobby Grich, Doug DeCinces, Johnny Oates, John Shelby, Larry Sheets, Eddie Murray.

"Cal Ripken came to us with top credentials," he said. "All the scouts liked him. He was courteous, clean, well behaved, and didn't act or look like a bum. As a ballplayer he kept on improving, both in the field and at bat."

Statistically, however, it wasn't a very impressive year for Cal and Bluefield. When Bluefield beat Kingsport 10–7 on August 5, its record was only 16–25, registering its fourth win in its last 18 games. Cal went 1 for 5 that day, a typical game in a struggling season.

John Shelby was a Bluefield teammate, an outfielder who was Baltimore's top selection in the 1977 draft. After a career with Baltimore and Los Angeles, Shelby was named a Dodgers farm manager for 1994. He now manages the AA San Antonio Missions of the Texas League. He was at the Pawtucket farm in 1992, trying to battle his way back to the Majors. "Cal has been the best friend I have in baseball," he said. "We hit it off from the start. When we met in Bluefield, Cal was a young kid, skinny, very talented. He never wanted to come out of a game. He came to play, and that literally meant all the time.

"Cal struggled at Bluefield. When things went bad, he always turned to his dad for advice. He had the highest regard for his dad."

Cal senior told *50 Plus* magazine that he provided a long-distance dial-a-coach service to his son. "I would call him up, basically, to lift my spirits," said Junior. If Cal was hitting weak ground balls to the infield or popping up to the outfield, the father would ask, "Are you seeing the ball?" and then follow up with specific advice.

How effective was all this? Said Cal junior, "Sure enough, I'd go into batting practice, do exactly what he said, and I came out of the slump."

Cal turned to Richie Bancells for off-field advice. In fact, Cal began a career-long professional relationship at Bluefield with Bancells, who was also making his way through the Orioles farm system. "Richie was our trainer," said George Fanning. "He was an awfully nice fellow, very competent and professional. Like Cal Ripken, he was willing to learn and make it to Baltimore. I can't recall how close Cal was to Richie at Bluefield, but with Cal's concern of staying fit and playing all the time, there is no doubt that Cal benefited from Richie's presence on our team.

"Cal kept on improving during his rookie season," Fanning continued, "but the raw statistics were not that overwhelming. He did not make the Appalachian all-rookie team." In 63 games, Cal hit .264, with 63 hits and 24 RBIs in 239 at bats. Cal had only eight extra-base hits.

"But the most amazing stat," said Fanning, "was that Cal had no home runs, after that preseason blast. Everywhere Cal has played, he has hit home runs. In Baltimore he hit 20 or more home runs his first 10 seasons, but not a one at Bluefield. And you can't blame it on our park. The dimensions are very friendly for the hitter— 335 down both the left and right fields and 365 to center."

Cal was clearly dissatisfied with his performance, so he joined the instructional league when Appalachian League play ended. He came to sharpen his skills and gain added experience under the tutelage of Jimmy Williams. Following instructional league play, Williams filed his report for the Baltimore Orioles:

"This boy has the tools to play in the Major Leagues. He is a good low-ball hitter." But there was room for improvement because the youngster "lets up on his throws, and he never sets up ahead on the pitch."

Having packed away his bats and glove at the end of the instructional league, Cal went back to Aberdeen for the brief off-season respite. "Although he was a celebrity in town," said David Easter, "Cal did not forget his high school buddies. We would go out for beers to local taverns like Tom Hooligan's."

Situated in Appalachia in a rural, tranquil atmosphere, Bluefield was not made for partying and frolicking. In 1979, Cal moved to different surroundings: Miami, Florida, the O's Class A affiliation.

It was hard work for Cal, not beach play and sunbathing. Miami Orioles manager Lance Nichols had a serious mission—to repeat as champions of the Florida State League. Cal was greeted in Miami by a familiar face—Junior Miner, now a Miami coach after managing Bluefield to a 29–40 mark, worst in 1978 in the Appalachian League. "Lance Nichols was an ideal manager to play for," said Miami teammate John Shelby. "He demanded hard work and did not go for any clowning. This was perfect for Cal."

Now a scout for the National League's expansion Colorado Rockies, Nichols looked back at 1979 from his home in Dodge City, Kansas. "I had a chance for much discussion with Junior about our team. Some 20 of our roster players had been with Junior at Bluefield. We knew Cal Ripken hadn't proven himself. You certainly couldn't say he had a sure ticket for the Major Leagues. The Baltimore Orioles were not down in Miami looking Cal Ripken over to set up a Major League timetable."

Cal played shortstop at Aberdeen and at Bluefield, but early in the season Nichols decided to move Cal to third base. Miami had Steve Espinoza, a first-year sure fielder, available for short. His third baseman Bob Boyce, the 1978 Appalachian League MVP, separated his shoulder before camp broke and did not recover his batting form, and his fielding also suffered.

Nichols recalled taking some heat for the move, but he defended that decision. "I was criticized for moving Cal to third," he said. "But it was the right move. When we began the season, I observed that Cal was having some problems at short, so naturally I decided to shift him to third. As soon as he went to third, he made plays that he or nobody else on our team could have made elsewhere. He became settled in that position. Third base was a perfect fit for Cal and for our team.

"One of the first plays I remember him making was diving for a ball, but he was never totally on the ground. His aggressive fielding made our team much sounder."

Nichols and Cal were pleased with his development. "After I played third for a while," said Cal, "I liked it better, too. At third you can knock down a ball and still have time to throw the batter out. At shortstop, if you don't make the play cleanly, you don't have a play."

While team play improved, 1979 was not a fun year for the Miami O's, especially at Miami Stadium. On May 9, Cal had 2 hits, but the O's, despite 12 hits, lost to Fort Lauderdale 4–3. They were a 9–15 last-place team, with a 6–7 home record. Miami Stadium had a capacity of some 9,500, but only 336 loners came for the game.

The continued microscopic attendance did not surprise Nichols. "Miami has been a football town for a long time," he reasoned, "and the Florida State League never drew well. That year we also had a Hispanic entry, the Amigos, that siphoned off some fans." Nichols was more concerned about the ongoing string of injuries. As the season's midpoint neared, Bob Boyce was back home in Cincinnati, and three of the top pitchers were nursing assorted ailments. Last year's champs were 26–42, ensconced in the cellar.

Cal was a bright spot for Nichols in that gloomy season. "We began the season with 20 players 20 years or younger," related the manager. "Cal and outfielder Grant Headford, two months younger than Cal, were not even 19. So you expected inexperience to be a problem. However, Cal was a very intelligent player who picked up things quickly. He had comprehension beyond his age.

"You had to admire his attitude and work habits. He was fully committed to winning. He was confident but unassuming and not cocky to the point of arrogance. His baseball philosophy was, 'If I'll do it, I'll do it well.' On days off, he would always practice fielding and hitting. Although he never pitched for me, he would also practice his pitching, just in case he was pressed into action, and also to improve his throwing accuracy from third."

Cal senior was delighted with Junior's development. "He got off to a slow start," Rip told Ted Hendricks of the *Havre de Grace Record*, "but he's coming around now. I think he's right on schedule. It's important to remember that he's playing with guys two or three years older than he is.

"I think Cal has the desire it takes to play the game. I've been in this business a long time and I've seen a lot of players who had a lot of physical ability. . . . But they lacked desire and that kept them from being good ballplayers. . . . It is true that in statistical terms—which are overrated anyway—Junior did not seem to do well in Bluefield and at the beginning in Miami. However, you have to evaluate a player by the tools he has shown. Does he have the ability, the stomach, the guts? When I looked at Cal—his hands, the way he fielded the ball, the swing, the projected power, I was very satisfied."

Cal's progress was visible statistically. After an ineffective beginning at the plate, he was up to a team-leading .295 by August and was the league leader in doubles.

But there still was a power shortage. Miami Stadium had friendly dimensions: 400 to center and 330 down both lines. Cal went through Bluefield without a homer and through June in Miami still did not have a homer in pro ball. His inaugural four-bagger came on July 2, and the occasion was auspicious for the Miami O's. The O's outlasted the West Palm Beach Expos when Cal put one in the left-field bleachers with two outs in the top of the 12th. Cal accounted for the only run of the game by victimizing Gary Abone, who toiled all 12 frames.

"Cal was still growing, or more accurately, filling out his physical frame when he came to Miami," said Nichols. "The ball started coming more sharply off his bat. His hits were beginning to carry. He hit one particular shot that went to the wall on one bounce. You could hang four stars on that one. His hitting was outstanding during the latter part of the season."

When the season ended in late August, Cal had managed five homers and put up very solid batting credentials: a .303 batting average, 119 hits in 105 games, a league-leading 28 doubles, and 54 RBIs in 395 at bats. And, yes, Cal played in all the O's 105 games. All this earned him a spot on the Florida State League All-

Star team. He was named the All-Star shortstop because he began the season at that position.

Cal joined a stellar group of All-Stars who would later become Major Leaguers, including league MVP Steve Balboni, Nick Esasky, Lloyd Moseby, Rafael Santana, and Bob Ojeda.

According to Nichols, Cal had a Major League "mentality" even if all the skills were not apparent. "When I would tell Cal something, whether about his hitting or fielding, he would apply it immediately. That's the Major League way," explained Nichols. Cal's approach was Major League, but his September performance at AA Charlotte certainly was not. He could produce only a .180 batting average, with four extra-base hits, three of them homers, in 61 at bats. Cal's manager was Jimmy Williams, who managed Cal a third time in the instructional league after Charlotte finished its season.

Cal had only eight home runs in two minor league years, but Williams saw the potential when he filed his report for Baltimore on Cal, who played both short and third for him: "Cal Ripken, Jr., has all the tools . . . bat is good . . . hits for power."

Cal's mediocre performance at Charlotte may say more about the difference in quality between Class AA and Class A. "The jump from A ball to AA ball can not be measured as just one step up," explained John Shelby. "The maturity and skills of the players on the AA level are much more advanced than the players below them. It does take time to adjust, but Cal was determined, and he succeeded."

Cal hoped to get off to a good start in 1980 for Charlotte, and he was buoyed by the excellent spring he was having at the O's training camp in Miami. He was hitting home runs and smacking line drives. The third-base job was his. "I know I can hit home runs," Cal told Glenn Rollins of the *Charlotte Observer*, "but that was part of my problem when I got to Charlotte last year. The first day up there, in batting practice, I hit a lotta balls outta the park. Boy, the ball just jumps out compared to Miami.

"I got into uppercutting the ball, and got into a rut. I started like 0 for 15, I think, and then I was worryin' about it, and it was a mess. I got out of it when we went on the road, but then we came home for a series and the season was over.

"This year I'm just concentrating on hitting the ball, and if I make good contact, I'll get some homers naturally."

Jimmy Williams had become very familiar with Cal junior. He was his manager at Charlotte twice, at the end of the 1979 season and in 1980, and twice in the instructional league in 1978 and 1979. Now retired after a long career in the Orioles organization as minor league manager and coach, Williams is a close friend of Cal senior's. Speaking from his home in the Baltimore suburb of Joppatowne, Williams recalled that Rip asked him in spring training about Junior's possibilities for 1980. " 'Well, the Charlotte home run record is 21,' I told him, 'but I'll be surprised if Cal doesn't hit at least 25.' I guess I turned out to be a pretty fair prophet."

Cal junior fulfilled his hopes of a flying start for 1980. Both Cal and Charlotte were impressive. At May's end, Cal was second to Steve Balboni with 11 homers, and the O's had a 2.5 game edge over Columbus.

"You have to credit Cal's power development," said Williams, "with the continued development of his physical strength. He was hitting the ball more solidly, hitting more line drives. There was one game early in the season, I believe it was against Memphis, when Cal hit a line drive that cleared the shortstop's head and sailed right over the wall."

By mid-June, Cal had 15 homers, more than halfway to fulfilling his manager's prediction. Added to his homers was a team-high 20 doubles, 37 RBIs, and a .277 batting mark.

"I still don't know if I'm a home run hitter or just a doubles hitter," Cal said of his emergence as a power hitter. "When I hit those three home runs last year at Charlotte, I got to thinking that I could hit some if I played here. But this spring, I finally got it through my head that you don't know if I'm a home run hitter or just a doubles hitter. . . . " As for his manager's home run prediction, Cal responded, "I'm not shooting for any particular number of home runs, but if I keep hitting the ball solidly, I imagine I'll hit some. I'd be happy if I got 25."

A very satisfied Williams filed his third report for the Baltimore Orioles on Cal Ripken: "Cal Ripken, Jr., is very good . . . good swing . . . hits low pitch . . . some fielding problems with the change of positions." Williams explained that he had switched Cal between short and third, which was being filled by Cal's Miami teammate Eddie Rodriguez. "One of the reasons, and it was not insignificant, for Cal's fielding problems," explained Williams, "was that Crockett Field was owned by the local Federation of Wrestling. After some wrestling matches, the field was in poor shape."

"A definite Major Leaguer," Williams concluded his report on Junior. Williams was also highly pleased with Cal's performance off the field. "Junior was always in the clubhouse after the game to review the game," he said. "It would not surprise me if somewhere down the line Cal became a playing manager."

Cal continued his superior play during the second part of the season, leading Charlotte to the league championship. He proved Williams a "genius" by hitting 25 homers and earned All-Star honors with 28 doubles, 78 RBIs, and a .492 slugging average.

After the season, Williams dispatched a report on Cal—his fourth and last evaluation—to Baltimore. "Cal Ripken, Jr., is now back at short," he wrote. "He does it all but run. It is only a matter of time that he makes it to the Major Leagues."

Williams's thoughts were voiced earlier in the season by Charlotte catcher John Buffamoyer. As he was watching Cal smack drives out of the batting cage, the catcher marveled, "I think he could play in the big leagues right now."

Low-keyed as always, Cal senior was content with Junior's play but would not outright predict his making it to the Majors. "Double A is the breakpoint in the minor league chain," he said. "If you can do well here, you have the chance to go on and later make it to the Major Leagues."

Why the great improvement powerwise between Charlotte and

Miami-Bluefield? "Simple," said Rip, "Cal has grown two inches and gained 25 pounds."

Rip took time off from his Orioles third-base coaching duties to see Junior for himself when he traveled to Charlotte in midseason to present the budding Oriole with the trophy as the 1979 minor league Class A Shortstop of the Year.

A somewhat nervous Cal had but one single and made two errors at short. Nevertheless, Senior was the proud father. "He can do a lot of things. Cal junior can hit better, run better, field better than I could as a player. He's bigger and stronger. The one thing he can't do better is play soccer. I'm still the best soccer player in the family.

"I feel Cal has the tools to reach the Major Leagues. I only hope I'm still coaching at Baltimore when that comes. I want to be there." If that day was to come, Senior would "welcome him as a baseball player. . . . I hope if he has problems, he'll come to me, and if I can help him, it will not be as father to son but as coach to player."

While Junior's offensive stats were impressive, Cal was not fully happy with his total performance. He did lead the Southern League third sackers in fielding—a .933 percentage, handling 415 chances with 28 miscues. "I am not satisfied with my fielding," he said. "I am still making dumb errors."

When Cal got down on himself, he dreamed of a future life in the Majors. "When I would get down on myself, I thought about what it's like in the Majors, what it's going to be like when I get there, and it makes it easier.

"I would also think back to my childhood days. I was always at the park with Dad. I would shag flies and play catch with the guys on the teams. Now, when I watch a big-league game on television, I'll see guys I used to play with."

There were moments of doubt, but it was at Charlotte that Cal Ripken, Jr., gained the confidence that he would make it to the big leagues. "Charlotte was where I went from saying I hope I make the big leagues to I'm gonna make the big leagues," he recalled.

He added to his newfound confidence by playing winter ball for Caguas in the Puerto Rican League. Winter play "could have been traumatic" for the youngster, recalled Caguas manager Ray Miller, now a Pirates coach. "Each team was made up primarily of Triple A and Major League regulars, including some fine pitchers. J.R. [Cal Ripken, Jr.] did a job on the Braves' Gene Garber. He also handled Bob Owchinko of the Padres and Steve Trout of the White Sox. . . . That pitching could have traumatized him. Instead, he was third in voting for Most Valuable Player in the league, and now he knows he can hit."

Miller added that Cal looked better at his age than did either Eddie Murray of Baltimore or Mike Schmidt of the Phillies at comparable ages.

Playing against teams with players from Triple A and the Majors, Cal hit 6 homers, had 38 RBIs, and posted a .279 batting average while capturing his team's MVP award.

3

ROCHESTER: ONE STEP FROM THE MAJORS

At the age of 20, Cal Ripken, Jr., moved to AAA Rochester, one stop away from the Major Leagues. Cal went to spring training in 1981 on Baltimore's 40-man roster. *Miami Herald* sports editor Edwin Pope looked at the six-four, 205-pound youngster, called him "Kid Rip," and described his handling a bat "something like Paul Bunyan twirling a wagon-tongue."

Manager Earl Weaver liked what he saw, but he still sent the youngster to the minor league camp in Miami at the end of March. "I was glad to have you in camp," Weaver told a disappointed Cal. "You did a lot of good things. Now go to Rochester and put stats on the board like you did at Charlotte, and I'll see you soon."

This treatment was consistent with Baltimore development policy. During its 20-year affiliation with Rochester, Baltimore brought up only Dave McNally and Jim Palmer without Red Wings experience. "We'd rather have a kid stay down an extra year than take him up a year too soon," philosophized farm director Giordano.

That spring the Baltimore media played up a fabricated rivalry with O's third sacker Doug DeCinces. DeCinces recalled the would-be rivalry from his general contracting offices in Irvine,

California. "Cal and I found the stories very amusing," he said. "I would joke with Cal, 'Hey, I once saved your life. Now you're taking away my job.' Actually, it was déjà vu. I gave Cal pointers in fielding in 1981 just as I had done in 1972.

"When the media didn't create attention with this 'third-base competition,' they would remind everybody that I succeeded Brooks Robinson. So now they said I was playing between two legends: Brooks and Cal Ripken, Jr.

"Actually, I always felt that Cal would have an excellent future in the Major Leagues. When you come into this game, you know that sooner or later someone is going to replace you. In 1981, he had a better chance of doing that than anyone else had."

But that did not satisfy Cal in the spring of 1981. He was even more displeased about sitting on the bench at the Biscayne College minor league training complex. An annoyed Cal sat under a tree, shelved by a persistent minor injury while his teammates played the Richmond Braves. "I've never worried about this stuff," he told Glenn Rollins of the *Charlotte Observer*, "but this nagging little injury bothers me. What if Doug got hurt tomorrow, and I wasn't ready to go up? What if this shoulder thing stays and stays?

"I don't know. Sometimes guys get right to the edge and don't want to go any farther. I don't want that to happen to me."

Doc Edwards now manages the Albany Diamond Dogs of the newly formed independent Northeast League. The 1981 Rochester Red Wings skipper remembered the unhappy camper. "Tom Giordano and I were both insistent that Cal not play unless he was fully healthy, whether it meant missing the balance of spring training. We felt that Cal was a rare player. We saw him as another Eddie Murray, who played for Rochester in 1976 and next year, at age 21, was up with Baltimore. With players like Eddie and Cal, you don't take chances on their health."

Edwards added that Weaver wanted a full year's play for Cal. Sitting on the bench in Baltimore was not acceptable. "We wanted Cal to play for Rochester an entire season," said Edwards. "Earl

Weaver was quite clear that he would not bring up Cal unless he could be in his lineup every day."

Great things were being predicted for Cal. "As good as Cal appeared now," said O's coach Ray Miller, "he's far from what he's going to be." Many national publications flatly predicted that Cal would be the 1981 American League Rookie of the Year. "No minor leaguer received more publicity after the 1980 season than Cal," said Edwards. "In Rochester, the press said that Cal was its best Major League prospect since Bobby Grich and Don Baylor. And the players were also impressed. Frank Robinson compared his home run potential to that of Atlanta's Bob Horner. I remember one occasion when the Pawtucket Red Sox came out of the clubhouse to see Cal take batting practice."

Six Charlotte grads joined Cal on the spring roster: Brooks Carey, Drungo Hazewood, Dave Huppert, Dan Logan, John Shelby, and Don Welchel. "They have all accepted me because of my ability, not because of my father," Cal told Ted Hendricks.

Cal senior and Cal junior were anxious to play down their relationship that spring, which marked a first: father and son on the same roster. "There isn't any father-son relationship here," the elder Rip firmly told the media. "I managed 14 years in the minors, including 1967 right in Miami, and saw hundreds of kids. They're all my sons, more or less. On this field or on this club, my son is just another ballplayer to me. I have a job and a life and so does he."

However, the senior Rip conceded to Edwin Pope that Miami life had brought father and son together for evening dining. "Yeah," chirped the budding Oriole, "and I picked up the bigger check."

The dinners and togetherness ended in March. Cal turned realist. The press had fed his imagination and hopes, but he knew that Doug DeCinces was set—for the time being—in Baltimore. "Yeah, I read all that stuff," Cal told the *Sporting News*. "I knew there was no room for me in Baltimore this year, especially if Doug's back was okay, but I started to believe what I was reading."

Cal's attention was now directed to the opening of the International League season. After four games, Cal was 5 for 13, with two homers. "We got off to a good start," said Edwards. "Columbus was generally considered the best team in the league, but we had a top-quality team and played exciting ball. Eight of our players made it to Baltimore: Cal, Bob Bonner, Tom Chism, John Shelby, Mike Boddicker, Jeff Schneider, Al Ramirez, and Dallas Williams. We sent a few to other teams. When you add players with previous big-league experience, you can see we had a talented club."

The 1981 season featured Billy Ball for the Oakland A's and manager Billy Martin and Stick Ball for the New York Yankees and manager Gene "Stick" Michael. So Rochester sports scribe George Beahon asked, "Does that mean the Red Wings are playing Medicine Ball for Doc Edwards?"

Perhaps it wasn't medicine ball, but Beahon or anyone else would have needed the appropriate rhetorical prescription to describe the rigors of April 18. When the Red Wings came to bat in the first against host Pawtucket in Rhode Island, all anticipated a pleasant Good Friday baseball combat. What unfolded was the longest game in baseball history. Appropriately, Iron Man Cal Ripken, Jr., was part of this endurance hardball—every inning, every minute of it, a harbinger of the future.

Rochester carried a 1–0 lead into the last of the ninth when Pawtucket knotted the score to send the fray into extra innings—many of them. The Red Wings were all smiles when they sent across the tiebreaker in the top of the 21st, but smiles vanished when the Red Sox matched that one.

They dueled for 32 innings. Finally, at 4:07 A.M., after eight hours and seven minutes, now being observed by a hardy surviving audience of 20, the game was stopped—but only after a frenzied call to International League president Harold Cooper, who said, "Enough."

The Orioles and Red Sox farmhands had rewritten history, topping the old record of 29 innings played on June 14, 1966, between Miami and St. Petersburg in the Florida State League. When Rochester returned to Pawtucket on June 23, Major League baseball was stalled in a players strike. The longest game became the biggest and only attraction in the baseball world. The resumed marathon was the magnet for 54 newspapers, three television networks, countless radio crews, and broadcasters from throughout America and as far away as Britain and Japan. There wasn't much to observe and record. After 19 minutes, Dave Konza ended the drama (or agony) with a bases loaded, none out single.

There were joyous hitting days for Cal between April 8 and the close of the marathon on June 23. "Cal Ripken, Jr., grew up in a baseball world," said Doc Edwards. "The park was part of his everyday life. It was the intangibles that distinguished him at a young age, things that you could not put in a box score. On the field he was a thinking man's player who brought a relentless work ethic to the game. Early in the season he was the first to arrive for what he thought was extra batting practice. Instead, he was the batting practice pitcher for his teammates. It mattered little because he hit three home runs that day."

Edwards was referring to the April 27 game against Charleston. Cal returned from a 5-for-23 road trip and wanted extra BP, but three other slumpers showed up, too—Mark Corey, John Hale, and Drungo Hazewood. Cal volunteered to pitch to them and was left with zero time in the batting cage before the game. But it didn't matter, because that day he became the 13th Red Wing in history to crack three round-trippers in a game. The victim was Mike Paxton, formerly with Boston and Cleveland. Cal drove a fastball to left in the first inning, a curve to left in the sixth, and fastball to center in the seventh.

"I never had the chance to hit three homers," an excited Cal told the press. "Whenever I hit two in a game, my second one came in my last at bat of the game. . . . I was looking for all three pitches. I've always been a pretty good guess hitter. I figured I'd get a fastball when he was behind two-and-oh. Then the next time, with a guy on second and first base open, I felt he'd give me a curve. The third one just got away from him."

Charleston manager Cal Emery was impressed but not surprised. "I saw him in the instructional league in Florida last year," said Emery, "and he is clearly improved. He's a lot stronger now. . . . A lot of our guys at Chattanooga saw him."

Edwards offered his own analysis of Cal's hitting. "There is a difference between guess hitting and thinking at the plate," he said. "Cal didn't just guess at the plate. He could figure out a pitcher's pattern. Rip has great talent. It's just as simple as that."

Cal provided Edwards with a unique baseball experience on May 31 against Pawtucket. "I've been in pro ball for 35 years," said Edwards, "but that was the weirdest game I've ever seen." Rochester averted defeat in the ninth when Cal hit a two-run homer to tie the game at 7. The Red Sox countered with two tallies in the top of the 10th. The Red Wings came back with a pair and kept the inning going with two runners on base.

Edwards continued the narrative: "Then [Pawtucket manager] Joe Morgan stunned everybody in the park by loading his infield with five players, hoping to foil Cal. So what did Cal do? He slammed a three-run boomer into the seats."

A defensive Morgan stood behind his strategy: "When he hits it over the fence, you can't say the strategy was bad."

Talking of his two homers, Cal said, "Some nights when you're batting, the ball looks very small. Tonight, it looked very big."

While Rochester was enjoying a good season, Baltimore's brass huddled to find a replacement for Lenn Sakata, who had sprained an ankle and was placed on the disabled list. Weaver and the coaching staff voted unanimously for Cal Ripken, Jr., as the replacement. But general manager Hank Peters and Tom Giordano decided on Red Wings shortstop Bob Bonner.

The feisty, outspoken Weaver voiced his unhappiness to Ken Nigro of the *Baltimore Sun*. "Bonner can play and our minor league people know what they're doing," said the Earl of Weaver.

"But it seems to me if we need a guy like Ripken, who can hit the ball out of the park, he deserves a chance. Our main need is freakin' runs, and don't let anybody kid you. Hell, if Dan Graham [catcher, third baseman, designated hitter, with poor fielding skills] can hit home runs, he's liable to be at shortstop."

Bonner's promotion was not lost on Cal. During a Toledo road trip he told Glenn Rollins, "I admit I get a little excited, a little edgy, when I see people around me going up. It kinda makes me bear down though."

Upon Bonner's call-up, Cal was back at short. "We were fully aware that Cal had played shortstop and done well," said Edwards. "Bob Bonner was the International League's Rookie of the Year in 1980, so we realized that he might be headed for Baltimore. How nice it was to have another shortstop like Cal ready to take over."

Cal, however, was surprised by the switch. "They didn't talk to me about shortstop," he said. "I wish somebody had told me they were thinking a little bit that way, 'cause then I'd have been taking extra ground balls at shortstop every day."

It was, therefore, not surprising that things did not proceed well initially. "When Bobby went up," said Cal, "they switched me cold, and I got some tough chances and made some errors. The Rochester fans are real demanding, and they got on me pretty good. It's not like Charlotte, where they're all pullin' for you, almost no matter what you do."

Cal promised to do better. "But I could play short in the Majors," he reasoned. "If I play it the rest of the season and in winter ball, I'll be okay. I guess I'll take ground balls in both places [short and third] from now on, just to be ready." There was no need. Bonner was back in Rochester two weeks later.

Cal continued his consistent power hitting. Through June 4, he was batting .315, with 15 doubles, 13 homers, 42 RBIs, and a sizzling .632 slugging average. All his homers were at Rochester's Silver Park, obviously very convivial for Cal with its comfortable dimensions: 320 down left field, 315 down right field, and 415 out to the center-field bleachers. The power production led to his being compared to a combination of Ernie Banks, Bob Horner, and Mike Schmidt.

Even considering a friendly home stadium, how does one explain the rise to power of a youngster who went his first season without one homer? "I just got stronger as I matured," explained Cal. "I was a late bloomer. I hope I'm still not finished growing. . . . I might not get any taller, but I'm still filling out, and I should get stronger."

Naturally, Cal was very satisfied with his self-evaluation at midseason. "Each year I set a goal of hitting .300," he said, "and then I'll take whatever comes in the homer department. Last year was the first year I really exploded in the homer department, so I still don't know what I'm capable of. That might have been a fluke last year.

"So far, I've been able to pull everything, even the outside pitches. I haven't had to think about taking those pitches to right field. I'm proud of my hitting and work real hard at it."

Cal kept up his impressive hitting during the second half of the season. Into the third week of July he had 17 home runs, 61 RBIs, and a .294 batting average. He led the Red Wings in games played, at bats, runs scored, hits, doubles, home runs, RBIs, and batting average. "I definitely thought he was a candidate for league MVP," recalled Edwards. "He basically carried our ball club."

It was not premature to think about Cal Ripken, Jr., as a Major Leaguer. It would not be long, argued John Kolomic in his July 19 article in the *Rochester Democrat Chronicle* titled WINGS' STAR THIRD BASEMAN IS MAKING ORIOLES FIND ROOM AT THE TOP.

"He was a professional all the way," said Edwards. "He just wanted to get better. He had his priorities established, and from what I saw being in the Major Leagues was number one on his list. When you look at his year in Charlotte and what he did at Rochester, you see tremendous growth and development, beyond the numbers. The pitchers in Triple A are so much superior."

While Cal had grown baseballwise, personal maturation still lagged, according to Kolomic. "While the man in him is taking over Cal junior," wrote the columnist, "parts of the boy remain. He takes losses hard and often sulks on the bench while his teammates are still in the clubhouse."

However, no one could fault Cal for his work ethic. "Cal always came to play, always prepared," said Edwards. "He was a great competitor; in short, a joy to manage." Cal played every game at Charlotte and at Rochester. "You've got to work hard to get to the big leagues," said Cal. "You can't go messing up down here. Some guys stay out late at night, but I get tired enough just playing the game."

Brooks Carey can vouch for Cal Ripken, Jr. He roomed with Cal in Bluefield, Miami, Charlotte, and Rochester. "If we were on the road, and you wanted to find Cal Ripken, you went to his room. That's where he would be," said Carey. "Cal realized where his future was and how much money he could make, and all the fame. He did not take his eyes off that."

Carey's opinion notwithstanding, money was not a motivating factor for Cal—at this point in his career. Cal did not even have an agent. "I don't think so," he responded to a media question about the drive for money. "It's just that everybody looks up to you when you're a big leaguer. That's as high as you can go . . . I want respect. That's what I always wanted."

In the successful year of 1981, the question about Cal Ripken, Jr., was not *whether* he would make it to the Major Leagues but *when*. "The only pressure is what I put on myself," he said. "I don't know if I can play in the Majors until I get there. . . . I just do what I can one step at a time."

4

INAUSPICIOUS DEBUT

Cal Ripken, Jr., sensed that at any moment he might take that final step in his journey to Baltimore. "Cal kept calling home," said Vi Ripken, "asking whether Rip or I had heard anything, and we kept on saying we hadn't."

The call came August 7. Cal got the news as the Orioles prepared to host a series with Kansas City. "I was excited when I got the call about midnight," said Cal.

The Baltimore front office had originally planned to keep Cal at Rochester for all of 1981, but the labor-management strife knocked 50 games off the baseball calendar. When play resumed, the owners decided on a second season, with the winners of the first season playing the winners of the second for the right to qualify for the League Championship Series.

The Orioles were second in prestrike play but were making a determined bid to place first in the second, 51-game season and play the Yankees, who finished two games ahead of the Orioles in season one.

To strengthen the O's in their pursuit, they brought up Cal and Jeff Schneider and sent infielder Wayne Krenchicki and pitcher Steve Luebber to Rochester. "With a 51-game season staring us in the face, we have to have the strongest team possible," said Hank Peters, the Orioles general manager. "We feel that Ripken and Schneider make us the strongest team. We have an obligation to the fans and the players to put our best team on the field." Peters described Cal as a "mentally tough kid. He's had a good upbringing and knows what pro sports are all about. He's made all the adjustments at every level, and we think he's ready."

Added Peters: "You see a player of Cal's abilities come up for the first time, and you start envisioning he and Murray at the corners for the next decade or more. That kind of power gets you pretty excited."

Was Cal's promotion influenced by Baltimore's third-base coach? From Cal's earliest days in the minor leagues, the media reported about player unhappiness with his being favored because of his father. "It was never the case," said Doc Edwards. "Cal Ripken, Jr., always earned everything on his own merits. Cal never let these reports bother him. He was in clubhouses before as a youngster. He knew what had to be done: go out to the field, forget it, play your best."

Understandably, Krenchicki and Luebber were displeased and did not hide their feelings. While Luebber sensed his demotion was imminent, Krenchicki, a utility infielder throughout his journeyman career, was caught by surprise. He received word from Weaver only a few hours before the press announcement. "I didn't expect it to happen," he said with an air of annoyance. "I just don't care to be going back to Rochester. But they want to look at Cal. . . . They still have to pay me. I guess I'll just stay in a hotel and go fishing every day."

Even for a stoic like Cal senior, Dad was surprisingly unmoved by Cal's milestone. Wasn't Cal's achievement a dream come true? Certainly not, Senior told the media. When Cal made it big—and only then—would he be excited. "It's not a thrill for me," he said. "Naturally, I'm proud, but the ultimate goal is to establish yourself and be in the Major Leagues for a long time. When he does that, I'll be proud. . . .

"I don't dream at all. I know people say you have to have dreams, but if you can't do it, there's no use in dreaming about it."

Senior was not a dreamer but a realist. So he was on the phone to congratulate his son and offer him advice. "I was joking with him about needing some help from [Orioles batting instructor] Ralph Rowe," said Rip. "But other than that, I can't remember a lot of what we said. I know he was very happy. He shows his excitement more than I do. From the stats he has put on the board all the way through the minors, he should be able to supply some weapons for us."

Cal drove down from Rochester and came to Memorial Stadium on Sunday, August 9. "I had a workout with Dad," said Cal. "It was just like it used to be. I put on my uniform just like I used to when I was in high school. Most of the guys on the Orioles know me, and nobody said much," said Cal.

Cal's arrival in Baltimore reunited him with former manager Jimmy Williams, who had moved to Baltimore as first-base coach. "Cal's not only made every jump in a higher league," said Williams, "but he also has improved each time."

Another eager greeter was Ralph Rowe. What would he do with Cal Ripken, Jr.? Responded the Birds' hitting guru: "Leave him alone and just hope he keeps hitting the same way he hit in Rochester. . . . Teams will be trying to find weaknesses, and he'll be facing different pitchers, so you know that somewhere along the way he will have some problems. I hope he doesn't try too hard to make good right away. . . .

"Some pitchers will punch him out a time or two. Oh, but just wait. I've seen [Rod] Carew and [Lyman] Bostock come through the minors and Murray, and I'm standin' here tellin' you that someday—this year, next year, whatever—Cal Ripken is gonna be a superstar."

Aside from the Ripkens, most of the media interrogation was directed at Doug DeCinces and Earl Weaver. Did the former feel the newcomer was a threat? How would the manager play Cal Ripken, Jr.?

DeCinces was a bit testy when questioned about turning over the hot corner to the youngster. "The only speculation comes from you guys," DeCinces snapped at reporters. "It's not coming from anyone else. The only thing I have to worry about is my back, and even with those problems, I think I'm doing pretty well. I'm second on the team in RBIs and second in home runs. If you're asking me if I'm afraid of losing my job, the answer is no.

"All I have to do is concentrate on staying healthy. If I take care of that, I don't have to worry about anything else. I'm sorry if I sound bitter, but that's all I've heard the past few days."

DeCinces reminded the media that he had been through a similar situation when he first arrived in Baltimore. "You've got to remember," he said, "I was the guy who had to come up behind Brooks Robinson. I was the heir apparent and all that junk. Now I'm supposed to be pressured by some guy behind me. All that is just media hype."

He knew Cal well, respected him; there were "no hard feelings" between Cal and himself. "I'm not taking anything away from Cal junior," he said. "I've seen him play, and I don't think there's any doubt he's got a future in the game of baseball. But by the same token, he's not going to step on my toes."

The immediate future of Cal Ripken, Jr., and Doug DeCinces was in the hands of Earl Weaver. Before Cal set foot in Memorial Stadium, Weaver was unequivocal about his plans for Cal. He would replace Krenchicki and would be put in the lineup as needed, but not as a replacement for DeCinces. "I will use Cal Ripken, Jr., like I used Krenchicki," Weaver announced to the curious media. "He will do things Krenchicki did. If somebody falters, we'll put him in there and see what he can do. . . . The ideal situation would be to put him out there 50 days and see what happens, but we're a contending team. Here you have to hit your way on the team."

The media persisted. Why not put Cal at third and place the back-plagued DeCinces in left? No chance, answered Weaver. "You have to move pretty fast in left, too."

While Cal was obviously thrilled to be in the Majors, he was not gushing, aware that his contributions might be limited. "I thought I might get a chance to play," Cal reflected. "But any way I'm used will be all right with me."

Since turning pro, Cal had only sat on the bench for any length of time during his call-up to Charlotte from Miami at the end of the 1970 season. How would the future Iron Man cope with Major League benchwarming? "I played a couple of games at Charlotte," he recalled, "got hurt, then had to sit and watch. That was a hard feeling, but this isn't the same situation. This is the big leagues and Charlotte wasn't. I think I can handle it."

The opposition on August 10, 1981, was Kansas City. Relating his pregame feelings to the *Havre de Grace Record*, Cal said, "At the beginning it didn't feel much different from Charlotte or Rochester. The only way it could be different was to go out there and play and see George Brett at third base and Willie Aikens at first. . . . I saw some people on the Kansas City roster that I played against recently, and that made me feel more at home. Everyone wanted to see me do good. I'm from the area, and that was part of it. I just hoped they didn't expect too much too soon."

To dispel any thoughts of hostility between the two, Cal and Doug took infield practice together as 20,000 fans awaited the first pitch. Cal made his Major League debut that day—not as a starter, a pinch hitter, or even a defensive replacement. It was the least expected scenario—as a pinch runner. Speed has never been a major element in the Cal Ripken, Jr., arsenal.

The Royals battled the Orioles 2–2 into the bottom of the 12th. Weaver turned to a stunned rookie: "If Singy [Ken Singleton] gets on, you are going to run for him." Sure enough, Singleton opened the O's 12th with a double—the Birds' first hit since the first.

The potential winning run in Baltimore's first poststrike game was carried by Cal Ripken, Jr., in his maiden appearance. The drama was prolonged when Renie Martin gave Eddie Murray a free pass.

Cal spoke about his debut to Glenn Rollins of the *Charlotte Observer*. "When I was announced and went in as a pinch runner, It wasn't as big a thrill as I thought it would be. I thought it would be at bat or in the field. Anyway, it happened so fast. They were screaming, but it was for Singy. I'm sure nobody was yelling for me."

He did admit being "a little nervous and fidgety" in the dugout. "Once I went in I was just trying to concentrate on the situation rather than to be awed by it."

KC manager Jim Frey instructed Martin to test the rookie, so the righty whirled and tried to pick Cal off second. "I was thinking," said Cal, "that with first and second and nobody out, I had to run on a ground ball and not get doubled off on a line drive. And no way I was gonna get picked off. Not with Dad coaching third. I don't take a big lead against anybody."

John Lowenstein ended the drama, smacking a Martin serve into the righty-field corner. As Cal turned third, he saw Dad gesturing like a windmill and raced home without a throw. Cal junior had brought home the O's first win in the new 1981 season.

Two weeks short of his 21st birthday, Cal had made it to the bigs and appeared in his first game. But was he "mature" enough, in the baseball sense? He observed Doug DeCinces, Eddie Murray, and Ken Singleton as they walked back to the bench after striking out, without a word leaving their lips. How would he respond?

Not well, he found out quickly. After a rainout on August 11, the O's hosted the Royals for a twin bill. In the first game, a 10–0 laugher, Weaver sent Cal in for his fielding debut, a late-game shortstop replacement for Lenn Sakata. Cal got his first start, at third base, and first at bat in the nightcap. His first opponent was Paul Splittorff. "I struck out in the first inning," he recalled, "and then kind of lost control. Luckily, I wasn't thrown out of the game. I saw myself on the news highlights that night. I was shocked. 'This is awful,' I said. I had to work at it to contain my feelings. The idea of image began that evening, when I looked at myself."

Cal also failed in his turn at the plate against Jim Wright before being replaced by DeCinces. The Birds hung on to win 4–3.

Cal's first Major League hit came at Memorial Stadium on Sunday, August 16, against the White Sox. Cal started at shortstop and singled against reliever Dennis Lamp. However, the O's were topped in 10, 8–7.

True to his word, Weaver used Cal sparingly and in spots. The lack of activity was unnerving to Cal. "I sat and my timing was a little off," said Cal. "And you can't experiment from the bench. Sitting and watching, I got bored. I was really upset. I said, 'Why couldn't I stay at Rochester, get in the playoffs, and at least help the team win. At least play every day.' But after much thought, I adjusted and thought, 'I'm up here and I'm getting my feet wet.' I got to see everything, and next year maybe I won't have any question marks."

Cal was used less as the season headed down the stretch. After September 11, he didn't make a plate appearance and, in fact, appeared in only two games, both as a pinch runner.

His sagging spirits received a temporary lift in early September when he was named the 1981 International League Rookie of the Year. "Wow, that's great!" responded the exuberant Oriole to the phone call in the clubhouse. "The International League had so many good ballplayers and so many good first-year players. It really is an honor. It makes it worth all the hard work you put in."

Indeed, the league had fine players. The MVP, Brett Butler, and Most Valuable Pitcher, Bob Ojeda, have had durable, successful Major League careers. Other stellar performers included Dave Righetti, Von Hayes, Pat Tabler, Wade Boggs, Jesse Orosco, and Bruce Hurst.

Cal put up impressive stats in 114 games: .288 batting average, 31 doubles, 4 triples, 23 homers, 75 RBIs, and a .535 slugging percentage.

Unfortunately, none of this transferred to his September record in Baltimore, which showed but 5 hits in 39 at bats, a .128 batting average; no extra-base hits and no RBIs. Cal put on his glove for 18 games: 2 errors in 12 games at short and 1 error in 6 at third.

Baltimore fans had little to cheer about. The Orioles, in season two, as in season one, finished two games out of first, except that this time it meant a fourth-place finish. For the second consecutive year, the Birds did not qualify for the playoffs.

5

ROOKIE OF THE YEAR, 1982

After watching the postseason on the sidelines, Cal Ripken, Jr., put aside the frustrations of August and September and packed his bags for winter ball. Once again he played at Caguas for Ray Miller. He was joined by Rochester and Orioles teammate Jeff Schneider.

"There were upcoming stars and established big leaguers among the teams," said Schneider. "If there ever was a doubt that Cal would be a big name, a big star in the Majors, the answer was far and away a decisive yes that winter. He consistently hit line drives and displayed superior power. Cal had an unbelievable streak when he hit about 14 home runs in 13 games."

Schneider lauded Cal's approach to the game. "Cal's father and later Earl Weaver instilled and intensified Cal's desire to win. But Cal's determination to always play, to never come out—that was his mental toughness and discipline. There was one blazing day when the temperature soared toward 100 degrees, and Ray Miller came to take Cal out. But Cal insisted in no uncertain terms that he was not leaving the field."

Schneider also spoke about an important career development that winter. "The switch for Cal from third base to shortstop happened that winter," he said. "Although Cal did not play short for Baltimore immediately, the change was set in motion that winter. Cal was both an excellent third baseman and shortstop. Simply put, he is a tremendous athlete who brings many fine qualities with his glove, among them quick reactions and great anticipation."

When winter ball ended, Cal led the league with 49 RBIs and was named Caguas's MVP. "He's very intelligent, too," glowed Miller, "like a young Singleton. He's a low-key guy whose voice doesn't carry like his father's does. But he'll make people notice him. I just wish he were my kid."

Cal was very satisfied with the winter experience. "I went down there to prove to myself and to others," he said, "that I could handle a better grade of pitching. It was worth it."

His future in Baltimore clarified somewhat when the Orioles said farewell to half their infield: Doug DeCinces, who was traded to California, on January 28, 1982, with Jeff Schneider for outfielder Dan Ford.

Cal admitted that he reacted joyfully to the DeCinces trade. "Honestly and selfishly," said Cal, "the first thing I thought when Doug was traded, 'Now I can play third base for the Orioles.' But I really wished it would have been somebody else but Doug leaving, but he was the third baseman."

A euphoric Cal Ripken signed his first Major League contract the second week of February. "I'll tell you," he said, "I'm going with a lot more confidence, and I'll be a lot more relaxed because they've practically handed me the job, and it's mine unless I hand it back to them."

He had set two goals, he told Ted Hendricks of the *Havre de Grace Record*. "The first part is to get to the big leagues," he said, "and the second part is to stay there and do well. I've achieved one part, and I'm not going to stop now."

In his first game as heir apparent to third base, Cal lined two doubles and a single to help his father defeat coach Elrod Hendricks's team, 4–2, in a March 3 intrasquad game. The

Orioles veterans took a quick liking to Cal, said Hendricks, a longtime bullpen coach who also serves the O's in their community relations programs. "You know why he was such a damn good kid?" related Hendricks. "He didn't forget where he came from. He could have been big shotting around here like a lot of other guys did. But he still went back up to the minor league camp at Biscayne College to visit the guys he played with in the minors."

Orioles second baseman Rich Dauer identified closely with Cal because Cal senior was his first manager in pro ball and, more important, because he faced the same situation in 1977. Dauer joined the Kansas City Omaha affiliate as coach after a 17-year career with the O's as player and coach. From his home in Hinckley, Ohio, he compared Cal's rookie year with his own:

"When I came to the Orioles' spring training camp in 1977, I had been given the second-base job when Bobby Grich signed as a free agent with the Angels. Like Cal I came up late the previous year and did not do well [4 for 39], just as Cal did not do well. When I began that 1977 season, I was afraid. I was trying to do well so fast. I was pushing. I was pressing."

Dauer was the International League batting champion in 1976 but began 1977 going 0 for 26 and 1 for 41. "I was very lucky," said Dauer, "that I had great guys like Brooks Robinson and Lee May around. They saw my slump was eating me apart, and they were always there to help me. You can't make it in the Majors by yourself."

Why did Cal fare badly in 1981? The incomparable quality of big-league players and the "partiality" of umpires were two elements, observed Dauer:

"There's nothing to compare to the jump from Class AAA to the big leagues. You're playing against guys who have been around 10 years, who know the game inside and out. Also, the umpires know who the veterans are and who the rookies are. The rookie isn't going to get the close call.

"Cal would go to the plate after being called up and look at the first pitch in the strike zone. Then home plate would grow two or three inches to favor the pitcher."

Hopefully, 1982 would be better—much better—for Cal Ripken, Jr. On March 25 Cal drew an 0-for-3 collar against Cincinnati. But he had already knocked in 12 runs in the Grapefruit League, as many as Eddie Murray had amassed during the entire 1981 exhibition season. Cal had played more than any other Oriole and also, expectedly, had been interviewed more than any other Oriole.

Also, to no one's surprise, Rip senior attracted an army of interviewers. Writing in the *Washington Post*, Thomas Boswell spoke of the affection that the Orioles had for Junior. Many O's had known the rookie since he was a youngster. More important, they admired Dad. "The son is looked on as the father's just reward," observed Boswell. Cal senior had paid his dues, and his son was the payoff:

"Little Rip is his reward for all the batting practice he has pitched, all the towering foul pops he has fungoed, all the pitchers he has warmed up, all the buses he has ridden while his wife of 25 years and four children were left behind."

Calmly, unemotionally, Cal senior noted that over the years he had many baseball sons, had given Cal junior little advice, and would not start now. "I don't have to talk to Cal now about the great opportunities he has in front of him. When he was in Bluefield and Miami and Charlotte and Rochester and Puerto Rico, I wasn't there then. I've never been able to watch him at any level, even Little League. Why should I start talkin' at him now? He's got his job. I've got my job. . . .

"No, I haven't talked to him yet. He's got his friends. All of our baseball life has been on a professional level. The father-son thing is overplayed. Hell, I managed Eddie Murray and Rich Dauer and Doug DeCinces . . . in the minors. I was a father to all of them."

Rich Dauer seconded Rip's views. "He couldn't have looked after me better if he was my own father," said the O's second baseman. . . . I'm sure if the son had gotten hurt or something, the fatherly instinct would have come out, but Rip senior treated his son the same way he treated me. We were all his kids." Senior repeated for the press what he told them when Cal was brought up in 1981—come back years later when he could evaluate his son's career:

"It's not what he'll do this year but what he'll do over the next 15 years. You measure a player by his whole career, what he learns, what he does under pressure. Am I proud of him? Well, sure, I'm proud of him as my son. But, as a ballplayer, ask in 15 years."

A longtime friend of Rip's and admirer of his son, Earl Weaver agreed: "The only important thing is to look at the book at the end of the season and see if he's hit 25 home runs rather than 5, or 86 RBIs rather than 26."

While Senior and Weaver spoke of Cal, Junior diverted attention to his brother, Billy. The 17-year-old was pitching at Aberdeen High and hadn't lost a game in two seasons but like his sibling had his future in the infield. "Billy might go pretty high in the draft," said Cal. "I'd love for the Orioles to take him. That would be okay, wouldn't it? Having your father and brother with the same team?"

All stories about Cal referred to him as a rookie, but he wondered: he had been called up last August. Little Rip went to the record book: "A player shall be considered a rookie unless, during a previous season or seasons, he has (1) exceeded 130 at bats or 50 innings in the Majors, or (2) accumulated more than 45 days on the active roster of a big league club prior to August 31."

Convinced of his status, rookie Cal was determined to make good in his "fresh" debut. "This is like a new life," said Cal, "a new challenge, a big opportunity that I'm not going to pass up. . . .

"My last two years, I've started out really hot and continued right through. I count on myself to get off to a good start. It's a new league, just like any other step, from Double A to Triple A, just a little bit tougher."

When Cal was not in the field, he was involved in the community, a commitment that has been unchanging throughout his professional career. Cal accepted the honorary chairmanship of the Walk America/Superwalk in the March of Dimes campaign. He posed for the *Havre de Grace Record* with smiling Maryland March of Dimes poster child Lynn Soltys. More than 5,000 Harford County residents turned out for the 30-kilometer trek from Harford Community College to collect pledges for research and medical services programs.

In later years, Cal articulated his philosophy of communal responsibility. "I recognize that as a baseball player I am a public celebrity, and willingly or not I am a role model for many, especially youth," said Cal. "I take this responsibility very seriously. I remember very clearly what baseball players meant to me in my growing years and how they influenced my life and career. It may be a burden, but if people perceive me as a good role model and feel I have contributed to their lives, then I'm happy and gratified."

Cal contributed to the opening day happiness of Birds fans. The largest regular crowd—52,034—filled Memorial Stadium for the opener on April 6, against Kansas City. Batting sixth, Cal gave the O's their first lead of 1982 with a two-run homer off Dennis Leonard—his first Major League homer, first extra-base hit, and first RBIs. Cal added a double and a homer for a three-for-five day in the Orioles' 13–5 victory.

After his sizzling 1982 debut, Cal went into a prolonged slump. On May 1, after 18 games, Cal was hitting a pathetic .118, a meager seven hits in 60 at bats. Most of the Birds also carried tired bats, as the Orioles endured a nine-game losing streak until Eddie Murray rescued them with a two-homer game against the White Sox.

Would Cal be benched? Would he be sent down to Rochester? "There seemed to be a sense, something in the air that Earl Weaver was only one game away from either benching Cal or sending him down," recalled infielder Lenn Sakata, now a farm team manager in Japan for the Chiva Lotte Marines. "But deep down Cal knew he was staying."

"It seemed like I was in Earl's office every other day, having a meeting," Cal said. "The best meeting I had with him was when he told me not to worry about going back to Rochester because they didn't have anyone to play third base in my place. He told me to go out and play my own game and not worry. It relaxed me."

"The next Brooks Robinson" received much sympathy in the Baltimore media. After all, rookies, no matter how outstanding, had to experience a period of adjustment.

Big Rip, who tried to distance himself—in the public eye—from his son's glory and downturns, admitted to having a breakfast talk with his son. "Almost all young hitters go through this same thing," observed the father. "They go into a little slump, and they go to the plate trying to get a hit instead of trying to hit the ball. Rich Dauer went through it when he came up, and even Singleton went through it last year."

Dad did offer a diagnosis for Cal's case. "It isn't a mechanical slump with Cal," said Rip, "and the pitchers aren't overpowering him. But 90 percent of batting slumps are caused by your mental approach, and that's what Cal is fighting now. I asked him if he could hit, and he said, 'Yes.' I said, 'Well, damn it, get up there and hit the ball. Go back to the basics.' I said early in spring training that the thing to do was to stick him in the lineup. Let him play, and he'll take care of the rest. He'll have some trouble, but he'll adjust."

From the day Cal reported to Baltimore, batting coach Ralph Rowe predicted greatness for Little Rip. Retired since 1984, Rowe recalled Cal's slump, from his home in Newberry, South Carolina. "It was very understandable that Cal Ripken, Jr., had troubles early in his career, in 1981 and 1982. He was so young and had a great desire to impress quickly. At first he hadn't determined for himself that he was a Major Leaguer.

"But you knew that he would get out of the slump and go on. He had the right attitude, plenty of heart, super eyes, and, Lord, how he did grow physically over the years."

The slump spilled over to the personality of the usually personable rookie. "Cal was a pleasure to be around," said Rich Dauer, "but he was something else during that slump. I had to listen to all his whining about how much he hated baseball and wanted to quit."

Scott McGregor and Mike Flanagan lockered next to Cal. The former remembered the effects of the horrendous slump. Scotty McGregor, now Pastor McGregor, spoke from Rock Church in Towson, Maryland. "Cal didn't smile for three weeks," he said. "The closer Cal got to the park, the worse mood he was in. To stir things up, I would ask him, 'J.R., why are you so moody? What do you have to be unhappy about? Hey, you're in the Major Leagues.' "

Floyd Rayford roomed with Cal and dealt with Cal's poor start in his own way. Presently a coach for the Phillies' Class A Batavia affiliate in the New York-Penn League, Rayford tried to inject humor into those trying days. "Cal and I played together at Rochester in 1981," said Rayford from Batavia's Tampa spring camp. "We always liked to kid each other. When he went into that slump, I told him, 'Cal, snap out of it. I am your roomie in your rookie year. If you don't make it, people are going to blame me. If you don't snap out of it, I don't want you for my roomie.'" To tease Cal, Rayford would threaten to have Doc Edwards pitch batting practice to him. "Cal could never hit in BP off Doc," explained Rayford.

Humor alone could not snap Cal's slump. Enter Reggie Jackson. The Hall of Famer was not one of Cal's favorites at first, according to Jeff Schneider. "Cal did not like Reggie Jackson when he first came up," said Schneider. Perhaps it was because of reports of his show-off nature or arrogance. However, that changed in early 1982.

Jackson was in Baltimore with his Angels team for a weekend series with the Birds. When Reggie played for Baltimore in 1976, he knew Junior as the teenage son of O's organization veteran Cal senior. "Hey, kid, I want to talk to you," Jackson approached Cal. "I know what you're going through. . . . "

But Reggie offered more than the same old advice. Reggie offered flattery, encouragement, and practical advice. "The Orioles traded away a fine player in Doug DeCinces so they could bring you up," spoke baseball therapist Reggie. "You look like you're fighting yourself. Everybody is probably telling you to do this or that. So just know what you know you can do, not what everybody else tells you to do. Stick with what got you here."

Reggie's advice was just the Rx for Cal's batting ailment. "I don't know why," said the surprised rookie, "but it just clicked. It jolted me." On May 2 he singled twice. "It was what my dad had been telling me all along," Cal would say later, "but I guess I had to hear it from someone else to believe it."

Something eerie happened the next day, May 3, on Cal Ripken, Jr.'s, march to stardom. In his second at bat against Seattle rookie Mike Moore, Cal was beaned in the head by a 91-mile-an-hour fastball from the righty. He left the game under his own power and X rays were negative. His helmet prevented serious injury and perhaps saved his life. There was a hole in his helmet the size of a silver dollar.

Roomie Floyd Rayford finished the game at third base, won by the O's on Mike Flanagan's masterful three-hitter.

The May 4 box score between the O's and Mariners is historic. The name of Cal Ripken, Jr., is missing—he was nursing the effects of the beaning. That was the last day Cal was not in an O's box score. (He missed one other game later that season, the second game of a twin bill.)

"I replaced Cal for that Seattle game," said Rayford, "and I'll never forget how he gave me that look from the bench. It was like he was saying, 'You have no right to be playing in my place, and you can bet I'll be back quickly.' Nothing could keep Cal out of the lineup. If he twisted an ankle, he would be on a machine and back in the lineup."

Cal was back the next game—after a travel day—on May 6 against California. Once in the lineup, he started hitting, and there was no stopping the rookie. The Moore pitch "just made me all the more determined not to be intimidated," said Cal. "I got mad after I was beaned. Maybe it got me going."

After further reflection, Cal attributed his improvement to maturity of attitude. "Perhaps I wasn't prepared for what awaited me in my rookie season," he said. "I think a cockier person would have been better off at the start because he wouldn't have been in awe of the Major Leagues as I was. I was timid and scared of the whole experience—not so much the guys I was playing with as with those I was playing against—like Jackson and [Dave] Winfield. I remember in spring training, the first time I hit against Goose Gossage. I thought he was really throwing smoke. When I got back to the dugout, the guys said he wasn't even letting it out."

Through July 1981, Cal had missed three games—the only games he has sat down in his Orioles career. The last game Cal missed was May 29, 1982, the second game of a Memorial Stadium doubleheader against the Toronto Blue Jays. Cal played the first game and was replaced by roomie Rayford in the nightcap. "I took some ribbing from Cal," said Rayford, "of course, in a good-natured way. Who would have thought that Floyd Rayford would be the answer to the trivia question, Who was the last Oriole to play in place of Cal Ripken, Jr., before his Iron Man Streak began?"

Cal closed May with another milestone—his first big-league stolen base. The hometown fans saw Cal steal home on the front end of a double steal off the Texas Rangers' Jon Matlack. Sakata was on first base.

"I was certainly not what you would call a base-stealing threat," related Sakata. "I didn't steal many bases in 1982 [he had only seven], and Cal is not what you'd call a speedster. However, he is a smart runner who knows what to do. What happened that day was that Al Bumbry swung through the pitch, I stole my base, and Cal ran home."

Ray Miller offered the following explanation: "This was one of Earl Weaver's trick plays. With a runner on first and third and a lefty on the mound, the runner on first takes a big lead, and the pitcher lobs the ball back to first. At some point, the runner on third will take off for home. That's what happened on the Cal Ripken steal."

On June 4, Jim Dwyer pinch-hit for Cal in the ninth inning at Minnesota. On June 5, Cal began an amazing consecutive-innings-played streak.

As Cal's average climbed, he savored early season heroics. Cal victimized the Yankees at Memorial Stadium on June 11 by driving in three with a long homer and a single. But there was more drama the next day. After the New Yorkers had rallied to tie the game at 3, Yankees left-hander Shane Rawley walked Gary Roenicke in the eighth. Cal slammed Rawley's next pitch over the center-field wall for his sixth homer.

"Curtain call," shouted the crowd of nearly 35,000. As the rookie came out of the dugout, Dad did not turn around to share in the glory. "Sure, I'm very proud of him," said Dad. "For him to go out and hit a home run in the eighth inning, sure, that makes me very happy."

Rip quickly went into an unemotional stance and articulated again his spiel about being a baseball father to many. "I keep an even keel," he said. "I don't have to keep anything inside. I managed 14 years in the minor leagues. I had so many young guys that you believe they were all my sons."

Cal took special pleasure in home run number seven at Cleveland on June 22. The three-run blast against righty Tom Brennan helped fashion a 7–0 Baltimore victory. Cal did not fare well against Brennan when he hurled in 1981 for the Charleston Charlies. "I didn't hit him at all last year," said Cal. "He threw a lot of tricky stuff. I might have had problems now if I didn't face him last year. But last night I put good wood on his slider."

Before Cal got his bat moving, his big-league stats showed a .121 batting average, 12 for 99 in 41 games over two seasons. His solid, consistent hitting took him from a near-bottom average to a .270 mark in July that also produced the awaited power potential.

In pushing his average to .272, Cal reached parity with Doug DeCinces, who had an identical mark in the third week of July. They matched each other with 12 homers; with 50 RBIs, DeCinces had only two more than Cal.

Experts had questioned DeCinces's ability to stay healthy enough to play every day, but through July he had missed only one game. "I know there was much doubt about my ability to stay free from injury, which was certainly a factor in the Orioles' decision to trade me," he said. "I certainly proved them wrong, and it was a career year for me, with 30 homers and 97 RBIs."

With his slump far behind him, Cal looked back dispassionately. "The fans and media expected me to hit a home run every time I came to bat," he said. "And I was trying to please Earl Weaver, a very demanding manager. I'm glad he was, because I'm better for having gone through it. But I was also trying to help my teammates and keep my head on straight. It was rough."

Cal was sensitive to his dad's insistence on minimizing any help he gave his son during his rookie season. Cal treated it humorously. "It was comforting having Dad there when I was going bad," he said. "Plus, it saved me a lot of money. In the minors when it went bad, I always had to call him long distance to talk."

Obviously in better spirits, the midseason Cal Ripken, Jr., was able to return to his personal form. "Beneath all that outward seriousness," said Dauer, "Cal was a practical joker. You couldn't be off guard, and you couldn't turn your back on him." Scott McGregor remembered "a crowded clubhouse where Cal and brother Billy ignored everybody and everything and went about playing their made-up games, such as tapeball, games that went up and down lines, and other silly games."

There was never more horseplay than in the room shared by Cal and Floyd. "One form of relaxation we enjoyed," said Rayford, "was wrestling. We never stopped wrestling. It began in the room and continued in the clubhouse. We would hit each other in the ribs. Anything was fair play. Once, Coach Ray Miller and Eddie Murray were angered and told us to cut it out.

"Once in our room, the maid knocked to come in to clean. We paid her no attention and kept on fighting. I'll say one thing about Cal: when he leans on you, it's like a building has collapsed on you. Often, I experienced this when Cal woke up, pushed the bedding on the floor with me in it, and jumped on top of me."

Having busted his slump, there were now serious demands on Cal. He was in the limelight and in demand. "Cal's Gals" and "Cal, Rip One" banners began flying in Memorial Stadium. He started making commercials, including a milk promo with Dad. It ended with Senior saying: "Drink your milk, Cal." It took great acting for Senior to be "emotional." "See?" said the senior Ripken. "They wanted me to get excited."

The joyous rookie days were tempered with the sobering reality of fame. "Maybe now I feel like a businessman," he told *Sports Illustrated*. "I certainly run up more bills than before. There are a lot more demands. I don't know; before, life just seemed much simpler. Life as a phenom means that everything you do is magnified. Sometimes, you feel like you shouldn't be ridiculed for every little mistake. It seems so serious."

Vi Ripken was not prepared for Cal's fame. She had baseball smarts but was not ready for Cal Ripken, Jr., to be the baseball sensation of 1982. " 'Is he that good?' I asked Rip. 'Yes, Vi, he's that good.' I didn't understand all the fuss about Cal. I was not ready for the world to take him away from me."

By July the direction for Cal's sensational career had been fully charted, with a major assist by Earl Weaver. Cal's hitting was now on course. His consecutive innings and games streaks proceeded.

On July 1, Weaver decided to move Cal to shortstop. There had been nothing wrong with Cal at third. To the contrary, he had gone 44 games without an error. Unfortunately, the two-base throwing error on June 15 on a grounder by Milwaukee's Mark Brouhard led to the go-ahead runs in the Brewers' victory.

What was behind Weaver's thinking? The manager reasoned that it was more difficult to find a good-hitting shortstop than a good-hitting third baseman. Said the Earl: "It's always been easier to find a third baseman who can hit the ball out of the park than a shortstop who can. You never know. Rip might be a great short-stop. He's played the position before."

While visiting Toronto in July 1993, Earl amplified on his de-cision to move Cal. "I was an organization man," he said. "Been with Baltimore my whole career. Did what they said and didn't mind doing it, either, but this time I put my job on the line. Fire my butt out of here, I told 'em, but as long as I'm here, the kid's at short every day."

Weaver's wisdom was questioned. Wasn't Cal too big and slow to be a shortstop? Cal senior called the move "phenomenal." He added, "Cal would have been a terrific third baseman, so why move him? That's what people thought. But Weaver knew even if Cal were slow and didn't have the range, he would catch the ball."

Weaver did not ask Cal junior, and he did not seek the opinion of second baseman Dauer, who had played alongside Orioles field-ing wizard Mark Belanger from 1977 until Belanger's departure before the '82 campaign. Dauer missed the Blade. Said Dauer, "Anybody would miss Mark Belanger. You're talking about the greatest shortstop in the world. He never put you in a bad position with his double-play throws. . . . He'd put you where you should be to make the play. . . . I never had to think out there. If there was any question in my mind, I'd look at Blade, and he'd have a finger out, pointing which way I should move."

Dauer was thrilled about the prospect of having Cal play along-side him. "We had gone back a long way since Cal was a youngster. He had early lessons from Mark. Cal had good working habits, and with his hitting troubles behind him, he could make a solid contribution to our defense. I was prepared to do all that I could to make Earl Weaver look like a genius."

Cal replaced Sakata, who had inherited Belanger's position. "Cal was very fortunate to break in at short with Rich Dauer next to him," Sakata recalled. "I never looked at myself as the next Mark Belanger. It would have been pointless and arrogant for anybody to feel that way. While I was at short, Rich gave me all the help and encouragement that I needed. He was one of the best." Dauer was certainly that. In 1981 he led all American League second basemen in fielding percentage (.989), with only five errors in 459 chances. During the 1980–81 season he played 76 consecutive games without making an error.

Sakata was also pleased that he would still be in the lineup. "When Cal went to short, I moved to third," said Sakata. "Cal had done a great job at third, so why not give him a chance at short?"

Cal took to his new position. To compensate for his lack of speed, he redefined the shortstop position to meet his own physique and abilities. In his own words, "I play the position the way I have to play it, and I do think that's different than anybody else. I can't get my feet to work as quickly as other shortstops, so I have to find my own ways."

Cal gave much of the credit to Dauer for adjusting to his new position. " 'Field it smoothly,' he told me. 'Throw it accurately. And if they beat it out, then it's a hit, not an error, and it doesn't bother me.' That's why I throw out so many batters by less than a step. Even umpires ask me, 'Do you do that on purpose?' "

The negative in the move was Cal's batting. "It took away some of my offense when I moved to shortstop," lamented Cal. "Maybe a play would occur in the top of the inning on defense, and I would think about it on the bench instead of watching the opposing pitcher. I didn't separate the two at first, but then I realized they just wanted me to make the routine plays. . . .

"If I had been asked at the beginning of the year which position

I preferred, the answer would have been third. But I really started to enjoy shortstop. . . ."

At third base Cal made 6 errors on 223 chances (.973); he was nearly as good at short (.972), making only 13 errors on 457 chances in 94 games.

With the reinvigorated defense, the Birds were positioned fully for an exciting Eastern Division struggle. Harvey Kuenn took over the fifth-place Milwaukee Brewers at the beginning of June and steered them to a seven and one-half game lead by late August. Perhaps to motivate his team, Earl Weaver announced his retirement effective after the season. It worked. Weaver coaxed extraordinary performances from Jim Palmer, Eddie Murray, and rookie Cal Ripken, Jr.

The Birds played at a torrid 33–11 pace over the last 44 games. Cal delivered many timely hits: his 18th homer, against Jon Matlack to help beat Texas, 8–6 on August 21, and a homer and four singles in a 10–3 rout of Texas the next day. The O's completed the sweep on August 23, 8–3, as Cal hit a two-run homer. On September 14, Cal hit a grand slammer against the Yankees that wiped out a New York lead and brought a 5–3 victory and a sweep of the doubleheader. "I saw a hanging curve," said Cal after victimizing Mike Morgan.

Cal continued his heroics the next day with a double that tied matters against Ron Guidry in the sixth inning before the O's took the contest 8–5. It made a winner of Don Welchel in his Major League debut. Welchel had been Cal's teammate when they had their first professional experience at Bluefield. "I was very happy," an excited Welchel told the press, "that Cal had a big part in my first win. We go back a long time." The O's won again the next day against the Yanks, 3–1, the first time since 1962 that the Yanks had been swept in a five-game series.

Cal had quite a season against the Bronx Bombers. His 17 RBIs against them were the most against them by any other Oriole since 1970.

The Orioles stayed close to the Brewers the rest of the way.

They were three games back when they traveled to Milwaukee for a critical three-game set, starting September 24. After a 15–6 Milwaukee rout, the O's came back to win the last two games. The series' second game featured Cal's 25th homer; the rubber game was won on a go-ahead single by Cal and a sensational throw by longtime friend and teammate John Shelby.

With the tying run steaming toward home plate, Shelby rifled a one-hop strike toward home plate, where Rick Dempsey completed the double play. "I played only for a brief while in 1981 and came up late in 1982, but it was a big thrill to be in that pennant race," said Shelby. "In fact, that last month was the most exciting of my baseball career because of the tightness of the baseball race that went down to the wire. I was also glad to see how far Cal had come. He was doing very well, and under pressure. I consider Cal my best friend in baseball."

Cal helped Baltimore end September on a winning note with a dramatic come-from-behind win at Memorial Stadium, 6–5 against Detroit. Cal had a run-scoring single in the O's four-run ninth. Earlier, he had hit his 27th homer, tying him with Murray for rookie homers by an Oriole.

The frenzied race came down to a season-ending four-game battle in Baltimore with the Brewers. Three games down, the O's could only win with a sweep. They won a doubleheader on October 1; in the nightcap Cal hit a homer to set a new Orioles rookie mark. The Orioles tied for the lead on October 2 by clobbering the Brewers 11–3. The crowd of more than 45,000 chanted, "Ain't no stopping us now."

However, Milwaukee dominated what should have been a classic pitching finale between Jim Palmer and Don Sutton, 10–2. Cal was a silent 0-for-4. But he was far from quiet down the valiant but futile O's stretch drive. In the last 44 games only Murray with 46 drove in more runs than Cal's 31 and out-homered him 13 to 11.

Only 11 of Cal's 28 homers were hit at home; however, over the years, he would thrive in Memorial Stadium. Eddie Murray, Brooks Robinson, and Boog Powell have hit more in the park, which had friendly dimensions: left field, 309 feet; left-center field, 390 feet; center field, 410 feet; right center, 390 feet; right field, 309 feet.

Cal outdistanced all rookies in homers, RBIs (93), total bases (284), doubles (32), runs scored (90), games played (160), and at bats (598). All this was accomplished under the added pressures of a heated pennant race and a midseason move to shortstop.

Cal would be even better, predicted Jim Henneman of the *Baltimore Sun*, saying he would become "one of the league's biggest stars." According to Henneman, in 1982 there was only one other superior shortstop: Robin Yount, who was "probably the most complete player in the game."

Yount won the AL Most Valuable Player Award honors, and Cal Ripken, Jr., was named the league's Rookie of the Year by the Baseball Writers Association of America. He became the fifth Oriole to win the award. Previous honorees were 1982 teammates Eddie Murray (1977) and Al Bumbry (1973), as well as Ron Hansen (1960) and Curt Blefary (1965).

While there was no surprise in Cal's selection, there was some amazement that Cal took 24 of the 28 first-place votes and four second-place votes. Cal beat out Kent Hrbek, Minnesota's classy first baseman and other fine rookies: Wade Boggs, Ed Vande Berg, Gary Gaetti, Dave Hostetler, Von Hayes, and Jesse Barfield.

"I was surprised by the margin," Cal admitted. "Hrbek had a fabulous year and I got off to that poor start. I figured I had a legitimate chance, but I thought it would be close," he told Ken Nigro of the *Baltimore Sun*. The Orioles had promised Cal that "they would call me around eleven o'clock [Tuesday night, November 23] if I won, and I counted every second starting at ten. Finally, at eleven they called. . . . It was a relief to me more than anything else because ever since the season ended people have been asking me when the Rookie of the Year voting would take place. The more everyone talked, the more I expected it, and I felt I was setting myself up for the big letdown."

Cal was surprised by the margin, but Minnesota owner Calvin

Griffith was shocked at the outcome and outraged by the margin. Griffith called Cal's selection "an out-and-out travesty." Unlike Cal, Herbie was steady throughout the season. Griffith had a legitimate beef. Herbie hit .301 to Cal's .264 and had more hits (160 to 158) and a higher slugging average (.485 to .475). Cal had one more RBI and five more homers than had the Minnesotan. Griffith called for a change in the rules so that "only experienced, knowledgeable writers are entrusted to vote."

Orioles general manager Hank Peters heartily endorsed the vote: "I can't think of any rookie in the league—and this is not to take anything away from a lot of other fine players—who's achieved all the things that young man did this season. He has a chance to be one of the finer players in the game."

6

MVP, 1983

Cal Ripken, Jr., would have loved a division title, an American League pennant, and a World Series championship ring. But he was glowing nonetheless as he reflected on his rookie-of-the-year season. The thrill lost some of its edge when Dad was passed over as the choice for the Orioles manager in 1983.

Speculation and rumor abounded after Weaver announced his intended resignation during the 1982 season. Cal senior was a strong candidate because of his many years of service to the Baltimore organization. As the decision process unfolded, Junior reacted diplomatically and avoided the bait. He spoke of a long career with the O's. "I've always been an Oriole deep down inside," said Cal. "At this point in my career, I'd like to play in Baltimore for 20 years; that would make me happy. . . . "

Cal felt fortunate that Dad was not his manager during his horrendous early 1982 slump. "It would have been hard," reflected Cal, "if he had been the manager this year, considering the things I went through earlier in the season. He would have been up for plenty of criticism for leaving me in the lineup, whereas Earl was a veteran manager and didn't get anything like that."

The Orioles said that they were looking for a seasoned manager with years of organizational experience. Cal Ripken, Sr., fit that description. But when the decision was announced on November 12, Joe Altobelli was chosen. A reserve first baseman for parts of three Major League seasons over seven years, the 50-year-old Altobelli served the Yankees as coach during the 1981–82 campaign. What impressed the decision makers most were his service to the Orioles—14 years—and his minor league managerial record. Five of his teams finished first, including in 1980, with the Columbus Clippers, the top Yankee farm team.

Rip senior never expressed his disappointment publicly. Ten days after the decision, Junior received word of the top rookie award. He wished he could relate the happy news to "manager Cal Ripken." However, no bitterness was apparent.

"Naturally, I was pulling for my dad to get the job," he said. "I felt he was qualified to manage the Orioles, and I feel bad that he's worked hard all his life but doesn't seem to get the breaks like I have. But I'm not angry. You can't say Joe [Altobelli] doesn't deserve the job, too. You can't afford to hold grudges in this game."

Cal's business was targeted to the next season. He conferred early with Altobelli. Cal insisted that he not be shuttled between short and third. The manager agreed. Cal had the job as Orioles shortstop. Altobelli and Hank Peters both praised Cal. "He's some kid," they chanted.

Peters had a more challenging off-season assignment than praising Cal. Junior would not be eligible for salary arbitration until 1984. "Cal had a great season, and he'll be dealt with in a very fair manner," promised Peters. "I haven't had any contract discussions with his agent [Ron Shapiro]. But I don't anticipate any problems."

Cal sought to divert attention from the contract talks. The most important thing was to play baseball. However, Cal was next to the last to sign, in early March. (Storm Davis was the last.) "I just came to Florida to play baseball," Cal told interrogators. "I think the contract thing has been blown out of proportion. I would have signed for anything. I just want to play baseball. The numbers are a nice thing to see, but it's not that important to me."

An eager Cal was anxious for 1983 to begin. "It's been one of my better spring trainings," he reflected. "Last year I had to prove myself and win a position. This year it's more a matter of getting my arms and legs in shape for the season. I'm just gearing up for the season to start."

The Kansas City Royals came to Memorial Stadium to open the 1983 season. The crowd was large, nearly 52,000, and the weather accommodating, but the Orioles didn't respond. The Royals prevailed. Cal drove in one of the Orioles' runs. "It's not the start of the season I'm worried about," said Cal. "It's the finish."

Opening day hype over, the experts wondered whether Cal would be plagued by the sophomore jinx. Not a jinx, argued Steve Stone, former O's hurler and Cy Young Award winner whose career had ended with an elbow injury. He predicted that Cal would be "the most dominant player in baseball within five years."

Cal paid no attention to all talk of a jinx. In fact, he felt he would do better. "Talk of the sophomore jinx was all around me," said Cal. "It was very popular. . . . I thought of it. Everyone wanted to know, 'How are you gonna handle it?' Well, I never believed in the sophomore jinx. I have felt comfortable from the start of the season. For one thing, I knew the pitchers better."

Talk of a sophomore jinx ended as Cal experienced no early season slump. The Birds flew high all season. They were never more than three games out of first; they were in first place for 115 of the season's 181 days. This was accomplished despite long stays on the disabled list by star hurlers Mike Flanagan and Jim Palmer.

Cal shredded thoughts of a sophomore jinx with many key hits. A two-run homer (June 6) against Toronto propelled the O's atop the AL East. A five-RBI day (June 15) with a homer and a double brought the O's back after a 7-0 deficit to Milwaukee. Cal victimized Brewers hurler Tom Tellmann, as he had done the previous week. "It was the same pitch he threw me last week," said Cal.

After his day against the Brewers, Cal's stats included 11 homers and 40 RBIs, both Orioles highs.

Altobelli had a "simple" analysis for Cal's avoiding the sophomore jinx. Speaking from Rochester, where he is now the Red Wings GM, Altobelli called Cal "a natural athlete with intelligence. Those guys don't have jinxes. They keep on maturing and improving.

"In the case of Cal, there were many pieces that came together in his second year. He was stronger, and his mental toughness became even tougher. There is a certain mental disposition that you have to carry with you for 162 games. You have to travel half the time, leave your family, live out of a suitcase. All this comes with the added pressure of performing at a Major League level. Cal met this challenge well, and even better in his second year.

"There is also no doubt that Cal played better the second year because we put him at short at the start and told him that's where he'd stay. When Cal was set at short, we knew that with his batting skills many of the offensive records were going to fall for the shortstop position."

Cal went on a tear in mid-July. On July 13, he led the O's to their fourth in a row with a grand slam off the A's Tim Conroy. Cal golfed a low inside pitch that barely went over left fielder Rickey Henderson's glove. It was Cal's 14th homer—his second career grand slam—and boosted his RBI total to 51.

The appreciative fans asked for a curtain call. "I knew it was high, but I thought Henderson caught it," said Cal. "Then the umpire signaled a homer, and I was happy to say the least, but it was only in the fourth inning, so I tried not to get excited."

Four Cal Ripken hits on July 20, including a single that broke a seventh-inning tie, helped the O's top Seattle 4–2 and put them in a first-place tie in the Eastern Division. Cal became the goat on July 22 when he booted a seventh-inning grounder that led to a 4–3 loss at Oakland, knocking the Birds out of first. But Cal rebounded as hero the next day in a 7–3 victory at Oakland, hitting his 16th homer and bringing his hitting streak to 16 games.

It seemed Cal and the Birds could do no wrong. The American League president overruled the umpires in the historic pine tar incident involving George Brett. The Yankees lost the ruling and the game and lost first place to the Orioles, who jumped to the top with a half-game lead.

Baltimore's catcher Rick Dempsey is now manager of the Albuquerque Dukes, the Dodgers' AAA entry in the Pacific Coast League. "Cal took the American League by storm in 1983," he recalled. "Certainly, there were pitchers who had faced him in 1982 and made or tried to make adjustments against him. But Cal was determined and worked hard to offset their adjustments.

"For example, in 1982 he was primarily a pull hitter, but pitchers realized this and made appropriate adjustments in 1983, and they began pitching him away. Cal then went with the pitch and hit a great number of doubles to right center."

As Cal's roommate during the 1983–84 season, Dempsey saw a side of Cal that few did. "Cal Ripken, Jr., was not the reserved person that the media now projects," he said. "He was rambunctious and playful. I tried to interest him in boating and surfing. But Cal nixed that because he wanted to play catch on the boat.

"When we were in the room we would wrestle for hours, and he often got me in a headlock. That kid was as strong as a bull. We crawled under the table in the kitchen and put hammerlocks on each other. Because of the way Cal jumped me from behind in hotel rooms, we gave him the name Geronimo.

"If we were not wrestling, we schemed pranks. We would booby-trap other players' rooms. Perhaps our favorite target was the room of broadcaster Tom Marr, when we were on the road. We got the key to his room and did all sorts of things, such as placing pine needles under the sheets, wetted his pillow, stuck his shaving lotion to the bathroom counter with Krazy Glue, and papered or put cellophane on the toilet seat. The best trick was taping his arms and legs to the chair when we caught him sleeping in Seattle. Best of all, he could never prove we did it.

"The idea was to have fun, and boy did we ever."

But Dempsey remembers Cal best as an intelligent player. "Cal was always a very good thinker. He watched the pitchers. No one would know the hitters better. No one had better hands at short."

The Orioles closed July with a 6–0 victory over Detroit, their fifth straight, giving them their best July ever (19–7), allowing them to remain in first. However, August began inauspiciously: seven straight losses, toppling them to fourth on August 12.

Cal Ripken brought the O's out of the doldrums on August 13. He already had an RBI double against the White Sox's Jerry Koosman when he came up in the eighth in a 2–2 game. Junior decided the game with his 17th homer, which frustrated Kooz's bid for career win number 200 but, more important, lifted the O's into third, one game from the top.

Cal's timely hitting that day was the catalyst for the Orioles' roaring stretch. They won 33 out of their last 43 and the division title. Obviously, the Orioles won with more than Cal's bat and glove. They had Eddie Murray, Ken Singleton, Gary Roenicke, John Lowenstein, Dan Ford, and Al Bumbry—and more—and a pitching staff with the second lowest earned run average in the American League. However, observed Al Bumbry, "Cal Ripken was at the center of our team. Having been a rookie of the year myself, I know there are many pressures on you the second year, from fans, management, and myself. The year that Cal had in 1983 was a great pickup for the team."

Cal was phenomenal down the stretch—and throughout the season—but so was Eddie Murray. They got to know each other well if only because Cal batted third and Eddie fourth. But Cal "forced" himself on Murray because the youngster saw the veteran as a role model. Cal spoke of the first baseman as "a perfect role model to follow. He got to the big leagues when he was young, and he jumped right in and did well. When I looked at him, I wanted to get to the big leagues and do well like he did. I wanted to be consistent like he was."

Vi Ripken pointed out that Murray was very "sensitive" about serving as a role model. "Eddie Murray has never wanted to be anybody's role model," she said. "What he does, he does because it's the right thing to do or the proper way to behave. If a child seeks a role model, he or she should look at parents or teachers, or community leaders. But if someone looks up to him and sees the positive side of his career, that is fine."

There was much to look up to for fans beyond Murray's stats. He had been involved with United Cerebral Palsy, the American Red Cross, and the New Holiness Refuge Church, just to name a few. He regularly purchased 50 upper box seats for every home game and gave them to underprivileged youths. In honor of his late mother, he donated $500,000 to support an Outward Bound camp program.

In his media relations, Murray has projected himself as an unfriendly and occasionally confrontational individual. In seven Major League seasons Murray had achieved a reputation as a very private person. But he opened up to Cal and at times ran interference for him. "It's not fair to Cal," he told the media, to compare the youngster to him. "You're talking about something I've already done. That's putting a lot of pressure on him, isn't it?"

Eddie Murray was good spirited, cheerful, and humorous when speaking about his friendship with Cal. "It's a puppy forcing himself on you," Murray told Murray Chass of the *New York Times*. "He's very playful whether you want to play or not. He picks you up and tries to headlock you. Every time we go out and warm up, he hits you over the head with a forearm."

Murray sought to help the youngster when he struggled. Said Murray: "Cal kept waiting for the pitchers to throw breaking balls the way they did in the minors. But they were throwing him fastballs, and he was taking them for strikes. I told him they want to see if you can handle the fastball first. He was too smart for his age because he was looking for breaking balls. Up here you have to prove you can hit the fastball before they throw you the breaking ball."

Cal was also smart enough to realize that he could learn from teacher Murray but not imitate him. Cal stressed the methodical and deliberate; Murray did not. "I like to figure out situations," said Cal. "I think about what the pitcher has that day and what he might throw me. The other guy [Murray] just goes up and hammers the ball. I can't do that. He has such extraordinary talent that he can do that. Sometimes it's hard to figure out how he does that. Sometimes after he hits a home run, I'll ask him if he was looking for a certain pitch. He says, 'No. I just saw it fall out of his hand and swung at it.' He would say, 'When I'm hitting good, that's it.' "

To test their hitting abilities, they had a friendly bet on who would strike out more in 1983; the loser would pick up the tab at the restaurant of the winner's choice. The youngster lost to the veteran 97–90. "I lost," Cal yielded, "but I'm filing a grievance. He didn't play the last few games. It should be prorated. But it's my own fault. I should've taken off the games where I struck out three times." A hopeful Cal looked forward to a dinner "where they don't have a price tag on the menu."

Teammates spoke admirably of Cal and Eddie. "They were two of the most devastating hitters of the American League in 1983," said Dempsey. "There was an imposing lineup up and down to back them up, but they were the catalysts of the team, and they were so good that we were there to make them look good."

Veteran Ken Singleton offered his observations: "I think Cal came on a little faster, but then Eddie Murray didn't have Eddie Murray behind him. When he was breaking in, I thought Cal would raise his average 10 to 20 points this year. But he's really been amazing. As far as Eddie is concerned, I think he's the best clutch hitter in the league."

As the Detroit Tigers chased the Orioles, manager Sparky Anderson also kept his eyes on Cal and Eddie. "Aw, it's more than the numbers," said Anderson. "Murray and Ripken do more for that club. It's the way they carry themselves. See, they're not above the rest of the guys in the clubhouse. That's so important. Those two guys have never given the Orioles a bit of trouble. . . . The other players look at those two, the top bananas, and they say to themselves, 'Well, if these two aren't gonna give the club any trouble, I'm sure as hell not going to.' "

After the Ripken-Murray comparisons ran their course, the media came back to an old standby before the Orioles-Chisox playoff: father and son Ripken. The press gathered around Senior Ripken as the O's worked out at Memorial Stadium. Baseball's proudest dad had to concede that "he's my son." While hitting grounders to Cal, he told the media, "I have tried not to think of our father and son relationship. The media has finally made me conscious of the relationship. They've made me realize he's my son. Because of all the questions."

Dad told the press that Cal now had a home in Cockeysville, about 20 minutes from Memorial Stadium, so they had not gotten together often during the season—in fact, only five times, all while the Orioles were on the road. "One of us would call the other," he said. "If both of us were free, we went out to eat together. You know he's young and all that. I don't want to interfere in his life."

At this point in Cal's career, continued Senior, there was little need to advise Cal. "He has his head screwed on straight. Once in a while he may say something like, 'Did I get out in front a little too quick on that pitch?' I'll say, 'Yeah.' That's all I ever have to say to him. He knows how to take it from there."

But Dad did admit to one notable exception, in September. Junior told Dad that he had sprained his left hand. "Put some tobacco juice on it and use the top hand. Let's go," ordered Dr. Ripken before the game in Minnesota. The Rx worked. Cal collected 5 hits and 13 total bases, a new Orioles record.

A sprained hand . . . nothing could stop Baltimore in 1983. Cal continued his fine play in the League Championship Series. After LaMarr Hoyt halted the O's 2–1, the one run driven in by Cal, Baltimore won three straight. Cal had a nifty 6 for 15, a .400 clip for the series.

In a series dominated by Orioles hurlers, Cal was not at the center with his hitting, but he was at the center of a near fracas in Game 3. O's pitchers had already hit three White Sox batters in the series. To balance things, Rich Dotson hit Cal in the hip in the fifth. Murray's voice was the most recognizable as yelling erupted from the Birds' bench.

Cal has been perceived as affable and pleasant, but he could be as tough and leathery as Rip Senior was. "If I think a pitcher hit me on purpose," Cal said, "I'll remember it every time I face him the rest of my career." After the Dotson hit, Cal, like the old-time players, went briskly to first without rubbing the hurt. He shouted to the hurler, "Is that as hard as you can throw?"

Dotson had his own explanation for reporters. "You don't want to hit anyone in that situation," he explained, "but you give a message. They hit three guys in three games after they hit ten in 162 games, so you think about it. It doesn't mean they're throwing at us, but they are hitting guys. When you do that, there's going to be some retaliation."

Seasoned White Sox backstop Carlton Fisk had a chat with Cal during his next at bat in the seventh. "We just cleared the air a little bit," said Fisk. "I talked to him and got a few things straightened out. Will it be forgotten? No, I don't think it will be forgotten, but I don't think it will have a bearing on tomorrow [Game 4]."

Fisk had that right. Dotson gave up six runs in five innings; the White Sox lost the game and were eliminated in the next contest.

"Bring on the Phillies," clamored the Baltimore faithful. Understandably, Cal got caught up in the excitement and frenzy of the World Series opener, at Memorial Stadium, with President Ronald Reagan in attendance. "It's the same game it always is," Cal tried to tell himself. "But I looked up there and I wanted to see the President. But on a ground ball, I didn't think I better make this play or the President will think I'm no good."

The O's lost the first game but stormed back to capture four straight. Cal was flawless in the field, but at bat he would rather forget his only World Series performance: 3 for 18 (.167), one RBI, and no extra-base hits. However, Orioles fans will always remember that Cal Ripken, Jr., snared the last out of the World Series off the bat of Garry Maddox.

Joyfully, Cal slammed the ball down on the turf. The celebration had begun. In the victors' dressing room, Cal senior was caught pouring beer over his son's head. Was he finally acknowledging the relationship between father and son, queried a reporter. Dad downplayed the incident. "I just happened to pour beer on his head," nonchalanted Senior.

Years later, Ray Miller still is not convinced. "I never really accepted Rip's public pronouncements that there was nothing special when Junior did something outstanding. Perhaps, accidentally, the pouring of the beer on his son's head was the real Cal Ripken, Sr., expressing himself."

When it came to celebrating, Senior expressed himself in his own way. In Aberdeen the home folks set their celebrating in motion. Banners were hung from I-95 overpasses to greet the team as it traveled by bus from Philadelphia to Baltimore. The owners of George's Chicken on Route 40 in Aberdeen got caught up in the spirit of Orioles magic with a sign underneath Biscuits and Breakfast: "We Just Love Those Birds."

"It was great to see all the fans come out to the games this year and share the fun," said Cal junior as he reviewed the crowd of 250,000 who lined Baltimore's streets for a parade honoring the Orioles. "It was even better to see them all come out and celebrate." Priming up for a local celebration, Aberdeen mayor Ronald Kupferman exulted, "Let's have one big bash and be done with it. I'd rather see one concerted effort."

Activity boomed for the Cal Ripken Fan Club. "It's gone faster in the last week than it did in a whole year," said Ruth Burnette. "I've had parents calling me asking how they can sign their kids up. The kids see other kids wearing the T-shirts in school, and they want to know how they can get one."

Father and son had coordinated answers for the local press. "It takes 25 ballplayers to win and we left spring training with the idea of using all 25," Senior told Tom Hendricks of the *Havre de*

Grace Record. Similarly, said Junior, "We had a team effort and we won the World Series because of it."

How exciting was it for father and son to share in the championship? Not so special, proclaimed Senior. "I haven't given that any thought. It's very nice to be on the same ball club. Cal had a fine season and was a major contributor." Likewise, insisted Junior, there was no added satisfaction. "I'm sure it's satisfying for him because he works even harder than the players, but there's a level of professionalism there. He's a coach, and I'm a player." Susquehanna county executive Habern W. Freeman proclaimed November 7–13 to be Ripken Week in Harford County. The Ripkens were "symbolic of the kind of people we are in Harford County," beamed Freeman. Unable to attend the celebration, Cal wired in his message: "I feel very fortunate to have grown up in Harford County as part of the Ripken family."

The celebrations at an end, Aberdeen and baseball fans everywhere wondered who would win the Most Valuable Player Award. While Carlton Fisk had an outside chance, the experts predicted it would be either Cal or teammate and friend Eddie Murray. Cal led the Majors with 211 hits, an Orioles record, and 47 doubles. His 121 runs scored topped the American League. His 76 extra-base hits were only exceeded by the Expos' Andre Dawson (78). He was runner-up in total bases, 343, to the Red Sox's Jim Rice. Cal hit .318—third best in Orioles history to Ken Singleton (.328 in 1977) and Bob Nieman (.322 in 1956). Cal hit 27 homers and knocked in 102 runs, the most ever by an Orioles shortstop.

Defensively, he fielded at a .970 clip with 25 errors in 831 total chances, an American League high. He was also the number one AL shortstop with 534 assists and 111 double plays.

Murray hit .306, with 33 homers and 111 RBIs, a .538 slugging average, and 115 runs scored.

The first baseman had finished second to Robin Yount in 1982 and had fifth- and sixth-place MVP finishes in 1981 and 1980, respectively. Murray would not comment publicly, but those close to the star were convinced he hungered for the award. Murray tried to end the discussion by telling the media, "I don't think about it. I can tell you that. And I don't ever remember a time in my career when I did. [The baseball writers] are going to vote the way they want. So it don't matter what I think. . . . But I'm still not gonna think about it."

Likewise, Cal refused to be drawn into MVP discussion. "I just want to feel I've done my part for the team," Cal responded simply.

However, the thought of winning was on Cal's mind. The announcement would be made on Tuesday evening, November 15. "Billy and I were playing darts at my home," Cal recalled. "My dad was going crazy calling me. Dad said that he was trying to keep busy by working around the house, but his mind kept wandering.

"The news came at 11:10, and I called Dad."

No sooner had the Ripkens heard the news than Cal and Vi arrived in Cockeysville, with a bottle of champagne.

Cal edged out Murray, with 15 first-place votes and 322 points to his teammate-friend's 10 first-place votes and 290 points. Fisk had 3 first-place votes and 209 points. It was the first time since 1966 that AL teammates had finished 1-2 in the voting. That year, Frank Robinson, Brooks Robinson, and Boog Powell—all Orioles—took the first three spots.

Cal became the first Major Leaguer to win the Rookie of the Year and MVP in successive seasons. Fred Lynn had won both in 1975. Cal became the fourth Oriole to win the MVP, following the Robinsons and Boog Powell, the last Oriole to take the award (in 1970).

The media pressed the winner: Why did he win? Had he discussed the voting with his teammate? "I played every inning of every game," reflected Cal, "and I played a position like shortstop that, until lately, hadn't been known for offense. It's a pivotal position. . . .

"And Eddie was hitting behind me, so I didn't walk a lot [58 walks, none intentional; Murray had 86 walks]. Most pitchers, if they got behind me 2–0 or 3–1 said, 'I can't walk him because Eddie's up next.' That helps a lot."

Cal said that Eddie and he had never "formally" discussed the award, "but we knew one of us would win it . . . and I can honestly say that if he'd won, I'd be the same happy man that I am today."

After more thought, Cal elaborated for John Woodin of the *Havre de Grace Record*: "It seemed like the MVP should hit 40 home runs, have 120 runs batted in, and do everything else well. But during the course of the season, people told me differently. Being on a team that wins is important, and what you do to help that team plays a big part.

"I did my share for the team. I pulled my load this year. But so did all the players. I could share the MVP with the whole team, and I will."

When the ballots were all counted, Murray was said to be driving across the country. He called the Orioles office, who released this statement: "I've been asked many times how I would feel if Cal Ripken, Jr., won the Most Valuable Player Award. Well, I feel like he deserves it, and I hope he does it again and that the Orioles win the world championship again. . . . I know of no better teammate and friend than Cal Ripken."

An elated Earl Weaver heard about Cal's selection on his way to a Miami golf course. He gave the media an "I told you so." "That really made me happy," chortled the retired skipper, "because I made a shortstop out of him. Strange the way things work out."

The Ripken Fan Club had an upcoming banquet at the Aberdeen Moose Lodge, and the award added a perfect touch. "That's nice," Cal said, reacting to the excitement in town, especially among youngsters. "Those kinds of things make you feel very special and proud. . . . The biggest compliment a ballplayer can get is to have someone emulate their style. I'd love to have someone say they're Cal Ripken, Jr., when they're batting right-handed or playing shortstop. That's the best thing you can get out of this game. That definitely has to make you feel good."

*   *   *

Aberdeen is overshadowed not only by Baltimore, but it must compete for attention with many other small towns outside the big city. Baltimore meant Babe Ruth. Now Aberdeen had Cal Ripken, Sr., and Cal Ripken, Jr. Actually, the Ripkens were added to its first sports hero, Irv Pankey, a three-sport star at Aberdeen High, later cocaptain of Penn State's football team, followed by 11 seasons with the Los Angeles Rams and Indianapolis Colts. He played tackle on one of the best offensive lines in league history and had a key role in helping Ram Eric Dickerson break O. J. Simpson's National Football League single-season rushing record. Pankey, whose mother lives in Aberdeen, has been active with victims of child abuse, the Boys Club, the Girls Club, the Special Olympics, and the American Children Diabetes Association. According to Cal's baseball coach, George Connolly, "We at Aberdeen are proud of the wholesome life in our community. For youngsters—and others—the best proof is that when you have athletes like Cal Ripken, Jr., and Irv Pankey go out and make it big, they don't forget their roots. More important, they're the same outstanding people they were before they left our community."

He spoke in detail to Thomas Boswell about his celebrity status. When he was young, he thought Major Leaguers "were gods, so to speak. If a kid wants to look at me like that, that's all right with me. But I don't want to disappoint him. I'd like to be considered . . . perfect . . . in that kid's eyes."

When Cal came to Nashville to receive the MVP award at the winter baseball meetings, drug charges had been leveled at a number of baseball heroes. Reporters quizzed Cal about his comments about being a role model. What did it mean to be "perfect"? Cal laid out his thoughts for the media: "I can do one thing well—play baseball. There might be a surgeon, or someone else, who does his job as well as I do mine. . . . So I don't feel I'm above anybody else. . . . I can do one thing and I'm lucky that people like to watch it."

The more appearances Cal made, the more assuredness he gained. "I seem to be opening up," he said. "People who heard me last year say they can't believe the change. They say I actually look like I'm enjoying myself. I'm still too nervous to eat before I talk. But now I've relaxed enough that after I finish I can eat dessert. . . .

"Last winter, I thought the people were, maybe, there as critics, to see if I could speak, or whether I was a dummy. Now I realize that they're really on your side. I still talk too fast, but I'm learning to tell my stories more slowly. I really do enjoy meeting people."

But no appearance was as difficult as the luncheon honoring him in Baltimore as the Advertising Club's Man of the Year. Tributes were issued by President Reagan, the governor of Maryland, the mayor of Baltimore, and Orioles officials. Cal had to address a large audience, but the most important listeners were Cal and Vi Ripken.

After receiving the award, he let loose a sigh: "I have to speak now, huh? I am confident on the field before 50,000 people, but I still need plenty of help speaking. . . . It was always my dream to be an Oriole, and it came true."

Then he turned to the table where his biggest fans, Cal and Vi, were seated. "I've never said thank you enough to my parents, especially my mother. She was the one who always took me around to the Little Leagues and other places so I could play baseball. Everybody thinks it was my dad, but he was always away in the summer. Other kids' dads would be there, but with me it was Mom. She knew more about baseball than my coaches. She was always there when I needed her. I just want to say how much I appreciate it."

Cal finished to tumultuous applause, but the congrats for the speech and honors and for the raising of Junior went to Cal and Vi Ripken. "That's Cal. He's something special" was Vi's impromptu response.

7

THE SLUMPING BIRDS: 1984–85

Cal Ripken, Jr., was basking in the afterglow of an MVP season. He was adapting handsomely to the postseason appearances and had become the darling of the media. However, more than three months into the off-season he realized that the business of baseball was not all delightful and, in fact, could be discomforting.

How would Cal fare in the business-oriented baseball market? What about milk endorsements? Or in a more jocular vein, some Jockey underwear à la Jim Palmer, another Ron Shapiro client?

"Uh, I don't think so," retorted an amused Cal to the last suggestion. "My basic job is still to play baseball," he said. "I'll do as much this winter as is physically possible. But I want to get some rest. I don't want to run around so much that I'll be distracted." All baseball business would be entrusted to agent Ron Shapiro.

The most pressing issue of baseball business was Cal's contract. Baltimore GM Hank Peters spotted Shapiro at the Advertising Club dinner and humorously opened talks.

"Okay," began Peters, "we all know about the .318 batting average, the 102 runs batted in, the 121 runs scored. Let's forget about them and consider the important things.

"Cal did not steal a base in 1983. He stole three in 1982. He

had five triples in '82, just two in '83. And his home run production fell off from 28 to 27. Obviously, he is not running as well,
or hitting with as much power."

Shapiro was hardly amused. Having played for two years, Cal
was eligible to go for arbitration for each of the next four years.
The Orioles did not choose the arbitration route. Instead, an agreement was reached and a contract inked on February 1, 1984. The
four-year pact would run through 1987, at a reported $1 million
annually.

Orioles tradition dictated that contract signings merited only a
news release. However, a press conference was in order now. A
Ripken was involved, and, more important, this was the Orioles'
largest commitment ever to a player of Cal's age.

"We have never given a multiyear contract to a third-year player
before," said Peters. "But eight years ago we had never given a
multiyear contract, period." Why the change?

"We are rewarding Cal's exceptional performance over the past
two years with an exceptional contract," Peters explained. "He has
certainly demonstrated that he is one of the top players in the
Major Leagues today. The long-term deal will allow Cal to concentrate solely on baseball for the next four years, and we are very
pleased that we were able to reach this agreement."

The exact amount was a bit fuzzy. It was not $1 million per
year, reports clarified, but "about" $1 million. Three years earlier,
Eddie Murray had agreed to a six-year contract, becoming the O's
first member in the millionaire's club. That came in his fourth year
with the O's. Because he was also a client of Shapiro's, it was
assumed that Cal's contract would not exceed Murray's during the
remainder of Murray's contract.

"To me, it showed that the Orioles are committed to maintaining the tradition of winning," said a delighted Shapiro, "because
they had to do a lot of soul-searching on this one. They had to
dig down deep."

Maestro Shapiro not only guided Cal's contract through Orioles
management, but he continued to orchestrate a program for Cal's

communal involvement to project the proper image for the rising star. The following announcement accompanied the signing:

Cal would purchase 25 tickets for every 1984 O's home game and distribute them to underprivileged youngsters and senior citizens in his native Harford County;
Cal would make a substantial contribution to the Harford Center, a day-care program for retarded citizens near home-town Aberdeen;
Cal would make a major contribution to the Baltimore School of Performing Arts.

The long-term lucrative contract intensified the spotlight on Cal to a much greater degree than had his winning the MVP Award. This was new for Cal, and the unaccustomed millionaire lost some of his placidity, even getting a bid edgy. "I don't like to make people mad," he said. "But when it starts to interfere with why you're here in the first place, well, I don't know. Everybody makes a bigger thing over a contract than what you are as a person. People want to seize on my new money. There's an implicitly negative thrust to questions—as if they don't want you to last. Maybe they want you to last, but maybe they'd like you to be a little bit of a disappointment, too. . . . But if I react to any of that, then I'm being defensive."

Cal knew that he would have to accept this part of baseball. He also remembered his dad's experiences as a minor league manager. "All this extra stuff, this media stuff, is part of the game, I know," Cal said grudgingly. "In the minors we learned to play baseball. You weren't educated to know about this part of it. Mom and Dad brought me along in everything else. We would talk about things at night. I'd watch my dad. I mean, he had to read the paper the next morning, too, and he'd say, 'Damn, so-and-so should never have opened his big mouth to that reporter last night.'"

With his contract, Cal was now a bigger celebrity in Baltimore. The loss of privacy was one price of fame. Aberdeen High class-mate Ron Keithley recalls meeting Cal for dinner at Christopher's.

"Cal's BMW was spotted," said Keithley, "and the crowd gathered. When I came out, I was mobbed by autograph seekers. They refused to believe that I was not Cal or, at least, his brother, Billy. Even after I took my license out, they would not believe me."

Cal vowed that he would put aside all distractions and concentrate on the business of playing in 1984. "I'm not going to go out there and be complacent, that's for sure." For starters, he looked forward to playing every day. The previous season he played every day "because I avoided a major injury. Sure, there's a selfish part to it, a guy who wants to play every day for his own gratification. But he could hurt the team. I look at it as, if I am healthy and able to play every day, I should play, and I took a great deal of pride in playing every day. And it wasn't easy."

He also promised to perform better in 1984. How could Cal improve on his MVP year, Altobelli was asked. "You don't expect anybody to improve on that type of year," the skipper answered.

However, Cal made 25 errors in his first full Major League season at shortstop. "That's what I wanted to improve on this year," he said, "cutting down on the number of balls I threw over Eddie Murray's head. I figure we either have to work on Eddie's jumping ability or my aim. Most likely my aim, because it's tough to catch a ball 12 feet over your head."

Cal's long-range goal was to play 20 years for the Orioles and "have children imitate and idolize him and say, 'I'm Cal Ripken,' " he told Paul Hendrickson of the *Washington Post*. "The best thing that can be said about an athlete in my opinion is that he's consistent and does the job time after time. I've done a lot, but I would never say I can't improve. I can be a better glove, I can be a better kind of hitter. If I don't bat .318 again this year, some people will say, well, he didn't improve, but in fact my stats might be better all around, y'know?

"In my short career, I've already met players who didn't seem to want it enough. Sure, they could stay up here on their talent, but sometimes talent is not enough. It's your working habits. It's your desire. Then it's your talent."

Even with less than two full seasons at the position, Cal Ripken, Jr., had reshaped the traditional view of the shortstop: a small, speedy player who could put his bat on the ball, a pesky hitter, a table setter. The most notable exception to the spray-hitting short-stop was Ernie Banks, who amassed 512 career homers. This is what Weaver had dreamed of when he moved Cal to short in 1982.

After a full off-season schedule and spring training, Cal was burst-ing with excitement on the eve of opening day. "What you want to do," he told Paul Hendrickson, "is have everything ready inside you to peak. That's exciting."

Excitement filled the opening day crowd of 51,000 at Memorial Stadium, boasting a game between last year's division winners. President Reagan threw out the ceremonial first ball and stayed long enough to see Cal hit a homer off the 1983 Cy Young awardee LaMarr Hoyt. However, the White Sox had already tallied two off Scotty McGregor en route to a 5–2 victory.

Cal had previously hit 55 homers, but this was the first one over the right-field porch at Memorial Stadium. The opposite-field blast just cleared the fence, aided by a swirling wind. "Quit calling it cheap," beamed Cal. "It wasn't cheap.

"It seems so many go out like that. I've seen guys like Robin Yount hit 'em there, and the guy from Kansas City [Leon Roberts] got one there opening day last year. It was a ball away, and I leaned in and hit it. I thought it had a chance to go off the wall. I was trying to judge where Harold [Baines], the right fielder, was going for it, and he kept going back and back. It was a good current, but it wasn't cheap."

While Cal was excited about his first homer of the season, the World Series champs had little to cheer. They lost their first four. Cal sparked the Birds to their first win, 6–3, on April 10, with two homers—third time in his career—and four RBIs.

"We're not too excited about this first [victory]," he said. "We won't be excited about the second or third or fourth. We'll be excited about the big ones—like the one Scotty threw in the World Series."

On a personal level, however, Cal was eager to talk about his opposite-field power. He hit a right-field homer off rookie hurler Bret Saberhagen. "It was a breaking pitch," said Cal. "That's the position every hitter likes to be in. I was looking for a breaking pitch. I remember his big breaking ball from spring training. I swung late but hit it hard."

Cal offered Kent Baker of the *Sun* an analytical review of his hitting development. "If you take my career year by year, it would go like this," he said. "At Bluefield I hit to all fields and could not hit it over the fence. [Cal had no homers at Bluefield.] The next year at Miami, it was the same, and my average rose. Then, all of a sudden my body started growing and the power started coming. I became home run conscious, and went from occasionally going to right-center to always pulling." At Rochester, Cal went the other way again, with this result: continued power and a rising batting average.

Cal opened 1984 impressively, but life was horrid for the Orioles collectively. Their 1–6 record was their worst start since 1955. After 10 games, they were 2–8. For those 10 games Cal had 4 homers, 13 hits, and 8 RBIs in 33 at bats. "The main thing about the game is to win," said the always competitive Rip. "It really doesn't matter what you do individually if the team isn't winning. There's no consolation prize for losing. You either win or you don't."

Signs of hard times: The Orioles lost their next two games. Owner Edward Bennett Williams gathered his troops on April 20 to be inspired by his oratorical skills. The Birds won their next two home games against Minnesota. Altobelli was moved by the owner's performance. "He told a short, biblical-type story," said the manager. "It was a simple message that, win or lose, everything passes in life. . . . It was so eloquent that I felt I should have applauded after he finished."

Cal had been swinging an inspired bat, but he could have applauded too. "We're not a ball club that has a lot of meetings. [It had been Williams's third meeting in five years of ownership.] But I got a lot out of Mr. Williams's talk. When you're in the middle of a losing streak, a team needs something uplifting, and Mr. Williams always says something that makes sense and makes you relax."

The revived Birds won seven of their next ten. Cal helped fashion a 3–2 win over Texas on April 29 by evening the score in the sixth with a triple and later scoring the winning tally on Murray's single. Too late, however. The Tigers had begun the season on a record-setting pace, with 12 wins in their first 13 games. By late May they were in cruise control in the Eastern Division, with a 35–5 mark.

Cal's success and busy schedule was not at the expense of his community. The Orioles shortstop visited the Harford Center in Havre de Grace in May to make good on his promise. He presented the center with a $5,000 check for a physical therapist to work with handicapped children. "I wanted to do something for as many people as I could," he said. "I can think of no better thing than to come back to Harford County, to try to do something for the kids where I grew up."

The visit was a great success, noted Maggie Green, chairman of the center's board of directors. "The kids had been looking forward to seeing Cal for a long time."

The Orioles could not catch the Tigers, but on May 6 they reached .500 for the first time in 1984 with a 6–1 victory over Texas. Cal achieved his sixth career four-hit game. More noteworthy, he became only the second Oriole to hit for the cycle, accomplished with a ninth-inning homer off Dave Tobik (Brooks Robinson had performed the cycle feat on July 15, 1960.)

Cal took his achievement in stride on that muggy afternoon in Arlington, Texas. "I hadn't been feeling that good," he said. "I had been swinging at some bad pitches. What does it mean? It means four hits. Where they all go is luck." Cal's average had gone "down" to .314, with no RBIs in four games.

"I was overswinging for a while," he continued, "and lately I've been getting in a lot of two-strike situations. That's good for me because it forces me to look at the ball."

Cal insisted he was not thinking homer in the ninth. "Maybe in the on-deck circle you think it'd be nice," he mused. "But when you get to the plate, you just think of hitting the ball hard." However, Altobelli said the entire Orioles bench started rooting for Cal after he doubled in the seventh. "It's quite a feat," said the skipper. "He told me last night he was in a slump, but he said it was just a little thing. His words were, 'I'll get out of it.' "

He did, and so did the Orioles, now at 14–14. "Hallelujah," raved the elated manager. "It was a pretty long haul for us, yet we made it in a short span of time. Listen to our clubhouse. There's a little different sound out there."

The sobering reality: Detroit won in 12; Baltimore was still nine games out of first. "It is too early to start looking at the standings," reasoned Cal. "If we win 100 games and don't win the division, we can't say anything."

The Birds played winning ball through May and raised their mark to 28–21. But the Tigers were still hot, keeping the O's in third place at May's end, 10½ games out. Baltimore took two of three from Detroit, winning the rubber game 2–1 on June 3, the margin coming on Cal's sacrifice fly. The Orioles had now won 25 of 34 and were nine and a half behind the Tigers.

However, the O's could not continue this pace. Detroit crushed the Birds 8–0 and 10–4 in Baltimore on June 10, and they fell 11 back. They lost in 11 to the Yankees, 5–4, and plummeted 12 games behind the Tigers, the furthest they were back in four weeks.

The Orioles were no better by mid-July, Cal's effort notwithstanding. His production in five post All-Star break games earned him American League Player of the Week. During the period he batted .476, with 4 homers, 8 RBIs, and 23 total bases. On July 17 he pushed his average up to .301, the first time he had exceeded .300 since June 20. In the past 17 games he had pasted the ball at a .362 clip. He was among the leaders in runs scored, hits, triples, extra-base hits, home runs, total bases, slugging percentage, and game-winning RBIs. He led shortstops with a .986 fielding percentage and had gone a month without committing an error.

Cal continued to contribute, but the Birds continued to fall. After a three-game skein, Cal contributed three hits to help beat Kansas City 4–3. Cal's two-run homer launched a five-run inning on August 1 that helped top Texas 7–2. But the O's stood at 58–48, 13½ out of first.

The O's began September 72–61, still 13½ behind. They lost their reign as world champs when the Tigers clinched the Eastern Division on September 18. The Tigers had clearly outclassed all opponents. They led the division from day one; that feat had last been done by the famed 1927 Yankees. Baltimore never reached 100 victories as Cal and others had hoped. (Detroit won 104.) Instead, the O's settled for a fifth-place finish with an 85–77 record, 19 lengths from first.

Perhaps it was not an MVP year for Cal, but it was clearly outstanding by any yardstick. He batted .304, with 27 homers, 86 RBIs, and 103 runs scored. Only once was he hitless for three consecutive games. He led the team in batting average with runners in scoring position—.311 (46–148). From June 27 through September 1, he batted .355. Deservedly, he was named to the AL All Star team, for the second consecutive year.

Defensively, Cal continued to improve. He established a league record of 583 assists, breaking Roy Smalley's mark of 579. His total chances, 906, were tops and the most since Leo Cardenas reached that number in 1969. Cal also ranked first in total chances without an error—only Ozzie Smith had a higher figure during the past four decades—and in taking part in double plays.

Cal's excellence in the field was detailed by two outstanding infielders of the 1970s and 1980s, Bobby Grich and Rich Dauer. The former had a long, solid career, first with Baltimore, then in the '80s with California. Like many other Orioles of the '70s, he played in the minors for Cal senior. Presently a minor league instructor for the Oakland A's, Grich spoke of the young Ripken from his home in Long Beach, California.

"In his first years with Baltimore," said Grich, "Cal established himself as one of the game's best hitters, but not enough was said about his defense. . . . Defense is very overlooked and underrated by the public. The most important and difficult defensive positions are shortstop, second base, third base, catcher, and center field.

"Cal did not have the range that some other shortstops had, but he had a very strong arm, knew the hitters well, and knew how to position himself. When he was younger, he learned from Mark Belanger. By learning from Mark and watching him play, Cal then developed his own style. He reminds me of a tall Eddie Brinkman [who played shortstop and other infield positions in the '60s and '70s, primarily for Washington]. . . . Cal developed his own distinct style, which is carrying the glove low and keeping movements to a minimum.

"When Cal's offensive contributions are added to the defense he gave the Orioles up the middle—and he was doing this every day and for a while every inning—you realize what a phenomenal player Cal was during the '80s."

Playing alongside Cal, Rich Dauer experienced the flowering of Cal Ripken, Jr., as Major League shortstop. "What he showed me," said Dauer, "was excellent range and an arm that was as strong as any other shortstop, if not stronger. . . . On simple plays, Cal set accuracy as his priority and lobbed the ball sidearm. When it came to the pivot throw, Cal clearly was at his strongest. He dropped down and threw in submarine fashion. Imagine how intimidating that must have been for a base runner faced with a throw from a person as large as Cal."

Cal's strong arm was responsible for many exceptional plays, Dauer commented. On one play, third baseman Wayne Gross and pitcher Storm Davis were crossed up on a bunt heading toward the mound. Hurrying in from short, Cal picked up the ball 40 feet from the plate and threw out the runner at first. "When was the last time you saw that happen?" Dauer ended rhetorically.

Had success changed Cal Ripken? the fans and media asked. "Some people wonder why I haven't become more flamboyant," reflected Cal. "They talk about the money. But I don't even know what the money is. It's just a number to me. I look at it this way: I have a talent, and I'm lucky people like to come to watch me.

"People look at you funny when you play ball. They think, 'This guy's had some degree of success; he must be a big shot all of a sudden.' And it does happen to some guys. They'll go out and buy a big car or a huge ranch or a house or something. . . . But all that was never that important to me. I don't know why . . . but it wasn't. I don't think I've changed at all."

Fame carried with it responsibilities, Cal realized. It was impossible to meet all the needs and wishes of the public. "The tough part is turning people down in things," he said. "This is my hometown, but obviously I don't have time to be everything. I can't be running myself around and then expect to be able to have my full concentration and strength to play baseball. . . . If some nights you don't want to be bothered, you just don't go out."

Cal enjoyed being famous. "Some players don't," said Cal, "but I don't think there is any hard part to that." What was difficult, however, was acting responsibly, because the public did not forgive the famous easily. According to Cal, "The thing about being known is that if you ever do anything wrong, people are never going to let you forget it. You see it all the time, all around the league. . . . What will happen to me if I do something wrong? I don't know. I haven't thought about anything like that."

No need to worry, an assured Shapiro said, because Cal was a "natural. He could deal with public pressure and would be easily forgiven. Cal is a natural person," said the agent, "and when someone is a natural person, meaning they are what you see, they have an easier time dealing with the pressures.

"All heroes are human, and how the public reacts when he fails them depends on the way the individual has approached his her-oism. Cal has not elevated himself to the status of a hero in his own mind or in his actions."

Before Cal left for spring training, he spoke of long-term and short-term goals. "Once you get to the big leagues and establish yourself, you feel better yourself," he said. "But when you look at a whole career, I've gotten three full years, and I want to play 12 or 15. I've scratched the surface. . . .

"My only goal is to leave a mark. I'd like it if after I'm retired, I'm in a bar and there's a nice play on the Game of the Week and I overhear some guy say, 'That so-and-so is a good ballplayer, but he's not as good as ol' Ripken was.' "

With the approach of spring training, Cal thought of 1984 and goals for 1985. "When I first moved to third," he recalled, "I thought it was temporary. I'd started to like third base, and I considered myself a third baseman. Now, I think shortstop is a little more challenging. When I was a third baseman, I felt like a spectator, just like people in the stands. At third you can only occasionally dive and make the great play. Shortstop is where more of the action is. Playing shortstop gives you a chance to use your brain on every pitch. It's a position that keeps you in the thick of things."

While Cal was now settled at short he still heard criticism that he was playing out of position. "I still hear it a little," Cal said, "because I'm still gaining my five pounds each year. I've gained five pounds every year since I've been in pro ball. I was six foot two and 180 when I went to Bluefield." In 1985 he was six foot five, 220 pounds.

How would he seek to improve his fielding? "I want to know where I should be on every hitter," responded Cal.

As for hitting, Cal had a list of targets for improvement. "I think I became more patient, especially toward the end [of 1984]. I tried to hit bad pitches sometimes just to help the team. I learned that sometimes you need to take a walk if that's all you can get. . . .

"I want to know the strike zone better," Cal said, which was translated by the *Sun*'s Richard Justice as knowing "every umpire's particular zone."

Cal said that self-improvement has always been an ongoing regimen, on and off the field. "I take [the game] home with me, because you're always thinking how you can get better. For instance, maybe there's a play I didn't make—say, a ball in the hole I threw away. Should I have held it instead of throwing? Did I do the right thing? If I don't take it home with me, if I don't think about it, maybe I'll make the same mistake again."

What drove him? Insisted Cal, "Money aside, it's still personal pride. The money is the business part. The game is still what matters."

With a lock on shortstop, Cal looked forward to spring training. "I can go at my own pace," he said. "It's not as mentally taxing. It's more enjoyable." Nevertheless, he could not be complacent. What if his skills diminished? "It's true what they say about ballplayers," he said. "You always think you're going to wake up one day and your ability will be gone. That's why there will always be some doubts when you come to spring training. You see a guy who's been consistent, say, for five straight years, and all of a sudden he's coming off a .220 season, for no apparent reason. You think about that all the time. You think about getting in a rut someday, getting in such a bad slump that you never come out of it."

If Cal wanted to stay vigorous, people wondered, would he continue to play in every inning of every game? He had already played in 3,931 straight innings, covering two full seasons. Only seven had accomplished that iron man feat, the last, Tigers first baseman Rudy York, from 1940 to 1941. "You can always find reasons to stay in a game," Cal answered logically. "If you're losing 10–0 and hitting the ball, you want to play because you're hot. If you're losing 10–0 and not hitting, you want to go up and try to find out something that will help you in the next game."

But doesn't mental and physical fatigue impair performance?

Not necessarily. "Sometimes you have your best games when you're tired. You can't tell," countered Cal.

Certainly, the Orioles needed an everyday Cal if they wanted to improve on their 1984 fortunes. They were strengthened by the addition of Fred Lynn and Lee Lacy to their outfield. Lacy injured his hand and did not start the season. The Orioles got off to their best start since 1979 by taking the first two at home against Texas, but it might have been the worst beginning in franchise history. For a few moments, the seemingly indestructible Iron Man was down.

In the top of the third inning of game two, the Rangers loaded the bases. Gary Ward led off second base. Baltimore moundsman Mike Boddicker suddenly whirled toward second to pick off the Texan. As Cal took the throw, his spikes got caught on top of the bag, and he turned his left ankle.

"Cal let out a painful yell," recalled Altobelli. "Fortunately, Boddicker took a moment for Cal to pull himself together and then threw a third strike past [Pete] O'Brien so Cal could return to the dugout. 'Can you continue?' I asked. He said, 'Yes,' and I went along with that.

"Hey, I knew what was at stake. First, the consecutive innings meant a lot to Cal. It would mean a lot to me if it were me. But the most important thing was how his playing or not playing affected the team. I'm sure Cal realized that the inning streak would have to end sometime.

"It also might be me who eventually would have to sit him down. These are the tough decisions a manager has to make. It can be a dark and lonely job. I was the guy who released three very popular Orioles: Palmer, Singleton, and Bumbry."

Cal had gotten to his feet, limped around for a minute, and then went to the dugout after O'Brien fanned. The ankle was wrapped between innings. It swelled up and stiffened, but Cal never left the game.

"Yeah, this was the first big scare, huh?" Cal told reporters after the 7–1 Orioles victory. "I never thought of leaving the game," said the wounded Bird. "I just like to go out there and be involved in the action. I don't want to sit and have someone else do my job. Heck, I remember when I played basketball and soccer. I hate to be substituted for." Cal left Memorial Stadium for precautionary X rays at the Greater Baltimore Medical Center. Fortunately, there was no fracture, but orthopedist Dr. Charles Silverstein ordered Cal off his feet for at least 24 hours. "Day to day," the Orioles announced. Dr. Silverstein would evaluate Cal's status after 24 hours.

It was impossible for Cal to play the Orioles' next game on April 11. But the heavens were smiling on Cal Ripken, Jr. The next Orioles game was against the U.S. Naval Academy in Annapolis. The Orioles lost 4–3 while Cal had a busy day away from the field. He was on crutches and off the ankle and had a therapy session at Children's Hospital with alternate hot and cold treatments. He was also measured for a light custom brace to support the ankle.

Cal "has a high pain threshold," Orioles trainer Richie Bancells said, but he was unwilling to speculate about Cal's status. The ankle was still sore.

On the day of the night game with Toronto, attention was directed at the quartet of Lenn Sakata, Dr. Charles Silverstein, Joe Altobelli, and Cal Ripken, Jr. Sakata remembered the "anxiety." Said the Orioles utility infielder, "I had not played short on any regular basis since 1982. It was not my regular position. I was much more comfortable at second and third. When Todd Cruz was traded that spring I knew that I was the emergency replacement at short. So I began working out just in case.

"But playing short is much different than playing other infield positions. I needed more time to get used to playing short again. However, when there was a chance that Cal might not play, I had to tell myself, 'If you can play the infield, you can play anywhere in the infield.'"

The orthopedist did not make a recommendation, but Dr. Silverstein delivered a favorable report. "There was marked improvement," he said.

The decision was up to manager Altobelli, who would have to turn in his lineup card. He would not make a commitment, but he told the media, "I'm optimistic that he's going to play. I haven't even given another lineup a thought. Well, you know what it would be anyway, but I won't think about it until I know."

Eight years later, Altobelli said, "Yeah, it was my decision, but the will and ability to play had to come from Cal." The media would get word at 5:00 P.M., April 11, three hours before Scott McGregor faced Jimmy Key at Memorial Stadium. Cal said he would be on the field.

"It's funny," he told the media when asked about his streak. "I heard during the introductions today that I was tied with Eddie [Murray, who had played in 444 consecutive games]. First time I heard it. So it's kind of imperative I get back in the lineup, huh?"

Cal fielded questions about his condition as he took part in pregame drills, ankle taped lightly, with no brace. He was never asked about being a designated hitter, which would have preserved the game but not the innings streak. "[The game streak] doesn't concern me that much," he said. "It gets bigger and bigger in other people's minds the closer I get to the [Orioles] record [Brooks Robinson, 463], but the point is if I think I'm able to play, I should play."

He offered full details of the injury and recuperative process. "I've never really hurt it in baseball, to be honest. I've done it a number of times that weren't sports related, like slipping in a hole or slipping on the ice in the dark and in [high school] baseball and soccer, and this time it came back a lot better than the other times, with freer movement and less pain.

"If the X rays said nothing was wrong, I knew I'd be in there. I've been walking around on it all day, and I don't see much problem with it. I tested it out a little bit, and there was no pain whatsoever. I spent six of those hours at Children's [Hospital] in therapy; then I went home and iced it and did a couple of things I was supposed to. I've had a lot of hot and cold [treatments] the last couple of days, and it feels better."

Wasn't he worried about favoring the ankle on a difficult play? "In the course of a game," answered Cal, "the body takes over, and you don't think about that. Besides, you don't feel any pain until the play's over."

Cal endured, and all enjoyed that day. The Orioles beat the Blue Jays 7–2. Cal went two for three, with one RBI and one run scored. In driving in the second run, Cal ran hard to first after smacking the ball off Key's foot. Third baseman Garth Iorg picked up the ball barehanded and threw to first, but a hard-running Cal beat the throw.

The Birds did well in the opening stages of the season, but the early going was not that smooth for Cal, who did not hit his first homer until game 6, on April 16 at Cleveland. Two days later he made two errors that opened the gates for an 11–5 Tribe win. The Orioles won in Texas on April 24, but Cal got into a heated argument with home plate umpire Dale Ford upon being tagged out by Don Slaught after Cal tipped the ball in front of the plate.

Dad jumped into the argument and got the thumb from Ford, which might have preserved Cal's consecutive-inning streak. However, Altobelli observed, "Don't read too much into Father protecting Son. Cal senior has a short fuse." His record bears that out: 30 ejections as coach and manager.

The Orioles clung to first with a 9–6 mark on April 25. The Orioles beat the Tribe at home again the next day, and Cal had his first game-winning RBI. When they dropped the next game to Cleveland 10–4, the Tigers slipped into first with a win over Milwaukee.

The Orioles regained first as they went into May. The month proved auspicious for Cal but not for the team. On May 3 he tied Brooks Robinson's O's consecutive-game streak of 463 and crowned the team's 8–7 victory at Minnesota with a game-winning homer in the eighth and two singles. Cal became the all-time Bird Iron Man on May 4, but the Orioles lost to the Twins 8–6.

Cal and the Orioles capped a very successful weekend on May 5 by taking the rubber game from a team that had won 10 straight and had been baseball's hottest club. In that game Cal went 5 for 6—his second career five-hit game—and knocked in four runs. The 10–5 victory propelled Baltimore to a one-game lead over Toronto. He came within inches of a club-record six hits. In the third inning he smashed a grounder off the glove of third baseman Gary Gaetti, who made a quick recovery for a force-out at second.

After beginning the season 4 for 24, Cal went 21 for 55 in the last 10 games, with 4 homers, 13 RBIs, and 8 multihit games. His average soared from .167 to .337, seventh best in the AL.

Twins hurler John Butcher absorbed much of the pasting. He had a career 5–0 mark against the Orioles until he met up with Ripken. "Cal's an awesome hitter, all the way around," he said. "It has been a while since he got to me like that. He has a great eye-hand coordination, and he just knows how to play the game."

Cal had become the terror of the dome. (Lifetime he is above .340 in the Metrodome.) "It's a little darker here than it is outdoors," he said, "but I seem to see the ball good. Maybe I can concentrate on picking up the ball after it leaves the pitcher's hand. There's no doubt this is a hitter's park, and even if you're swinging bad coming in, it picks up your confidence. The turf is very fast. It's a nice feeling."

Cal had also been swinging well in the Seattle Kingdome. How would a dome in Baltimore suit him? "Nah, I'd rather play outside," Cal said playfully.

But the thought intrigued Altobelli. "I think that you guys might be writing about a potential .400 hitter in a dome," argued the manager.

But Cal did promise to visit the dome soon. He kept his word, returning to Minneapolis as the starting AL shortstop for the July 16 All-Star Game.

Unfortunately, the Orioles would look longingly at this May dome series. They left 15–8, one game in first. A little more than a week later they lost to Kansas City 5–2, on May 13, falling out of first, and never again reached the top except for a tie on May

20. In fact, the Orioles' fortunes deteriorated steadily. They were five games out on June 1; by mid-June they fell to fourth. After starting 18–9, they went 11–17.

The ax fell on Joe Altobelli in the midst of a five-game losing streak. The World Series champions manager in 1983 had gone to a fifth-place skipper in 1984. Altobelli was stunned by the removal despite reports that his job would be in jeopardy if the Orioles struggled in '85.

Cal Ripken, Sr., had hoped his time had come to manage the Orioles. It did—but only for one game as interim manager on June 14. Earl Weaver was plucked from retirement. When a family commitment kept the Earl away for one game, Senior made his managerial debut. The Orioles won 8–3 and ended their losing streak.

Senior's brief moment of glory as coach and manager was observed by the *Evening Sun*'s Melody Simmons, who described the manager for the day as having a "Christmas-morning look on his face . . . the evening's purist, a Cinderella in spikes."

Once again Senior was passed over. When Altobelli was selected to succeed Weaver, Son and Dad had little response. But this time there was keen disappointment behind the polite, correct statements. Senior thought he was the choice.

Junior made no attempt to hide his unhappiness. "I am disappointed from a personal standpoint," he said. "He is definitely qualified to manage. And someday someone might just realize that. He knows more about baseball than anyone else I know. But I'm sure his time will come."

Dad tried to be more tactful and philosophical upon hearing that Weaver was returning. "I guess I was a candidate for the job—at least that's what everybody wrote in the papers," he said. Senior added with cynicism after a one-game tenure, "Here's the thing. When you sign a contract to manage, you also sign a contract to be fired. That's all there is to it."

He ended the questioning with Rip realism. "I don't think I have anything burning inside of me to be manager," he said. "I guess that after 29 years of working for the Orioles, I'd want to manage. There is no question about that. However, I still feel I am a young man, and I didn't get that upset two years ago, and I don't get that upset now. I'd be happy managing, but I'm tickled to be a third-base coach right now."

Once Weaver was back, "Cal turned another page," said Vi Ripken. "There wasn't any sense dwelling on it and crying over spilled milk. We really put it out of our minds."

It was easy for Senior to move on because Weaver was only named as Baltimore manager through the '85 season. GM Peters also made it known that "anyone is a candidate for the job at this point." Moreover, Peters praised Senior as an "old professional."

Weaver was brought back to work wonders. As the All-Star Game approached, the Orioles were only 41–38 and were not contending with Toronto. Weaver had no magic wand. In fact, the Birds fell even lower in the standings. On August 8 they were swept by Toronto, and at 53–52 were in fifth place, 14½ from first.

Cal could not help the team advance. In mid-July he put together a seven-game stretch in which he hit .429 (12 for 28). But Cal and the Orioles were frustrated as the season wore on. On August 22 Seattle's Matt Young shut out the Orioles. Junior became embroiled in a fourth-inning called strike by Dale Ford. Enter Dad and another ejection.

The Orioles played better ball and entered September 68–60, but that only merited fourth place, 12½ games out. Cal had a big Labor Day game, leading the Orioles with two homers and six RBIs to crush Oakland 12–4.

The reality of September 1985 was that Baltimore was reduced to spoilers. In past years Ripken and Murray had hit well against the Yankees, but in 1985 they combined for only four RBIs and a .182 average in eight Orioles losses to New York. On September 20 the Orioles and Eddie and Cal got their revenge by beating the Yanks 4–2 and pushing them further back of the Toronto Blue

Jays. The deciding runs were driven in by Cal and Eddie in the seventh.

Losing pitcher Rich Bordi threw one too many sliders to Cal, who lined a 3–2 slider to left field for a single and the tiebreaker. "I threw him four or five sliders in a row," said Bordi. "He's too good a hitter to do that. They wanted me to throw breaking balls to him, but I could've thrown a curve ball instead of a slider. But the one he hit was about three inches outside and down. Still, he pulled it to left. You're not going to hook that pitch unless you're looking for it."

The Orioles played spoiler that evening, but the Yankees rebounded to win 97 games, finally falling two games short of the Blue Jays. The Birds could do no better than fourth at 83–78. The Birds were only 53–52 for their spirited and colorful skipper.

Cal's batting average dipped to .282 from .304 in 1984. But it was a superstar season. He knocked in 110 runs—only in 1991 did he drive in more. He hit 26 homers, his fourth consecutive 20+ season. For the third straight year he scored 100+ runs (116), topped only by Rickey Henderson's 146 for the Yankees. Cal hit .321 with men in scoring position. Eddie Murray tied Cal with 15 game-winning RBIs. In 12 other offensive categories he was either first or second on the Orioles.

The continued fielding improvement of shortstop Cal was seen in the stats, notably in two league-leading categories: 123 double plays (the most in his career) and most putouts, 286. And a report on the Iron Man Streak: Cal joined a very select group having played every inning for three straight seasons. (Mickey Vernon of the Washington Senators achieved the feat in three seasons, but not consecutively—1942, 1947, 1953). To find three-season iron men, one has to go back to early-20th-century Boston. Red Sox outfielder Buck Freeman played from July 28, 1901, to June 5, 1905, 534 straight games without missing an inning; likewise, teammate Candy LaChance did not miss an inning at first base over 424 games, May 23, 1902, to April 28, 1905.

8

A TRIO OF RIPKENS

The Orioles won the World Series in 1983, failed to qualify for the postseason the next two years, and then continued their decline with three consecutive losing seasons—1986 being the first losing season since 1967. Cal Ripken, Sr., was not named manager for 1986. Junior was still under contract and kept a low profile during the 1985 off-season.

When Weaver was brought in to take over for Altobelli in 1985, the media reported that the Earl would only stay on to the season's end. However, with little fanfare Weaver was asked to come back. Baltimore had been the American League's most successful team for the past 20 years. They had won six pennants; no other team had won more than three. Weaver had led the Birds to four of these flags. The Orioles brass hoped Weaver would lead the team once more to glory.

Optimism was guarded at the start. After 14 games the 1986 Orioles were 8–6, a game and a half out. Cal had his first game-winning RBI at Texas, knocking in two for a come-from-behind 3–2 victory. Cal combined at Cleveland with former Bluefield teammate Larry Sheets for home runs that beat the Tribe 5–2. On April 29 they combined at Chicago for five RBIs, including Cal's third homer, for an 8–1 victory over the White Sox. The Orioles ended April two and a half games out, in a three-way tie with Boston and Cleveland behind the Yankees.

The Orioles continued their fine play into late May. They won an exciting game against California and Mike Witt, 2–1, at Memorial Stadium when Cal hit a two-run, two-out homer in the seventh. Cal's fifth homer made the Birds 7–3 in one-run games and winners of 9 of their last 11 games. It was also a big game because he had gone 6 for his last 36.

"It's a step in the right direction," said Cal. "Anytime you can win that way it's great. Witt is one of the toughest pitchers in the league. He is always nasty. You're never happy to face him four times in a game."

A disappointed Witt explained, "I got it up." Cal called it "a mistake pitch. When he drops down, he is very effective. But it doesn't break as much as the one he throws three-quarters. I've chased that pitch many times in the dirt. But he left this one out over the plate."

The Orioles were playing at a similar pace to their late May 1985 showing. After 37 games, they were 21–16, four out and in third place; in 1985 they were 22–15 and in second, one and a half out. However, the Orioles were confident. They were winning the tough games, and they did have Earl Weaver from the start. They finished strong in May. A pair of two-run homers by Sheets and one by Cal gave Baltimore an 8–6 win in Oakland. The O's had won 15 of 18. They finished May 27–17, three and a half back and in third behind the Red Sox.

Cal kept up his consistent hitting in June, highlighted by a 17-game hitting streak. However, the Orioles stumbled. They lost seven of eight and were seven games out on June 21. They ended June being swept in Baltimore by the Bosox, who now led them by nine and a half games.

The ill fortunes of the Birds could be attributed in part to pitching woes. In 1983, Baltimore had the lowest earned run average in the AL East. But in 1985 and 1986, Baltimore had the highest

ERA with the exception of Cleveland. Now the proprietor of a Mexican food concession at Memorial Stadium, former O's reliever Tippy Martinez recalled the decay of Orioles pitching, which he blamed in part to injuries. "In 1985 I was in 40 games [actually, 49]," he said, "but in 1986 I was out almost all season with a shoulder [14 games and 16 innings]. Storm Davis was also injured that year. Dennis Martinez was injured early in the year and was traded to Montreal."

Injuries crippled the Orioles hill staff and were also responsible for continued lineup changes. Twelve Orioles spent time on the disabled list, which produced 141 lineup changes, including nine third basemen and six second basemen.

As the O's began losing, an air of unhappiness pervaded the team, according to Floyd Rayford. "It wasn't the Orioles of the early '80s," he remarked. "New players came in, but it was not a good mix. The chemistry was bad. Players complained. The winning attitude disappeared. The loss of Al Bumbry and Ken Singleton after 1984 was damaging. They were the soul of the team."

In particular, Rayford cited Eddie Murray as the most unhappy camper. The first baseman suffered an injury and missed a month. In his place the Orioles brought up Jim Traber, who immediately became hot. Murray was not doing his best to get back in shape, an irritated owner Williams told the media.

"Eddie was completely unhappy with the situation," said Rayford, "and asked to be traded. He was dissatisfied with the attitude of the players and management. Eddie had meant so much to the team for so many years. You could not criticize his work ethic and dedication. In one stretch he played for 444 straight games and played every game for four seasons [but not consecutively]."

The losing and the dissatisfaction got to the Earl. After the O's were shut out in Chicago before the All-Star break, he turned to his troops: "Gentlemen, we stink." Before leaving the clubhouse, he finished his speech: "The whole team needs to spend the All-Star break in the hospital. The few guys who are healthy aren't hitting. Except the kid [Cal Ripken]. Do you know the kid hasn't

had also put in many years for the Orioles. He wanted the job. Frank Robinson was also very interested in managing Baltimore."

The Ripkens were convinced that Senior would finally get his chance. Vi Ripken was afraid that the overwhelming support for her husband among the public and the media might backfire.

"I was worried that there was overkill in the media," she recalled. "I am not saying that I was unhappy with the support for Rip, but you didn't want the other side to be forced into a corner, where they are being railroaded into appointing Rip."

Much was being reported in the media, continued Vi about Cal's reaction to the possible nonappointment of his father. "A lot was said and written, much of it not true, about how Cal might react or what his thoughts were," she said. "What was true was Cal had said, 'I think my dad should get the job' or he said, 'I'm not the one who makes the decisions.' But Cal never said that he would leave when his contract was up if his dad didn't get the job. Cal could not leave that way."

A decision was expected soon after the season ended. "The waiting game was not the easiest one to play," she said. "It was no secret or surprise that Rip wanted to manage. But he only wanted to manage the Orioles. Once he was offered it he would accept it."

Although Vi was willing to go along with her husband's eagerness to accept the Orioles reigns, she had reservations. "On the one hand, I told Rip, 'If you think you can do the job, go for it. But was this the time to take the job the way this team has been going, the way certain players have been performing? If they don't improve in a year or so, would that be all she wrote?' "

Cal Ripken, Sr., did not have long to wait. No sooner had the season ended when the Orioles announced at an October 6 press conference that their third-base coach was now their manager. GM Hank Peters said that Senior was selected because he was capable of reversing the Orioles' fortune. "Cal is not getting the job," said Peters, "just because he has been a loyal employee for a long time.

Cal is getting the job because we think he's the one who can turn this team around and get it heading back in the right direction."

Peters later admitted that Rip was his choice when Altobelli was dismissed in the middle of 1985. Owner Williams, however, had the final word, and he had wanted Weaver. Williams now joined the Rip bandwagon. "Rehiring Earl Weaver was the biggest mistake I've ever made in baseball," he said. "[Rip] handled himself with such class and loyalty in different situations that you had to be impressed."

The owner cited the team's 1984 trip to Japan. "We were on the plane 17 hours going over," mused Williams, "and he never loosened his tie once. You had to be impressed with that kind of discipline."

The entire Ripken family was thrilled with the good news. "I'm glad he has it and hope he'll do well with it," said matriarch Clara Ripken, 89, Senior's mom. "I wanted to be there [at the news conference], but I have arthritis so bad, I was better off staying at home."

A joyful Senior responded with humor. "There should be no doubt in your minds," he said, "that I'm very, very happy. . . . They said in Aberdeen that it will be a cold day in Aberdeen when he gets this job. Boy, it was cold this morning. [Former Orioles coach] Billy Hunter used to say, 'It's great to be young and an Oriole.' I'm both."

How would he compare himself with the incomparable Weaver? queried a reporter. "Number one, I'm taller," the manager answered quickly. "The difference between Earl and me is that he raises hell when we're winning, and I raise hell when we're losing. But really there's not much difference between me and Earl."

Much of the questioning at the conference concerned the role of Junior in his dad's selection, his future relationship with his son, and Cal's chances of being moved to third. Rumors had spread that Cal would play out his option if Dad were not hired. "That statement was never made," insisted the manager. "He wants to be here. Whether I get the job, whether I get fired, it has no bearing whether he will be an Oriole. As his old man, I know that. As someone who has watched him play, I know that it has no bearing."

Stories had circulated that Senior would only get the job because of his son. "Now that I am hired, there is nothing for him to say about that," said Cal senior. "His job is to go to the ballpark and play. He doesn't have time to get caught up in anything else."

The Orioles had an excellent third-base prospect, Craig Worthington. Because Cal and Worthington both had had good years (Worthington in the minors), it was surprising that there was speculation that Cal would be moved to third. In fact, rumors circulated that Senior had been named manager on condition that he move Junior to third. "If you're asking me if that was a condition under which I took the job, no it was not," Senior said firmly.

However, Cal senior did not rule out shifting Junior. "I was asked if it was set in concrete that Cal stayed at shortstop," he explained. "And I told them it wasn't. It's something we'll have to decide after we see what happens."

In other words, if Worthington was not the answer at third base, Cal would consider the move. "We've talked about it," said Senior, "and Cal has always said that he would make the move if it would help the club. He's always said that."

As expected, Dad was low-key in looking forward to managing his son. It would be the same as managing Eddie Murray or any other top-quality player. "Any team could use a guy who hits 25 homers and drives in 80 to 100 runs every year. I wish I had 24 of them, whether it's Cal Ripken or anyone else."

Reporters wondered whether Senior was committed to maintaining Cal's consecutive-inning streak. "If I could see that far ahead," reflected the manager, "I would be able to tell you a lot of things we'll do next year. But there's a possibility that Cal junior will be rested. But when you sit in that office day after day and fill out the lineup card, then you go out and lose a game 4–3, you wonder if the guy you left out could have gotten a hit that would have given us the game. But I like players who come to the park ready to play. He prepares himself."

The manager revealed that he might move Cal—in the batting order. In 1985, Cal batted third, followed by Murray and Lynn. Weaver switched Cal and Lynn in 1986 because he felt that Lynn would hit into fewer double plays. Senior leaned to the 1985 lineup. "I'm going to do some research on it," he said, "but it seemed to me that we were more successful that way [with Cal batting third]. We got Freddie to give Eddie some protection, and we know he can drive in runs."

Third base, catcher, and second base were problem positions, according to Senior. He intimated that son Billy Ripken might solve the infield problem. "We have good reports on some kids in the system," beamed Rip. "Yes, the reports on Billy [Ripken] are good. Maybe we can fill a hole from within. . . . "

The conference over, euphoria turned to realism in the Ripken home. Cal was given a one-year contract with an Orioles team that had finished in the cellar. "Rip was fully aware of the shortcomings of the Orioles team he was invited to manage," said Vi Ripken. "You also would like to have a little more security, too. But he never hesitated. In life, when you get the opportunity, you have to take it. You never know if that opportunity will ever come again."

Vi added that Rip had the proper baseball temperament to do well. "We think he is a good communicator and teacher," she said. "And with his hard work and other qualities, everything should come out all right."

Mrs. Ripken also said that Rip's personality would allow him to deal effectively with baseball's pressures. He left the game at the park, she observed. "There's a little more mental stress as a manager, but he'll handle it. I don't think he'll take the losses any harder. He didn't sit around and mope or shout at me when he was a coach. And I don't think he will now.

"It'll be like before. After one or two losses, he certainly wasn't affected, but after a string he might get a little testy. That's because his mind is always working, wondering what he could do to prevent [losses]."

For several years Cal Ripken, Jr., had responded to questions about the opportunity of playing for his father. He had nothing to say for now. Billy Ripken spoke for the Ripken boys. "I'm kind of worried about him," said Billy, "considering the shape the team is in and the way Major League managing goes. But this is what Dad wanted. He never played the political field for other managing jobs elsewhere. He could never pass up this opportunity."

The managerial decision process at an end, Cal left for Japan with a U.S. Major League all-star team. Cal shared shortstop with the Cardinals' Ozzie Smith. The United States won six of seven against a team of all-stars from Japan's Central and Pacific Leagues. The Oriole topped the American batters by going 7 for 14 with 2 doubles, 2 homers, and 6 RBIs.

Upon his return, Cal busied himself with community work. Under sponsorship of the Bel Air Athletic Club, Cal and Larry Sheets organized a celebrity volleyball tournament, which raised $5,000 for the Cystic Fibrosis Foundation. Cal helped open Aberdeen's K Mart in Beards Hill Plaza and donated his $2,500 appearance fee to the Aberdeen High School athletic department.

Senior, Junior, and Billy Ripken gathered in January 1987 to announce the establishment of the Ripken Memorial Foundation, at a banquet hosted by WAMD Radio's Jim McMahan at Aberdeen's Colonel Choice. Located in Aberdeen Town Hall, the foundation assembles memorabilia from the Ripken family and other local professional athletes.

Manager Ripken used the occasion as a forum for 1987 Orioles baseball. "I know these guys can get the job done," Senior said of his Orioles. "I may be hardheaded, but that's what I believe. We'll be a competitive team." The Orioles would be "playing Orioles baseball again," meaning there would be fewer mental and physical errors.

Billy Ripken was placed on the Orioles' 40-man spring roster, so, naturally, an entire new set of questions was initiated for Cal junior. How would the dad-manager and brother-infielder relationships affect his play? If Billy made the team, would Cal be moved?

Junior would be unaffected, said Senior. "He'll be the same guy. He's been the same guy since he came to the big leagues. He'll be the same guy 10 years from now. . . . [The Ripkens' playing together] will have no bearing whatsoever. [Cal's] a professional. He has a job to do. Young Billy has a job to do. We don't think about the family part."

The Orioles shortstop did not hide that it would be "exciting" to play on the same infield with Billy. But Dad had taught them how to handle that possibility. "From a family perspective," said Cal, "it's pretty exciting. Playing on the same team as my brother is something I've always looked forward to."

No "professional" problem would occur, added Cal. "Dad taught us to approach it that way because he always did. I don't see any pressure. . . . It's a growing process. My father would talk to me until he was blue in the face, trying to make a 40-year-old from an 18-year-old, but it's a learning process."

Senior was the ultimate baseball teacher. He helped write the Orioles way, a guide for minor league managers and coaches with instruction on how to teach the Baltimore system. What mattered most were the fundamentals: bunting, hitting cutoff men, hitting and running, backing up bases, and the like. One of Senior's star pupils was Eddie Murray. While Murray's minor league manager in 1974, Rip converted the first baseman, a natural righty, into a switch-hitter, and Murray went on to become one of history's best.

On March 5, 1987, Cal Ripken, Sr., delivered his state of the Orioles address in the Miami locker room. "I wish you could have heard it," said outfielder Mike Young. "He said he wanted us to laugh and have a great time like Orioles teams have had in the past. The difference is that when we go out on the field, we have to tend to business. He said baseball was a matter of doing two million little things. You do the little things and you never have to worry about the big ones."

Presently Pastor McGregor, Scotty McGregor has always appreciated inspiring talks. "[Rip] was so filled with energy and enthusiasm," the pitcher recalled. "We had been hearing the same tired, flat speeches for years. It was a breath of fresh air to hear something different."

Eddie Murray, Mike Flanagan, and others who had played in the minors for Rip had already seen the real Senior. They were inspired more by the action that followed those words. "We seem to be getting back to doing things we used to do," pitcher Flanagan said. "We go through every drill methodically now. We don't take anything for granted. This franchise was built on defense. As pitchers, we always complained about not having enough runs, but that means we took the defense for granted. But the last couple of years have made us realize just how important it was."

For Cal junior, the locker room inspirational did not surprise. He had seen his father as leader—in the home, in the minor league ball fields and clubhouses. "I couldn't help but wonder," reacted Cal, "what everyone else in the room was thinking when he was talking. Many of them had never seen him like this before, but the guy who talked to us is the dad I've always known. He's at his best when he's in charge. . . . Some men were made to follow and some to lead. My dad's a leader."

What Cal did not know was whether his father would keep him at short or move him to third. Baltimore signed veteran free agent infielders Rick Burleson and Ray Knight during the off-season. Third base had been a glaring Orioles weakness for some time. Cal took a professional, team-first attitude. "I used to perceive it as people attacking me, like I couldn't play shortstop," he said. "I got defensive. That's not the case now. If they tell me we're a better team now with me at third, I'll grab another glove and play."

If Billy made the team, he could play on one side of Cal, at second base. Since his arrival in Miami, Billy the Kid had already made his free spirit known. Because of his mischievous reputation, he was often blamed for pranks pulled off by his older brother. The *Miami Herald* featured a color photo of the three Ripkens. An unknown prankster clipped the picture and posted it on the club-house bulletin board complete with an original caption: THE PEP BOYS: MANNY, MOE, AND JACK.

In a split-squad game, Cal and Billy formed the double-play combo for one team. As the Ripkens posed three abreast afterward, Junior reached behind Dad to twist the cap sideways. An annoyed father unhesitatingly turned to stare at the assumed culprit—Billy.

However, Billy was not in camp to impress with his light antics. He did not have the potent bat of his brother. But he was an excellent fielder who had led Southern League second basemen in four fielding categories in 1986.

The Orioles ended the infield question: Billy was sent back to the farm, and Cal was set again for short.

Added to the endless questions about the Ripken family and the infield shift were questions about Cal's contract and about his consecutive-innings streak. Cal was in the last year of his four-year contract. Would that affect his play? "A contract can't get a hit," Cal retorted. "It is gaining importance in my mind," Cal said, referring to the streak. "People say a day off will help, but I don't see how coming out in the fifth inning of an 11–0 game will make you refreshed for the next game."

However, Cal's spring hitting had little vigor. In 21 Grapefruit League games, Cal hit only .157. Why had this happened? After all, during the post-1986 visit to Japan, veteran Hiroshima Carp third baseman Koji Yamamoto put Cal on the right path. "How come you changed your batting stance?" asked Yamamoto, who had last seen Cal in the Orient in 1984.

Cal then went back to holding the bat straight up like he had held it several years back. "With my stance, the right elbow had become so low," Cal said, thanking Yamamoto, "that the hands could not execute a powerful snap over." The results were great in Japan. "My hands started flying through the zone," said Cal. "I hit two homers the day Yamamoto told me." But the magic seemed gone in Florida.

The Orioles' optimism also vanished. They began the season

dismally, losing seven of nine at one stretch. At April's end they were 9–12, nine games out and in fourth place. Rip's managerial start was woeful, but Cal had a marvelous beginning.

On May 6 he hit a three-run homer that sparked Baltimore to a 6–0 win at Minnesota. Cal had nine homers and 30 RBIs. His last nine hits had been for extra bases, including four homers. However, he was troubled about the performance of the Orioles in past years: poor beginnings and horrid endings. "I've had a tough time dealing with the way each season has ended the last three years," he lamented. "The motivation, when you're not playing for a true winning reason, just wasn't there. You need an approach that works no matter what."

Cal was leading the league in eight batting categories, featuring a better-than-.500 average, 14 for 27, driving in runners in scoring position. Orioles coach Terry Crowley, now a Minnesota coach, was impressed. Observing Junior in batting practice, he remarked, "He hasn't hit a ball bad in 15 minutes. He's talented. But he's even more dedicated."

Aware of the pressure on Dad because of the Birds' subpar play, Cal said, "You can't blame Dad for the team's play. Dad is a great instructor. Look at what he's done for me."

The shortstop's star status reached beyond the baseball world. Morganna Roberts, the exotic dancer from Columbus, Ohio, better known as the Kissing Bandit, had begun her career in Baltimore at age 13. Since 1970 she had targeted a number of baseball stars—she would go to the park, elude security, jump out onto the field, and kiss her selected hero. Her conquests have included Johnny Bench, Steve Garvey, Pete Rose, and Nolan Ryan. She claimed Cal Ripken, Jr., on May 2.

Cal and the Memorial Stadium gathering took it in stride, but the Orioles manager of stadium operations, John McCall, was not such a good sport. "If you or I went out on the field, we'd be arrested just like she was," he snapped. "The fans pay money to see the game. They don't need to see Morganna, the exotic dancer, cavorting on the field."

The Orioles fans were pleased that the quality of play had picked up. On May 25 the Orioles nipped the Oakland A's 4–3 to complete a sweep and finish their West Coast trip with an 8–2 mark. They were 24–20, five out of first. The Birds returned home to continue their winning ways. On May 27, Cal drove in the tiebreaking run with a two-out, sixth-inning single to beat California 8–6. Cal's seventh game-winning RBI of the young season enabled the Orioles to slip into third place, four behind the Yankees. The next day the O's hit four homers, including one by Cal, to win an 8–7 thriller against California in 12 innings.

The Orioles of Cal senior had become an exciting team. They had clouted 48 homers in their last 19 games; their 56 round-trippers in May was a Major League record. An ebullient Hank Peters remarked, "We've corked all the bats, put everyone on weight programs, and juiced up the baseball. . . . The important thing is, we're in a position now where we can be a factor in the race."

However, a June swoon knocked Baltimore out of the hunt. When the Orioles lost a four-hours-plus 11-inning 8–5 game in Toronto, it was their seventh loss in their last eight games. Cal hit his 15th homer against the Red Sox on June 9, but the O's lost 2–1, their fifth straight setback, dropping them to 27–30, nine games out and in fifth place. The skein reach nine on June 12 when Toronto beat them at Memorial Stadium 8–5. The Birds had sunk to 27–33, 12 games out and in sixth place. Cal helped end the slide the next day with his 16th homer as the O's prevailed against Toronto 8–5.

Looking to end their losing ways, the Orioles resorted to wearing orange jerseys for the first time in three years. However, this was not the Orioles way that Cal senior had taught. All spring he had stressed fundamentals, but his forces, Junior among them, deserted him on June 16 at Yankee Stadium.

The Orioles lost 6–5, giving away leads of 2–0 and 4–2. In the sixth inning second baseman Alan Wiggins failed to cover second on a routine grounder and was late on a throw to first. An unhappy manager moaned after the game, "People that don't make mistakes win. People that make mistakes lose." He told the media after a team meeting, "I'm just trying to get people to come out here and play the game like it's supposed to be played. I'm going to work at that."

Baltimore fell 13 back, and their 28–36 start was their worst beginning since 1955. In the midst of that disappointing loss, Cal reached two milestones: his 1,000th Major League hit and his 829th straight game, tying Eddie Yost for seventh place on the iron man list.

The Orioles lost again the next day to the Yanks 6–3, prompting a story by David Falkner in the *New York Times*, headlined LOSING IS STRANGE FOR RIPKEN. Falkner wrote about the 30-year man of the Orioles organization who had been a vital cog of a team that had won more games than any other franchise during the past three decades. "Ripken had not only been a loyal servant," wrote Falkner, "but perhaps the most skilled of a skilled ensemble of baseball minds."

Pitching was the root cause of the Orioles' problems. Their 4.00 Earned Run Average was third highest in the American League. They finally got a pitching gem at home on June 24, as Dave Schmidt shut out the Yanks 4–0. Homers by Cal, Eddie Murray, and Ray Knight ended a string of nine straight losses to the Bronx Bombers.

That victory was one of the rare joyous moments of early summer. The Birds spent July 4 in the Minnesota Metrodome but did not celebrate. They lost their sixth straight, 4–1, for their 29th loss in their last 34 games. They stood at 31–49, 19½ games out and in sixth place. Both Cal and Murray had a chance to tie or drive home the winning run with runners on second and third in a July 9 home encounter against the Twins. Jeff Reardon struck out both sluggers to preserve a 3–2 win. It was the Birds' 32nd loss in 37 games.

In the midst of this misery, the Ripken family made history during the weekend preceding the All-Star break. Billy Ripken was brought up from Rochester to replace Rick Burleson, let go by the team. The slick-fielding Billy had done well with the bat in Rochester, hitting .286, and had an eight-game hitting streak.

When Billy joined the Orioles on July 11, it was the first time in Major League history that a manager had two sons on the same team. Previously, there had been only two other manager-player father-son combos in the Majors: Connie and Earle Mack (Philadelphia A's, 1910–11, 1914) and Yogi and Dale Berra (New York Yankees, 1985). Only three times before in baseball history had three members of the same family wore the same uniform at the same time: Jose, Hector, and Tommy Cruz, St. Louis Cardinals, 1973; Felipe, Jesus, and Matty Alou, San Francisco Giants, 1963; George, Harry, and Sam Wright, Boston Braves, 1876. (Hal McRae has managed his son Brian with the Kansas City Royals, from 1991–94; and since 1992, Felipe Alou has managed his son Moises with the Montreal Expos.)

Cal and Billy made history playing alongside each other that July 11 evening against Minnesota. The game itself was not eventful. Billy was 0 for 3 with a walk; Cal was 0 for 4; Baltimore lost 2–1.

The three Ripkens were major news for prideful Aberdeen. "The Ripkens of Aberdeen became the nation's first family of sports," boasted the *Havre de Grace Record*. When he heard rumors of Burleson's departure, Billy knew he would soon be in the Majors, he told reporter J. M. Eddins, Jr. "It has gotten to me a bit," he admitted, speaking of the wave of questions about the baseball family. "You get a little tired of answering the same old questions, most of which have nothing to do with baseball. Stuff like, 'What's it like playing with your brother and your father . . . ?' All I know is what I have been working for as far back as I can remember. Now I have my chance."

His big-league stay was not guaranteed. Charlotte's Pete Stanicek was ready to step in if Billy faltered. "This is my dream," said Billy, "but I will not stay here just because I want to stay here or it looks good in the papers. I have gotten my shot, and I have to do something with it."

Cal Ripken, Jr., was an established star; Billy now had his chance. The *Record* headline of July 15, 1987, played to this theme: BILLY IS STARTING ANEW . . . and . . . CAL IS STARTING AGAIN. The shortstop was heading for his fourth starting assignment in the All-Star Game. He beat out Detroit's Alan Trammell by more than 850,000 votes.

The Ripkens helped bring better times to the Orioles after the All-Star break. Billy hit his first Major League home run on July 19, propelling the O's to a 5–1 victory in Kansas City, giving Baltimore their first four-game sweep ever there. On July 22, Cal hit his 16th homer and drove in three runs in Chicago to help the Orioles win 11–6, their seventh straight victory. On July 23, Baltimore beat the Royals at home, 2–1. Cal drove in both runs, while Billy continued his hitting streak, at eight games.

Cal was also the hero on July 24, driving in the winning run on an eighth-inning sacrifice fly, leading to a 3–1 victory. Baltimore won again on July 25. Their 11-game winning streak, 10–0 since the All-Star break, was their longest since 1978. They had inched their way to 13 games out of first. Was a miracle in the making?

The Royals brought the Orioles back to reality on July 26 with a 4–0 two-hitter. Another streak ended later at Cleveland, with a 4–3 loss; Baltimore had won seven straight on the road. After renewed hope, the Birds finished July with a 47–56 mark, 16 games out of first.

Losing ways resumed in August. A three-run homer by Cal on August 7 helped the O's break a four-game skein, 9–2, in a home game against Texas. But the Birds were 49–50, 16 games out of first. Cal hit a two-run homer on August 12 at home against Cleveland, but Baltimore lost 8–6 and fell to 51–63, 17 out.

Both Cal and the Orioles struggled in August. He went homerless for 12 games until he hit number 23, a three-run shot at home against California, in a 9–5 win. The month ended for Baltimore with a 60–71 record, 18 games from first.

The remainder of the season was agonizing. For Cal and the Orioles, September 14 was especially painful. The Birds were being clawed by the Blue Jays in Toronto, 17–3. Cal was left on base to end the O's eighth, so Billy reached for his brother's glove to bring it out to short, since the O's were taking the field. "That's the wrong glove," Senior told his son. Surprised and shocked, Billy insisted, "No, this is Cal's." Once more Senior said, "That's the wrong glove."

It was the end of Iron Man Cal's consecutive-innings streak of 8,243. Cal and his glove remained in the dugout as Ron Washington went to short for the bottom of the eighth. That was Washington's only appearance at short that season—in fact, it was the only time Washington ever played there for the Orioles. The last time Cal had been replaced was on June 4, 1982, when Jim Dwyer pinch-hit for him against the Twins' Terry Felton. There is no official listing of consecutive innings played, but no baseball historian has challenged Cal's record.

Before the game, Cal was at a season low .249 batting average. In the first 34 games of 1987 he had hit .333 with 11 homers and 34 RBIs; in the next 108 he struggled at .222, with 13 homers and 53 RBIs. He entered the Toronto contest with one hit in his last 12 at bats and seemingly broke the slump by going 2 for 4, including a double and two RBIs.

A surprised Cal was told by his father in the top of the eighth that he was going to the bench. The O's owner and the GM had long voiced the opinion that the innings streak should be ended. "I've been thinking about it for a long time," said Senior. "I wanted to take the monkey off his back. It was my decision, not his."

Cal told the media that the timing was "perfect," in a game out of conceivable reach. Did Senior do it because Cal had been fatigued? "No, the guy's big and strong. Playing the innings and playing the ball games wasn't wearing on him."

The Streak had become a "burden," said the manager, because the media had relentlessly pursued and questioned Junior. "I want to take that burden off his shoulders. . . . Everywhere we go, someone wants to write a story about the consecutive-innings streak. I had to do it sometime."

This was the ideal game, concluded the skipper. "He wasn't going to hit a 20-run homer."

Ron Washington, Billy Ripken, and Cal Ripken, Jr., were asked for their thoughts after the massacre. A journeyman infielder who had toiled in Los Angeles and Minnesota, Ron Washington assured his place in baseball trivia: Who replaced Cal Ripken, Jr., when his consecutive-innings streak ended? "I didn't do anything," Washington smiled. "I knew what was going on. It's only natural that I was surprised. Everyone in here was surprised. I just grabbed my glove and ran out to shortstop. I was just hoping they would hit me a grounder. Nobody did."

"It might be for the better now," Billy reflected about the Streak's end. "I don't think anyone's going to surpass what he's done. There will only be one of those streaks. That one."

Father knows best, especially when he's the manager. Clearly unhappy on being given the word by Dad, Cal never thought of questioning the manager or appealing as son to father. "The manager has his say in the way the club is run," said Cal. "I'm a player. I do what my manager tells me to do. . . . It was a surprise, but I didn't feel I needed an explanation. . . . It just so happens, in this case, that the manager is my father."

The media wondered whether Cal was tired or whether all those innings had affected his hitting. His streak had become an issue, he said, only when his hitting fell off. "I described [questions about the streak] as being a hassle, but I regret using those types of words. They don't describe the way it was. It would only become a problem when I wasn't swinging the bat well or when I was in a defensive slump. People would come to me and say, 'You need a day off.'

"I have to defend myself and say I don't think that [fatigue] was the reason. It just seemed to be a common topic, a common question when I was slumping. I have never looked at the streak as a problem of any sort."

The innings streak now ended, Cal achieved a career first in Baltimore on September 25. In the first inning Yankee hurler Al

Leiter threw an outside pitch that umpire Tim Welke called strike three. Cal was tossed out (Dad had already had four 1987 ejections) and missed an 8–4 Orioles loss and Don Mattingly's record-tying fifth grand slam in one season.

"In my mind I didn't say anything to warrant getting thrown out," explained the ejectee. "I know from standing in the box. I heard pitchers say a lot worse and still stay in the game. I told him he missed two pitches, and he came to me and said I was out of the game."

Welke said he ejected Cal "for constantly arguing balls and strikes, shouting in my face. Then he whacked the brim of his helmet into my mask. Some guys say things, then walk away. But he came after me."

If Dad hadn't ended his innings streak, would that have affected both player and umpire? "I would hate to think that," argued Cal. "It should make no difference." It made no difference to Welke, who "didn't even know he had a streak going." Senior had no comment when asked why he wasn't tossed when he came out to argue.

Cal's end of the streak and first ejection were a prelude to the close of an unhappy first season for Senior. The Orioles rested in sixth, 67–95, 31 games back of AL eastern division winner Detroit. Larry Sheets looked for a cheerful note after the Orioles won their last home game, 8–5, on September 27 against the Yankees. "We sandwiched our season against a couple of wins." (The O's won their home opener in April.) But a sober manager rejoined, "But we didn't win enough damn games in between."

Senior had good reason for his unhappiness. The team's 51 home losses was an Orioles all-time low. Their 90-plus losses was only the third time in history that they reached such depths.

Cal Ripken, Jr., had also fallen mightily. His .252 batting average was the lowest in his six-year career. However, he had made notable offensive contributions: 27 homers, 98 RBIs, 97 runs scored, and a career-high 81 walks. He was the first Oriole in the '80s other than Murray to lead the team in RBIs. He also led the team with tying/go-ahead runs driven in and a .295 mark with runners in scoring position.

These stats were complemented by an outstanding season in the field. He was second in the league in fielding among shortstops (.982) and at one point played 37 consecutive errorless games. For the fourth time in five years, he led AL shortstops in assists (486) and was second in total chances (740) and double plays (103).

9

DISGRACEFUL FIRING

On Friday, November 13, 1987, Cal Ripken, Jr., married Kelly Geer in Towson United Methodist Church.

The romance between the six-foot blonde and baseball's most eligible millionaire began at the Corner Stable restaurant in Cockeysville. Kelly's mother, Joan, spotted Cal sharing a table with former Orioles outfielder Al Bumbry. Mrs. Geer asked Cal to give her an autograph for Kelly. He obliged and grabbed a napkin from the table. He wrote, "If your daughter is as attractive as you are, I would like to meet her," and signed his name. Other sources report a different inscription: "If you look anything like your mother, I'm sorry I missed you. All my best."

Delighted with her prize, Joan Geer eagerly called her daughter Kelly in College Park, Maryland, to convey news of the autograph. Kelly, an undergraduate at the University of Maryland at the time, listened politely to her mother's story, then reportedly said, "That's nice, Mom. But who is he?"

Some months later, Kelly and a girlfriend, Patty Buddenmeyer, noticed Cal surrounded by a crowd of 150 adoring girls. Patty later told the *Baltimore Sun*'s Mary Corey that Kelly had difficulty approaching Cal: "She must have stood up and sat down ten times before she got the nerve to go over to him. And Cal must have had a million women around him." When Kelly finally did attract Cal's attention, she introduced herself by saying, "You met my mom a couple of months ago." "What do you do?" Cal asked. She told him she worked for an airline. Cal concluded, "You're Kelly."

Cal's courtship of Kelly began with a lunch date. He continued his pursuit of her through systematic wooing that peaked with a birthday party during spring training in Florida. His personal birthday surprise for Kelly involved hiring a limo to chauffeur them around, buying a bottle of vintage Dom Perignon to toast her, and putting a longhaired Japanese puppy on the backseat to be his special gift to her. "He's very romantic," Kelly told Sylvia Badger of the *Baltimore Evening Sun*. "Best present of my life."

Cal proposed to Kelly on New Year's Eve, and she accepted. Kelly then left her position at the Piedmont Airlines VIP Lounge to oversee preparations for the big day.

Kelly asked her sister, Holly, the proprietor of Holly's Boutique in Olney, to attend her as maid of honor. Cal Ripken, Sr., would serve proudly as his son's best man. Baseball fan Oscar de la Renta, father-in-law of Cal's teammate Fred Lynn, designed Kelly's wedding dress.

The prospective bride had long dreamed of a double-ring ceremony, but Cal junior already wore World Series and All-Star rings. The clever lovers found an answer to the dilemma. As Aberdeen minister the Reverend James Chance pronounced them man and wife, Kelly slipped on Cal's hand a gold band thin enough for him to wear on the third finger of his left hand along with one of his baseball rings.

After a European honeymoon, Cal returned and busied himself with the Orioles' charity basketball team and with his ongoing community activities.

When Cal arrived for 1988 spring training, he found a club embroiled in debate over whether he should be moved back to third base. Ray Knight no longer played for Baltimore. Other possible third basemen were Craig Worthington, utility player Rene Gonzales, or Billy Ripken.

As the discussion of the lineup continued, Cal had little to say on the matter. "It's not a big deal," he asserted. "I used to think it was a slap in the face, people thinking I couldn't play shortstop. I don't look at it that way anymore."

Owner Williams had remarked that at age 27, Cal was still growing taller. Williams's view was seen by Cal as perhaps jeopardizing a double-play combo possibility of Cal and his brother. "That's the way everyone approaches it," responded Cal. "Size has always been the reason for the argument all along. Even in better years, people would say, 'He'll play shortstop for a few years and end up back at third.' It's all because of size."

Billy saw a similarity between Magic Johnson of the champion Los Angeles Lakers hoop team and his brother. "If Magic Johnson can play guard," said Billy, "[Cal] can play short. They're the best at what they can do."

Clearly the tallest shortstop in the big leagues, Cal stood literally head and shoulders above all other shortstops, even though athletes were getting taller and bigger every year. The average size of the other 13 projected AL shortstops was six feet, 172 pounds.

However, Cal trusted the manager's skill and expertise in designating the players in the 1988 lineup. "I'm here to help us in any way I can. The manager's here to guide the players to winning. It's his choice. If it'll make us a better team, I'll go over there and make the same transition I did six years ago."

Junior saw the problem not in terms of *where* he played but *how* he played: how to improve his own performance and focus better if the team fell behind. In June 1987 the O's fell out of contention, continuing a slide that began May 29 and ended on July 5, amounting to a 5–30 tumble. Attempting to beat the division teams seemed a possibility, but by June they had only 11 victories against division rivals above them. For Cal and the other Birds, he explained, "That was the difficult part, finding a reason to play."

Cal analyzed his own performance: "I tried to do a little more than I was capable of. I tried to be the one that made us win. In hindsight, that was the wrong thing to do." Rip agreed. "He was guilty of the same thing a lot of the hitters were. He tried to go up to home plate and do too damn much. And when you do that, averages fall off."

Having grown up with Cal, Billy understood the shortstop's dilemma. "He's a perfectionist," said Billy. "He saw his average going down the ladder, and he was pressing more and more. He was probably going up to home plate saying, 'I've got to get a hit.' That's not how you go about hitting. You go up there trying to hit the ball hard. When he didn't, it affected him. I could see that."

The Orioles may have had their troubles as a team, but the fans continued to love the Ripkens. When Cal senior spoke at an enthusiastic annual banquet of the Cal Ripken, Jr., Fan Club, he recalled the tough times of the past but also looked ahead. "We have a future. It was a bad year, no question about it. But everything is uphill from here on down the road. I used a word in October '86 when I got the job: 'patience.' I think I stayed with patience through the course of the year. In 1988 we may have to have a little bit of patience also. We just can't go from the bottom to the top in the snap of a finger. We have to improve the pitching. We are trying to do that."

The skipper pleaded with the fans to keep the faith. "We are going to do everything," he promised, "to improve our ball club in 1988. Have patience and stick with the Birds and root for the Birds."

The Orioles had been baseball's winningest franchise from 1957 to 1987. Perhaps that spirit had motivated Cal senior in his fan club speech; it may also have prompted his spring training announcement to his team—and the world: "Damn right we're contenders."

Despite the bravado, Senior understood that the Orioles would be rebuilding in 1988. "The Orioles experienced a downturn in the early '80s," he said in 1993. "We lost good scouts, and the good talent was not coming in. The scouts we had were able to sell our organization, and, therefore, we could get talent as well as anybody if not better. Now, we had an influx of new people."

He counseled patience as a good motif for 1988: The team needed it; the management needed it; Cal junior needed it. "The word *hope* is not in my vocabulary," said Senior during the summer of '93. "From the start, my goal has always been to win the World Series. Vince Lombardi said, 'Winning is the only thing.' I would change that to 'Winning is everything.' "

Baltimore opened the season at Memorial Stadium, hosting Milwaukee in front of 52,395, the O's largest regular season crowd. Besides the gate, nothing else went the Birds' way: the Brewers walloped the home team 12–0, the O's worst opening loss ever. Trying to draw something positive from the debacle, Senior observed, "We did make it through the ball game without anyone getting hurt."

Fans comforted each other with cliches and platitudes: "Tomorrow is another day." But games two, three, four, five, and six brought losses two, three, four, five, and six—and still no victory. Roland Hemond, who had become the Orioles' GM in November, had run out of the advised patience. Cal senior got the bad news on April 12.

The firing caught Cal senior by surprise. Suited in his uniform, he sat at his desk in Memorial Stadium, ready to make out his lineup card. "Roland called me to come to his office," said Senior, "and he told me I was being relieved. . . . I'm disappointed, no question."

Senior thought that he and owner Williams had a mutual understanding that 1988 would be "a rebuilding year," a season in which no one expected a lot from the O's. Williams had "decided he was going to roll over my contract for 1988 and said he wanted me to have the chance to manage a decent club," Senior recalled. "So it was agreed to be a rebuilding year. We had many meetings based on trying to educate people to do the right things. I kept telling them we were signing too many soft-teasing pitchers. The fastball is baseball's best pitch, always has been, always will be."

As manager of the Orioles, Cal Ripken, Sr., had a 68–101 record, including his one game in 1985. He had managed longer than any other skipper in Orioles minor league history. Hemond, who had left Chicago for Baltimore, rewarded all this loyalty by handing Senior a pink slip after six games. The new GM set a modern Major League record for speed in firing a skipper after the season opener. *Sun* reporter Bill Glauber called the firing "unintentionally cruel."

Hall of Famer Frank Robinson, former Orioles player and now front office executive, succeeded Ripken senior to become the tenth Orioles manager in the club's 35-year history (excluding Weaver's second tenure and Senior's interim game). Hemond claimed that if Robinson had turned down the job, Rip would have remained as skipper. The GM also told Rip that he could stay in a front office post with the Orioles. Still stunned and amazed at being sacked, Senior could only immediately respond, "I hadn't even thought about that. Right now, it's just tough."

In an interview in his home years later, Senior admitted, "It was very difficult to accept. I had been in the organization. I had worked my way up to the big leagues. I spent my life with the Orioles."

Vi Ripken had her own perspective on her husband's firing. "Six days into the season, my husband lost his job," she said, "and I thought everyone lost their minds."

Cal senior revealed that he had not discussed his firing with Robinson—he had not even seen him. But Senior had become aware of other rumors. "I did hear that Edward Bennett Williams told Frank that I would be fired even if [Frank] did not take the job. However, I never heard the report that said the opposite: if Frank had not accepted, I still would have the job."

The Orioles front office fired Ripken senior intending to restore the team's winning tradition. Yet Robinson carried a cumulative 450–466 record in his two previous managerial stints, with San Francisco and Cleveland. Robinson's third stint as skipper in 1988 began with a 6–1 loss to Kansas City. Even a new manager couldn't keep the O's from its seventh consecutive loss.

The local media seized on the firing. RIPKEN OUT, headlined the *Havre de Grace Record*. "Cal is baseball personified," said Jim McMahan of WAMD Radio in Aberdeen. "He may be down, but he's not out. He's done a lot for the community, and now it's time for the community to show its support for him and the family." Members of the community rallied to the cause of the ousted manager. The move angered former Aberdeen town commissioner Jerry Nolen. "It was a hasty removal," said Nolen. "He wasn't the one responsible for the players the team traded for and for those who haven't performed up to expectations."

The Baltimore Orioles fans, front office, and players wondered how Cal and Billy would handle their dad's firing. The last firing of a manager who had a son on the team occurred in 1985. Owner George Steinbrenner gave the pink slip to Yogi Berra after 16 games, while Yogi's son, reserve infielder Dale Berra, remained on the team.

Friends and admirers of the Ripkens' knew how the family felt about baseball, so the headline RIPKEN BROTHERS HANDLE FIRING JUST LIKE DAD—AS PROFESSIONALS to Jim Henneman's story in the *Baltimore Evening Sun* did not surprise them. The reporter revealed that Hemond had spoken with the Ripken brothers when they arrived at the park on the day he dropped their dad. "I don't blame them if they're hurt by this," said Hemond. "That's the way it should be. I certainly can understand. But I'm sure they have the same makeup as their father, always giving it their best. They are both so highly professional with a great understanding of the game they were raised in. They can understand it." The short time the Ripkens worked together in the majors "was beautiful."

Cal and Billy drew closer that sad evening. "Cal and I always spend a lot of time together before a game," said Billy, "but I guess [last night] it might have been a little more than usual." Billy had missed the phone call informing him of the firing, but he had heard the news on the radio two minutes before coming to the park. Junior heard word of the dismissal from his father before the ballplayer left home.

"It wasn't a long conversation," said Cal. "He just wanted me to know before I heard it from anyone else." Rip told his son to go out, "bust his rear end, keep his head up, and play"—and pass the message on to Billy. Cal delivered Rip's message to Billy during the pregame huddle. "Mainly, what I told him," said Cal, "was that anything he had to say to make sure he thought it through. I reminded him that anything he said would reflect on him and the family."

Confronting the reality of their father's firing proved difficult for the brothers. As Henneman reported, "For the first time in their big-league careers, Cal junior and Bill walked into a club-house, put on their uniforms—and probably felt naked in front of the baseball world."

Throughout the questioning from media, players, and fans, Cal refused to second-guess Hemond's decision or show any bitterness toward management. Playing under those conditions "was kind of eerie," said Cal. "You can't prepare yourself for something like this. You feel bad because you know somebody in your family feels bad."

But Cal remained a realist. "My job is still the same," he said. "You've got to do the same thing day in and day out. I've been doing the same thing so long that I've been able to block out the distractions. . . . [The firing] is a hard-core reality in base-ball. That's the way the system works. I can't do anything about that. . . . Professionalism, work ethics—I know it sounds trite, but that's what [my father] taught us—that there's a certain way to do things, a way to go about it, and you do it, no more or no less, regardless of the circumstances."

Nor did the younger Billy feel any bitterness. He fielded the questions well, but without concealing a note of frustration. Dad "waited so long to get the job. Then he finally gets the team, and we stink." With the game still 45 minutes away, Billy yielded to the emotional strain. "I'd have to say right now, yes, it's going to be tough," said Billy. "But when 7:35 rolls around, I still have to do what I have to do. I consider myself a professional. I play the game only one way—that's hard, that's to win. When 7:35 rolls around, that's what I'm going to do."

The O's lost again that night, but Billy's ground ball had moved Joe Orsulak to third. From there, Orsulak later took advantage of Cal's sac fly to score the lone Orioles run.

Billy had just started his first full season with Baltimore, and he thought it out of place to comment on management's judgment. "I can't start getting involved in front office decisions in my second year. Maybe in my 12th year. Hopefully, I'll have a 12th year." The front office action would have a resounding impact on Billy Ripken and his relationship with Cal Ripken, Sr. "When he was the manager and I was a player, you couldn't call it a father-son relationship," Billy said. "Tomorrow, I'm going to speak to him as a son."

The next day, before game time, Billy decided to change his uniform number from 3 to 7, the number his dad had worn when he managed. "I just didn't want to see anybody else wear it," Billy explained. "I'd be lying if I said I didn't feel something." Billy had no idea of how long it would take for him to get over the hurt Rip's firing had caused. "I won't know until I've done it," he noted.

Hemond had spent his first 11 years without discarding a skipper. As if to regain their allegiance after firing their father, Hemond turned his attention to the Ripken boys and observed: "They have great work ethics, great dedication—that's why they are the players they are. To me, they're all baseball. They have great respect for the Orioles organization. I hope it's not tarnished by this. They're such good people. I hope they understand."

Junior felt hurt and "bothered" by the firing long after the initial shock had subsided. "Even 0–6," he said, "it seemed like we were in a few games. Then my dad was let go, and there was a bigger sense of chaos that developed. It makes you ask yourself, 'What's going on?' It wasn't a matter of understanding the firing. It was a matter of accepting it. And that took time. . . . I just wanted to win, to make everyone go away, to go on with the season."

Orioles management may have thought that a shift in leaders would quick fix the team's troubles, but it didn't work out that way. News of Atlanta's opening 0–10 and tying a National League record buoyed the Orioles' spirits. They carried their enthusiasm into Baltimore on April 15, where Cleveland nipped them 3–2. Cal drew an 0 for 3 in that game, making him 0 for 21 that season.

Now the Orioles counted 10 opening losses and shared the opening frustration of the Chicago White Sox of 1968, who also had started 0–10. Only the 1904 Washington Senators and the 1920 Detroit Tigers had begun a season more dismally.

Baltimore faced Cleveland again, this time in 41-degree windy weather that resulted in a chill-factor temperature of 15 degrees. The grueling game ran into extra frames, but the Cleveland team finally toppled the O's 1–0. The Orioles' season record now stood at an abysmal 0 for 11.

Cleveland also won the next contest, extending the O's losing streak to 12. Cal was now 0 for 29 and showing pathetic season stats: 2 for 43, .047, with no homers.

Cal senior revealed that ever since Junior was a boy, he had taken losing especially hard because "he always had the desire to excel and to win. He was highly competitive, and that's one of the reasons he has done so well." Vi Ripken recalled that once in a Little League game "Cal got so upset because one of his teammates had not come through. I had to explain to Cal that his teammate was trying and doing the best he can. You have to accept that."

None of the O's could accept the fact that they had each fallen into a slump, but that's what the stats seemed to show. The team batting average was .186, with only four homers. Eddie Murray, Terry Kennedy, and Jeff Stone had individual batting averages of .152, .156, and .031, respectively. Billy Ripken and Larry Sheets shared top billing for the most RBIs—each of them had four. The GM tried to reassure the Orioles players. "We've scored 17 runs in 12 games," said Hemond. "When that happens you suffer. The crazy thing is we have good hitters. When you have good hitters, you ride out the storm, and they'll bust loose." However, the storm would not pass over a ball club that managed a team earned run average of 5.43. Mike Morgan, the staff ace, held a 3.65 ERA, but the four other starters showed 8.44, 7.84, 5.73, and 5.63.

On April 19 in Milwaukee, for the first time the O's had more than a one-run lead, but their 3–0 first-inning lead meant little when the Brewers canned them 9–5 and sent them to a record-tying 13-game losing streak. Cal had his first homer on only his third hit of the season. When asked about the mood of the team, the usually communicative Cal replied tersely, "At this point, I don't have much to say." Brother Billy viewed the situation more optimistically. "We've had some good pitching coming into Milwaukee," he said, "and that's encouraging. Our hitters will come around. We know this can't go on."

But it did. ORIOLES GO FROM BAD TO WORST, read the *New York Times* headline after the O's lost to the Brewers 8–6 and fell to 0–14. The Orioles had now tied the franchise consecutive loss record—set in midseason—of 14.

Hurler Mike Boddicker, a now-losing hero of the '83 World Series and other important frays, offered his thoughts on the O's ignominious record. "I don't give a damn about no records," he said. "All I want to do is win a ball game."

The situation could be worse, some scribes pointed out. The O's losses in their last five exhibition games didn't count in the tally.

Kansas City swept by the O's 3–1 on April 24. The Orioles scored their only run on Cal's second four-bagger of the season. The team now stood at 0–18; rival teams had outscored the Orioles 114–34 in those 18 games.

"We were pathetic," said pitcher Scott McGregor. "We were the laughingstock of the town." It got to the point that the veteran hurler was crying between starts.

"This was the first time in my life that I would have a sense of what's going to happen wrong," Scotty said. "You'd feel it come over the team in the third or fourth inning. The thing was, guys were saying, 'This is pathetic.' But there was nothing they could do. It was a horror story."

The O's next traveled to Minnesota for a bout with the Twins. Before the game, President Reagan called Frank Robinson to encourage him and to urge him to keep his chin up. "Hang in there," said the chief executive. "I know what you're going through."

Robinson retorted, "No you don't, Mister President."

The Orioles fell again, 4–2, in the opener of their series.

Baltimore owner Williams had persevered through six cancer surgeries only to watch his team's nightmarish decline. "I suffer for Ed," said Hemond. The GM also realized how the O's losing streak affected the folks in the bleachers. "The fans watch us to get pleasure or relax or get rid of frustrations," Hemond said. "When you play like this, you feel like you aren't providing them with what they are entitled to."

Strange practices and bizarre rituals began to surface in the ranks of Orioles boosters. One Baltimore disc jockey went on a nonstop broadcasting vigil, vowing not to get off the air until the Orioles put one in the win column. Roland Hemond superstitiously sat in a different seat each inning, trying to change the team's luck. Other players wore their caps sideways or their uniforms inside out, making every effort to break the streak of bad luck that had plagued the team.

As a before-game token of faith and encouragement, one fan sent a dozen roses to outfielder Ken Gerhart. His teammates draped the roses over Gerhart's locker. Jim Dwyer observed, "They're sending us flowers like this was a funeral parlor." Gerhart's dozen blossoms didn't help the O's performance.

Another hopeful fan, commiserating with manager Robinson, sent him a lapel pin that read, "It's been lovely, but I have to scream now."

Echoing the sentiments of Robinson's pin, Junior welcomed a

new reporter assigned to stay with the Orioles until they won one. "Join the hostages," Ripken said.

Even the cynics applauded when the O's won 9–0 in Chicago on April 29. IT'S OVER! HONEST! THEY WIN! screamed the *New York Times* headline. The pundits could now stop speculating whether the Birds would surpass the record of the Louisville team that had lost 26 in a row in 1889 in the Major League American Association.

The victory depended on many heroes. President Reagan kept on calling to rally the team on; Bob Rivers, the nonstop disc jockey, persisted in this mission; Roland Hemond wore the champagne-splashed suit he had last donned in Chicago in celebration of the 1983 Western Division championship; Mark Williamson gave up only three hits in six innings; Eddie Murray put Baltimore ahead in the first inning; and Cal Ripken, Jr., had four hits, including a double and home run.

The Birds did not make merry. The teammates felt relief, not joy. "I'm not in a celebrating-type mood," Cal said. "One and 21. That's not good. That's not a reason to be jumping around and celebrating."

The O's yielded their one-game streak to Chicago, 4–1, in Comiskey Park. Once again the Birds had set another dubious record: the lowest modern-day mark for any one month—1–22, .043, eclipsing the 2–28 of the Athletics in July 1916.

The Orioles had attracted nationwide attention and won widespread sympathy, yet Cal shrugged it off. "You like publicity," he said. "But not for this reason."

The publicity gradually subsided, especially after their second consecutive win, on May 22—a 7–2 triumph over Seattle, aided by Cal's seventh homer. Their third straight win—7–3 over Oakland on May 23—featured Cal's eighth homer.

Despite these homers, Cal had gone 14 for 89 since May 9. Although his average had dropped from .316 to .230, he welcomed Jack Morris to Memorial Stadium on June 6 with a four-hit day as the O's pounded the Tigers 5–2. The homer against the ace righty, whom Cal had pounded for a .370 career average, gave the Orioles their first two-run-or-more homer since September 30, 1987. When the O's again beat Detroit, 7–3 on June 7, they passed another season milestone: it marked the first time since April 10–12, 1987, that the team had won a series against an AL East opponent. They had lost 25 series and tied three.

The Orioles' poor performances in recent seasons and their hasty dismissal of Cal senior caused rumors to fly throughout Orioleville. Cal junior would not resign from the Baltimore team but the team would trade both him and Billy. Cal would stay with the O's because he wanted to stay on the same team as his brother. Bad blood existed between Cal and Robinson, his dad's replacement, because a slumping Cal refused to take advice from the Hall of Fame hitter.

Robinson reminded Cal that rival teams often started such stories of trade talks and that those items did not necessarily originate with the Orioles. "These rumors come from other people," said the manager. "When that happens, you sit and listen."

General manager Hemond, however, found it difficult to contend with the gossip. "It's a tough one," the GM said, "and I don't know how to handle it, really. The rumors emanate from other cities, and I don't know. That's why we have tampering rules, because people shouldn't be throwing names around. Sometimes I strongly resent it; it just depends on how it's handled. If somebody asks you if you'd be interested in a player of that caliber, you'd be crazy if you said you wouldn't."

Hemond praised Cal for his response to these rumors. "I think he's just handled it well," said Hemond. "He just concentrates on his play."

Rumors notwithstanding, the Orioles still had an immediate problem: Cal's contract ended after the 1988 season. Robinson put off signing Junior, saying, "It's too early now. . . . There's plenty of time, [but] we can't wait until the end. I would think that the All-Star break would be a good time for preliminary talks, a feeling-out period. And then you'd try to get it done by September, or at least not too deep in September."

Amid the continuing swirl of rumors, on June 25, in a 10–3 Orioles loss to Boston, Cal reached a personal milestone. He made his 1,000th consecutive start for Baltimore. Only Lou Gehrig, Everett Scott, Steve Garvey, Billy Williams, and Joe Sewell—iron men all—had played in more consecutive games.

In four of the past five years, Cal had led all Major League shortstops in home runs, RBIs, and slugging percentage. For the fifth straight year the American League chose him as the starting shortstop in the All-Star Game. He went 0 for 3 in the AL's 2–1 victory at Cincinnati's Riverfront Stadium, but in the field he sparkled even more than the Wizard of Oz, the Cardinals' Ozzie Smith.

RIPKEN WAS, OH, SO SMOOTH AT SHORT, read the headline of Ken Rosenthal's report for the *Baltimore Evening Sun*. "Cal has become the great shortstop that he is by being in the right place at the right time. His backhand one-hop stab in the hole and rifle throw to nip Will Clark in the second inning dazzled as the gem of the evening."

Cal saw the call for a fastball and knew the hard-throwing Minnesota pitcher Frank Viola could not be pulled by Clark. Ripken moved into the hole between short and third. "After the ball's hit, it becomes a reaction," Cal explained, "but the decision where to play . . . was made before he made contact. I had a hint it would be hit to that side. It gave me the advantage to move over a little bit."

Clark and Viola lauded Cal's play. "The guy looked like he had been standing there a hundred years," raved the San Francisco star. "It was just a great play. I thought it was going to go through the hole."

Viola also voiced his admiration for Junior's skill: "I thought it would end up over the left-field fence. He hit it so hard. It was a heckuva defensive play."

"It was a joy to play behind those pitchers tonight," said Cal. "When a pitch was called for in a particular area, I had confidence

Cal junior keeps his eyes on the camera while Billy sits on mother Vi Ripken's lap, seated in the stands at one of Cal senior's games, Aberdeen, South Dakota, 1964. (Courtesy of Vi Ripken)

Cal senior managed the Tri-Cities' Atoms (Washington State) for a time. Here he is pictured with his team and their kids. Cal senior kneels in front; with him *(from left)* are Cal, Fred, Billy, and Ellen. (Courtesy of Vi Ripken)

Cal's first little league team. The future Major Leaguer is the second player from the right in the second row. (Courtesy of Vi Ripken)

The world's greatest shortstop started as a pitcher. He is shown here practicing his hurling for his high school team, the Aberdeen Eagles. (Courtesy of Vi Ripken)

Fielding for the AAA
Rochester Redwings.
(Courtesy of Vi Ripken)

Welcome to the Majors,
son. Senior shakes
Junior's hand as he
rounds third. (Kevin
Allen)

Billy Ripken signed with the Orioles in 1982—his senior year of high school. Behind him *(left to right)* are Cal senior, scout Jim Gilbert, and brother Cal. (Kevin Allen)

Cal senior looks pensive on opening day, 1987. (Kevin Allen)

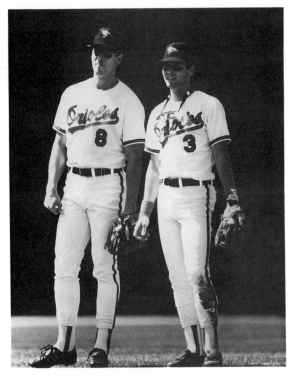

A trio of Ripkens in the dugout. Billy's first day in the Majors, June 1987. (Kevin Allen)

In the field, Billy played second base to Cal's shortstop. (Kevin Allen)

Cal senior stands over his two sons— every day is family day at Memorial Stadium. (Kevin Allen)

Cal goes airborne over the Twins' Gary Gaetti, May 1989. (Kevin Allen)

Taking a swing against Seattle, in 1994. (Kevin Allen)

Thumbs up! Cal in shades, with the Baltimore Elites hat. (Kevin Allen)

Jack Dunn IV presents the Jack Dunn Community Service Award to Cal and Kelly Ripken, January 1995. (Kevin Allen)

The hardest-working man in baseball. (Kevin Allen)

the pitch would be in that area. Viola was pitching so well that I could almost tell where the hitters were going to hit it."

Cal said the All-Star Game "was fun," certainly a welcome change from the Orioles' woes and his dad's firing. Junior found even greater happiness on July 27 when he agreed to Baltimore's offer of a three-year contract for $6 million with an option year. "I'm relieved," said the signee. "I'm established in Baltimore, and I enjoy playing there."

Cal's delight with the contract translated into success at bat. After he had signed the agreement with his team, Cal hit homers in four successive games and seven homers total in the seventeen games that followed the pact ratification.

In a rare display of excellent pitching and hitting, the O's beat the A's 10–4 at home on August 20. Cal had two doubles to give him 439 extra base hits since 1982, second only to Dale Murphy's 464 over the period. In his previous nine games, Cal had 11 hits and reached base safely in 21 straight games.

But come September, Cal and the Orioles began to sing an old refrain. When the O's succumbed to the Yanks on the first day of fall, September 21, their defeats totaled 97, tying the record set in 1955 for the second-most losses in club history. The 100 losses the club had suffered in its 1954 edition had set a record that held for 34 years, but the O's cracked that one, too, in a double loss at home to Detroit on September 25.

Cal's power production had fallen off. In another O's loss on September 29, Cal hit his 23rd homer, off the Yanks' Rich Dotson, after weathering his career's longest homerless streak—30 games. The entire Orioles family felt the end of the season had not come too soon, as the team dropped the curtain on a 54–107 record, approximately one win in every three tries.

The season's team and personal disappointments and frustrations had taken its toll on Cal. His hit total, 152, fell off for the fifth straight year and ranked lowest in his seven-year career. He also had a career-low 49 extra-base hits and a dismal .264 batting average, with a meager 81 RBIs.

However, his 81 RBIs and 23 homers topped the stats for Major League shortstops for the fifth time in six years. Cal joined Hall of Famer Ernie Banks as the only shortstop to hit 20 or more homers in seven straight seasons. He was only one of five Major Leaguers to slug 20 or more homers in each of the past seven seasons. Cal drew a career high 102 walks and led the American League with 10 sacrifice flies.

While his fielding did not win him a Gold Glove, he led the AL in putouts (284). He turned 100+ double plays for the seventh straight year. His fielding percentage, .973, was identical to that of 1987 and had been higher only in 1986.

Cal's performance reflected his baseball maturity in the trying 1988 season: he had overcome the pain of his father's dismissal and the misery of his team's defeats to emerge as a true professional.

Cal senior and Vi watched their sons' struggles as part of the Orioles in 1988, but only from afar—on a television screen, never at the park. The Birds brought Cal senior back for the 1989 season, and he stayed with them through 1992. However, the unexpected firing had shattered the unquestioning trust that had once existed between the Ripkens and the Orioles.

10

BOUNCING BACK: 1989

Cal looked forward to a restful off-season after a very trying 1988. Kelly and Cal had been married nearly a year, settling in a 15-room mansion in the Worthington Valley north of Baltimore. "Cal's a real homebody," said Kelly. Their social friends were Billy, fiancée Candace Caufmann, and Eddie Murray.

Kelly felt she was a "lucky woman," wrote Randi Henderson in the *Baltimore Sun*. "I'm lucky because I've met someone who's so genuine and sincere and caring. It has nothing to do with him playing baseball. He's one of a kind."

Kelly and Cal were caring people who found a most meaningful way to benefit their community. In November 1988, they announced a gift of $250,000 to inaugurate a literacy program to be housed near Memorial Stadium.

The Cal Ripken, Jr., Lifelong Learning Center has been modeled after adult reading programs offered by other community groups. The center works closely with the Baltimore Reads Foundation, a joint public-private group that aids Baltimore's adult literacy project. As many as one in four Baltimoreans is at least marginally illiterate.

"I belong to a book club. I love to read," said Kelly, a board member of Baltimore Reads. "I couldn't believe the number of people who were missing out on that."

According to Maggie Gaines, executive director of the Baltimore Literacy Corp., those enrolled in the 20-hour-a-week, six-month program at the Ripken Center "benefit from the understanding and expertise of professionals—literacy specialists, educators, and social workers. Since its founding, the center has enabled some 200 people win the battle against illiteracy."

Louis Kendrick learned to read in his late thirties. He told *USA Today* in 1992 what the Ripken Center meant to him. "I can even write a letter now," he told Greg Boeck. "It means people like the Ripkens care." With the Ripkens in attendance, Baltimore mayor Kurt L. Schmoke accepted a White Award from President Bush in 1992 for demonstrating that "reading is the first step."

Senior and Vi Ripken also enjoyed the off-season. Three months after his firing, Cal rejoined the Orioles organization and was named a coach again after the season ended. Fred Ripken had difficulty understanding why his dad returned to the coaching lines. "It was a political move," said Fred, referring to his dad being fired to bring in Frank Robinson. "I was shocked by the firing, and even more shocked when Dad went back the following year."

The man who relieved Cal of his managerial duties, Roland Hemond, was among the speakers at the Annual Ripken Fan Club Banquet. His remarks were part praise, part apology. "It was a tough year for the Orioles, a tough year for me, and a tough year for the Ripken family," said Hemond. "There was a lot of trauma, and I respected them for the way they handled it. I will never forget it."

All the Ripkens were in attendance. Orioles public address announcer and former Brooklyn Dodger pitcher Rex Barney said it best for the assembled: "There's not a family like this in Harford County or anywhere else."

Senior was back in Miami for spring training with number 7 returned to him by Billy. The bitterness was not gone, but he did not want to dwell on the past season. "Sure, no one would be happy about being fired after six games," Senior reflected. "No, I thought we were building a ball club, and I thought I was going to be the manager. But that's water over the dam. That water is downstream. It's probably in Mississippi by now."

He was still the same Rip, too old to learn new ways. "I'm going to be the same person no matter where I am or what I'm doing," he said. "If I'm out there hunting sharks, I'll bark at the damn sharks, that's for sure."

Things had not changed for Senior, but the winds of change blew over Miami. Cal was being considered for third base, while Billy had no assurances that the second-base job was his. Manager Robinson was giving rookie Juan Bell a shot at short. What irritated Cal was not that he might be switched but that he did not learn of the plan directly from Robinson. Quite a change from the past years when Dad was the manager.

"It's amazing to me," said Cal. "Things can change so dramatically in such a short time. But that's real life. And not just in sports. You don't want it to happen, but it happens, and you learn that you have to handle it."

Cal was concerned about his shortstop position, but equally worried about Billy keeping the second-base job. His dream was to play for 10 years or so with his brother, in the same way that baseball "brothers" Lou Whitaker and Alan Trammell performed with the Tigers. In a practical sense, Cal felt that communication between shortstop and second baseman was important for cutoffs, steals, bloop hits, and the like. That communication came only with familiarity and was "one big reason why we are able to turn the double play."

No matter what the Orioles decided, Cal would accept the decision as a professional. That's what Dad had taught. "As long as I can remember my dad," said Cal, "he always did his job in a professional manner. He preached to us the right and wrong things. He'd say, 'This is how you'd do it. There's no sense doing it halfway.'"

As a professional, Billy was elated that Dad was back. Billy, who had sunk to .207 in 1988, looked at Dad as his personal hitting coach. He also relied on his brother, who told him, for example, what to expect from a certain pitcher and where to play a particular batter. Now he could again go to Senior and Junior. "When I need some help, I know who to go to," said Billy. "I go to both of them."

About Cal moving to third, Billy jested, "I'll just have to talk louder. With him at third and me at second, I'll scream over to him. I can scream, you know that."

The three Ripkens were reunited, but good friend and valued teammate Eddie Murray was gone. With his trade to the Dodgers, the Orioles were bereft of his bat and leadership. How would the Orioles replace a power hitter like Murray, the Major League's most consistent, productive RBI man of the '80s?

Father and brother aside, Cal was closer to Eddie than to any other Oriole. Cal had adjusted to Dad's firing, so he would cope well with Murray's departure. "Cal's got through it," said the first baseman. "He'll be fine. He doesn't have anything to worry about—except having somebody on base and having somebody behind him who can hit. We had some good years together, some great years. But things went bad, and I got blamed."

Cal was his only friend in adversity, Murray told Ralph Wiley in *Sports Illustrated*. "I know Jackie Robinson went through hell," said Murray, "because I know what I heard around Baltimore from so-called fans. I can't tell you what it did to me. I've never shot a gun in my life, but I was told things that made me want to get a gun and kill somebody. I couldn't talk to anyone but Cal."

Murray was especially embittered toward Williams to the extent that he did not attend the owner's funeral.

According to Cal, Eddie had been "hurt" by the media attacks. The media had attacked Murray for not taking care of himself as well as he could; for not playing with emotional intensity; for playing first base apathetically, e.g., not diving for balls; for rarely sliding on the basepaths. "Eddie's been hurt," said Cal. "We live in a world where success is determined by statistics. Eddie and I would have stats going in every September. But at one point, players from other teams came out and told us that their pitchers were fined if they gave Eddie or me a pitch to hit and we beat them. It's hard to be productive like that. In all good baseball sense, you should take your walks. But it's hard to deal with because you want to hit. So you start to expand your strike zone. . . .

"Eddie Murray set a higher standard for me while he was here. I benefited from playing with him, and hitting in front of him. I didn't fully realize how much until he left. But I know he's been hurt."

After the previous year's debacle of April '88, the Orioles had a modest goal: winning their first game on April 3—quickly. In full view of President Bush and guest Egyptian president Hosni Mubarak, the Birds won their season opener at home. They beat Boston 5–4 in 11 innings. Cal's three-run homer in the sixth had given Baltimore a temporary 4–3 lead. Baltimore beat Boston again 6–4 on April 6, the first home series they had taken from the Bosox since September 1983. The O's ended another futility streak—eight road losses since September 1988—with an 8–1 victory, April 9, against Minnesota.

The Orioles were 4–4 after eight games, not impressive, but they were 21 games and 26 days ahead of last year. When they beat Minnesota on April 22 at Memorial Stadium, 4–1, they had attained an 8–8 mark, but they were the only Eastern Division team at .500—and that was good enough for first place, the first time since May 11, 1985.

The Orioles continued to play well and increase their lead. However, Cal went into an 0-for-13 slump at the end of June, as the Blue Jays came to Baltimore trailing by six, on June 27. Cal's hitting was not a factor that game as the Orioles combined to wallop the Jays. But the "Ripken way" of playing, the Cal Ripken work ethic, was very much in view in the ninth inning. The Jays were trailing 16–3.

Toronto's Tony Fernandez slap-bunted a ball past Orioles third baseman Craig Worthington. Suddenly Cal tore out for the ball down the left-field line. Without turning his back toward the infield, he slid across the grass, barehanded the ball in midslide, made a perfect throw to second base, and collapsed face first into the grass. Fernandez had to be content with a single.

Did the play have any importance with the Orioles up by 13? Could he have injured himself? Cal always hustled no matter the score. That was the "Ripken way."

The next day, June 28, Cal broke out of his slump with three hits, including the tiebreaker, his eighth homer in the eighth, for a 2–1 victory. The Orioles good luck charm was in the stands, President Bush, who had now seen three Orioles games—all won by Baltimore. The Orioles ended June 43–33, five and a half games in first. The scene shifted to Toronto on July 4. Led by Cal's homer, three RBIs, and Dave Schmidt's pitching, the Birds prevailed 8–0. They won the next day 5–4, giving them a 47–34 mark, a six-and-a-half-game lead at the midway point of the season. A year before, they were 24–57, 26 games out of first.

The Orioles faltered in July. Their 5–17 post–All-Star Game record matched the record of the 1975 Pirates for the worst record during 20 or more games for a team in first place during that entire period. They were beaten in Minnesota 10–6 on July 27. It was their eighth straight setback, within one defeat of tying a Major League mark of the longest losing streak by a first-place team. They prevailed at Kansas City on July 28, 4–3 in 11 innings, averted the records books, and hung on to their four-game lead.

The losing continued into August. They began the month with 13 losses in 14 games. A seven-and-a-half game lead on July 19 had melted to only two on August 2. The Orioles looked to Cal for power and experience. He was the veteran among players who had never experienced pennant pressure.

"The difference between this club and the 1983 championship team," said Cal, "was that the 1983 team was a veteran team with a few younger players sprinkled in. It was a team more settled, more sure of itself. We had losing streaks in 1983, some big ones, same as this team; they're part of every summer. Your confidence goes up when you win and tends to go down when you lose. We knew that then. But this team has to find out about that the only way they can, by going out and playing."

The Ripken brothers provided leadership on August 2. After being down to the Bosox 6–0, the Orioles rallied to win in Boston, 9–8, on Cal's late-inning hit. Cal (three) and Billy (four) combined for seven hits, an AL mark for hits by brothers; it fell one short of the Major League mark by the Pirates' Waner brothers, Paul and Lloyd, who had three and five, respectively, on June 25, 1932.

August 7, 1989, was memorable for Cal Ripken, Jr., but not for something he would boast about. He was ejected for the second time in his career. "It was like running God out of Sunday school," said home plate umpire Drew Coble.

Cal was up in the bottom of the first inning against Minnesota at Memorial Stadium. Two Orioles had already been fanned by Roy Smith on called strikes. Cal got two called strikes and then turned around to voice his unequivocal disagreement to Coble. The argument began rather gentlemanly, but Coble got into Cal's face when the ump found the player's epithets to be very unsuitable.

Manager and Dad rushed out not to save Cal, who had already been ejected, but for damage control, to avoid suspension because of bumping an umpire. An enraged Cal pushed his father and the manager around and tried to get at the umpire. He continued to scream at the umpire, and Robinson, Dad, and on-deck batter Keith Moreland restrained the shortstop. Dad led Junior off the field.

Cal left the field, his streak of 1,003 consecutive innings at an end. It was also the first time since June 5, 1982, that Cal had been pinch-hit for. Rene Gonzales joined Jim Dwyer as the Cal Ripken pinch hitters. Cal had been at short in the top of the first and had batted in the bottom of the frame, so there was no question that the consecutive-game streak of 1,198 was not disturbed.

The Orioles fans made the evening unforgettable and miserable for Coble. "Kill the umpire" was a refrain that at times became frightening. "That was a miserable two and a half hours for a guy to be put in a situation like that," moaned Coble. "I had stuff thrown at me. . . . I won't forget it for a long time. I couldn't call a pitch that was right. They disagreed with everything."

Coble had a some harsh words for Cal. "I just think it was horse _ _ _ _ of Cal to do what he did," said the umpire. "He can argue balls and strikes, but he can't get away with calling me what he called me. I don't care how bad his club is going." (The O's lost 4–2 but at 57–53 remained two games in first.)

Dad and Robinson perhaps prevented suspension and preserved the fourth-longest consecutive-playing streak in baseball history. Would a suspension have been an "interesting" way for the streak to end? a reporter asked Robinson. "It wouldn't have been interesting," replied Robinson. "It would have been terrible."

Cal refused to discuss the incident, but during the off-season he looked back at the "disturbing" moment. "I felt horrible about being thrown out," he said. "I didn't feel I handled it right. I felt I was provoked. . . . I wanted to say a lot about it then, but when you have time to think about it, you know you should have been able to hold your temper, to say something else. It wasn't so bad at first, but when I look back at it now . . . I was ranting and raving. It was just all temper."

Cal has been called the Iceman, a player with little fire or passion. He realized that he had acted out of character. "Every competitive player has that fire," he reasoned, "but how you control it is the question. I have to release it in my own way. I never throw a helmet or bat at a game when a youngster might see it. So imagine my losing control in front of many youngsters, especially that boy from Virginia."

Certainly, there was no one in Memorial Stadium more crushed by the ejection than a youngster who had traveled from Virginia just to see Cal play. "I got thrown out in the first inning," sympathized Cal, "and the kid cried the whole game."

Cal promised to keep his anger out of public view. "What I do I do out of the park," he said. "I would come into the clubhouse, venting my frustration by slamming a bat into a chunk of rubber. When I lose it, it is a controlled atmosphere, when no one knows. Instead of throwing a helmet down and being mad at yourself, you come in and take some swings at the tube. Fifty thousand people don't see you hit the rubber. Only your teammates do."

Cal had no need to be angry in August. While during one stretch he had only 13 hits in 70 at bats, he drove in 14 runs in 18 games. The Orioles played well in August and closed the month at 72–62. Unfortunately, Toronto played better ball and tied the Orioles for first on August 31.

On August 17, Cal contributed a homer to help beat Toronto 11–6. But the home fans cheered loudest for his playing in consecutive game 1,208. He passed Steve Garvey on the iron man list; only Everett Scott and Lou Gehrig were ahead of him. Knowledgeable Birds fans were aware of the Streak, but never before had the Streak gone public.

A crowd of 40,147 watched a video tribute in the sixth inning, "Happy 1,208th." To the accompaniment of Madonna's "Lucky Star," everybody stood and cheered. Cal responded; he came to the top of the dugout and tipped his cap, the words "thank you" seeming to leave his lips.

"I was caught off guard" by the crowd's action, said Cal. "Through the course of the Streak," he continued, "I've tried to play it down. It doesn't seem as big at this point in my career as other things—winning a world championship, the team doing so well this year. To play in consecutive games is an individual accomplishment. Team-oriented goals are much more satisfying. I've played it down. I didn't really figure anyone else was noticing it either."

Cal was pleased with the reception given him by the home fans, but he continued to stress that what mattered most was the Orioles' rebounding from the horrendous 1988 campaign. When he signed a new contract in 1988 he said that he was ready to "live with what happens," a reference to the team's continued losing pattern.

It was different in 1989, he said. "The last few years, there haven't been too many really exciting at bats. When you get your concentration so keen, you can phase out 50,000 people screaming and yelling at the top of their lungs. When you lose, it never builds up to that point.

"This year it's totally different. It even started on opening day, that at bat against Roger Clemens [a three-run homer]. He's one of the best pitchers in the game. The fans are going wild. You get that feeling. You could almost sense this season would be different.

"As the season has gone on, I've had quite a few of those at bats. The importance of driving in runs is so big, your concentration's so keen. It's almost like there's a fear factor involved. You're so wound up, so high-strung, you're almost nauseous. The electricity has come back to the game."

Baltimore had occupied or shared first for 115 of the season's first 150 days, the most ever by a team that had finished last the previous year. But the Birds began September inauspiciously. They were walloped in Chicago 10–1 and fell from first when Toronto triumphed.

They remained one game out on September 5 when Cal homered and later doubled home the tiebreaking run in the seventh, to give the O's a 3–1 victory at Memorial Stadium against Cleveland. The victory was even more satisfying for Cal, whose 20th homer gave him one more record: the first shortstop in baseball history to hit 20 or more homers in eight consecutive seasons.

Cal kept the Orioles in the race. On September 11, Cal drove in three runs, two on a homer, to lead the Orioles at home past Chicago 6–2. Cal had three homers and ten RBIs in his last nine games to keep the Orioles only two games out of first. They were only one game back on September 21, despite an early September 2–12 road trip. Their record of 83–70, already 29 wins more than in 1988, was the tenth-best single-season improvement in Major League history.

Their last home stand, which went 6–5, set back their chances. What hurt especially was their final home series, against the Yankees. They could have tied Toronto on September 24, but Chuck Cary blanked them 2–0. "We played good baseball," a disappointed Cal said. "All of the games were close. It could have been a great home stand, but it was only a good one. . . . Every loss hurts. You can't watch the scoreboard and hope Toronto loses. The fact is you have to go out and play well."

Baltimore had a final chance in a dream end-season matchup against the Jays in Toronto. The Orioles could force a playoff by winning two or an outright division championship with a sweep. However, they lost the opener 2–1 in 11 and saw their hopes crushed when Toronto came back to win 4–3 the next day.

When the season began, almost no one expected Baltimore to challenge for, let alone win, a division crown. Without question, Cal was the veteran who kept his team in the race: by playing every day, by his consistent hitting, by being the centerpoint of the league's best defense.

However, Cal took heat for not contributing offensively down the stretch. Entering the season's final weekend, he had managed only seven hits in 55 at bats in the last 16 games, when the Birds could have overtaken the Jays. He hit .257, the fifth straight year he was under .300. In 14 bases-loaded opportunities, he hit safely but once. Only once, September 4–5, did he enjoy consecutive RBI games. In 1988, Cal had 102 walks; with Murray gone in '89, he had 57.

However, Cal dominated the game with his glove, committing only eight errors during the 1989 season. During one stretch he went 47 games without an error. The streak ended September 24 with a throwing error, only his second of the season. He led AL shortstops in putouts (276), assists (531), total chances (815), and double plays (119). Despite these amazing stats, he was edged out for fielding percentage by Tony Fernandez of Toronto, who posted a .992 percentage. Cal's .990 percentage was equaled or topped only four other times: Fernandez (1989); Cal (.996 in 1990); Larry Bowa (.991, 1979); and Eddie Brinkman (.990, 1972). While Fernandez played in 140 games, most on Skydome plastic, Cal played in all 162 games, primarily on dirt and grass.

11

A FIELDER FOR THE RECORD BOOKS

Rachel Marie Ripken was born on November 22, 1989, and Cal and Kelly now looked at his baseball future in the context of fatherhood. He limited his public appearances and sharply reduced his interview schedule. Interviews and photographs were now off limits in the Ripken home.

"We'd always heard everyone say, 'Wait till you have kids. Your life will change,' " Kelly Ripken told Patrick A. McGuire of the *Baltimore Sun*. "It kind of renews the vows you said when you were married. It makes you appreciate each other all over again. That's what having a family is all about. The emotion you pour out over this little bundle of joy."

"You have a different outlook on life," Cal said. "Everything else in this grand scheme of things. . . . I mean, this [Rachel Marie] is what's important."

Cal involved himself fully in Rachel's care. "Cal's changed Rachel's diapers and fed her even before I did," said Kelly.

Cal had been very accommodating at the park and in the clubhouse, but things would not be the same. "If my wife and baby come to the game," Cal explained, "I might have to change my routine after the game and say, 'I have to get home now. I'll be happy to sign tomorrow.' I have a responsibility to the baby now."

His new life brought Cal a fuller realization of life and his place there. "As you grow older," he reflected, "you find out that there's other things as important as baseball. The latest example is life. The whole secret of life is life itself. Life is totally different when you have a baby. You recognize your priorities. I don't want to sound like a philosopher by any means, but it's just a growing process. I'd like to think of myself as a good person and a good family person. When you're here at the stadium, you're a baseball person. When you leave here, you're not. Well, you are, but you're not."

New priorities aside, Cal was still a "baseball person" away from the park during the off-season. He reflected often about next season and his role on the team. It was difficult to endure three consecutive losing seasons from 1986 to 1988, but it taught Cal about winning. "I feel fortunate to know the losing side," he said. "Maybe you appreciate winning more. Maybe you're a better person for experiencing defeat as well as success. If you only see one side of it, you don't have the full picture."

For the Orioles to do well in 1990, according to Cal, they could not expect him to carry the team; for him to do well, he had to be a patient and "stubborn hitter."

As the Orioles began the '90s, Eddie Murray, Ken Singleton, and Jim Palmer were only memories. The team would build around Cal Ripken, Jr., he was told. "The hard-core reality is," said Cal with displeasure, "I'm not the type of person who can carry the team. . . . When they said during this whole rebuilding process that they were building around me . . . I thought it was unfair. I mean, it made me feel good that they thought that much of me. But it's all a myth. No one player makes a difference in baseball. In football yes, and in basketball. In baseball you're one of nine. In baseball you only go to bat four times a game. Maybe you get four plays a game. It's a group of individuals playing collectively as a team."

Cal also was averse to being called a leader. The manager, the person who made the decisions, was the leader, according to Cal. "Sometimes the word *leader* can go to a person's head. I kind of think my presence was my biggest contribution last year. I think I had a stabilizing effect on younger players, especially down to the wire. But the only thing experience gives you is an opportunity to share that experience. If [leadership] is defined as being stabilizing, then that's part of the role."

Throughout his professional career, Cal worked hard to improve his skills. He was displeased with his performance during the past five years. Junior had last driven in 100 runs in 1985. He had last hit .300 in 1984, when he had last achieved both.

Cal often replayed—in his mind and on the screen—a 1983 video featuring Reggie Jackson. The future Hall of Famer was giving a brief résumé of all the Orioles and Phillies players as part of ABC's World Series telecast. Speaking of Cal's 1983 year, he said, "Ripken had a great year. It very well could be a career year. He might never accomplish this again."

Reggie's remarks haunted Cal over the next six years. "Statistically, what he has said has kind of held up," admitted Cal. "I can't argue the point, although I know I'm now a much better player than then. But his comments . . . I think about them all the time. You wonder if you'll ever put together a season where everything seems to go right again. . . . "

Cal consoled and strengthened himself with the words of Denver Broncos quarterback John Elway, who suffered losing two Super Bowls in the '80s. "I'd rather have the opportunity to fail than not have the opportunity," Elway remarked. Cal agreed. "I can contribute," he said. "I still do it. I still go up there. I still keep battling."

To improve his contributions, Cal put the priority on patience for 1990. In the previous year he had become restless when the opposition pitched around him. "They tell you not to get impatient where you try to take it into your own hands," said Cal. "But I was so gung-ho. You just want to contribute. You want to drive in runs. You say even though they're pitching around me, I'll expand the strike zone. When you strike out, pop up, you can't believe that you were that stupid. For a moment you thought you could rise to the occasion. Maybe in minor league ball you could get away with that. But the level of play here is too good to give the pitcher a bigger strike zone. He sees what you're doing, and he says to himself, 'Now I don't have to throw the ball over the plate at all.'

"I fell for the trap. You know, the other teams have scouts, and they were telling people, 'Ripken will swing at anything.' But you convince yourself that maybe it's better to swing than not. You're guilty of trying to help the team win."

The best hitters were determined, and that was Cal's goal for 1990. "Sometimes you have to be stubborn," he said. "You say, 'I know this pitcher will throw me the breaking ball.' For two at bats, he only threw fastballs, but you are stubborn and wait for the curve and you hit it. The pitcher eyes you with amazement as if to say, 'How could you be looking for that?' "

Cal had not done as well as he wanted in 1989, but the Orioles had exceeded expectations. If Cal had a better season, perhaps the Orioles would do better, too. It did not start off that way. After their first 18 games, the O's were four games out, in the Eastern Division basement. During one stretch, they lost five straight and suffered 14 consecutive hitless innings.

Even when Cal got his stroke going in May, the Orioles hardly improved their standing. On May 12, Cal hit two homers at Oakland, numbers five and six, that decided the game 3–2 for Baltimore. However, the Birds stood at 13–17, five and a half out, and ended May 21–26, four behind and in fifth place.

The Orioles' fortunes suffered in part because in late May, Cal became mired in an 8 for 57 slump. Baltimore won three of their first four games in June, and Cal hit a sacrifice fly for the deciding run at Milwaukee, in a 6–4 win. That moved Baltimore to three out of first despite a 24–27 record. But Cal continued to struggle. On June 13 his batting average was down to .209; in 59 games he had a mere 30 RBIs and seven homers. Manager Robinson dropped him from third to sixth in the lineup.

"I was as frustrated as I've ever been, in 1990," said Cal. "I was at rock bottom, thinking I might be through. I mean, it wasn't a matter of being tired. I just wasn't myself at the plate.

"I had developed bad habits, trying to do too much, and the more I fought it physically, the more it became a mental problem."

Robinson sought to aid Cal by telling him of his own troubles in 1965, with Cincinnati. (He ended the year with 33 homers, 113 RBIs, and a .296 batting average.) Said Robinson, "The more you fail, the more you search, the farther away you get, the more doubts creep in. The mental part is worse than the physical. You start to feel alone, as if you're the only one who has ever gone through it."

Agent Ron Shapiro related that Cal felt he was letting Baltimore down—not only the team, but also the city. "How do you satisfy everyone who knows you, thinks they know you, and feels you're part of their life? It was as if Cal felt he was letting the family down."

Cal gave the family something to cheer about in a 4–3 June 12 home victory against Milwaukee. Baltimore's Iron Man played in his 1,308th straight game, moving him past Everett Scott. Now only Lou Gehrig, with 2,130, was ahead of Cal as baseball's all-time iron man. A day before passing Scott, Cal told a *New York Times* reporter, "It wasn't a goal coming to the big leagues that I wouldn't miss a game. You just try to prepare yourself each and every day and go there. Eight years later, it has evolved into this."

How appreciative were the Baltimore fans about this achievement? Ironically and sadly, the Baltimoreans did not stand up and cheer. Instead, Cal was soundly booed. Forgetting about his milestone and taking note of his low batting average, any fan with smarts had to consider his phenomenal fielding. He had made only one "unlucky" error thus far in 1990, on Friday, April 13. In fact, the day he passed Scott, he also broke the Orioles record of his mentor, Mark Belanger, by handling his 242nd consecutive errorless chance. *Sports Illustrated* criticized the ungrateful fans. UNFAIR RIP, cried the headline. "For a streak that impressive, the fans should have carried him off the field."

Discontented Baltimoreans continued to grumble. The Birds lost at home, 5–3, to Cleveland on June 26. They had lost five in a row and were 31–40, in sixth place. They had occasion to boo Cal, who made an error in the first inning, his first miscue after 67 games and 296 chances. Cal was charged with an error when a throw from center fielder Mike Devereaux went off his glove.

The Orioles beat Cleveland the next day 6–3, and Cal came up a bigger winner. His streak was resurrected through the conscience and investigative work of official scorer Bill Stetka. He was not fully satisfied with the error he gave Cal on missing Devereaux's cutoff throw, so the scorer spoke with players and coaches from the Indians and Orioles. He also reviewed the play on videotape. It was Devereaux's throwing error, Stetka decided.

From the moment an "E" was flashed on the scoreboard, the Ripken miscue became a cause célèbre among the players and the media. After the game, Rich Dauer, then a Cleveland third-base coach and former teammate of Cal's, advised Baltimore Orioles public relations director Rick Vaughn that the error belonged elsewhere. "Richie told me that he wouldn't take that error," said Vaughn. "I just told Bill [Stetka] maybe he needed to talk to people to be sure. I didn't pressure him at all."

Dauer offered the media a detailed analysis of the play. "I saw a throw that was very off line [in the relay assignment]," said Dauer. "The third baseman [Tim Hulett] was going to have to come off the bag to get the ball.

"I never even thought of it as being an error on Ripken. If it was catchable, he was going to catch it. I don't believe a guy should get an error for trying to intercept something that's already gone haywire."

Tim Hulett agreed. "It was definitely off line," he said. "Devo [Devereaux] got under the throw a little bit, and it sailed on him.

Rip had to take a couple of steps to the left. Had the ball gone through I would have had to make a good play to catch it."

Stetka spoke to the two principals, Ripken and Devereaux. " 'I had to jump for the ball,' Cal told me," said Stetka. " 'If you think it's an error, I can take it. I'm a big boy.' "

Devereaux was a bit fuzzy about the play. "I know I had to get in there in a hurry," related the outfielder, "and the ball could have been off line. It happened so fast. I don't like to put anything on anybody else. Just say I had to seriously rush. . . . Normally, errors are pretty much black and white. It either is or isn't, but in a few cases, there are questions, like this one. Scoring sometimes boils down to judgment, and that's what this was."

Having gathered all the information, Stetka reversed his ruling, gave Devereaux the error, and explained his decision: "Basically, it was because it took more than ordinary effort to try to stop the ball. That's why it was changed. Obviously, if he didn't try to stop it, the run would have scored, and the ball might have ended up in the dugout. . . .

"I'm sorry this came in the middle of the streak. If Cal were not this close to the record, not this much would be made of it. But everybody with a good view of the play agreed that Cal had to go a ways, reach, and leave his feet."

The reversal gave Devereaux his second error on the play: the first for bobbling the ball on Chris James's single. "I had already ruled that James was not entitled to a stolen base," said Stetka. "Now, I had added another error."

Nearly three years later, June 24, 1993, as Stetka scored the Orioles game against the Tigers, he summarized that historic reversal. "I spoke to coaches, players on both teams, and then studied the videotape," he recalled. "It was the Indians who first questioned the error on Ripken. Candy Maldonado shook his head when he first realized Ripken was given the error. Chris James also called it a throwing error. When I spoke to Dauer and Hulett after the call, I realized the call had to be reviewed."

What all this meant was that Cal still had a shot at Ed Brinkman's record of 72 consecutive errorless games (May 21–August 24, 1972). On June 29, Cal surpassed Belanger's Orioles record of 69 flawless games. Cal tied the AL record on July 1 in Minnesota, in a game won by Baltimore 6–0. He stood alone on July 2 by handling two chances, both ground balls hit by Gary Gaetti.

Cal enhanced his personal triumph with a homer and a run-scoring single. However, all this did not prevent a 4–3 Orioles loss in the bottom of the ninth. The loss put a downer on Cal's record-breaking Sunday. "It doesn't seem so good because of how the game turned out," he said. "It was a tough game to lose when we had a chance to win it."

The next challenge was the Major League record of New York Met Kevin Elster, 88 consecutive errorless games (July 1988–May 1989). On the way toward that record, Cal established a Major League record for consecutive errorless chances by a shortstop when he cleanly played a grounder at Texas by Jeff Huson leading off the first. Cal surpassed Brinkman in handling his 322nd consecutive chance without an error. The July 5 milestone, an AL record, was dampened a bit with a 3–2 Orioles loss.

On July 16 both the host Orioles and Cal succeeded. He handled his 385th chance at shortstop, snapping the Major League mark New York Giant Buddy Kerr set during 1946–47. The Orioles crowned the day with a comeback win against Texas. Good luck charm President Bush and Mrs. Bush were on hand.

Kevin Elster's record was tied by Cal on July 19 at home against Chicago. Cal had now handled more than 400 consecutive chances without an error. He broke out of a 1-for-11 slump and knocked in two first-inning runs with a double that set in motion a 4–1 victory. Cal's triumph shared headlines that day with Pete Rose's being sentenced in Cincinnati to five months in prison for income tax evasion.

Two record breakers were in the lineup July 20 in Texas. Nolan Ryan edged toward a milestone by beating Baltimore 5–3 for his 299th win. Cal now held the Major League record for consecutive errorless games by a shortstop. His 89 straight errorless games also tied an AL record: consecutive flawless games by an infielder other than a first baseman. The mark was set during 1964–65 by Orioles second baseman Jerry Adair. When the streak reached 91 on July 25 in Chicago, Cal passed three second basemen: Hall of Famer Joe Morgan, Manny Trillo, and Adair. But he still had a long stretch to reach Ryne Sandberg, the Cubs second baseman who set the standard for infielders with 123 consecutive errorless games.

After Cal broke Elster's record, the right-field faithful in Memorial Stadium hung up a banner that read, "Cal Knows Shortstop," à la Bo Jackson. However, Cal preferred playing on the road during his fielding streak because there was less attention paid to his streak on the road. "Games mounted up without people reminding you of it," he said. "You didn't have to hear it, see it, or read about it. You could put it out of your mind."

Four more games and Cal's streak ended on the road, in Kansas City, on July 28. In game one of a doubleheader, Cal booted a fifth-inning ground ball off the bat of Royals left fielder Jeff Schulz. Cal went to his right but could not handle the ball cleanly. There was no hesitation by official scorer Del Black: farewell to 95 errorless games and 431 chances.

There was no television that game, so there was no benefit of instant replay. However, Black insisted that a clean pickup would have gotten Schulz. Manager Robinson agreed. "He still has a throw to make," said Robinson. "I don't know if he would have gotten him or not. I was watching the play in the hole. It was a tough play, but he had the ball and dropped it, didn't he?"

It was not a routine play, Cal insisted, without challenging the scorer. "I didn't think it was real easy," said Cal. "I had a chance to throw him out, but the ball was hit deep, and it was spinning away from me. To make that play, I would have had to set myself before I threw it. I think if I caught the ball, I could have gotten him."

With the streak over, past and present managers offered their thoughts on the record breaker. "Because he was such a good player and because he insists on playing every day, you know that Cal was going to break all kinds of records before he retired," said Joe Altobelli. "He's got soft hands," raved manager Robinson. "He makes the hard plays look easy and the easy ones look easy. He's not flashy, but he does it all."

Cal did not forget his mentor, Mark Belanger, in the celebration of his records. "Mark always told me to watch the guy playing my position when I was sitting in the dugout," he said. "Mark would always tell me, 'If that shortstop does something wrong, tell yourself you won't do that.' In particular, he told me to watch Alan Trammell. He felt that Alan was one of the best ever at his position. I then got into the habit of checking other guys out. I still do. Mark Belanger was a master shortstop. His voice, advice, and inspiration have always been with me."

The streak emphasized the fielding standards that had been set by both the Orioles and by Cal. Baltimore had entered the doubleheader—which they split by winning the second game—with but one error in their last 14 games and had not made more than one error in a game since June 26. In his last 154 games Cal had only three miscues and only two throwing errors in his past 296 games, going back to 1988.

In addition to his fielding feats, Cal set new marks in the iron man category. In a home twin bill on July 13 that they split with Minnesota, Cal became number one for playing consecutive games at one position. He played his 1,308th game at short, one more than Everett Scott, also a shortstop. The first 27 games in Cal's streak was at third base; his last start there was on June 30, 1982. Iron Horse Lou Gehrig had played 885 consecutive games at first base. Gehrig had also played shortstop and the outfield and had maintained his streak as a pinch hitter.

Cal played every day: he fielded superbly, but he did not hit consistently in 1990. In fact, by mid-July, Billy was outhitting his brother, batting .280 and headed for his best year. Because of his good year, said manager Robinson, Billy did not have to be concerned about his brother's exploits. "You're only overshadowed when you're having no success. Now nobody wants to say anything about Billy being here because of his brother. He's having a hell of a year."

Despite a cold bat, the Orioles played well in July. They had the best record in the league since the All-Star Game break and won 17 of 28 that month. They were in third place but only four back. However, Orioles fortunes soured in August. They finished the month 60–70, falling to fifth place, 14 games out.

The fate of the Orioles worsened in September. On September 6, the O's lost at home to Seattle, 9–5. They were swept in the series, had lost 17 of 21, and had sunk to 60–75, 15½ out of first. The race came down to a struggle between Boston and Toronto. All that remained for the Ripkens were personal achievements and for the Orioles to play spoilers.

After being no-hit at home by the Red Sox on September 18— and failing to score in 71 of their past 83 innings—the Orioles came back in the seventh to win 4–1 and drop the losers into a first-place tie with Toronto. It was Cal's body, not his hitting, that prevented Red Sox hurler Tom Bolton from escaping a disastrous four-run seventh.

With one out and Cal at first, Craig Worthington slapped a soft liner to Jody Reed at second. Reed had an excellent chance to double up Cal, who had wandered off first. Reed threw the ball straight at the bag. Cal moved back toward first, and the throw hit him in the buttocks. "Ripken is a big dude," moaned Reed. "It was a tough play all around," lamented Sox manager Joe Morgan. "If [Reed] threw the ball to the outfield side of the bag, [Ripken] was a dead duck."

The Orioles played their last game of the season, at home, on October 3, a game that would be meaningful if Boston lost and Toronto then beat the Birds to tie for first. However, Boston won, and the O's ended the season on a winning note, 3–2. But it was a disappointing year for Baltimore, finishing at 76–85, 11½ games back and in fifth place.

Cal Ripken, Jr., had vowed to improve on his 1989 offensive performance. In that sense, the year was a great disappointment. His .250 average was the lowest of his career. His totals dropped off in hits, RBIs, and runs scored. He batted a pitiful .204 with runners in scoring position. Only Steve Sax and Mike Greenwell had done worse than Cal's 20 percent success rate among batters with 150 or more opportunities.

The Orioles finished fifth; Cal didn't hit .280. Nevertheless, his offensive stats were still quite respectable. He led the Orioles in nine offensive departments, among them homers, 21; RBIs, 84; hits, 150; runs scored, 78; doubles, 28 (tied with brother Billy); triples, 4 (tied with Steve Finley) at bats, 600; intentional walks, 18; and game-tying/go-ahead RBIs, 39. His 21 homers marked the ninth consecutive year he had hit 20 or more homers. Cal was the only shortstop in the elite group of 12, among them Joe DiMaggio, Reggie Jackson, and Ted Williams.

Moreover, the season's end augured well. In the last 102 games, Cal batted .274 with 14 homers and 54 RBIs.

When it came to his glove, no one could challenge his superiority. He set eight all-time fielding records for a shortstop—notably, most consecutive games without an error, most consecutive chances without an error, fewest errors (three), and highest fielding percentage (.996). Added to his .990 in 1989, Cal owned two of the five highest percentages for a shortstop in Major League history. (Together Cal and Billy made only 11 errors, the fewest by a keystone combination in Major League history among those who played two-thirds of their teams' games at second and short.)

For the second consecutive year he won the Most Valuable Oriole Award. Would his peers award him his first Gold Glove?

12

MVP REDUX: 1991

The Orioles fans had another restless postseason. For the seventh consecutive year, the O's concluded baseball after 162 games. No Oriole won the Most Valuable Player Award. No pitcher earned Cy Young honors. But at least, Orioles supporters thought, Cal Ripken, Jr.'s, wondrous 1990 fielding would bring a Gold Glove to Memorial Stadium.

It did not come. Instead, the distinction went to the White Sox's Ozzie Guillen. The exact vote is never announced, but reports claimed that the vote was overwhelmingly for Guillen. "It was a crime," bellowed Tim Kurkjian in *Sports Illustrated*. Texas manager Bobby Valentine was highly displeased by the vote of fellow managers and coaches, "embarrassed by the actions of my peers."

As usual, the public Cal did not reveal his unhappiness. "I didn't really get my hopes up," he said, "but to be honest, I'd like to win one of those things someday. . . . Granted, it's not too flashy and not too noticeable, but I still have to go out and play the way I play."

Why did Cal lose? According to Brooks Robinson, Cal played short so gracefully, without effort, that few paid attention and respect to his performance. "Cal is not as dazzling, not as spectacular [as Guillen]," he said, "but nobody plays the position like he does. Nobody puts as much thought into playing the position. He's the best I've ever seen when it comes to playing the hitters, and I think that's the reason his defense is overlooked. . . .

"He doesn't fit the mold of a shortstop because he's not small and flashy. The defensive part of the game is definitely taken for granted, and it's a shame. . . . There's a lot to think about when you're playing shortstop, but most guys don't do it. They just go out and play the position and let their instincts take over. . . . Cal has an idea on every pitch to every hitter. I've never seen anyone with the ability to play off the pitcher and hitter the way he does.

"I guarantee you that if he was playing third base, he'd be sensational. No one knows the game like he does. Cal is one of those guys who does everything the way it's supposed to be done. It's something that was bred into him. He is the consummate pro."

Baltimore-based freelance writer William J. McKenna argued that over the years Cal's bat had outshone his glove and, more important, his detractors had not accepted Cal the shortstop because he did not fit their concept of the shortstop. Said McKenna in *Tuff Stuff*, "Ripken himself believes that for many years his offense has overshadowed his work in the field and people are just beginning to notice his glove work. A more cynical theory. . . . Some purists in the game have, and presumably always will maintain, that Cal, at six foot four and 225 pounds, is just too big and too slow to be a shortstop. He doesn't make enough spectacular plays, they believe, and he belongs at third or perhaps even at quarterback."

The Ripken Fan Club decided to correct the perceived injustice. It created its own trophy and gave the award to Junior at the annual banquet in Aberdeen's Moose Lodge. "Junior should have gotten the Gold Glove, especially when he had only three errors all year and Ozzie had 17," snapped fan club vice president George Travers.

*　　*　　*

The season was long past; the awards were done with. Cal returned to his off-season regimen of preparing for the next campaign. During the past four winters, Cal, teammates, and friends played basketball three nights a week at Baltimore's Bryn Mawr School. His house was now completed in the Baltimore suburb of Reisterstown, with a full gymnasium: basketball court, weights, and batting cage.

Cal played basketball with the intensity and drive of a participant in an NBA final or World Series seventh game. A man possessed on both boards, he was ferocious on defense, harassing the player he was guarding.

Cal needed to excel in all he did. "It's amazing how Cal could be so determined with nothing on the line," said Orioles teammate Mike Flanagan. "I was very determined myself when I first began playing pro ball. However, pro ball is so demanding that I could not transfer that drive to other areas. What did it matter if I won in Ping-Pong? Often, we would all be so tired, and we would like to quit. Cal would become angry that we were all so tired."

Flanagan could not explain Cal's drive on the baseball field. "The guys are zapped out after a game," he said, "and Cal's in back of the bus, yelling and whooping. I've yet to see him sleeping in a corner."

As Cal prepared to pack his bags for spring training, he spoke of the strange experience of the past season. He was booed by hometown supporters, but as an Orioles fan himself he understood their actions. "It might have happened a few times," Cal admitted, "but when you've played in front of a lot of people for a long time, you don't really hear it. I know I've been booed from time to time. People come looking for entertainment. It's a response to not being entertained. I try to put myself in their position because I consider myself to be an Orioles fan. They've seen you when you're in first or second every year, and now you're in a rebuilding period. There is a certain amount of patience, but they want to get back to these days [of winning]."

Cal displayed that eagerness at camp. He had the bounce, energy, and euphoria expected of a rookie. "I was bouncy and jumpy as a kid," said Cal, "but that's good. I think people notice that I like to have this uniform on."

Cal credited skipper Robinson with lifting his spirits. The shortstop ended 1990 with positive thoughts from his manager. "Mentally, you start to question yourself," reflected Cal. "Your confidence is on such a roller coaster that whenever you go into a slump, psychologically, you start to think, 'Is this a trend that will continue for the rest of your career?' "

Frank Robinson to the rescue. "He went on to tell me stories about how back in 1965 he wasn't doing very well and started to wonder if he'd get another hit. He went on to have some of his best years after that.

"That doesn't sound like much, but it was enough to give me the confidence to go back to the drawing board, and I went into the off-season with a game plan."

Teammate Brady Anderson was impressed with Cal's approach. "He doesn't ever want to lose, even in those tiny games," said Anderson. "He makes up games, like sockball, which is baseball played with a taped-up sock in the hallways during rain delays. He's sweating his butt off, then goes out and gets two hits.

"In spring training we have the 12-minute run. You don't have to try. He tries. He comes to me before the race and tells me how we're going to run it. When I won, he got very angry at me. He insisted that I went out too fast. I ruined him."

Cal had never won a Gold Glove, but his reputation was set in the spring training camps of Florida and Arizona. A survey of managers and front-office executives, reported in the *New York Times*, placed Cal among the game's top players, along with Don Mattingly, Yankees; Robin Yount, Brewers; Ryne Sandberg, Cubs; and Rickey Henderson, A's.

"The great thing about Ripken," said Yankees manager Stump Merrill, "is that everybody says he should be playing third base, but all you see him do is get to the ball and throw the guy out.

All I know is that he's always in the right spot for us at the wrong time."

Frank Robinson lauded his shortstop as a thinking man. "Quietly, in his own way, he'll ask you questions about situations and give his opinions on it," said Robinson. "And he doesn't just ask you questions and accept quietly. If he has an opinion, he'll let you know about it. I like that."

The question about the 1991 Orioles was whether the addition of Glenn Davis and Dwight Evans would strengthen the Orioles. Very little. Davis spent April on the disabled list. After 16 games, the Birds were 6–10 and in last place. However, Cal was off to a sensational start. On April 14 the Orioles socked it to the Rangers in Arlington, 11–4. Cal had two homers, a triple, and a single for seven RBIs. It matched the biggest Orioles RBI-game since Murray's seven-RBI output against the A's on May 18, 1986.

"I can't say right now . . . it's too early to tell how they're pitching me," said Cal. "But I do know I'm more relaxed. . . . In the past I have tried to overachieve, and when you try to overachieve, the pitchers expand your strike zone."

The clear improvement in Cal's bat was also evident to manager Robinson. "He's hitting the ball hard. He's more relaxed mentally, and he doesn't feel he has to carry the entire team."

On April 28, Cal had four RBIs to help the O's trim the Brewers 5–4 at Memorial Stadium. After 16 games Cal had a .350 batting average, with 20 RBIs. "The way the season unfolded, my confidence just grew," said Cal. He had been experimenting since his batting average dropped to .209 in June 1990. "I've been trying a lot of things ever since, but generally I've gone back to the basics, spread out a little bit. It has just carried over through the winter and spring training."

He was now trying to use the entire field. "That comes from waiting a little longer," explained Cal, "and seeing the ball a little better. You can make solid contact going the opposite way."

Cal's revived bat did not translate into an improved Orioles team. They were beaten at home on May 16 by Oakland, 6–3.

Even President Bush, who had brought the Orioles previous victories, could not help. He attended with Mrs. Bush and their guests, Queen Elizabeth and Prince Philip. All left after two innings, convinced the Orioles would not overtake the early A's lead. They were right. The Birds fell to 11–19, in last, eight and a half games out.

Orioles management had also seen enough. Frank Robinson was removed after the O's compiled a losing record. Johnny Oates did not make a memorable debut on May 24. They lost at home to the Yankees, 7–1, a game punctuated by a forgettable Cal Ripken fielding performance. Cal made only three errors in 1990; on May 24, 1991, he made two errors in successive innings—dropping a ground ball and later throwing errantly to home. He had not endured a two-error game since June 4, 1987.

"My managerial debut was not easy," recalled Oates from his Petersburg, Virginia, home. "We lost four straight and I lost nine pounds. I was down to 174 pounds. I had not been that thin since the late '70s when I was a catcher with the Dodgers." Oates and Baltimore won at home against Cleveland, 5–2, on May 28. But the Birds still remained in last, 14–26.

The Orioles and Cal Ripken, Jr., were both consistent in June. Baltimore continued to lose, and Cal continued to hit. The O's opened the month by winning three of four in Boston, but they lost two one-run games, June 3-4 in Minnesota. At month's end Baltimore was 29–43, 11½ games out in the cellar.

On the other hand, Cal's bat kept booming. "Every time I look up," said Oates, "he's on base." In the losses to the Twins, Cal had two three-hit games and raised his league-leading batting average to .359. In the latter part of June, however, Cal struggled with an 0-for-16 slump and fear of a prolonged decline set in. (His previous longest slump was an 0-for-29, in April 1988.) On June 23, Baltimore was in Kansas City for a doubleheader, and Cal's first two at bats increased the skein to 0 for 18.

However, the skein ended on his third at bat, a bloop single. That day might well have been Cal's most important during the

1991 season. He pounded out six hits in his next nine plate appearances and surged back to .350, the highest ever by an Oriole so late in the season. After the twin bill he was back again on top, replacing the A's Harold Baines as the AL's leading hitter.

His day's production: single, RBI triple, double, and single, and in the nightcap, two singles. Cal now had a league-leading 33 multiple-hit games.

He tried to play down the 6-for-10 performance. "It's only one day of the season," said Cal, "and 10 or so at bats out of 600. . . . There's still plenty of time to slip into bad habits. I hope I don't, but it's not like I don't have to worry about it anymore because I had a pretty good day today."

The doubleheader reunited Cal and Royals hurler Mike Boddicker, former teammate of the shortstop's at Bluefield and Baltimore. He was amazed at Cal's offensive success in 1991. "He's simply been scary," said Boddicker. "Cal has always had a tendency to slip into some bad habits, get overanxious, and try to do some things he shouldn't be doing.

"But I've watched him on TV earlier in the season, and I've seen him here, and he's just doing everything right, period—no flaws and no holes in his swing. I'm not saying he's going to end up the season hitting .360 and 45 home runs, but I'm saying that there are going to be some huge numbers under his picture in the scoreboard once the year is done."

The huge numbers continued. Cal had three hits in Cleveland to help the O's topple the Tribe 7–2 and raise his league-leading batting average to .355. When the O's returned to Baltimore, he helped his team beat Boston 7–3 with his 16th homer.

"Hitting is basically about waiting for as long as you can," Cal said, trying to explain his 1991 exploits. "There were times last season when I wasn't waiting, where I was jumping out with no idea as to where the pitch was going to be or even what kind of pitch it was. I was anxious, and I committed myself to the swing way too early. . . . [Now] I'm patient. I'm selective, and I'm waiting. . . . They're little changes, not big ones."

For the first time Cal publicly admitted that he had been under the tutelage of Frank Robinson, who shortly after leaving the managerial reigns returned for a second stint in the front office. "It's nothing I did, and there's nothing I said to him that Cal didn't already know," asserted Robinson in refusing to take any credit for Cal's 1991 offense. "The whole difference is that Cal Ripken has had a good, solid fundamental hitting base since spring training, and he's avoiding some of the pitfalls that have gotten him into trouble before."

After 67 games, Cal was on a pace for 34 homers and 109 RBIs. In addition to leading the league in batting, slugging percentage, and multiple-hit games, he was second to Joe Carter in homers, second to Cecil Fielder in RBIs, and was among the leaders in hits, total bases, doubles, and on-base percentage.

At the All-Star break Cal had a .348 average, with 18 homers and 54 RBIs, the first shortstop to be leading the league so late in the season since Lou Boudreau (.361) in 1947. The sweetness was marred by the Orioles, who were in last, 14 games behind Toronto. "It's a lot less fun when you aren't winning," Cal said. "But there's nothing I can do about it except do my job as best I can. I'm hoping things can turn around. I'm not saying we can overtake the Blue Jays, but there's still a chance to make this a respectable year."

The 1991 All-Star Game was in Toronto, but the Blue Jays' success had no relationship to Cal's feelings about the summer classic. He was selected to start his eighth consecutive game, but initially he showed little enthusiasm. Perhaps it was the hype, the endless questions about his consecutive-game streak, or analyses of his late-season slumps, but Cal had not felt comfortable in past years about the festivities and the game.

This year, however, was different because of the Skydome home run hitting contest. The Tiger's Fielder hit mighty blasts that had height and distance, but Cal had 12 homers in 22 swings. One of the blasts hit the window of a sky box in the fourth deck.

Practice made perfect. On All Star Game day, July 9, Cal delivered a three-run homer, the winning blow, to give the AL a 4–2 victory and him the MVP Award. The homer was only the third hit by an AL shortstop in All-Star history.

The victim was Cal's former teammate Dennis Martinez, who had moved to Montreal. "I threw a slider that stayed up," said Martinez. "You don't make mistakes like that, especially to Cal now. He's in some kind of groove."

Losing manager Lou Piniella added his plaudits. Piniella had seen Cal in his rookie and MVP years while the former was playing for the Yankees and later when he managed the New Yorkers. "Not only is he an outstanding shortstop," said the Cincinnati manager, "but he can hit the ball for power. I don't know how in the world he keeps going. He plays a tough position, a position where you can get hurt, and he just stays in there and does his job."

The MVP Award, added to his home run contest feat, told Cal that this was the harbinger of a very successful year, from the beginning to the end of the season. "Everything seems to be going my way," Cal reflected. "That [All-Star Game] has always been a nerve-wracking experience, but after the home run contest, everything fell right into place."

During the home run contest, Cal joked, "I'm going to see if we can do something about getting these [12 homers] to count." Unfortunately, the Orioles continued to flounder. On July 20, they were 37–52, 17 games out; on August 8 they were 43–64, 18 out; on August 31, they were 53–75, still 18 out.

Cal's great year proceeded after the All-Star break. On July 19, in a 4–1 Orioles home win against Seattle, Cal attained two milestones: he played in his 1,500th consecutive game and slammed his 20th homer. He became only the eighth player to hit 20 or more homers in his first 10 seasons.

"The 1500 is a nice big round number," said Cal about the Streak. "But I really don't know what it means. I'm proud, but I try not to get caught up in it."

However, Cal expanded his comments about the Streak: "I'm proud of the accomplishment and the achievement. At the same time I don't look at it in the same way everybody else looks at it, probably because I can't afford to.

"The real reason I've played this long is not because I set out to do it; it's just I wanted to go and play, be in the lineup. It's symbolic of the way I approach the game. And I've been lucky enough to stay away from injuries. Now, if I got caught up in it and think of [the Streak] the way everybody else does, then maybe I change my approach, and I don't want to do that."

Late in July, Cal still led the league in hitting, as he had done—with the exception of one day—since June 4. He led the league in three other offensive categories and was among the top 10 in 10 departments. His .988 fielding percentage led all shortstops.

Obviously, Cal was among the game's superstars and among the Orioles greats. In fact, Baltimore fans considered Cal the second greatest Oriole of them all. Brooks Robinson placed first in the *Evening Sun* fan survey, topping Cal, 38.5 percent to 25 percent. They were followed by Eddie Murray, Frank Robinson, and Jim Palmer.

Cal and the other Orioles did their best to give their fans grace, style, and, most important, a few more victories. For the first half of September, they played near-.500 ball. On September 11 the O's swept the Yankees in a three-game set at home and crept to within two and a half games of fifth place. They beat the Indians at home 4–3 on Cal's sacrifice fly in the eighth and now were a game and a half out of fifth. They lost to Boston at Fenway Park on September 18, 7–5, and remained a game and a half out of fifth.

Cal put one more achievement in his dossier. His 30th homer placed him in the elite circle of Ernie Banks, Rico Petrocelli, and Vern Stephens—shortstops with 30 or more homers in one season. Banks achieved this feat five times; Stephens, two.

Sadly, the Orioles did not finish in style. Their record of 67–95 gave the Birds a sixth-place finish, 24 games out of first.

Only Cleveland finished behind them. This tied the team for their fourth worst record in franchise history.

The Orioles rang down another losing season, concluding their schedule at home against the Detroit Tigers. But the poignant drama was not just the end of another bitter season but a farewell to Memorial Stadium. "If you're a baseball fan of any character, Memorial Stadium was a great stadium," Cal told Peter Richmond in his book *Camden Yards and the Building of an American Dream*. Richmond called the park "the big leagues' next-to-last neighborhood park, tucked among the city's rowhouses and graced by the trees that grew behind the scoreboard."

Cal had fond memories of Memorial Stadium. As a high schooler he made the short trip from Aberdeen to Baltimore, hitting balls in the Memorial Stadium stands, dreaming that one day he would be part of Orioles history. He would sit in the stands, shouting "Ed-die, Ed-die" with the rest of the crowd, cheering for the popular first baseman.

The last series with the Tigers brought together two mutual admirers for the finale at Memorial. Ever since he had made it to the bigs, Cal paid a lot of attention to Alan Trammell. "He's the player I've tried to emulate, especially in the field," said Cal. Interestingly, Cal started at third and moved to short; Trammell began at short and later in his career played at third.

Trammell had been paying attention to Cal's explosive year. "It looks to me," said Trammell, "like he's getting his bat through the strike zone longer, compared to when he kind of hooked the ball. But his other numbers, besides the average, have always been there. Everybody notices now because of his average. He's had a great year, right from the start.

"When that happens, you get the feeling that they can't get you out. That's a great feeling. I think that's what happened to Cal— and he's had such a great year."

October 6, 1991: The Orioles trailed the Tigers in the bottom of the ninth, one out, and perhaps the last batter ever in Memorial Stadium history at the plate. Who else at the plate but the great

Oriole facing Frank Tanana. The Hollywood script called for a final booming homer off Cal's bat. But it could not be worse: a 5-4-3 double play.

"I'd rather have gotten a hit," lamented Cal. "I grounded into a double play." Jokingly, Cal said, "I'm only as good as my last at bat. . . . It was difficult to stay focused. I wouldn't be human if I did. I kind of went outside of myself and tried to do more than I could. In the back of my mind, I wanted to hit a home run. And that's the worst thing you can do."

Cal's swing ended the relationship between the Baltimore Orioles and Memorial Stadium, at 5:07 P.M. (although an Orioles farm team played there). Emotions poured out after the game at a tribute for more than 100 past and present Orioles who returned to their playing positions in the field, attired in their uniforms. They trotted out to the accompaniment of heart-wrenching music from the movie *Field of Dreams*.

The Robinsons came out first: Brooks, then Frank. All the other O's received tributes from most of the game-time crowd of 50,700. The last player to come out onto the field was Cal Ripken, Jr., Baltimore's icon, the authentic, majestic link, the last great Oriole of 33rd Street, in Memorial Stadium. The last Oriole to sprint out of the dugout was Earl Weaver.

Cal Ripken, Jr., was the "one link to the great tradition," wrote Ken Rosenthal in the *Sun*. "The one man with a sense of it all."

Cal's most devoted fan loved every moment of the tribute. "I thought," said Kelly Ripken, " 'That's a nice touch, that's a nice touch.' "

Stoical as was his wont, Cal could not hide his feelings at the news conference. "It's kind of an empty feeling," a subdued Cal said as he left Memorial Stadium.

13

CONTRACT WOES

When the 1991 data were tabulated, they added up to what everyone knew about Cal Ripken, Jr. He had an incredible year. Junior achieved career highs in three categories: batting average, .323; homers, 34; RBIs, 114. His 210 hits were one short of his career best. He led the Majors with 368 total bases (only six other American Leaguers have had as many total bases in the past 51 years), 85 extra-base hits (only the ninth player in the past 50 years to reach that total), and a career-high 73 multihit games. His 46 doubles and .566 slugging percentage were second best in the Majors.

No big-league shortstop had ever achieved 30 homers and 200+ hits or 30 homers and 40 doubles. Ernie Banks—twice—was the only other shortstop to hit .300 with at least 100 RBIs and 30 homers. Cal became the tenth player in AL history to hit more than 30 homers and strike out fewer than 100 times. In this select group are Don Mattingly, Ted Williams, Joe DiMaggio, and Al Simmons. The last righty batter to achieve that feat was Al Rosen, in 1953.

Defensively, Cal was equally spectacular. For the second straight year, he led AL shortstops in fielding percentage at .986.

He also led the league in four other categories: putouts (267); assists (529); total chances (807); and double plays (114). His fielding set the tone for a record-breaking Orioles fielding season. They led the Majors in fielding percentage, committed the fewest errors, and became the first team in history to make fewer than 100 errors in three consecutive seasons.

With all the stunning records in his portfolio, it was a no-brainer that Cal earned the Louis M. Hatter Most Valuable Oriole Award for the fourth time. He led the O's in 14 offensive categories—everything except triples, sac bunts, and stolen bases. Only four other Orioles—Jim Gentile, Frank Robinson, Boog Powell, and Eddie Murray—had hit .300 with 30+ homers, and 100+ RBIs. Cal's .323 batting average had been topped only by Ken Singleton's .328 in 1977.

The awards season focused on two contrasts: Cal's year of achievement and the awful campaign of the Orioles—sixth place, 67–95, 24 games out. Sportswriters and broadcasters gave Cal his first award, on October 17: the Associated Press Player of the Year, outpolling the Tigers' Cecil Fielder and the Pirates' Barry Bonds. The award stresses individual achievement rather than value to the team.

"Obviously, it's a big honor," said Cal. "I feel very good about it. Most people measure our seasons—at least I do—on how the team has done. It was not the best year for the Orioles, but I got back to the consistency I had before. That was the best thing about the season.

"This year I got back to the level of efficiency I was used to. The best thing about this year was being able to go out there and be consistent on a daily basis. My batting average reflected that."

Managers, coaches, and players chose Cal over Fielder and Bonds on October 22 as the *Sporting News* Player of the Year. Cal became the first player in the 55-year history of the award to win the honor while performing for a team that finished below .500.

Baltimore beat writer Peter Schmuck took up the cudgels for Cal in the weeks before the MVP balloting. Cal was deserving, irrespective of what the Orioles did. "Ripken may have played on a sixth-place team, but he played at a level that few of his contemporaries will ever approach," said the *Sun* scribe, "and he did it consistently for nearly six months."

In discussing the MVP Award, other writers stressed the difference between the MVP and Player of the Year honors. The latter recognizes personal performance while the former requires selection on the basis of the actual value of a player to a team; number of games played; and general character, disposition, loyalty, and effort.

Shortly before announcement of the MVP awards, Cal received a perfect score in the ratings by the Elias Sports Bureau. The ratings were based on a two-year performance and were created during the 1981 strike settlement to divide players into classes for free-agent compensation. Cal achieved a perfect 100 score for 1990–91 by finishing first in each of seven categories: plate appearances, batting average, on-base percentage, home runs, RBIs, fielding percentage, and total chances. Don Mattingly (1986–87) had been the only player to receive a 100 rating previously.

The MVP voters, two beat writers from each team, agreed with the thinking of Peter Schmuck. On November 19, Cal Ripken, Jr., became the first AL MVP ever from a losing team. Two Cubbies, Ernie Banks (1958–59) and Andre Dawson (1987), had won the MVP as members of losing teams. In a tight race, Cal garnered 15 of 28 first-place votes for 318 points to edge Fielder, who had 9 first-place votes and 286 points.

"I don't think it can replace not having a winning season," reacted Cal, "because when you're an athlete in a team sport, the only thing that really matters is winning. Having gone through winning, I can stand up and say there's nothing like it."

Cal added, "It was a storybook season. It seemed like whenever I was out there on the field, I could do no wrong. Very rarely do you get that feeling as an athlete. . . . I don't know if I'll ever be able to duplicate what I did this year. I never had a slump. Everything I hit seemed to fall in."

At the press conference held at the nearly completed Oriole Park at Camden Yards, Cal compared winning the '83 MVP Award to this year's honor. "The first time I won," he said, "I was young and excited. I jumped into the big leagues, and we had a great season. Everything happened so fast. I don't know if I really understood it or appreciated it.

"This time, I've experienced the low points as well as the high points. I've been through tough times, like losing 100 games. To rebound the way I did this year, I have a very special appreciation for the award this time. . . . " Cal was the 20th player to win it two or more times.

There was joy in Camden Yards but bitterness, dismay, and wonderment in Detroit and Toronto. Cecil Fielder had now been denied the award twice. In 1990 he had hit 51 homers but was second to Rickey Henderson. In 1991 he led the Majors with 133 RBIs and tied for the Major League lead with 44 homers (with Jose Canseco). The Tigers had contended with champion Toronto for most of the season.

"They told me last year I had to play on a contender," the Tiger roared from his home in Arlington, Texas. "Now Cal Ripken, plays on a sixth-place team and they tell me he's an MVP. It's a shame the way things go down. . . . I'm not saying he didn't have that kind of season, but he played with a sixth-place team.

"It's a joke as far as I'm concerned. The way things were done this year I'm just done with it. If anybody put together two years like I did, they'd be MVP. So it's just a bunch of garbage."

Blue Jays fans wondered why Joe Carter, Roberto Alomar, and Devon White were slighted.

The controversy was aired out in the press. Was the award a popularity vote? How valuable was Cal Ripken, Jr., to Baltimore? With him, they finished sixth; without him, argued critics, they still would have beaten out Cleveland. Change the award from Most Valuable Player to Player of the Year, argued writers.

Toronto Star columnist Dave Perkins lambasted the award. How valuable was Cal to the Birds? Perkins asked.

"Well, absolutely and positively, Cal Ripken, Jr., has great usefulness to the Baltimore Orioles. Why, the Orioles were able to finish only 28 games under .500 and nestled comfortably into sixth place, within 24 games of the Toronto beloveds, with Ripken's great contributions included.

"Without him? No telling. They would probably have finished, oh, sixth. They'd never be as bad as Cleveland. They never would have gotten within 24 games of their first-place team in a weak division, though. So this makes Cal Ripken, Jr., the American League's most valuable player for 1991?"

Outrageously, Perkins suggested that Cal had won because of his hitting exhibition under the dome by winning the home run contest and All-Star MVP honors. But why, asked Perkins, should "a hot two days in July under the prying eyes of the league's press" be so important weeks later in MVP balloting for the entire season? Didn't Banks and Dawson win the MVP with losing teams? That proved, said Perkins, that until this year "only the National Leaguers had the corner on doing really dumb things with their votes."

Asserting that he wasn't partisan, the Toronto scribe chose Big Daddy Fielder. Without him, the Tigers would "have finished plenty closer to the Orioles than they would have to the Blue Jays."

The Minnesota press and fans had reason to feel slighted. The Twins made a triumphant reversal from cellar doormat in 1990 to World Series champions, yet their batting hero, Kirby Puckett, finished only seventh in the balloting. The case for the outfielder was made by Steve Koehler of the *Springfield News-Leader*. "The best guy on a second-to-last team won," said Koehler of Ripken. Joe Carter, who finished fifth in the vote, was more deserving. "Had Carter been out of the Toronto lineup," argued Koehler, "the Blue Jays would have been fighting with Baltimore for a cellar spot. Comparing Carter's value to that of Ripken's is like comparing gold to lead."

Clearly, according to the writer, Puckett was the MVP. "Puckett's .319 batting average, 15 home runs, and 89 RBIs, along with playing the role as leader during Minnesota's most improbable march to the world championship, made him the No. 1 MVP candidate in my book. . . . If not for him, the Twins fans would be crying in their Homer Hankies."

Manager Oates joined the battle. He agreed with critics who measured MVP value by the player's worth to the team. "No man in baseball could have been more valuable to the team," he said, "than Cal Ripken was to the Baltimore Orioles. From opening day to closing day, the stats speak for themselves. . . . The criteria should be, where would your team be without him? Well, where would we have been without him?" Answered Oates wryly, "Eighth place!"

Cal refused to be drawn into the controversy. "It's unfair for me," said the MVP, "to get involved in the specifics of the voting and the interpretation of the MVP. My job is to go out and do the best I can. Then, after your job is over, it's out of your control whether you win the award or finish second. But now that I've won it, I'm very happy about it."

When the controversy subsided, it was time for another award, with no postannouncement debate. At the end of 1991, Alan Trammell remarked, "I can't believe that [Cal] hasn't won a Gold Glove." Now, Cal had his first Gold Glove.

The Gold Glove was added to a remarkable collection of awards: the All-Star MVP, the American League MVP, and Player of the Year Awards of the *Sporting News* and the Associated Press. Only once had this been achieved in baseball history, in 1962 by Maury Wills of the Los Angeles Dodgers.

Sports Illustrated designated Cal Ripken, Jr., and Nolan Ryan as the only two ballplayers among a handful of athletes who were "living legends."

The only award Cal didn't capture was 1991 Male Athlete of the Year, presented by the Associated Press. Michael Jordan, who led the Chicago Bulls to the NBA crown, took that honor. Cal placed fifth.

*   *   *

Beyond his baseball value, Cal was literally valuable to Baltimore, according to the *Baltimore Business Reader*. His 34 home runs brought home $128,000 to the Reading, Runs, and Ripken campaign for Baltimore Reads. The total included monies pledged by Orioles fans and McDonald's, MCI, Black & Decker, and Colgate-Palmolive. "Everyone who went to bat for the future by pledging money for Ripken's homers," said the publication, "can count themselves as MVP's, too."

Cal coaxed fellow baseball stars to join him and Kelly in participating at a special weekend, signing autographs and auctioning memorabilia to raise funds for the literacy program. The Ripken Baseball Clinic in Aberdeen also raised some $17,000 for the Harford County Boys and Girls Club.

Cal's awards also brought gains for those capitalizing on his added fame. The Maryland State Lottery's new instant scratch-off game commissioned a Baltimore-based advertising and public relations agency to produce a television commercial that featured Viola Ripken. She is shown scratching a Baseball Memories lottery ticket and exclaiming, "Ooh! The boys aren't the only ones who can hit in this family."

Donruss Baseball Cards invited Cal to sign 5,000 cards for its 1992 series. In the meantime Cal's rookie card, in mint condition, jumped in value in six months from $25 to $75. Experts speculated that the card might eventually go for $500.

Chicago Processing minted 15,000 Ripken Medallions, with Cal's name, likeness, and uniform number, 8, on the front, and on the reverse side the words "1991 American League MVP."

For Cal Ripken, Jr., however, the phrase *awards bring rewards* had one central motif for nearly a year: a new contract. His contract ended after the 1992 season. Serious thought and discussion had been under way before the season of awards, before the Orioles said good-bye to Memorial Stadium. Management did not want Cal to bid farewell after 1992 to Camden Yards.

Orioles president Larry Lucchino kept a contract journal. Its first page is dated September 26, 1991, the start of a 333-day process. "We approached Cal's agent Ron Shapiro," Lucchino told me in a 1994 interview, following the sale of the Orioles when he was no longer president. "We met for lunch. Discussions were informal at first."

"But it should be pointed out that in the beginning we made a serious very fair offer of $20+ million. Our offer would have put Cal in the salary range of top shortstops."

In *Play Ball*, John Feinstein details the negotiations. "Lucchino's first offer was a long way from acceptable: two years for $10 million." "Totally untrue," insisted Lucchino. "John asked for my notebook and for Shapiro's. Ron gave his, but I felt that there were entries and comments that were not relevant and, therefore, kept my book. The result is certain inaccuracies in reporting the negotiations."

The Orioles went to the winter meetings in Miami and returned with many questions unresolved: no contract. In the midst of the troubled situation, reports had surfaced that Billy Ripken, Juan Bell, and Tim Hulett—who combined for a .240 on-base percentage in 1991, the lowest in the Majors for one position (second base)—would be packaged either to Montreal for Delino De-Shields or to Los Angeles for Juan Samuel. After his dad was fired in 1988 and Cal's contract stalled, would Billy's being traded be viewed by Junior as the ultimate injustice?

As a frequent guest on talk shows, Cal often had to field contract questions. "I've always maintained there are two sides to baseball," he responded with a pat answer. "There's the business side and the playing side. My job is playing . . . and that's the way I'm going to keep it."

Cal did not let the contract process disrupt his off-season regimen. Three times a week he closeted himself with his favorite batting "instructor," a 1932 Dudley pitching machine. "The best batting-practice pitcher in the world can't throw consistently for strikes," said Cal, "although my father would argue that it's the other way around."

Cal would soon leave his family for another season. In February, according to Feinstein, Shapiro, with Cal's MVP in view, countered with $39 million over 5 years. "In the beginning, they were not coming through with anything realistic," Lucchino said, challenging Feinstein's details. "They asked for sums which they did not really expect to receive."

Before Cal left for spring training, Lucchino engaged in creative contracting. He sent a three-page letter to Cal and Kelly to the effect that the Orioles were deeply interested in Cal staying in Baltimore. To prove that, the Orioles were prepared to make him the highest-paid shortstop in baseball. While Feinstein called the approach "unusual," Lucchino said, "I had told Cal that I would be writing him, so the letter was not unexpected." An impressed Shapiro reduced demands to $38 million.

Cal came to Florida still no closer to a contract. Brother Billy told reporters that Cal could have demanded to renegotiate the contract after his MVP year. "There have been a lot of players after a season like Cal who want to renegotiate," said Billy. "But he stuck with the terms of his contract. He never bitched, like a lot of players have."

The unsigned MVP refused to comment about the negotiations during the first day of full-team workouts at Twin Lakes Park. Matters were in the hands of Shapiro and Lucchino, he said. "My stand is I'm signed until the end of the year. I'm under contract. It's baseball now. I want to focus on baseball. . . . I don't want to talk about it, really. . . . My job is the baseball-playing side of baseball, and that's the way I want to keep it."

It was only baseball when the O's began their Grapefruit League schedule at St. Petersburg against the Cardinals and brought together arguably the Majors' two best shortstops: Cal and Ozzie Smith. "He's not a prototype shortstop per se," said a complimentary Smith. "At six foot four, 225, you think of him more as an outfield type, a third-base type. That speaks for his ability, to be able to hold down such a demanding position as shortstop. . . .

"When you do the offensive things he does, it kind of over-shadows everything you do defensively. Just like my defense over-shadows everything I do offensively."

While Cal tried to focus on baseball, Lucchino and Shapiro were immersed in the business of baseball. During that first week of exhibition baseball, Lucchino wrote Shapiro that he found it "puzzling and surprising that our first offer was inadequate." The Orioles' offer of $20-plus million for four years would now be upped to $30 million for five years. The Orioles would "make Cal the first $6 million man in the game."

"We were beginning to come together," Shapiro told Feinstein. Shapiro countered with $36 million and emphasized that neither he nor Cal was flexible about this figure. No one was flexible, and Cal remained unsigned.

"We had an understanding that the contract discussions would not be aired publicly," said Lucchino. "This was not to our advantage because the media got the impression that the Orioles were cheap and unappreciative of Cal. And when they printed dollars and cents, they were inaccurate."

The Orioles, especially owner Eli Jacobs, were assailed in the press. *Sun* columnist Michael Littwin called the owner "cheap." According to *Washington Post* columnist Thomas Boswell, "Jacobs simply didn't appreciate the enormous value, and the rarity of what Ripken had done in 1991 . . . how Ripken had put together one of the great seasons in the history of the game for anybody—including Babe Ruth."

Boswell also got his shots in at Orioles management in a lengthy feature. "Sometimes you wonder," he wrote, "if the Orioles believe [Cal has slipped in his skills] as you watch the excruciating and almost insulting way they dawdle all winter in contract negotiations with the best shortstop in AL history."

Sporting News columnist Greg Sprout, in his March 30 round-up, quoted an unnamed AL executive: "If you know Eli Jacobs as well as I do, there's no way he'll shell out $32 million to keep Cal for four more seasons. Eli is going to say, 'Thanks for the memories; we've really enjoyed having you.' And Cal can continue his consecutive-games playing streak with some other, richer team."

The *Sun's* Ken Rosenthal applied logic and simple economics. "If Barry Larkin [of Cincinnati] is worth $25.6 million and Bobby Bonilla $29.5 million [with the Mets], Cal Ripken deserves at least $30 million for five years," said Rosenthal. If things became hectic, he added, the Orioles might have to offer $35 million for five years. "But $8 million per year would even be crazier, and that might be what Ripken commands on the open market."

Why was Jacobs holding back? wondered Rosenthal. "You never know the whole story with Jacobs," said the columnist. "Are the Orioles on such a tight budget because he borrowed heavily to buy the club? Because his other businesses are struggling? Because he wants to sell the team?"

Everyone knew how much Cal Ripken, Jr., enjoyed playing in Baltimore. It had been a dream since his childhood. It was the Ripken way. On the other hand, it was important for him to feel the Orioles wanted him, and that could only be proved through a satisfactory contract. "Of course, we wanted to keep Cal. We appreciated what he had done on the ball field and off," said Lucchino. "He is an icon in Baltimore, and we did make him a reasonable offer right from the start. However, there was nothing to say he wouldn't leave. In fact, there would be less pressure on him if he played outside of his hometown community."

Putting aside the stalled contract momentarily, the media turned their attention to the opening of baseball's new wonder: Camden Yards. The inaugural was April 6, opening day for the Orioles.

The Orioles' new home was applauded for its architectural grandeur. It was a symbol of "a glorious new trend in baseball," wrote Bruce Jenkins of the *San Francisco Chronicle*. More important for Cal Ripken, Jr., stressed Jenkins and other writers, was that Oriole Park was crafted with Cal in mind. The dimensions were ideal for hitters, especially righties with power: 410 feet to deepest center, 364 to left center, 333 to left, 318 to right. Through his first ten years, Cal had compiled his best stats in the Minnesota Metrodome: 89 for 240, a .371 batting average, with 12 homers and 46 RBIs. The Oriole Park dimensions were similar to those at the Metrodome, especially the friendly wall in right.

Better days were ahead for Cal in Camden Yards, according to Boswell of the *Washington Post*, "now that he has finally escaped from Memorial Stadium, a hell-hole for a line drive gap hitter. Ripken never moaned, but for a decade, he's batted 30 points better on the road. Those 309-foot warped corners on 33rd Street let every left and right fielder shade a few steps towards the alley, stealing hits.

"Now Rip will move to Camden Yards, a park whose every dimension was designed, on purpose, to suit Ripken's hitting patterns."

Not surprisingly, Cal had mixed feelings about Camden Yards. It was like leaving a comfortable home. Memorial Stadium "meant a lot to me," said Cal. "I grew up as an Orioles fan, watching all the great players play. It meant a lot to me to walk out on that field for the first time as a player. It had a great tradition, and it's hard to lose that. But we have to close the book on that part of Orioles baseball."

On the other hand, Cal was "kind of excited about seeing the new park, but it really hasn't set in yet. When we get there and start playing, that's when it'll hit us."

That feeling thrilled the 44,568 spectators who were on hand for opening day. The majestic Camden Yards was described by Claire Smith of the *New York Times* as a "jewel in the heart of Baltimore's restored downtown harbor area." It was especially delightful for Orioles fans, who cheered the 2–0 shutout of Cleveland by Rick Sutcliffe. President Bush headed the list of VIPs and ran his record to 4–2 for Orioles home games. He was accompanied by Mrs. Bush and grandson George P. Bush.

Cal's bat was silent in the home opener. He improved at the Toronto Skydome opener April 10. He batted in one run in the Orioles' 4–3 loss, hitting a tough low slider from crafty lefty Jimmy

Key. More personally satisfying than the RBI was the warm and generous ovation the crowd gave the AL MVP.

This was no small feat, according to Jim Proudfoot of the *Toronto Star*. Local fans, the writer recalled, have been noted for being less than gracious to visiting celebrities, e.g., Kirby Puckett, Rickey Henderson, Wayne Gretzky, and Bobby Orr. "Now in saluting Ripken, they were rising for a change above hometown chauvinism," wrote Proudfoot. "And they were entirely correct in doing so. This is truly one of baseball's class acts, admirable in every way. Say, could it be Torontonians are learning to appreciate some of the game's finer points?"

Toronto's Jack Morris shut out the Birds 2–0 the next day. The only hit Cal had that day was on his left elbow, stung by a Morris pitch. After the 1992 season, Cal admitted, "It was an injury that was recurring," he said. "Every once in a while, I'd slide on it or make a throw and feel it in a certain area. It lasted a majority of the year."

The O's played well. They won 12 of 20 and were in third place, only two and a half from the top. However, Cal's start was inauspicious. He hit his first home run in game 20, after 72 at bats, his longest-ever home run drought at the start of a season. That home run was in his favorite park, the Metrodome, on April 28, helping the O's beat the Twins 10–5.

Perhaps he was not thriving in Camden Yards, but the Orioles loved their new home. They were 8–1 there, 15–8 overall, on May 2, and in first place. It was the latest they had been at the top since August 31, 1989. Cal had his first home run at Oriole Park on May 3 against Seattle as the Birds swept past the Mariners 8–6. Cal had but 2 homers, 12 RBIs, and a .258 average in 25 games.

Through his career, Cal had said that he would trade personal stats for the chance to be on a winner. In early 1992 that wish was being fulfilled. "When you're winning," he insisted, "you don't have time to think about whether you're hitless in your last 10 at bats. All you're thinking about is what you can do in your next at bat to help the team win. Your whole focus is on that one game.

You derive so much more satisfaction from winning than from anything else.

"There's nothing better than playing on a team that's winning, where you don't have to hit 30 home runs or drive in 100 runs. The only focus is what you have to do today to help the team win."

Neither Cal nor manager Oates was worried about his slump. "My confidence level is still high," said Cal. "Even though when you're going bad, you feel like you'll never get a hit. At this stage right now, I feel some things are coming along. I'm not too concerned.

"I've gone through home run droughts, RBI droughts, where I haven't gotten any hits, throughout my career. All I know is that it always seems to eventually turn around."

Counseled the manager: "Don't judge anyone on their start, or their finish. Cal's not swinging as consistently as he was last year, but before the season's over, he'll be there."

Cal compiled a 16-game hitting streak through June 8 and raised his average to .262, and his hits were driving in key runs. On June 2 he got the Orioles off to a good start at Anaheim by hitting a two-run homer off Mark Langston in a 4–2 victory. "It was a mistake over the plate to Cal Ripken," said the hurler, "and you can't make that mistake with Ripken." Cal pleased the home fans on June 5 by driving in the game's only run to nip Toronto in the eighth inning. That moved the Birds into first place by percentage points over the Jays. The O's lost the next day, but they recaptured first on June 7 with a 7–1 victory, led by Cal's three run-scoring singles against Toronto.

"I never worried about him," said Oates. "He's the one guy on the team where I know what I'll get from him."

But would Cal remain in Baltimore? The *Washington Post's* Boswell feared that just as Eddie Murray had left after feuding with owner Williams, Cal Ripken, Jr., could leave in disagreement with owner Jacobs. There had been "significant erosion" between Cal and the Orioles, wrote Boswell.

The Cubs had signed Ryne Sandberg at a reported $7.1 million a year. The Orioles should realize, advised Boswell, that their market compares with that of Chicago and they should make Cal the right offer. Despite a falloff from his MVP year, the Orioles should offer Cal a contract as if to say, "Relax, we appreciate what you've done. We're confident you'll keep doing it in the future. You don't have to prove yourself to us. We'll even take the risk you might get hurt before your old contract would've run out."

No offer had been made public. Nevertheless, Boswell offered Cal advice on his contract. Cal "needs to understand that the Orioles would be crazy to assume his '91 numbers will be his norm for the next five years. He needs to get out of the funk, start producing on the field, act like a leader in the clubhouse, and tell the Orioles he'd sign in a minute for $34 million for five years."

Shapiro refused to tell Boswell about the specifics in the negotiations, but he did not rule out that Cal could leave Baltimore. "Even though Cal and Eddie [Murray] are different people, they both have feelings and sensitivities that, in this case, have some parallels. Sooner or later, these feelings can't be ignored."

The Orioles had offered Cal $30 million for five years, reported Maske in the *Washington Post*, with a June 7 dateline. That figure sounded high, responded an unnamed American League executive. "But in this day and age when it's Cal Ripken you're talking about, that's just the starting point for the negotiations."

Lucchino would not be drawn into the numbers game. "We won't negotiate publicly," he insisted. Traveling at the time, Shapiro was unavailable for comment, but he told Feinstein, "It was a potential deal breaker."

July 11 was a very important day in the ongoing contract melodrama. Orioles traveling secretary Phil Itzoe delivered to Cal's locker a handwritten letter from Lucchino. "The Orioles want to sign you now," said the missive, "and get the matter behind us without further distraction and delay." The letter ended, "We look forward to reaching agreement now."

Feinstein maintains that Shapiro smelled the communication

coming but was unsuccessful in stopping its delivery. "Cal was struggling a little bit," said Shapiro, "and I was worried that he might get his hopes up too high if he read the letter."

Cal did get his hopes up, and an excited shortstop left for the All-Star Game in San Diego. He was an acclaimed All-Star and set a number of records for the midsummer classic. He was the leading vote getter in the Major Leagues, receiving the most ballots since Gary Carter in 1982. Junior passed Luis Aparicio as the first AL shortstop to start in nine games and tied Luis for most appearances, 10, by an AL shortstop.

While Cal did not star in the game, he received the Roberto Clemente Award as the player who best exemplifies baseball on and off the field. The award memorializes the Pittsburgh Hall of Fame outfielder killed in a plane crash while bringing supplies to earthquake-ravished Nicaragua in 1972. "I have never met Roberto Clemente," said Cal, "but everyone I have who did said he was a wonderful person. This is a great honor."

On the eve of the game, *USA Today*, under a Mel Antonen byline, told of Cal Ripken's refusing a $30 million offer. Cal conceded the possibility of leaving Baltimore. "I could picture myself playing elsewhere," he said. "You think those thoughts. They come into your mind. Ideally, you'd like to play in one place. Realistically, you have to be prepared for that not to happen."

Antonen asked Cal if the contract process had an effect on his on-field performance. Yes, he could "ignore" those thoughts. "The contract is part of the sport, but it will go away."

The optimism for a deal soon vanished. On July 23, Shapiro responded to Lucchino's letter with an offer of $33 million and an escape clause after three years to adjust to new market conditions. Lucchino did not accede.

"Certainly, the offers that Shapiro proposed were influenced by Don Fehr [representing the players union]. They felt, unjustly, that players were not getting what the market would bear," said Lucchino.

At midseason Cal had endured batting slumps, contract squabbles, and criticism of the Streak. On July 23, a sad note further depressed his spirits, Sam Hulett, son of Orioles infielder Tim Hulett, died after being struck by a car. Cal was especially sensitive to the father-child relationship. He admitted feeling guilty, traveling on the road and leaving Rachel behind. "She really became angry at me when I had to go away. On one home stand, every time I went to put her to bed, she said she couldn't sleep until Kelly came in to see her, because she knows Kelly isn't going to leave her like I do. That afternoon [following Sam Hulett's death], when I put her down for a nap, I had a long talk with her about how much I loved her and how hard it was for me to go away."

The contract was not signed. It did not become an "invisible" problem. The collapse of the negotiations was followed by a disastrous second half of the season. By the third week of August Cal was hitting .251, with only 10 home runs and 55 RBIs. He had gone since June 23 without a four-bagger, the longest power famine in his career. Throughout July and August, the O's clung to second place, usually two to four games from the top. In fact, the entire team was suffering a power famine. From June 23 on, Cal and Randy Milligan had but one homer in 380 at bats. They had 50 homers in 1991. The team had 27 homers during that period, 10 hit by Leo Gomez.

Why the slump? Perhaps the hit on the elbow by Morris in April and a hit in the back on July 3 by Twins lefty John Smiley had affected his hitting. However, the media sought to develop the relationship—if any—between the uncertainties and anxieties of the negotiations and their effects on Cal's at-bat performance. At first Cal dodged the questions, but he answered directly in mid-August. "It's not something that sits on your back every day," explained Cal. "You think something might be accomplished and the excitement level goes up. Then nothing happens and it goes down. Then there is a period of disappointment that lingers for a while. Then you get back to normal and it heats up again. It's a constant up-and-down ride."

After the season, Cal told John Feinstein, "I don't like to make excuses for the fact that I wasn't hitting, but I was distracted. It's easy to say why worry about whether you're going to make five or six million. Either way, I'm set for life. That's true, but that wasn't what it was about at that point. I just felt like the Orioles were playing mind games with me. Whether that was right or wrong, it was bothering me."

Lucchino takes strong exception to this analysis. "We made a fair offer from the start," said the Orioles CEO, "and we dealt with Cal with great appreciation for what he has meant to the team and to the city. If his hitting were affected by the contract, then why didn't he have a great comeback following his signing?"

Whatever the reason for his slump, his teammates and fans were concerned. Fellow Orioles asked Cal what had gone wrong. Veteran hurler Mike Flanagan, in what would be his last year in Baltimore, was sympathetic. He understood that negotiations meant human relations, not just dollars and cents. "That's your life out there," said Flanagan. "When you give your heart and soul out there every day, the last thing you want to hear in November was what you didn't do.

"Me, I just wanted to be paid what I was worth, but how do you determine that with a guy like Cal . . . ?"

Milligan, whose subpar 1992 performance led to his departure in 1993, felt that Cal and he had contributed even with their falloffs. "I don't think you could evaluate what Cal and I did just by the cold statistics," he said. Manager Oates took up the theme as it related to his shortstop. "Look at his 11-year career," said the manager. "He's a little off his career numbers, but not anything to be alarmed about. . . . Cal probably won't be happy with that because he demands so much of himself, but there are a lot of things Cal brings to the ballpark even when he's not getting a hit or driving in a run."

The July 29 contest at Yankee Stadium illustrated Oates's dictum. Rookie Arthur Rhodes blanked New York, but Cal made the big play—in the field. In the fourth, the O's were up only 1–0, with two out and Mattingly at first. Mel Hall singled to center field. Mattingly courageously galloped into third. Cal cut off outfielder Devereaux's throw before it reached third and quickly threw the ball behind Hall to catch the Yankee off first. End of inning and end of Yankees threats for the game.

Orioles fans were worried that negotiations would be broken off and then Cal would be gone from Baltimore in 1993. "Even if I decide to do that [break off negotiations]," Cal curtly told the *Sun*'s Peter Schmuck, "you probably wouldn't know about it." Not signing was not synonymous with not wishing to remain in Baltimore. "There have been assumptions made because I'm not signed—like I don't want to be here. A lot of assumptions are really unfair. It could just be that negotiations shouldn't be done until your contract is up. It could be a situation where these are just the games that are played in negotiations."

Agent Shapiro was being told by fans to get Cal signed. If Cal left Baltimore, he told *Legal Times*, he would hardly be the most likable citizen in Baltimore. "I don't feel it now," said Shapiro, "except when I'm walking through the stadium and people yell that Cal should sign. But I think most people understand that Cal should get what he's asking for."

Shapiro insisted that he would not let the possibility of Baltimore losing its icon "get in the way of the negotiations. My philosophy is that it's best for a player to have an identity with one city. But we have to do what's best [for Cal]."

Manager Oates had to do what was best for the team. The O's beat Seattle 2–1 at home on August 20. It was only their second win in seven games. During that stretch, the team hit a miserable .224. Cal had hit .169 in his last nine games. Oates dropped Cal to fifth in the batting order for the first time since August 7, 1990. Milligan was moved to the second slot, and Devereaux now batted third. "We want to get Cal started," said Oates. "Maybe this will make [the three hitters] more relaxed."

Cal was very agreeable. "Fine, it doesn't matter where you bat," he said. "Whatever lineup the manager selects is okay with me. We're all out to win."

Win they did the next day at Oriole Park against Oakland, 4–2. Cal—and Milligan—had no hits in the new lineup. On August 22, the O's lost 7–3 and fell to three out of first. Oates was testy during a postgame meeting with the media. How about the Ripken slump and the contract status? the media asked. "Enough already," the manager snapped. "Cal's an important player, but right now we can talk about more important things about the Baltimore Orioles than Cal Ripken, Jr. . . . I'm not talking any more about the slump, the Streak, or the contract. We've got a lot more things to take care of than that."

Oates told the persistent press that he hoped Cal's ninth-inning single on August 22 would help break a 7 for 47 schneid. "I'm sure he feels all the pressure in the world. If the Baltimore Orioles are going to win, he's going to have to contribute because he's a focal point. But he doesn't have to carry the load by himself."

Suddenly, with no advance notice, word came of the contract: $30.5 million over five years. At his option after playing days, Cal would have a four-year, $500,000-a-year contract. When the math was completed, it was a $30.5 million package. In short, Cal had signed the largest contract in baseball history, although Sandberg would earn the highest annual salary.

The "official" signing photograph showed Cal in Orioles uniform minus cap, with shirt-and-tie Ron Shapiro, Roland Hemond, and Larry Lucchino. More precise details were then given: $4.5 million base salary in 1993, $4.8 million in 1994, $6 million in 1995 and 1996, and $6.2 million in 1997. A $3 million signing bonus rounded out the package.

Shortly after he inked the pact—less than an hour before game time—Cal hurried to Oriole Park. Said Roland Hemond, "Cal was concerned that he wouldn't get back to the field in time for infield practice. That says something about him."

Oates learned of the pact only a few minutes before the signee arrived at Camden Yards. "That's great. He's in the lineup tonight," an unemotional manager said.

The contract was signed on the evening of Cal's 32nd birthday,

August 24. It was a done deal, PA announcer Rex Barney told the assembled crowd of 44,285. Lucchino and Hemond accompanied Cal to home plate as Barney told of the signing of "our beloved All-Star shortstop."

The historic announcement was made at 7:36 P.M. Cal acknowledged the applause and standing ovation of the crowd by taking his cap off. Baltimore then took the field against California. Cal celebrated a birthday and a contract, but he and the O's did not celebrate a victory. Cal was of little help in the 5–2 loss. In the bottom of the third, with the O's trailing 1–0, two out and one on, Cal stepped up and ended the frame. He bobbled a routine grounder in the fifth that helped the visitors load the bases and later take a 4–1 lead. In the bottom of the fifth, he hit into a double play. The birthday-contract celebrant was booed.

The signing of Cal Ripken, Jr., was the biggest story in Baltimore for days. Participants and the media offered their commentary. Fans had their say. What would it mean to Cal and Baltimore on the ball field? What would it mean to baseball in general?

Looking at the astronomical numbers, Cal said, "Those numbers to a normal person makes them shake their head. I shake my head all the time. Sometimes it's hard to explain how anyone can be deserving of that. Maybe there is no explanation. But there is a business side, and those are the salary figures that are thrown around. This is my talent; this is what I enjoy doing. . . . I never felt that I was underpaid. That contract [1988] gave me a tremendous amount of security, allowed me to do a lot of things financially. You sign a contract. I take the same view with the magnitude of this contract as I did with the magnitude of the other contract."

The bottom line for Cal: "I never pictured myself in another uniform. I'm from here. I'm an Oriole, and that's all I ever wanted to be. I just can't accentuate that enough."

Eschewing money discussions in the abstract or concrete, Ron Shapiro opted to dwell on Cal's strong loyalty to Baltimore and the strong commitment of ownership to the signee and to the fans.

Shapiro boiled it down to Cal's deep feelings never to leave his hometown. "It's much easier [to negotiate]," said Shapiro, "if you make up your mind to go on the market. But I knew in his heart that Cal didn't want to give in to that temptation. . . .

"There were difficult days, but Cal's deepest desire was to remain here. . . . I don't think Cal ever even thought about leaving. He grew up here watching Brooks Robinson and Jim Palmer play their entire career with the Orioles. It has been his dream to follow that tradition, and we weren't going to disturb that dream. . . . "

The much-attacked Orioles front office was lauded by Shapiro. "Reaching an agreement with the Orioles was a continuous objective of Cal's in this negotiation," said Shapiro, "and a truly unique and harmonious relationship between a club and a player has now been cemented. . . . It represents a significant commitment on the part of our owner, Eli Jacobs, to Cal and our fans. The best thing that happened was Cal's smile in Larry's [Lucchino] office after [the signing of the pact]."

Lucchino was relieved that the issue had been resolved. The Orioles had given Cal "fair value" and in so doing had proved their commitment to fans and franchise. "We think Cal Ripken is a first-ballot Hall of Famer," said Lucchino. "He personifies the best of the Baltimore Orioles organization, and we are pleased and proud that he will be performing for the organization for many years to come. . . . Make no mistake. This is a long-term commitment to Cal, to the city, and to the region—and it is a commitment to winning that should not be overlooked. . . .

"I thought it would be a sad irony if the longest applause at the 1993 [All-Star Game] was for Cal Ripken in another uniform. I didn't think that was the way the world should turn."

Now that the contract was in Cal's pocket, how would the star respond? The Orioles were locked in a pennant race with Milwaukee and Toronto. Could Cal step up his performance in the remaining 37 games? "Couldn't Cal have signed for $30 million back in the spring?" asked former O John Lowenstein, as an announcer for Home Team Sports (cable TV). "Now he's getting $30.5—all this misery this season for a lousy $500,000. He may be under more pressure now, feeling he has to live up to the contract."

However, Mike Flanagan felt Cal could deal with the pressure. "I don't know if I've ever seen anyone with the ability to be as completely focused as he does, despite all the distractions," he said. "He's an amazing person."

While agent Shapiro commented that the contract removed a burden from his client, he would not guarantee that the old form would magically come back. "It's impacted him," said Shapiro, "but this doesn't mean this will turn the switch on. It's a burden off him, though."

Kelly Ripken had endured the contract agony for months. "Now, I just hope I can enjoy the pennant race," Kelly sighed.

In July 1988, Cal signed a contract and proceeded to hit seven homers in the next 17 games. At contract signing time, Cal ranked 11th in batting average among shortstops with 250+ at bats. Looking to the next 37 games, Cal said, "I'm hopeful it will give me a fresh start. I'm not going to make any promises because who knows that [negotiations] might not have been the problem anyway.

"I could still get hot and hit 20 homers. . . . In my own estimation, I haven't done poorly. I just haven't done as well as I wanted to."

August ended with no power dividends on his contract. The Orioles closed the month at 72–58, two and a half games behind Toronto. On Labor Day weekend, as the teams geared for the stretch, the Birds had closed the gap to a half game. "We're happy where we're at," said a satisfied manager Oates. "But we can't sit back at the end of the season and say we're satisfied with winning 76 games. . . . Just because we weren't favored to win doesn't mean we shouldn't try to win it."

The O's made their run without a potent Ripken bat. Cal was hitting .245, with 10 homers and 60 RBIs. Cal's slack had been made up in part by Brady Anderson, who had scored 91 runs, driven in 91, and stolen 49 bases. Brady came to his teammate's defense. "Cal's had a few slumps," said Anderson, "but he's still a Gold Glove shortstop. He's still knocked, and he's still got good numbers, so he's an asset. He's not having an MVP-type season like he had last year, but it doesn't mean he doesn't contribute."

The Orioles' pennant hopes were set back when the Yankees swept them at Camden Yards, September 7–9. They fell three and a half back. The Yankees radio and TV crews criticized Cal. Cal's problem lay in his batting stance, according to the WPIX-TV team. Bobby Murcer and Phil Rizzuto were impressed with one stat: Cal's $30.5 million contract.

On a 3–2 pitch in the ninth, umpire Nick Voltaggio called ball four. Mocked WABC Radio's Michael Kay, "Voltaggio didn't have the heart to punch out baseball's highest-paid player."

Cal's Iron Man Streak, in light of his batting woes, was the most frequent topic of conversation during Cal's at bats. The Yankees telecasters cited the sentiments of broadcaster Tony Kubek, an excellent Yankees shortstop in his time (1957–65). The Orioles had no better shortstop on the team than Cal, so he belonged in the field. However, Kay and partner John Sterling debated the benching of Cal in view of his hitting and in consideration of his streak.

If Oates benched Cal, reasoned Sterling, the manager would be "assassinated." Kay would honor the Streak but remove Cal after the first inning. The Orioles wouldn't miss Cal; after all, they "were in the pennant race despite him." Added Kay, "If you're Cal Ripken, do you ask to be benched?"

It is reasonable to say that if Cal had his typical year, the Orioles would have fared better in the pennant race. Orioles fans knew this. The Birds were blown out of Oriole Park by the Yankees, 16–4, on September 8. Cal drew a round of boos after popping up in the sixth. Sterling was amazed. "He has played every inning . . . he got his tail booed. . . . But [the fans] have a right."

On Sunday, September 13, local sports celebrities Cal Ripken and near homonym Mark Rypien were solidly booed for their playing poorly with fat contracts. Washington Redskins fans did not like Rypien's quarterbacking. Orioles fans did not enjoy Cal's continued power failure, as the Birds were defeated by Milwaukee 3–1 to tumble five games back.

However, Cal did not take the boos personally. His father had also been booed in the past. His dad had told him: If you give your best, that's all that matters.

A year later, Senior offered his own perspective on the 1992 slump. "There are many things that go into a slump," he said. "It can be mechanical, and that can be fixed. Then, there is the mental side, and that is a little more difficult to fix. In 1992, Cal had to deal with continued interrogation and criticism of his contract, his game streak, and his hitting. You have to be in the proper frame to perform at your best. I have always said that one good thought is better than two half thoughts."

Cal kept playing (his streak had reached 1,700 games on August 25), but the O's continued to lose. During the weekend set with Milwaukee, with the Brewers taking two of three, Cal had gone 0 for 11 and had fallen to a .239 batting average. In his last 73 homerless games, Cal had hit .190.

It pained Oates to see the decline of his MVP. "Sometimes I look at him and still remember the first time I laid eyes on him when he was six years old," said the manager. "But he's not six anymore, and he's not 24. I've seen him the last four years. This year he doesn't look the same."

What was more painful for Cal took place on September 11, at Camden Yards, game 1,713 in the Streak. Cal doubled in the first inning against Milwaukee's Bill Wegman and twisted his right ankle rounding first base. He did not come out of the game and did not miss a beat, going on to the next game, September 12, against the Brewers. Still, it was one of three close calls for the Iron Man (the others being April 10, 1985, and June 6, 1993).

*   *   *

Cal stopped his homerless decline on September 14 with a four-bagger that helped the O's beat Kansas City at Oriole Park, 2–1. His 3-for-3 day also put an end to a 3-for-29 slump. He had gone since June 23—292 at bats—since his last round-tripper. Having found the range, Cal hit number 11 against Milwaukee on September 18, but the visiting Birds were trounced 12–4 and stood four and a half games out of first. They also lost the next game to the Brewers, 4–1, and were now five and a half behind Toronto—and for the first time since the end of May, they were in third place, trailing the Jays and the Brewers.

The Orioles salvaged one of four against Milwaukee and headed home to host Toronto for a critical three-game set. The O's offense had soured. For 15 consecutive games they had failed to score more than four runs. "It's a concern," moaned Oates. "The pitchers go out there thinking, 'If I give up but two or three runs, it could be too many.' " Fingers were pointed at Cal and Glenn Davis, who had combined for a pathetic three homers since August 14.

The series opener, on September 22, was memorable and disastrous for the Orioles and Cal senior. It featured a three-hour rain delay, an abortive O's rally, and at the end a crushing 4–3 Orioles loss. Down 4–2, the Orioles rallied for one in the eighth and in the ninth had the tying run, Tim Hulett, on third with one out.

Anderson hit a ball to Devon White in medium center. Coach Ripken held the runner back, preferring to rely on Devereaux, the O's most consistent hitter and run producer. He did not come through.

Senior's coaching decision was debated for several days. Not only had the O's failed to bring in the tying run in the ninth, but a tying run had also been thrown out at home on an eighth-inning ground ball. Manager Oates was obviously disappointed. "Ninety-nine percent of the time, I leave a game here when I go home," he said. "[September 22] was one of those that I didn't leave here. [The win] was there. . . . " Nevertheless, Oates did not question Ripken's call. "Senior had a tough decision. Put yourself in his position. . . . From where he was standing, White had a chance to throw [Hulett] out."

Senior was unequivocal in his own defense. "I'm looking right at the ball," he said. "You're not going to get the tying run thrown at the plate to end the game. The man is out at the plate if I send him. I guarantee it."

Cal junior later made a comment about the controversial coaching decision of September. "From an emotional standpoint," said Cal, "I guess it might be easy to think the pennant race came down to that play. It's easy to sit in the stands or sit someplace else and say so after the fact, but you have to look at the situation. I can look back at the whole season, and I can't find two decisions he made at third that were wrong."

The Orioles had been thinking sweep, but they now had lost the opener. The situation was desperate: six games out in third place, with 12 games left on their schedule (10 for the Jays).

Baltimore won one of three against Toronto. The O's slipped to six out with 10 games left. They never got closer to the top and never crept back into second place. For the record, they were eliminated from the race on Sunday, September 27, by losing 6–1 at Oriole Park to the Red Sox.

For Cal Ripken, Jr., hopefully the season's end was a foreshadowing of better times for 1993. He hit his 13th and 14th homers in a four-game series in Cleveland in October, to go along with six hits and seven RBIs. The RBIs were one more than he had had in all of September.

Was Oates previewing 1993? In the season finale on October 4, he pulled Cal out in the third inning to give playing experience to rookie Manny Alexander. Cal had never left earlier, except for two ejections, during his 1,734 consecutive-games streak. For those interested, Cal had played 15,658 innings out of a possible 15,783—99.2 percent.

Extensive analysis was unnecessary to show that Cal had had a subpar offensive season. His 72 RBIs were a career low. For the first time he failed to hit 20 or more homers. (He finished with

14.) His 44 extra-base hits were another career low. Among Orioles batters, Cal was only the fifth most prolific home run hitter and third leading RBI producer.

Cal made contact, but the bat was slow. In fact, he struck out only 50 times in 637 at bats. The American League's most productive shortstop, Travis Fryman (20 homers, 96 RBIs), struck out 144 times. Cal's low points eclipsed two offensive milestones: his 1,000th RBI, at Oakland on August 31; and his 268th and 269th homers in Milwaukee on June 23, placing him ahead of Brooks Robinson as the number one righty Orioles home run hitter.

Nor was the glove mediocre. He made only 12 errors in 744 total chances, a .984 fielding percentage, and won a second Gold Glove. He led the league in turning double plays (119), the sixth time he led the league in this category. He was tops in putouts (287), also for the sixth time.

14

THE BREAKUP OF THE RIPKENS

I've had a lot of problems," Cal Ripken said at the end of the 1992 season. "I wish I could explain them all away but I can't."

Cal was not the only Ripken who had experienced a tough campaign. Ripken senior was still the focus of criticism for the critical decision in Toronto not to send the potential tying runner home on a fly ball. And after hitting .230 with a mere 36 RBIs, Billy Ripken could not count on his own return in 1993.

Less than two weeks after the curtain had come down on the 1992 season, the Orioles had in effect put an end to Senior's 36-year association with the Orioles by removing him as third-base coach.

Second baseman Harold Reynolds, with Seattle since 1983, was signed as a free agent on December 1, 1992, a clear signal that Billy Ripken would not be back for another campaign.

The three Ripkens had been together for five and half seasons. Cal had played parts of 12 seasons with his dad as coach and manager. For the first time in his big-league career, Junior was the only Ripken in an Orioles uniform.

On Father's Day, 1992, Cal senior reflected about his baseball relationship with his sons, in an interview with David Ginsburg of the Associated Press:

"I don't even think about it. We just happen to be in the same business at the same place. Maybe years from now, when I'm reflecting upon things in my rocking chair, I'll smile about all this. But for now, they're just a second baseman and a shortstop on the ball club."

The *Baltimore Sun* reported that Senior would not be back as coach in 1993. Baltimore had offered him a newly created top-level position as coordinator of minor league field operations. Senior would serve as liaison between Oates and the O's six minor league teams, with the goal being the uniform teaching of fundamentals at every level.

Senior rejected the offer without comment. But after gathering his thoughts, he spoke several days later from his home in Aberdeen. "I read that I was retiring," he said, "but that's not necessarily fact. I never said anything about retiring.

"I didn't want to work anywhere else, but right now, I don't know what I'm going to do. I'm going to take my time and think about it. . . . I'm available for a Major League job somewhere. I'd be willing to sit down and talk to anybody."

Senior made it clear that working at the Major League level was the key to the future. "If somebody wants to talk about a job at the Major League level, I'll do it," he asserted. "Otherwise, I'll just wait and see what develops."

Rip had been Oates's first manager in professional baseball, and they had enjoyed a long, cordial relationship. In fact, Oates sought Rip's advice on becoming O's skipper in 1991. Oates came to the defense of his friend after the announcement of Rip's not being rehired.

In fact, GM Hemond said the matter "was an organizational decision," indicating that Oates had not asked for the move.

After Senior rejected the minor league post, Hemond said, "Obviously, we're disappointed. Otherwise, we wouldn't have offered him the job. We thought it would be a good position to utilize his abilities."

Hemond added in a prepared statement: "Cal Ripken, Sr., has played important roles in the many successes of the Orioles throughout his distinguished career in the organization.

"Players at all levels of development have benefited from his vast knowledge of the game and his teaching skills. We are all grateful for his many important contributions, and we wish him well in his future endeavors."

Behind the minor league offer and good wishes, there had been unhappiness over Rip's performance on the field and in the clubhouse. There was grumbling, notably from Oates, about the game the Orioles lost when the third-base coach didn't send in the potential tying run in the September 22 game against Toronto.

Senior addressed that game at the time of his dismissal. "I can't believe that had anything to do with [the release]," he said. "If you have any understanding of the game of baseball, you realize that a coach never wants a tying run thrown out at home plate. The ball wasn't hit that deep, and Tim Hulett is not a good runner. We had Mike Devereaux at the plate, and we had a chance to tie or even win the game. You don't take a high-risk chance at that point."

In March, Senior opened up to the *Sun*'s John Steadman and elaborated on his dismissal. He was summoned to a meeting with Hemond, Oates, and Frank Robinson. "Roland told me we have to move some people along [ostensibly to open opportunities for younger coaches]," said Senior. "He said he wanted me to coordinate the minor league camp and also I'd probably spend some time with the Major League club.

"I listened and asked him, 'Before you go flowering up that job, tell me why I'm not staying here.' He said again because 'we have to move some people along.' I asked him when he wanted an answer. He mentioned three or four days. I thought it out, reviewed it, and called back and told him I couldn't accept the proposal. They announced I retired."

As for his self-removal from the players, Cal senior vigorously refuted the charge. "That's wrong," he said. "The players never stopped coming to me asking for help. The biggest laugh I got was when I read in some newspapers that I sat in the back row of the bus to get away from everybody. Know why I sat there? So I could smoke cigarettes."

In a farewell tribute to Senior, *Sun* columnist Jim Henneman took note of the often-cited "cantankerous and stubborn nature" of Cal senior. And, true, the umpires and Rip had few kind words for each other. "He has a volatile side," said Henneman, "that can make Earl Weaver seem like an altar boy."

But give senior his due, said Henneman. He "worked harder at his job than anybody who has ever worn the uniform of the Baltimore Orioles.

"Nobody, not even Cal Ripken, Jr., whose dedication is a source of constant amazement to his peers, approaches his job with more diligence or tenacity."

According to Henneman's estimate, Senior threw about 25,000 pitches in batting practice every season and some 10,000 during spring training.

Farewell, concluded Henneman, "I'm going to miss the crusty old *$%&!—and I don't care if he likes it or not."

The Billy Ripken chapter was another matter. He was not included on their 15-man protected list for the November expansion draft by the Florida Marlins and the Colorado Rockies. For practical purposes Billy's days were over in Baltimore when the Birds acquired Harold Reynolds. Billy was "shocked" by the decision. While Billy had hit only .230 with 36 RBIs, he had made but four errors in 108 games and 538 chances for a .993 fielding percentage that tied for the league lead among second basemen; Reynolds made 12 errors in 677 chances for a .982 percentage. Moreover, in 1992, Reynolds had hit only .247 with three RBIs less than Billy had. However, Reynolds had a clear advantage in speed, averaging 32 stolen bases in his past seven years at Seattle.

Billy shared second during 1992 with Mark McLemore. Together they knocked in 63 runs. "That's a fair amount of production" from the number nine slot, said Billy. "We were not the reason we lost the pennant," Billy said, voicing his disappointment in not being tendered a 1993 Oriole contract.

While shocked by the developments, Billy was fully aware throughout his stay in Baltimore that he would come up short in comparison to his brother. Furthermore, his brother could not guarantee his tenure with the team. Billy told *Sports Illustrated* in 1990: "I hear 'em saying I'll never be as good as my brother. Sometimes I want to yell back at them, 'No s---.' They think I don't know that? They're telling the truth, so how can I get mad? Sure, I'd like to get in eight years or so. But I know my brother would never say, 'I want my brother here to play with me.' He wouldn't do that.

"We're two different people. On the field we're not brothers. We're teammates. My brother is a superstar. I just wanted to be a good professional baseball player."

There was no immediate reaction from Junior. He voiced his thoughts during an interview for the May 1993 *GQ* by Peter Richmond:

"It's disturbing. There's no understanding it. You try to explore all the reasons there could possibly be, and you come up with no reason. To a person of a certain intellect, it doesn't make sense all the way around.

"We've been raised in baseball. . . . We were raised to see it as a profession, not as a recreational sport, so certain things were expected. But as a baseball person—even from a marketing position—I don't understand it from any angle."

The Orioles, Cal agreed, had the "right" to let Billy go in favor of the better hitter, Reynolds. But baseballwise, Cal disagreed with their "logic." "I've played with a lot of second basemen," said Cal, "and Billy does things at second base that no one else does. . . . Historically, you build a team defensively up the middle."

Cynics and pragmatists suggested that the Orioles designed the strategy that Cal be signed before giving any clue that Dad and brother would later be discarded. To that thought, said Cal pensively, "If that were the case, that would be really sad. . . .

"I had to look at my contract from the standpoint of what was best for me and my immediate family. I refuse to believe that is what happened. If all those things were connected, I'd be pretty disgusted."

In the midst of the dismantling of the Ripkens in Baltimore, Cal was able to take professional solace from two postseason honors: a second Gold Glove and the Lou Gehrig Award.

"Of all my seasons in the big leagues, this was one of the most frustrating and difficult," Cal said at a Camden Yards news conference. "It makes me feel good to be recognized for something. When I look back on this year, this is a positive thing."

Cal became one of three shortstops in Orioles history to win more than one Gold Glove. The others are Mark Belanger and Luis Aparicio.

Cal said that he had always been able to separate his defense from his offense. "Some people, when their offense isn't going well, their defense suffers as well," said Cal. "With others, their defense rises to another level. I don't think either of those describe myself.

"I've always been able to separate offense and defense. When I'm out in the field, I don't want to think about striking out or that I hadn't been swinging the bat very well."

Despite taking home another Gold Glove, Cal put Belanger and Aparicio in a league of their own. The award is "a big pat on the back," said Cal. "But I don't go around saying I'm the very best. I think Mark Belanger and Luis Aparicio are the two greatest shortstops I've ever seen. I wouldn't put myself in the same category as those guys."

Cal's Gold Glove was presented to the shortstop at the Camden Yards November press conference by Michael Hirsch, a graduate of the Ripken Learning Center.

*   *   *

The start of the 1993 season was fresh, but the memories, the pain, and the questions were not new—they had begun with the dismissal of Cal senior. As Junior headed for Sarasota for his 13th season with Baltimore, the number did not suggest good fortune. "It's a little different," said Cal. "I don't know how to put my feelings into words. I'm used to having [my brother and father] here . . . It feels kind of odd, kind of strange. It hurts a little bit. I'm used to having my brother out there fielding ground balls, being social. In some ways, I felt lost out there."

Cal tried to inject some humor into the first day at Sarasota. When he was driven in a golf cart to meet reporters, he observed, "When you get older, that's what happens." Now that Billy was in Texas, Cal hoped to see him at some point in spring training. Cal senior had tried to give his son solace before he left Reiserstown. "The beauty of talking to my dad," he said, "is that he turns things around, and you end up feeling better than you did before you talked to him, even though you're trying to make him feel better. . . . He takes care of his son."

The new third-base coach was Mike Ferraro, whose managers in the early '70s at Rochester had included Cal senior. But at second, Cal would be working with a stranger. Cal came into Sarasota with Harold Reynolds. "We talked about general baseball things," said Cal. "The reality of the situation is I have to do my job as a baseball player. . . . I don't blame Harold Reynolds because my brother's gone. I enjoyed playing with my brother, but I have to be professional. Harold is the second baseman now."

Reynolds spoke briefly but confidently about the new relationship. "I'm sure it's strange for Cal," he said, "but I'm also sure he'll handle it. We'll do our best to work together."

Perhaps Cal handled it well, but in June he admitted missing his brother. Cal responded to a *Baseball Weekly* question submitted by Casey March, 11, of York, Pennsylvania: "I was sad and I'm still a little upset. Since shortstops and second basemen have to communicate a lot with each other, it was a great advantage having my brother there. I miss him personally, and I miss him professionally."

After the first day of full-squad workouts at Twin Lakes Park on February 26, the loneliness was more pronounced. "You grow up wanting to be a pro ballplayer, and you make it," said Cal. "Your dad is a coach, and it's against the odds that you're going to end up on the same team. Then your brother comes up, and the odds are against him making the Major Leagues. I feel like we beat the odds.

"It was kind of nice because baseball was something that separated us as a family. My dad was away a lot when I was a kid. Then it brought us back together, and my dad was there if I needed him, and my brother was there. It's still a positive, but there's some hurt that goes with it."

Cal senior told the *Aegis* in February 1993 that he had no job offers, primarily because the Orioles had classified him as "retired." And he'd be "the only one who'll decide when I'm retired."

At this point, Senior felt he could work for anyone, George Steinbrenner included. "I once thought I could never work for him. Now, I feel, hey, if you work for him and you're fired, you walk off with a lot of money."

Manager Oates was ready to confront and try to help Cal deal with his loneliness. "He and I talked at length," Oates said. "It's going to be different. He's probably going to be a little lonely. If I know Junior, the first few days are going to be rough, but he's a professional. I don't expect him to be clicking his heels about it, but I don't expect him to do anything different."

Cal went 1 for 2 in a 4-0 loss to the Cardinals at St. Petersburg on March 7. He had four hits in his first six exhibition-game at bats. He was starting to look like the old Cal junior. "I'm comfortable at the plate right now," he said. "I don't know what that means. I had a good spring last year, and it didn't do me too much good. You can be in a good groove at the plate, and then be in a bad groove all of a sudden. I'm not taking anything for granted. I just hope this keeps up, the way it did two years ago."

Cal was encouraged by Oates's plan to continue Cal as his everyday—literally—shortstop. At the end of 1992 the skipper had hinted that perhaps Cal would be an occasional designated hitter. While Oates wanted to give Cal some bench time, e.g., at the late stages of some games, the DH was out. "If he stays healthy," promised the manager, "Cal's going to start 162 games at shortstop this year. In the past, I've only taken Cal out of games when we were behind big. That might change a little bit. I'll look for some opportunities to get him a few innings off when it'll help, like before a day off, so he'll almost have two days off."

Oates elaborated on his plans for Cal. "How much rest Cal gets this year will be in direct proportion to how we play," said the manager. "For him to get rest, we'll have to play very poorly, or very well. If we're close all the time, he might not get too much rest."

Also factored in were Cal's potential replacements: utility infielders Mark McLemore, Tim Hulett, and Steve Scarsone. The Orioles' top shortstop prospect, Manny Alexander, needed more farm seasoning.

In 1992, Cal exited nine times; there were 16 early leaves in 1991; and he rested 11 times in 1990. If, as suggested by Oates, Cal were removed when the O's were trailing by five or more in the seventh inning or later, that would have meant 13 departures in 1992. If applied to large leads, that could mean 20 removals.

Cal inserted his own thoughts about playing in 1993. "I'm going to play the year, to a certain extent, with some nagging injuries. I don't like to mention them. I don't like people to think there is an excuse for everything. The fact is, you can't go a whole season without something, so I prefer just to go out there and play the best I can like I always have."

The Cal Ripken, Jr., contract was a recurrent theme during the spring. Discussions were fueled by the skyrocketing free agent signings and by the chapter in Feinstein's book. While Ripken's deal seemed monstrous in August, it seemed humble when Bobby Bonds signed a $43.5 million deal with San Francisco. Joe Carter matched Cal's $6.5 million average in a three-year package with Toronto.

Bonds's signing didn't upset Cal, but he did express regret about the negotiations process. "My only regret," said Cal, "is that I didn't handle my contract situation better. I regret not saying [to Baltimore]: 'No offense, but we either do it in spring training or we do it in October.' "

The Feinstein narrative of the contract process was written with the help of Shapiro's notes, so not all nuances are presented in the author's pages. Lucchino now insisted that the first offer was not $10 million for two years but $20 million for four years. Moreover, media reports claimed Shapiro's first move was not for $39 million but for $50 million.

Feinstein's narrative is sympathetic to Shapiro-Ripken and clearly stresses the unusual approach of Lucchino in going directly to Cal. "It can be important to talk to the player directly," Lucchino defended his modus operandi. "There is an opportunity for misunderstanding if you always go through a third party. We wanted to make sure there was no misunderstanding. We've done it before, and we'll do it again."

What price the extended negotiations? "Who knows?" said Lucchino. "He didn't have a Cal Ripken season. These guys are human beings, but they're also professional athletes. There is a stress and strain with contracts that does occur. If you ask me what would have been if he had signed right before opening day—which was everyone's goal—I can't answer that."

Cal always spoke of separating the business end from the baseball end. Having put the contract process behind him, Cal was eager as could be to begin season 13. "In a small way," said Cal, "I was relieved" when 1992 ended. ". . . It's always good to clean the slate and start over again this year. You can't change what happened last year. You can only work to make this year come out as good as possible. I'm looking forward to this year. I've readied myself, and I'm in good shape. Best of all, I've eliminated a lot of the doubts associated with last year."

*   *   *

For the first time in more than 15 years, Cal senior was not at opening day; neither was Vi. To accentuate the Orioles' dismantling of the Ripkens, opening day at Camden Yards featured Cal and Billy wearing different uniforms: Cal's Orioles versus Billy's Texas Rangers.

"I think it would have been rough on Senior, coming to the park," said Billy. "And it would have been rough on Mom, too." The Ripkens were probably at home rooting for Texas, said the flippant Billy, "wearing hats with *T*'s on them in the living room."

Texan George Bush had been replaced on the ceremonial pitching lines by rookie president Bill Clinton. President Bush had brought five wins and only two losses during his visits to Baltimore. Clinton did not do as well. The O's had a one-run lead in the bottom of the first, but Texas scored five in the third en route to a 7–4 win.

The severing of the Ripken family baseball ties was sharp and dramatic at opening day. The brothers chatted briefly the night before by phone. "Did you go to the park together?" a reporter asked. "Stop it," Billy snapped. "We live in different directions."

After pregame introductions, Cal was talking between the foul lines with Billy. Neither would reveal what was said. "That was brother stuff," said Billy. "You're not getting that on tape."

Veteran Harold Baines (241 career homers as the 1993 season began) came to Baltimore via Oakland after the '92 season. He was born, raised, and still lives in St. Michael's, Maryland. Neither Baines nor Cal received the loudest ovation. It was the returning Billy who received the loudest ovation. Both Billy and Cal were appreciative. "It was nice, real nice," said Billy. "It made me feel good, made me feel like the people liked the way I played here.

"I didn't know what to expect. I always felt the people genuinely liked me here—I just don't know how much. I was surprised [the applause] was that loud and that long. They really sustained it and I appreciated it very much."

No stranger to standing ovations, Cal was delighted, too. "I think it was an indication of their appreciation for the kind of player Billy is," said Cal. "He's the kind of player who's going to give you everything he's got all the time. It made me feel good, and I'm sure it made him feel good."

But the Baltimore chapter was closed, according to Billy. "I had a lot of good experience here. But that chapter of my life is gone. When you get released, you're not wanted. Now that I'm here with the Rangers and playing, it shows that somebody likes me, and that makes me feel good."

In practical terms, Billy Ripken at bat was a new experience for Cal, who had to determine how to position himself. "I've never played against him before, so I've got to evaluate him [defensively] just like any other player. That's what I was thinking [when Billy was at bat]. It wasn't like I was out there saying, 'Come on, Billy, get a hit.' "

Billy, like Cal, had to focus on the game when the first pitch was thrown. "I'm sure there's going to be times when I'm going to look over there and expect to see him," said Billy. "But right now, I've got other things to do."

What Billy and Cal hoped to do was to contribute so that their teams could begin 1993 on a winning note. In their first nine games, however, the Birds were 3–6 and in sixth place. Cal hit his first homer on April 16, in a 4–1 home win over California. Cal was hitting .282 but with a mere 3 RBIs. But at this point he had to be pleased; his average was up. And on April 18 he had the game winner against California when his 60-foot dribbler up the third-base line in the eighth was the 4–3 decider.

But the O's continued to lose. On April 24 they snapped a three-game slide with a 6–5 win at Kansas City, as Cal doubled home the tying run and Glenn Davis delivered the winning single in the eighth. The formula was welcome because the 3-4-5 hitters, Ripken, Baines, and Davis, had been in a combined 9-for-63 slump. Cal drove in four with a three-run homer and a single to lead the O's past Minnesota at Camden Yards on April 28, but the home team still remained last, 6–13 and seven out.

But manager Oates saw good things coming, in particular for Cal. "Junior's having a lot of good at bats right now," said the manager before the Birds lost on May 12 at home to Boston, 2–0. "I think he's swinging really well right now. He's going to all fields, hitting to right field a lot. I don't know how Junior hit before I got here [as a coach in 1989]. But since I've been here, when he's been hot, he's hit line drives to right field and left field. The last few days, he's hit everywhere from the right-field foul line to the left-field foul line."

Cal had a pathetic 22 for 111, a .198 average; but then he went on a six-game hitting streak, going 8 for 23, to elevate his batting mark to .246. In past hitting droughts, he had turned to his dad and to Frank Robinson, when he was the O's manager. Now he sought the counsel of O's batting instructor Greg Biagini. On consecutive afternoons in Toronto, Cal was on hand for early batting practice. "Two days in a row, that's unusual for him," said Biagini. "I don't think Cal's swinging that badly right now. He's hit some balls lately. I think he'll be fine."

But Cal was not doing well. The evaluations of Oates and Biagini notwithstanding, Cal had hit under .200 through May 23, since beginning the season 9 for 18.

To break out of his funk, Cal resorted to changing his batting stance, taking batting instruction, and rearranging his travel habits. When Baltimore played Milwaukee on May 22, Cal was only at .215 with two homers and 15 RBIs. In that game, he discarded his crouch at the plate and started standing straight up. "I used to hit that way all the time," he said. Standing straight up, Cal hit two homers in his first three games. "It's probably something that won't last," he said of the changed stance, "but it hasn't felt bad, and I've been swinging the bat good. I can get the bat through faster. Maybe I'll find the stance again, but in the meantime, I was frustrated, and I tried to do something."

One of these homers came at Yankee Stadium on May 24. His deep blast over the left-center fence in the seventh was decisive in the O's 8–6 win. *New York Times* writer Jack Curry was surprised. "When was the last time anyone saw Cal Ripken, Jr., hit a home run away from Baltimore?" Curry asked. Actually, it was his first road homer since October 3; however, until 1993, Cal had 137 homers on the road and 136 at home.

While Cal had only one blast in New York, he drove balls into the far reaches of the stadium that might have been homers elsewhere. Biagini applauded. "I don't think his skills are in decline," he said. "He's getting the bat head out all the time, and he's starting to drive the ball. Baseball is a game of adjustment and readjustment. Being able to adjust is the key to having success year after year."

Yankee Don Mattingly and Cal Ripken, Jr., came up together to the bigs in the early '80s, were fellow All-Stars, and had always appreciated each other's talents. "I watched Cal, and I thought he looked great," said the Yankees first baseman. "The ball jumped off his bat. I sat on the bench, and I told someone, 'He's having some good swings. [The new stance] looks good, to tell you the truth.'

"I've seen Cal change his stance over the years. He works in the cage at home all winter and comes to spring training every year with a different setup. I'm sure he'll continue to make changes to be successful. You know that a player of his caliber is not going to be happy batting .215 or .220."

Former roommate Rick Dempsey commented on Cal's batting stances. "When it comes to hitting, Cal and I shared little. But one thing I shared with Cal is changing batting stances. However, I changed my stance more than Cal has."

Not satisfied with a change in stance, Cal went into the batting cage on May 29 at Anaheim Stadium with Frank Robinson. Robinson was willing to help while recognizing that Cal felt sometimes more advice is worse than no advice. "Cal feels—like most good hitters—that he knows himself better than anyone else," said the Hall of Famer. "Sometimes, the more outside advice you take, the worse off you're going to be. He will try to figure things out himself first, then start listening to people. When he does look for help, he looks to people that know him the best.

"That's why he always went to his dad. He talks to me for a couple of reasons—because he knows I have done it, and because I'm one of the few people here who have known him for a long time."

The new stance and the instruction did provide results. He had a double and a home run in a 3-for-4 game against California on May 30.

Cal's improved performance was noticeable. At the end of June, Oates, Biagini, and Robinson put some finishing touches on the new stance: from crouch to upright, along with adjustments of the feet and bat. "We're just trying to get him to settle in," said Biagini. "He's trying to get comfortable, and I think he's done it. The biggest thing is that he's more upright. The other things are just minor adjustments."

Cal started perking up: 10 RBIs in the last 12 games; 4 home runs and 16 RBIs in 18 games; on base in 12 straight games. With all that, Cal's batting average reached .211 in the past 73 games, and .228 for the season.

While Cal struggled at the plate and was changing stances, a more troubling development surrounded the Baltimore icon.

AN ORIOLE WHO HAS TRULY FLOWN THE COOP, said the headline of a *Los Angeles Times* story by Gene Wojciechowski. The story dealt with Cal's removal from the team through separate transportation and separate accommodations. "You remember the knock on the Boston Red Sox: 25 players, 25 cabs," said the *Times* columnist. "Now comes the news that Iron Man Cal Ripken, Jr., . . . who lately has been swinging an iron bat, has been a little bit on the aloof side."

Instead of riding on the team bus, Cal was being picked up at the airport in limousines, and in certain cities he was staying in a hotel different from the team's. "What's next?" wondered the reporter. "A request for his own dressing room?"

Michael Kaye and John Sterling told New York fans of Cal's

doings on the May 24 broadcast. "He's separating himself from the team," an unsatisfied Kaye said.

The travel and lodging arrangements had been going on for some time, Ripken told the Baltimore media. "To be honest with you," he said, "I think it's something I have the right not to talk about. But since others have taken it upon themselves to make certain inferences, maybe it's better if I do. Sometimes, you feel if you don't say anything it'll just blow over—but maybe it won't.

"Nobody has come to me before and asked me about it. If they had, I would have explained that it was strictly a matter of security and privacy."

Removing himself from teammates was an "overblown" issue, Cal said. The other Orioles always knew where to find him. "And the limos are nothing more than a means of transportation—you can't get a car onto an airport runway.

"I think some people have the mind-set that this is like a Pony League team that is chaperoned while traveling. I don't think they understand what it's like. . . . But we don't have team meals or meetings at the hotel—the time we spend together is at the ballpark or when we go out after a game. And that doesn't change one single bit."

In addition to team separation, Cal sought refuge in the players' lounge or trainer's room. He also gave himself cover through Tufton, his own public relations firm.

When Cal senior cleaned out his locker in Camden Yards after his dismissal following the 1992 season, Junior took over the spot. Its proximity to the almost private exit proved valuable in getting the shortstop in and out during the trying days.

Cal said that he was being stalked by fans and professional collectors, so he had to make it most difficult to be found. "There have been instances," he said, "of people hanging out on the [hotel] floor, hiding behind soda machines, knocking on your door. . . . Even when you use an alias, they still seem to find out where you are.

"I don't like to go through that, especially when my family

travels with me, which is often. I don't know what others do, but this is the way I choose to handle it—by trying to avoid it as much as possible."

According to Cal, he was being hunted because of his pursuit of Gehrig's iron man streak. "I've always looked on myself as an unselfish, noncontroversial player whose only goal has been to work hard and play every day. I find it amazing that the Streak has evoked so many strong opinions and so much controversy. . . .

"The Streak seems to have become my own identity, and I have to deal with it in every city. The longer it goes and the bigger it becomes, the more it's an issue of management for me.

"I mean, I have only so much concentration. I can't use up 75 percent before I get to the ballpark. I have to protect a certain amount of my privacy. I owe it to the club and myself. . . . "

Neither manager Oates nor the front office was willing to change matters. "That's something negotiated between Cal and the club," said Oates. "It doesn't affect me at all." While not spelled out in the contract, the road arrangements were left to the discretion of Cal. But the agreement was not intended to be permanent, according to Lucchino. "We're aware of it, and it is my understanding," he said, "that it is a temporary situation because of the special burden on Cal when he's on the road."

Cal's situation was different from other Orioles players, according to GM Hemond, "and the other players recognize that. He's not out gallivanting or flaunting the freedom. He's using the privacy to prepare for the game."

Hemond praised Junior. "The only time you hear any criticism about Cal," said Hemond, "is when he's not hitting. It's absurd. His statistics aren't the only measure of what he means to the club."

The Orioles were worried that all the attention on Cal might affect his on-field performance. Everyone on the Orioles hoped that the fielding woes were only brief. Playing in Oakland on June 1, Cal let a grounder go between his legs, leading to a 4–1 Athletics victory. He made another error in that game when his one-hop throw to first could not be caught by David Segui. He made his third error the next day when he couldn't handle a sharply hit grounder. He had now made seven errors in 1993, which was on pace for a 22-error season. He had not made that many since 1985, when he had 26 miscues. Not only was Cal making errors, but after a 1-for-3 day, he was hitting .218. Oates justified the continual playing of Cal because of his fielding. "He's human," said an understanding manager. "It happens. Sometimes we take him for granted because he's so steady. He makes the plays so routinely. That second error [the throw on June 1], a lot of short-stops don't even try to make that throw. You try to make that throw, from short left field. Sometimes, it's not that easy."

The errors and the anemic batting average brought criticism from the baseball world. Was it proper for Cal to play every day when his hitting was off and his fielding had some lapses? San Francisco hitting coach Bobby Bonds watched his son take a day off despite his mighty hitting for the Giants. That gave Bonds senior a chance to attack Cal for refusing to sit.

"That's idiotic," he said. "If I were his manager, he'd be out of there. He's hurting the team and showing that personal goals are more important. He wants to break Lou Gehrig's record even if it'll cost Baltimore the pennant."

It was stinging criticism from one of the game's best hitters in the recent past. Cal responded tactfully. "Everyone is entitled to their opinion," he said. "That doesn't mean it's fact. It's not a one-man game. It's a team sport. In '91 I couldn't have done any more than I did and we finished fifth or sixth. If I was the key to this team winning the pennant, we'd have won it in '91."

It takes one coach to answer another one. O's coach Davey Lopes, who had a 16-year career primarily with the Dodgers, told Bonds and others to mind their own business. Only Cal can know about the Streak's adversity. Said Lopes, "One day off isn't going to make any difference to Cal physically. Only he can answer the question of whether the strain of the Streak is wearing him down. People like [TV broadcaster] Tim McCarver and Bobby Bonds are saying things about Cal being selfish. To hell with those guys. They're not part of this organization.

"Cal doesn't need outside people telling him what to do. He's a man. He'll know. It's a tough situation. . . . "

Amid the tumult of 1993, the Streak almost came to an end involuntarily. In fact, Cal was nearly convinced that June 6 would be the end. A Sunday brawl at Camden Yards in the match versus Seattle nearly put Cal out of action. During the 20-minute bench-clearing beanball battle, a horde of Mariners knocked over Cal and Leo Gomez, who were seeking to protect Baltimore hurler Mike Mussina.

Cal heard something pop in his right knee. "Nothing like that ever happened to me. Basically, I never had an injury." Cal told his wife Kelly that he wouldn't be able to play on Monday night. The joint was swollen, and he couldn't walk. "All day, I assumed I wouldn't play that night," recounted Cal.

"Couldn't you play one inning?" pleaded Kelly.

"No," said Cal.

Cal turned down her suggestion that he at least pinch-hit.

"But the Streak will be broken," said Kelly.

"Yes," said Cal, a bit unhappily.

"I thought that's [the Streak] what you wanted," said his wife.

"You, too?" he said.

In storybook fashion, the knee came around after all-day ice treatments. "People automatically believe," said Cal, "that the Streak has become me. Even the person closest to me in the whole world. . . . I'm here simply to play. However things work out is fine. The Streak just happened. I didn't ask for it."

The O's were on what turned into a 10-game winning streak, and Cal wanted to help even if he was hitting .218. Once the June 7 game was under way, said Cal, the knee "loosened up much better than I thought it would."

Cal was 1 for 2 with one RBI in the O's 3–2 triumph. He also waited out two walks. If Cal needed any proof that the injury was not serious, he got it in the ninth frame when the leadoff batter shot one to the hole. "When I planted and threw off my bad leg and nothing gave way, I figured it wasn't a serious injury. . . . I felt miraculously good. I must be a quick healer."

For the second time in four games, Cal flirted with a threat to the Streak. Cal was certainly fortunate that he was still intact after a June 9 battle against Oakland. Convinced that he had been thrown at in the first inning, A's catcher Terry Steinbach directed Bob Welch to throw hard and inside to Cal. After McLemore singled in the bottom of the first, Cal was knocked down by an 0–2 Bob Welch pitch. Cal threw up his hand, and the ball hit his left wrist and went off his jaw.

Two Orioles had already endured serious injuries through similar pitches. Catcher Chris Hoiles had his wrist broken in 1992; Glenn Davis had his jaw broken that same week in '92. But the O's and Cal had a scare and no more.

Cal showed his toughness during that first inning. Devereaux singled home McLemore, but Cal was tagged out in a full-speed forearm-to-the-jaw crushing collision at home plate. Cal jogged to the dugout as the A's catcher knelt for several minutes and then went to the dugout. Cold towels were applied to Steinbach's head. Steinbach left the game with a headache and dizziness. Cal had thus taken Steinbach out of the game with his crushing slide and had paid back the villain.

The collision also gave O's broadcaster Jon Miller the perfect answer for critics such as Bobby Bonds, who said that all that mattered to Cal was streak preservation.

Having twisted his knee during the Seattle brawl, Cal should have been cautious sliding home. "He looked like he wanted to hit [Steinbach]," said Miller. "He knocked him out of the game."

Miller added, "I'm amazed at the things that get attributed to Cal about the Streak, like the thing with Bobby Bonds. Every time there has been a brawl or near brawl, Cal has been one of the first guys out there. If the Streak is so important to him, what's he doing out there?"

The continued focus on Cal did not divert Baltimore fans from realizing that their Orioles had been playing well and promised to be in the hunt for the pennant. While Cal's offense was not consistent, he was still a valuable contributor with his bat.

When the Orioles beat Oakland 7–4 on June 9, it was the first time since 1980 that they had gone 6–0 on a home stand. On June 11 the Birds won their ninth straight, trouncing Boston at Fenway Park, 16–4. It was the first time that Baltimore (30–30) had been at .500 since opening day and their longest winning streak since an 11-game streak in 1987.

Cal went 3 for 5, including a three-run homer, his sixth, and an RBI double. Cal sparked a six-run fourth by slamming Jose Melendez's 1–1 offering into the left-field screen. "It was a slider that stayed over the plate," said Cal. "I hit it okay, but it might have been a Fenway homer. But I'll take it. I'll take anything at this point. . . . It's nice to get a few hits and knock in a few runs. It's been pretty much a struggle most of the year, so it's nice to get a few hits."

Both manager and hitting coach were quite pleased with Cal's Fenway performance. "Cal's going to get hits for you," said Oates. "That's why he's out there every day. There are going to be some days when he might not get some hits, but when you need the big hit, he gets it."

On June 18 in Cleveland, Indians manager Mike Hargrove opted to pitch around McLemore, who was hitting .294, and pitch to Cal, whose average was .214. The score was 1–1 in the seventh. The strategy backfired as Cal, 0 for 3 against Jose Mesa and in a 1-for-19 skid, slammed a 365-foot homer down the left-field line to give the Birds a 4–1 win.

It was not unique, according to Cal. "It's not the first time they've walked somebody intentionally to get at me," he said, "but it's been a little while.

"I wasn't insulted by any means. Mesa's had my number pretty good, and I haven't been going good."

Hargrove did not second guess himself. "When you got one

guy batting .294 and the other hitting .214, you have to do it," he said. "We got him out three times before.

"If I had to do it again, I'd do the same thing. McLemore's been swinging the bat well. Everything screamed for McLemore to be walked. . . . I don't care if the batter was Superman. You have to pitch to him in that situation."

A 6–3 win in Cleveland on June 20 gave the O's their sixth straight series. They had not done as well since 1986, when they won seven series. They were still eight out of first, but their level of play was markedly better. This was evident in their next series, at Camden Yards, when they swept league-leading Detroit.

Cal showed in a 6–2 win on June 24 that even in a slump he could still be a creative hitter. Cal had the decisive hit in the three-run first. With Mark McLemore on first, the Tigers guessed right on a hit-and-run play and called for a pitchout. But Mark Leiter did not throw the ball far enough out of the strike zone. Cal, despite having his bat tipped by catcher Chad Kreuter, deftly got his bat on the ball and sent a single to right field.

Cal's skills and craftiness notwithstanding, striking weaknesses were visible in Cal's offense. After drawing an 0-for-5 collar July 6 in an 8–0 O's win in Kansas City, Cal was at .215, the lowest he had been in his Major League career so late in the season.

In his slump, Cal did not have his onetime support system. "It wouldn't be far-fetched to say that when you look for your teammates and certain people for support when you're not going well, I've always had it in house," said Cal. To an extent Cal admitted he was envious of Ken Griffey, Jr., having his dad on the Seattle staff.

"I could see Dad and Billy, get a few things off my chest, and go on with the day. They had my best interests at heart. We all looked to each other for support."

His average was down, but on July 10, the Camden Yards folk saw Junior reach another milestone. A single up the middle off Wilson Alvarez was his 2,000th career hit—the 14th active player and 191st in history to reach that circle. To celebrate, Cal added another hit, an RBI, as part of a 6–0 gem by Fernando Valenzuela over the Chisox.

With less than a week to the All-Star Game, Cal—and others—reflected on his 1993 performance. *Baseball Weekly* was not ready to give Cal a spot on its All-Star roster. "The big show is in Baltimore, but Cal Ripken won't be on this squad." The choice was the Mariners' Omar Vizquel. "Averaging .275-plus, he won't kill us with the bat."

Cal was the fans' choice but not that of the managers. An Associated Press survey of Major League managers relegated Cal to the bench, along with other fan selections: Kirby Puckett, Wade Boggs, Gary Sheffield, and Ivan Rodriguez. Omar Vizquel and Travis Fryman were tied for Cal's spot. Cal had only one vote.

But *voting* fans decide the starting lineup. Cal had nearly 2,100,000 ballots cast for him, compared with less than 850,000 for the Tigers' Travis Fryman, who was hitting more than 60 points higher than Cal was.

At the All-Star break, Cal pushed himself up to .229; still, he had the lowest batting average among regular AL shortstops. However, he had more homers than any other AL shortstop. Only Fryman's 55 RBIs topped Cal's 45. When Fryman was in Baltimore in late June, he took a diplomatic approach. It was the fans' game, he observed, and the fans wanted to see Cal Ripken, Jr.

It was Cal's 11th appearance and 10th consecutive start, equaling Ozzie Smith's Major League record for shortstops. But Cal was not satisfied with his own play and even thought of not playing. "Professionally, it's a little embarrassing to me," he said, referring to his batting average. "I'd like to do something to feel I deserve to be here. Overall, it's been a frustrating first half, a disappointing one.

"I thought about not playing. Yeah, I thought about it, but you feel a sense of responsibility and obligation to the fans. . . . It's not an easy decision no matter what you do. I've wrestled with it."

The last time Baltimore hosted the All-Star Game, at Memorial Stadium, was in 1958, two years before Cal was born. His memories of watching the stars perform was in cities where Senior managed. "That night we'd have a barbecue and watch the game," Cal recalled. "It was special because it was a chance to see all the great players in one game."

Cal's mind-set changed as the game approached. "Being the starter makes me feel very good," he said, "because I haven't felt really good about myself this year. I had a bad start. Maybe I was trying too hard to make the All-Star Game because it was at home."

What Cal will treasure from the 63rd All-Star Game is a standing ovation of 20 seconds from the hometown gathering. Whenever PA announcer Rex Barney mentioned Cal's name, the fans howled their approval.

During six uneventful innings, Cal grounded to short in the first inning against Terry Mulholland, struck out in the fourth against Andy Benes, and grounded to third with two on against Steve Avery.

Nevertheless, Cal could only be pleased. He told TV commentator Jim Kaat after leaving the game that the thunderous ovation was "the greatest moment in my career."

Speaking of the All-Star Game love affair between Cal and the Camden Yards partisans, Morris Siegel of the *Washington Times* wrote, "When Baltimoreans fall in love, they fall in love for keeps and don't hide their enthusiastic admiration. They remember the good times with Rip."

The Orioles family—fans and other supporters—hoped that resumption of play after the All-Star Game would be the start of a new, super drive by the Orioles, sparked by Cal's resurgent bat. The Orioles did not succeed in their pennant drive. However, Cal fared well on two fronts. His batting improved significantly, but most important, Cal and all the Ripkens were blessed with the birth of Ryan Calvin Ripken on July 26.

To add to the joy of Cal and Kelly's second child, Cal was at his wife's side without compromising the Streak or ending it. Ryan's birthday was an off day for the Orioles. Cal celebrated the birth by clobbering a three-run homer the next day against the Blue Jays at the Skydome. Unfortunately, the Birds' bullpen gave the game away.

Before Cal's first child was born, Kelly and Cal decided that Rachel would be the name for a girl, Cal III for a boy. But that was nearly four years before. "I was very proud to have my dad's name," Cal told Erik Brady of *USA Today*. "But the name is so famous now, it's a different situation. It would be unfair to give a child that name. A kid should have his own identity from the beginning. There should never be any pressure to do what I do."

Growing up, Cal had the treasured experience of a close parent-child relationship with his dad, even if Senior was on the road so frequently. Now that he was a parent, Junior had another view of life. "Being a father, your perspective changes. You see things you never saw before. The most important thing in my life now is raising my kids in a normal atmosphere. That's almost impossible, but you fight to make it as normal as you can. . . ."

In its "Second Half AL Preview," *Baseball Weekly* prognosticated, "Don't be surprised if Cal Ripken gets hot."

They were right. Cal was hitting .215 on July 6; after that date he hit over .300, with 14 homers and 46 RBIs. He never went hitless in two consecutive games.

Jokingly, Cal said he felt "good" by going hitless in the All-Star Game. "I'm glad I didn't waste any hits in the All-Star Game," he said. "I've saved them for tonight, when it counts." Tonight was July 15, at home against Minnesota. Cal had two hits, featuring his 13th home run. The Orioles won 5–3 and climbed into a second-place tie with Detroit, only one and a half games behind the front-running Toronto Blue Jays. "I'm starting to regain my confidence. The changes I've made allowed me to have more reaction time up there. I am focusing on using my hands more. . . . When you get more hits, you feel more comfortable. If you're tense, you can't adjust in the same amount of time."

In the next six games, Cal raised his average from .215 to .232. As of July 19, he was on a 23-homer and 86-RBI pace, which approximated his career averages of 25 homers and 92 RBIs.

"The last game in Kansas City last week [July 21]," said Cal, "I found something in my swing, something that I think is helping me. I feel much better at the plate right now."

Orioles batting coach Greg Biagini was highly impressed. "His body is much quieter. His upper body is more upright, and his hands are now protecting the inside part of the plate. It's a combination of all these little changes."

The Orioles thrived, too. They took six of their first eight post-All-Star games and briefly enjoyed first place.

As improved as was Cal's bat performance, critics, nevertheless, argued that Cal needed a rest. They bolstered their point with the July 28 game at Toronto. In the battle for first, Cal bobbled a grounder by Tony Fernandez to enable Toronto to run off with a 5–4 ten-inning victory. It was his 12th miscue of the season, matching his 1992 total. Cal was also hitless in this critical game, and his batting average was down to .229.

Cal was not deterred. He had the 12th two-homer game of his career, on August 7, as the Birds beat Cleveland 8–6 at Camden Yards. Cal had 18 home runs and was on a pace to hit 26 homers and drive in 98.

Cal began the Orioles' next road trip, against Texas, by continuing to demolish their pitching with his 21st and 22nd homers. However, the Orioles still lost 5–4.

Cal finished August at .252; on May 28, he was hitting a puny .199. He was ready for September with a projected 28-homer, 99-RBI season, which exceeded his career average.

Cal Ripken, Jr., had impressed Frank Robinson and Johnny Oates. "His confidence level is up," said Robinson. "You can see it when he goes to the plate and in his approach to hitting. You get the impression that when he goes up to the plate he has the feeling that he's better than the pitcher. And that comes from having some success."

Manager Oates agreed: "I just think he's more relaxed. That only happens when you're having some success."

Fortunately, Cal Ripken's hitting was not the only story in Camden Yards. The Birds kept the pressure on the Blue Jays by blasting the A's at Oakland on September 12, 14–5. Cal led the O's to their 11th victory in 13 games, with four RBIs, including home run number 24. The Orioles were in second, a game and a half back.

However, that's as close as the Orioles would get. They had an especially disastrous road trip in mid-September that took them to Boston, Milwaukee, and Cleveland. The Orioles blew two leads late in the game in Boston, and after dropping a tough 6–4 decision at Cleveland, they found themselves five and a half games out.

The trip was particularly difficult for Cal, who had now played more than 1,880 consecutive games. In the first three games at Boston, he was hit by a pitch, crashed into the Red Sox catcher, and nearly dislocated his left shoulder in making a circus catch. In Cleveland, a sharp one-hopper hit an uneven spot on Cleveland turf and almost took his head off.

In the Fenway Park opener on September 13, Cal ranged far behind second base to rob Scott Fletcher with the bases loaded. "I felt a twinge in my left shoulder," said Cal after the catch. "I just stretched it out a little bit. It gave my shoulder a little twang. It doesn't affect anything else."

The next night, Danny Darwin hit him in the upper left arm. But the most threatening incident of the series was in the series finale, when Cal crashed into Red Sox catcher and former teammate Bob Melvin. Cal left the scene unharmed, while the backstop needed three stitches to close a gash above his eye.

Cal compared the Melvin collision to the collision with Steinbach earlier in the year. "With Steinbach, that was my only recourse," he said. "I don't think there is a textbook way to do it. Randy Milligan ran into Ron Hassey in Oakland [in 1991], and he was out for two months. There are all kinds of things that can happen."

Since the Streak began, from 1982 through the end of the 1993 season, there have been more than 13,000 entries on the Major League's disabled lists.

How has Cal been able to stay healthy? "He has been fortunate to avoid injury," said manager Oates, "but he doesn't avoid injury. He's banged up like everybody else. He plays with pain, and he plays well with pain." According to teammate Tim Hulett, "I think it's phenomenal that he has never had an injury that put him out. Obviously, his pain threshold is higher than the rest of us, and he plays with things others wouldn't. I think some of it is the way he plays the game."

"I suppose there is a luck component in everything," Cal said. "I have always said that I've been lucky to avoid serious injury this long."

Cal has long maintained that he does not shy away from potentially injurious situations. "I try not to think about that," he said. "If you play hard and concentrate all the time, that insulates you and protects you. When you're focused, you know there's a chance somebody is going to run into you at second base and you're prepared for that. You don't take for granted that you are going to stand up at any base, so you never have to slide at the last minute. When you're not paying attention, that's when you can be caught off guard."

The unexpected certainly happened on September 21 at Cleveland. Call it a bad bounce, a bad hop, or simply a bad break, but Cal and the Birds were victimized. Randy Milligan hit a ball over Cal's right shoulder for a two-run single to climax a four-run fifth that put the Tribe ahead for good. Cleveland manager Mike Hargrove was sympathetic about Cal's misfortune. "The ball Milligan hit almost took Cal's head off," he said. "You can't cuss it; you just know it's one of the hazards of sharing the field with a football team."

The end came soon for Baltimore. They lost two at home on September 26 to the Tigers and were mathematically eliminated from the race. Said a realistic and accepting Cal, "Once it's over, you reassess your goals. We've had a strong season and now we want to finish as well as we can."

Once more, the Orioles finished as also-rans, tied with Detroit for third place. Cal closed out his 11th straight season, 1,897 games, without missing a game. His statistics were better than those of 1992, but they were not imposing. He batted .257, and finished with a near-career-average 24 homers and 90 RBIs.

Cal was not the dominant Oriole he had been in previous years. He was surpassed in batting average, extra-base hits, and home runs by other Orioles. Jeff Sagarin of *Baseball Weekly* analyzed all players to determine the predicted runs per game if a team's entire lineup consisted of that particular player. RPG (runs per game) considered all offensive categories. In the group of batters with 502+ plate appearances, Cal finished 53rd out of 73 with an RPG of 4.55. Chris Hoiles (8.73), Brady Anderson (5.46), and David Segui (5.02) finished higher than him.

Cal also did not fare well in the annual rankings of the Elias Sports Bureau. Cal had had a perfect 100 in 1991, had dropped in 1992, and fell even further in 1993. Among shortstops, Cal ranked behind Tony Fernandez and Travis Fryman.

In more direct statistical comparison to other AL starting shortstops, Cal finished eighth in batting average behind Tony Fernandez, Travis Fryman, Mike Gallego, Ozzie Guillen, Greg Gagne, Felix Fermin, and John Valentin.

On the other hand, only Travis Fryman, with 97, drove in more runs, and Cal led all AL shortstops in homers. In fact, no Major League shortstop had more home runs than Cal did, and Fryman was the only big-league shortstop with more RBIs than Cal.

Obviously disappointed with his performance, Cal was still pleased that he had helped the Orioles in their consistent play throughout the season. "We had the experience of being competitive," he said, "and that's something to think about during the winter and take into next year."

15

UNFINISHED BUSINESS: 1994

Cal Ripken, Jr., approached his 13th full year in the Majors with some concern. Did his poor offensive performance in 1993 portend future problems? He conceded that things had become more difficult physically. "It's a lot harder in the off-season to work out," he said. "Keeping in shape takes a lot more effort than it used to."

However, he resumed his usual off-season regimen, working out in his own gymnasium—lifting weights, playing basketball, and throwing and hitting in a baseball cage. He also treated himself to two vacations, one in the Caribbean with his wife, Kelly, and another with the children in Disney World.

Nagging thoughts persisted about the Streak and about last year's disappointing season. "I don't want to become obsessed by [the Streak]," he reflected in idle postseason moments. "I'm only concerned right now with the first game of next season, and after the first game, it'll be the second game. I try not to look too far ahead."

In sum, Cal had to be especially pleased by two off-season happenings. The Oriole had become publicly pronounced as the greatest home-run hitting shortstop in baseball history. Cal was also pleased about the O's acquisition of Rafael Palmeiro, who had starred with the Chicago Cubs and the Texas Rangers.

Hall of Famer Ernie Banks had long been considered baseball's greatest home-run hitting shortstop, with a total of 293. (He had 219 while playing other positions.) However, the Elias Sports Bureau discovered in 1990 that 16 of the 293 round trippers had actually been hit while the Cubbie was playing first. Elias neglected to notify the Orioles. Once aware of the error, the O's held a public celebration at Camden Yards. Joining the ceremonies on February 9 was Banks, who had 512 career homers. Presenting the honoree with a commemorative bat, Banks said, "You have a young man here in Baltimore who is highly talented and a real professional. He is a true example of how to deal with success. I'm extremely happy that he broke this record because it gives me a chance to come back and be remembered, too."

Cal's memories were of July 15, the game in which he had passed Banks (without realizing it) with a blast off Twins starter Scott Erickson in Camden Yards. The 5–3 triumph made a winner of Ben McDonald. Cal's homer came in the bottom of the sixth, a fortunate blow for McDonald, who left after six frames. "I remember it," Cal said, "because the game was tied and Ben had developed a blister on his pitching hand. Ben pitched as well as anybody during the second half of last year, but he really was a hard luck pitcher. He was still the pitcher of record, and as I was going to the plate, Rick Sutcliffe came over to me and said, 'Hit a home run. . . . ' I didn't know if he said that to fire me up or what, but that was one time I went up to the plate and I tried to hit a home run. The first pitch was a breaking ball, and I laid off it. The next time I managed to get a pretty good piece of the ball."

The ball landed in the left-field seats, and the Orioles marked the location with a commemorative spot. Birds GM Roland Hemond was a bit unhappy that the milestone was not marked on July 15. "It would have been a great night for Cal and the fans to share," he said, "but it certainly doesn't do anything to tarnish the milestone."

For Cal, the ignorance was a blessing. "I'm kind of glad I didn't know. I'm the kind of player who puts pressure on himself in situations like that, so I probably wouldn't have hit another home run all year." Cal now had 289 homers as a shortstop out of a career total of 297.

Cal was assured of less pressure, at least at bat, when the Orioles signed Palmeiro as a free agent in December. An excited Johnny Oates mused at the news conference, "You could move Mike Devereaux back up to second and put Palmeiro in that third spot. You've got three guys in those 3-4-5 spots [Palmeiro, Cal Ripken, and Chris Hoiles]. Or you've got Harold Baines in there. That's a pretty good lineup, and all because of that guy in the third spot."

New O's owner Peter Angelos was opening his purse, and hopes for 1994 mounted. When the Birds came to camp, they had signed Palmeiro, solid-hitting Chris Sabo, and top-quality hurlers Sid Fernandez and Lee Smith. A pumped-up Cal Ripken arrived at Twin Lakes Park for the first full workout in Florida.

"It's exciting coming in spring training this year," he said. "This team was already good, and we added guys like Palmeiro and Sabo and Fernandez. Those are a lot of reasons to get excited.

"I'm a fan, too, and as an Orioles fan you can't help but get caught up with what could happen with this team. . . . As a fan my expectations are very high."

In addition to Palmeiro and Sabo, the Orioles fielded a lineup with the potent bats of Chris Hoiles and promising star Jeffrey Hammonds. No wonder scribes were writing about a relaxed Cal Ripken. "He's having the time of his life," observed David Hughes in the *Wilmington News Journal*. At the end of March, Cal was hitting .367. Because of the added punch, he felt less pressure.

"I think at times in recent years I've been guilty of trying to do more than I'm capable of, because I was the guy who was called on to carry the load . . . I've felt very refreshed this spring because the focus has been on the team's chances rather than on individual accomplishments. It's definitely been different. . . . People aren't so much asking me about what kind of year I'm going to have as they're asking what kind of year the team will have."

Indeed, it would be a different Orioles team from past years. "No one can pitch around us the way they used to," Cal said. "There's too much protection all the way through the lineup."

The World Series? It was 11 years since the Orioles' last appearance. "Cal's goal is to play for a winner again," according to manager Oates. "He wants so badly to go back to the World Series. He saw we were making moves this winter, and he wanted to know what was going on. He wanted to have input, and we value his judgment very much. So he and I would talk as to our needs and how we could help ourselves."

The shortstop spoke openly about another World Series opportunity. "Coming here to a team that has won championships, finishing second on the last day of the season in my first year and then winning the World Series the next year—that seemed to spoil me a little bit. It happened so early in my career that I don't really think I appreciated it as well as I should have. This time around, I have more of an understanding of what it takes to get there."

Cal had impressive numbers in Grapefruit League play: a .365 batting average, with 13 RBIs in 52 at bats, including two homers.

Baltimore had spent $44 million on free agents, so Orioles watchers had, in the words of a *New York Times* article, "extravagant expectations"—namely, a playoff spot, at the least. Fans roared on opening day, April 4, at Camden Yards, the loudest applause saved for demigod Cal Ripken, Jr. Cal delivered two hits in the Orioles' 6–3 victory against Kansas City.

Throughout April the Orioles played well as Cal contributed with timely hitting. The Orioles were 4–2 after beating the Tigers 7–4 in Detroit's home opener, fueled by Cal's two-run triple. He knocked in the go-ahead run at Camden Yards in an 8–6 win over Oakland, an April 25 game in which he starred with two doubles and three RBIs. The Birds routed the Angels at Camden on April 27, 13–1. Cal collected four hits in a five-RBI day, highlighted by his first round tripper of the season, to go along with three runs scored.

After 22 games, Cal had 19 RBIs, a .337 batting average, and 16 runs scored. He led the Birds with seven tying or go-ahead runs batted in and was hitting .458 with runners in scoring position. "Ideally, anyone would want to get off to a good start," Cal said, stating the obvious. He had done well in the second half of '93 and was merely continuing his ways. Part of the reason, he observed, was the straight-up style batting stance. "I seemed to have success with that, and I've tried to keep it in place."

Equally as important as stance maintenance, if not more important, were the rejuvenated bats in the O's lineup. Said Cal, "When the offense works as a unit and everyone is scoring runs, it helps to relax you. You know that you have protection around you, that they can't avoid pitching to you, and that is a big help."

Batting coach Greg Biagini agreed: "I think the supporting cast has something to do with it. You have to pitch to everyone in this lineup. You can't pitch around people, certainly not Cal, and that makes a big difference."

Said manager Oates, "It could be that he's seeing the ball well right now," he said, "or it could be the guys around him in the lineup. But there doesn't always have to be a reason. Let's just watch and enjoy him."

Cal batted .340 in April, an April average he exceeded only in 1984 and 1987. The 19 RBIs were only topped by his April production in 1987 and 1991.

On May 1 the O's stood at 15–9, two and a half games in back of the Bosox. Cal helped rally the O's for a 6–3 May 10 home victory over Toronto with his second homer of the game and two RBIs. The Birds had now won 10 of 13 and were only a half game back of the Yankees. It was their best start since they went 22–9 in 1970.

As for the Streak, it was quite unobtrusive, as the Orioles kept winning. "Hey, it's something we're glad about," said Palmeiro. "We want to win. But the Streak is going to be there. Everybody knows it. Cal just shows up and does his work every day. But he doesn't say anything and neither do we. When it gets to be that time, we'll deal with it and so will he."

Palmeiro, who lockers next to Cal, added, "Cal is a very smart player. He studies the game and prepares to play. That's why he has been so successful. He just doesn't go through the motions. He does what it takes to get an edge."

Reliever Lee Smith was a key factor in the Orioles' winning ways. Baseball's all-time save leader had played with one of the great all-time shortstops, Ozzie Smith. Still, he included Cal among the best. "I would not want to place rankings," he said, "but when you look at hitting, fielding, and all other qualities, the best shortstops I have played with and against are Ozzie, Cal, and Barry Larkin [of Cincinnati]."

While Cal had fallen off a bit, he was hitting a solid .290, with a team-leading 23 RBIs. The Orioles slipped a bit and had fallen to 24–17, four and a half behind the Yankees. However, both Cal and the Orioles had big days on May 24 at County Stadium against Milwaukee. The Brewers raced off to a 5-0 lead, but the O's charged back against Teddy Higuera with a four-run third and a six-run fourth. Two of the big hits were Cal's two-run, 300th career homer in the third and three-run double against reliever Jeff Bronkey in the fourth. All told, Cal had six RBIs in the 13–5 triumph.

The 300th homer gave Cal a celebrated place in Orioles history. He joined two other Orioles greats: Boog Powell (333) and Eddie Murray (303).

As the end of June neared, the AL East race had become a battle between New York and the pursuing Orioles. On June 25 the Birds stayed three and a half games behind the Yanks when Cal hit a tiebreaking two-run eighth-inning homer for a 4–3 victory in Toronto's Skydome. Cal's ninth homer, off Juan Guzman, gave him 50 RBIs for the season—in 71 games—to go along with a .296 batting average. Cal was leading the team in RBIs, obviously benefiting from hitting behind Palmeiro, who sported an average of .336.

June ended with a 4–2 road loss to Cleveland, which kept the O's four and a half games behind the Yankees. Cal had three hits, including his 10th homer, in the losing cause. Cal's stats in June were: a .354 batting average, 20 RBIs, and seven homers, the most he has ever had in June.

Cal finished off another back-to-back homer performance on July 1, in a 14–7 Camden Yards rout of California. His 11th homer and double were good for three RBIs.

His bat remained potent. On July 3 Cal hit a grand slammer— the third of his career—against the Angels in a 10–3 victory that brought the O's to within three and a half of New York. Cal's two RBIs helped the O's past Seattle, 5–2, on July 5.

At the All-Star break, Cal had put up numbers comparable to his better offensive years: a .306 batting average, 65 RBIs, and 12 homers among his 102 hits. In fact, the 65 RBIs were the most he has ever accumulated for the first half of the season. Truly an All-Star performance. With 5.1 million votes, he was second only to the more than 6 million ballots cast for Ken Griffey, Jr. A smiling Cal was featured on the July 6–13 cover of *Baseball Weekly*.

He added to his American League record for a shortstop by starting in the All-Star Game for the 11th consecutive year. He leads current AL players with 12 appearances. Cardinals shortstop Ozzie Smith made his 13th appearance, a record for the position.

Cal was informed of his All-Star election on July 3, the day of his big game against California. "I try not to make a big deal of what happens in one day," said Cal. "It was a big day for me, and I'm happy about it, but baseball has a way of bringing you down when you're on top. I try to keep an even-keeled approach. . . .

"It's a great honor every year to be an All-Star. I always have a great time. I wish every big leaguer could get the opportunity just once because it's a special event. It's more than a big game. It's a chance to be with the other guys in a special setting. . . . I've had some good first halves and some not so good over the years. It feels good this year to go to the All-Star Game knowing I'm doing well."

Not surprisingly, Cal played every inning of the exciting 8–7 10-inning National League win and collected a double in five at bats.

In 1993 much of the All-Star talk at the Camden Yards happening focused on Cal's batting woes and his consecutive-game streak. The attention was much less in Pittsburgh, and much more laudatory. The 2,000th game approached, but Cal was uncertain, he told reporter Mike Lopresti in Pittsburgh. "If you tell me," he said, "I'll try to forget it as soon as possible. I'm fearful that by knowing too much, you become obsessed with the game streak, rather than playing the game every day."

Among Cal's greatest admirers in Pittsburgh was the Florida Marlins' All-Star representative, first baseman Jeff Conine. He is the Marlins' iron man, having played 250 consecutive games for the second-year expansion team. He is also second among current players, more than 1,700 games behind Junior. Conine did not get into the game but simply sat on the bench and marveled at the Oriole Iron Man.

"For him to do it at his position, I can't even imagine it," he said. "It's hard to grasp. People have no idea, the toll it takes. It was hard to [play every game] just for one year. He's done it for 12 or 13."

Another All-Star, Yankees third sacker Wade Boggs, had played against Cal when they were in the International League. He, too, was amazed at the Streak. "I don't know how he's done it," Boggs marveled. "You'd think that he'd foul a ball off his foot or pull a hamstring going from first to third or something. It's just inconceivable he hasn't needed a day off."

Among the more interesting pieces in the Streak literature was an announcement by New York Yankees management that no changes were planned on the Lou Gehrig monument in Yankee Stadium. It speaks of the "amazing record" of 2,130 consecutive games that "could stand for all time." *USA Today* quoted Yankees director of stadium operations Tim Hasett about any changes: "I've not heard of any plans. I've thought about it because I know what it says. Change it? It might be either that or there will be a lot of pictures of Ripken standing next to it. That'd be easier."

Marty Naughton of the Yankees media staff also saw no monument rewrite. "Of all records, that was the most improbable to be broken. Certainly, we expected the iron man record to be for all time."

Perhaps Cal had not circled game 2,000 in his mental calendar, but Bird and Cal watchers knew that the milestone would be reached on Saturday evening, July 30, at Camden Yards against Toronto. How appropriate! The Streak began against Toronto, the innings streak stopped against Toronto, and number 2,000 would be recorded against Toronto. But a strange twist of fate from the sky happened on the way to 2,000.

The roof tiles fell down from the Seattle Kingdome, so games on July 18 and a makeup doubleheader were canceled on July 19. The Orioles played a day-night doubleheader against Cleveland on July 26, the day game a makeup for a May 7 cancellation. The following game, on July 27, was rained out, forcing a twilight twin bill on July 28. In effect, the Iron Man had three unscheduled days off in a 10-day period.

Unfortunately, the off days did not prove auspicious for Orioles fortunes. The O's dropped two to the Tribe on July 28—the first Indians sweep in four years—to stretch the Birds' losing streak to three and sink six behind the Yankees.

The Indians shortstop observed his counterpart closely during the series. Omar Vizquel had won the Gold Glove in 1993 and spoke of the dangers that await in the field. "So many things can happen," he said, such as base runners barreling into second, that make injury so much a possibility. "I think base runners respect him a lot. You don't want to take out a guy who has been playing 2,000 consecutive games. You don't want to come in hard because you got so much respect for the guy."

Cal did not see it that way, however. "I haven't really sensed that, because I haven't changed my approach one bit. . . . My size insulates me a little bit. . . . At times when someone takes me out, it's a collision he feels as well. Someone of lesser size might not have that deterrent."

The Blue Jays stopped the Orioles the next day, pushing Baltimore seven behind. The Birds ended their skein on July 30, ushering in game 1,999 on a winning note. The Camden Yards throng of 47,684 gave Cal a long and highly vocal standing "O" before the fifth inning. A tribute flashed on the board in center field to the tune of Prince's "1999."

For Cal, who went 1 for 3, the tribute was "awesome," but why the fuss, he wondered. "It's just one game," he matter-of-facted. The edge was also blunted by a 6–4 loss, dropping the home team eight behind the Yankees.

The Orioles left for a brief road swing, to open with game 2,000, at Minnesota. The Twins viewed the occasion as exciting, so they ran a large ad in the local press, "2000 and Counting," guaranteeing that a ticket would be a "collectible for years to come."

The Twins, mired in last in the AL Central, drew 27,712 to the park. As Hall of Famer Frank Robinson, the O's assistant GM, settled himself into his seat to watch the game, he remarked on the accomplishment. "This is history. Only one other player has reached 2,000 consecutive games."

These sentiments were shared by the Metrodome crowd as well as by members of the Twins and Orioles. When Cal came to bat in the first inning, the largely partisan crowd gave him a resounding standing ovation. Always the unassuming hero—but amid the sustained applause—he took off his helmet. Metrodomers insisted the ovation was as loud and as sincere as that given the previous year to hometown hero Dave Winfield upon recording his 3,000th hit.

Cal fouled out to end the first and had no hits on his milestone evening, but he made two sparkling defensive plays—most notably going deep in the hole to throw out Shane Mack to end the seventh—that helped preserve a 1–0 Orioles victory and complete-game shutout for Arthur Rhodes.

The Iron Man went about the game as but one day in the baseball life of Cal Ripken, Jr. Before batting practice he spent about five minutes signing autographs on scraps of paper, caps, cards, gloves, and everything directed his way.

"This is not something I set out to do," Cal remarked in playing down his feat, amassed in 13 seasons. "This is just a by-product of my desire to go out and play every day.

"I don't know what this accomplishment means. I know 2,000 is a nice round number. I'm just glad it means that my teammates can count on me. Beyond that, I don't know."

While Cal seemed stoical about game 1,999, he was a little more excited after game 2,000 during postgame interviews in the Gopher Room. The milestone was shared by his wife, Kelly, who surprised Cal with her presence in the Metrodome.

Stepping out of his usually reserved stance, Cal remarked, "It's nice to be recognized. . . . It's hard to put into words. It's one of those situations, you can't believe they're standing for one reason—and that's you."

Cal added that he owed his work ethic to his father, who taught him that "You can't contribute from the bench."

For that reason, there has never been a day professionally that he didn't want to play. "I never had a time that I had doubts," he said. "The fact of the matter is: some days you don't feel 100 percent. I've had some of my best days when I didn't feel 100 percent."

Cal was more enthused about the compliments paid his fielding during game 2,000. Holder of the Major League record for fewest errors in a season by a shortstop, the celebrant continued, "The biggest compliment that could be paid to me is that 'he plays the game as he did in his first few seasons.' My first few seasons, that was my goal. I've never been obsessed with Mr. Gehrig."

A line drive off the bat of Mike Devereaux during batting practice nearly hit Cal. He saw the shot at the final moment and got out of harm's way. The previous day he was hit on the butt by a Juan Guzman pitch in the sixth in apparent retaliation for the two serves that Orioles reliever Armando Benitez threw behind Devon White in the top of the frame. It was the 42nd time he had been plunked during his career.

All this reminded Cal how fortunate he was to have avoided physical injuries. "I've always felt if you play the game the right way, play full speed, and keep your concentration on, that insulates you against some injuries," he said. And don't forget good fortune. "When I think of all the odds of losing the Streak, I realize how fortunate I am and thank my lucky stars."

During the consecutive-game streak, more than 3,100 players have spent time on the disabled list. The previous week 75 were on the DL, including the newest entries, sluggers Andres Galarraga and Mark McGwire.

In response to my query about "losing" the celebration in Baltimore, Cal affirmed that he had some "regret" that the milestone could not be achieved in Camden Yards. The Streak "is very much a part of Baltimore and its people," he said. "They are there every day, whether it's going to work every day, going to school every day. . . . It means being there and knowing somebody can count on you."

The magical evening touched many of the other participants. Manager Oates said that he had difficulty remembering 1982, when the Streak began. "It boggles my mind to think of the stuff I've done in my life since he began that streak. My son hadn't even started school yet, and now he's getting ready to go to college." Manager Oates noted that he never had a conversation with Cal "exclusively" on the subject of taking a day off, but it was discussed "in the context of other concerns." Specifically, said Oates, the Streak came up after Cal twisted his right knee during the June 6, 1993, brawl between the O's and the Mariners. "I told Cal," he said, "that I would not play Cal if playing him would be detrimental to the team." As for suggestions that Oates let Cal pinch-hit or make a token fielding appearance, the manager snapped, "I wouldn't do that because that is not the way Cal wants his streak to continue. . . .

"I would not embarrass him with that. I would not even think of diminishing what he's done. That's not him."

Childhood mentor and '81 teammate Mark Belanger had other thoughts on his mind besides game 2,000. As special assistant to Executive Director Donald Fehr of the Players Association, Belanger wondered how long players aside from Cal would keep on playing. However, the great O's shortstop set aside time to praise the Cal Ripken he knew. "Incredible," he said in reference to the Streak. "Do you realize how strong Cal has had to be both mentally and physically . . . ?

"I have often spoken at clinics or talked with other players and brought up Cal as the example of the approach and attitude we would want all players to adapt. . . . The Orioles are getting a bargain with Cal. When you look at what he has done for the franchise on and off the field, you realize how much more he's worth than what he is being paid."

One of the newer Orioles—since mid-June—outfielder Dwight Smith said that a few weeks before he had observed a game of tapeball—involving hitting a wadded-up ball of tape with a Wiffle-ball bat—between Cal and Ben McDonald. "I don't see how the man doesn't get hurt," wondered Smith, "because he acts just like a little kid."

Twin players were also struck by the immensity of the Streak. First baseman Kent Hrbek, who retired after the '94 season, came in second to Cal in the 1982 Rookie of the Year balloting, which incensed the Twins front office. However, Hrbek was totally praiseworthy of the Oriole. "I never would have imagined that any human could play that many games in a row. When I played a few games in a row, I needed that day off."

Outfielder Kirby Puckett and Cal Ripken are two superstars who share many interests, including agent Ron Shapiro. "I have been close to Cal for 10 years," Puckett said. "It's unbelievable what Cal has done, and he will break that record. As for myself, forget it. Even with high school and Little League, I don't approach 2,000. . . . . It's even tough to play 10 in a row at our age."

Puckett is one of countless players who have never approached that rarefied number. Fewer than 200 players—past and present—have even been in 2,000 Major League games consecutive or no. Only six have played in 1,000 consecutive games. Thirty-one iron men have played in 500 or more straight games (Pete Rose and Charlie Gehringer each have two separate 500+ game streaks).

The adulation directed toward Cal on August 1 prompted my question in the locker room: "Are you happy that you will be looked upon as a role model at a time when athletes have failed in this role? And should athletes be responsible for their behavior off the field?"

"I will not say that athletes have an obligation to their fans and public to behave in a certain way," he responded. "However, I know how I looked up to baseball players in my youth. I molded my behavior on the examples of players like Brooks Robinson, Ken Singleton, and Eddie Murray, and of course, the examples of my parents. I see how people view athletes. The athletes are placed in a position of influence, and I will continue to take this very seriously."

At 2,000, what about the future? "I know it's a cliché," answered Cal, "but I'll give you my approach: 'One day at a time.'"

Cal added that he has matured this season in his approach to the media. "And having a good season alleviates discomforts" when he is questioned about the Streak.

When the O's arrived in New York for a three-game set, the media sought out the Yankees' Don Mattingly, like Cal the consummate team player and admirer of the Iron Man's. What did the Yankees captain think of the Streak? Said Mattingly, "We wonder how many times he was too banged up to go out there but did anyway. We wonder how many times he had a case of the can't-get-out-of-bed flu but got up anyway and played. You ask anybody. We're all in awe of what he's done."

However, another Yankees first baseman, a star of past days, had other thoughts. Tommy Henrich, 82, a former Gehrig teammate who lives in Dewey, Arizona, told the *Baltimore Sun*: "Because of my past history with the Yankees, Lou Gehrig and all that great tradition, I want that record to stay with the Yankees.

"But I'll tell you what. My hat is off to Cal Ripken if he pulls it off. It amazes me that a shortstop is doing it—that's the most amazing thing. There's more activity at that position than any except catcher. He's in danger every day, sliding into him."

The only thing that could be discomforting now was the threat of a work stoppage. On August 11 New York's WFAN Radio reported a conversation between Yankees second baseman Pat Kelly and Cal in which the Oriole was incorrectly identified as the team representative. Reportedly, Cal told Kelly that the impending strike had "taken off from his game" and caused him to lose "concentration."

However, the statistics did not reflect this. In nine contests after game 2,000, he went 14 for 40 (.350), with five RBIs and his 13th homer. His batting average was up to .315. In his last 38 games he had hit .369 (38 for 157). He was fifth in the AL with 140 hits. Although the Yankees had a fairly comfortable lead, the Orioles, winners of six of their last nine, had reduced the deficit to six and a half games. More important, they trailed the Indians by two games for the wild card spot in playoff competition.

The season for Cal and the Orioles ended temporarily when their August 11 encounter against the Bosox at Camden Yards was rained out. While the gathering waited out a rain delay of 2 hours and 16 minutes in the bottom of the third, Cal and catcher Chris Hoiles were playing catch in the rain-soaked dugout.

Cal's streak remained fixed at 2,009. An unthought-of phenomenon: Cal Ripken not playing. In the words of *Orlando Sentinel* columnist Brian Schmitz, "What's the most painful irony of the pending baseball strike? Putting Cal Ripken and work stoppage in the same sentence. These two things just don't go together, like Streisand and a sour note."

Toronto star Paul Molitor was queried whether anyone could approach Cal's 2,000-game streak. "The way the owners are making it sound," he responded, "it doesn't look like there's ever going to be 2,000 more baseball games."

Cal did have difficulty accepting the possibility of a strike. "I've never been through a work stoppage in the summer in my entire life," he said, "and I refuse to think about it occurring even now. If it does happen, I really don't know what I'd do."

The halt in the flow of the great American pastime left Cal downtrodden. "It's just sad," he admitted. "Deep down, nobody wants this strike, but we have to fight for what we've got, and though some people don't understand, maybe they will someday."

That being said, he was reluctant to say more about the strike or about his new regimen. He opted for a low profile.

Desperate for stories during the strike, newspapers calculated losses to owners and players. For those who cared, Cal's losses at $26,230 a day placed him fifth among big losers, behind Bobby Bonilla, Jack McDowell, Roberto Alomar, and Roger Clemens.

All stories of day-by-day losses mattered little when acting baseball commissioner Bud Selig announced on September 14 the cancelation of the season and postseason, killing the World Series for the first time since 1904.

For millions of baseball fans, those were the only facts that mattered. Individual records counted little. The records of a season unfulfilled clearly showed a superior Cal Ripken year: a .315 batting average (career third best) in 444 at bats, and 75 RBIs (topped on the O's only by Palmeiro's 76) in 112 games. His .985 fielding percentage was best among AL shortstops.

Beyond the cold stats, the TAG ratings, devised by Pete Taggert in order to seek to assess a player's total contributions (e.g., advancing a runner, catching a thrown ball without a chance), placed Cal 15th in AL Hitting and 7th in Total Contribution.

Among other postseason rankings: In Elias Sports Bureau rankings of two-year statistics, Cal placed third among AL second basemen, third basemen, and shortstops, behind John Valentin and Roberto Alomar. In AL Most Valuable Player voting, he finished 12th—the top Oriole—behind Frank Thomas.

The Streak remained frozen at 2,009, and one thing was certain: if and when he played game 2,131, Johnny Oates would not be penciling in the shortstop's name. Oates was fired at September's end. "I think Johnny has done a good job," Cal said. "There's been a rebuilding of Orioles baseball here the last so many years and Johnny's been a big part of that." Did he agree with the firing? Said Cal, "I'm just a player. Obviously, like everyone else, I have an opinion."

What it was he never said; however, he added to the volume of Streak literature with commentary on the labor danger facing the Iron Man. Cal was in New York on September 23, along with Eddie Murray and Dave Winfield, to urge the younger union members to continue solidarity throughout the stoppage. Would he play next season if there were no settlement and the owners used replacement players from the minor leagues? Or would he let his pursuit of the record end?

Responded Cal, "My general feeling is if it's replacement players, it's not Major League baseball, and I won't be playing."

He expanded on these sentiments to Mark Maske of the *Washington Post*. "I've told myself," he said, "that if it's supposed to end I need to be strong enough to let it end. If it ends for a good reason, I won't have any regrets. I won't look back. . . . I won't ask myself, 'What if.' I'll just let it end, and I'll move on. . . . It's my decision, and I've made it."

The official statistician of baseball, the Elias Sports Bureau, was reluctant to confront the possibility. According to Seymour Siwoff of Elias, "I don't like to talk about it. We're hoping it doesn't come to that." Pressed further, Siwoff ruled, "The Streak would be broken. We had the National Football League [1987 strike]. The owners used replacement players and all the consecutive-game records came to an end."

Red Sox general partner John Harrington spoke of the possibility of using replacement players for what he called "Professional baseball" rather than "Major League baseball."

Would that make a difference for Elias? "That's up to the baseball community," responded Siwoff. "It's their call. All we can do is go by what they say."

O's first baseman Rafael Palmeiro and locker neighbor of Cal's was vocal in his unhappiness. If the Streak ended with replacements, he said, it "would be terrible. It would be completely unfair. Don't the owners know they're messing with history if they do that? . . . They wiped out the World Series. Now they're going to keep Cal from breaking one of the most unbelievable records there is?"

The Orioles' decision to use nonunion players rested with majority owner Peter Angelos. He has "strong personal feelings" against using scabs. However, he would have to balance his opinion against the business responsibility he had to his partners. "Here's a guy who hasn't missed a game in 13 years and has a chance to break this impressive record," said Angelos. "I would view that as a very powerful disincentive."

Angelos, however, was unequivocal about fighting for the record breaker to be set in Camden Yards. Before the stoppage, schedule makers had projected game 2,131 for late June in Baltimore against the Yankees. Now, Cal would match Lou Gehrig on August 16 against Cleveland in Baltimore; the tiebreaker has been scheduled for August 18 in Oakland.

Upon notification, Angelos called the American League office and then wrote a "strongly worded letter" asking the league to "structure the schedule so that he can do it here.

"Obviously, we would do everything possible to see to it that the game in which Cal would break Lou Gehrig's record would be played in Baltimore."

Traditionally, the winter months have been designated as the hot stove period. Fans and the media collectively ponder trades, free-agent signings, prospects for the next season, and the like. In 1995 the hot stove became frigid as the baseball world wondered whether there would even be baseball in 1995.

How would all this affect Cal Ripken, Jr., and his Iron Man Streak? Angelos adamantly continued to tell his fellow owners that his team would not use replacement players. "This course," he said, "does a disservice to the game of baseball and the history of baseball in the country. This is our national game. This is no way to treat it."

Angelos said that he had the full support of O's general manager Roland Hemond and assistant GMs Frank Robinson and Syd Thrift. The three concurred that the use of replacements was "indefensible." Angelos did concede that adherence to his position could bring "certain penalties imposed under the constitution by-laws of the American League."

The penalties could be a fine of $250,000 a game, suspension, and ultimately confiscation of the Orioles franchise.

Behind Angelos's stubbornness is the Streak of his shortstop. "We have a special problem in Baltimore with the Cal Ripken Streak," he said, "an extraordinary accomplishment by Cal and one that we certainly will do everything to avoid harming."

To further protect their favorite son, the Baltimore City Council introduced a bill that would fine Major League Baseball $1,000 for each game played with strikebreakers at Camden Yards.

Could the union give special dispensation to Cal so that he could play if the impasse continued? At the close of 1994, Houston Astros reliever Todd Jones was widely quoted as saying that other players would understand if he continued his game streak. "This is a Halley's comet thing he's going after," said Jones. "It's safe to say that none of the union members would hold it against him."

Agent Ron Shapiro quickly put such thoughts to rest. "Cal Ripken will not be a replacement player," he said. "Cal Ripken has never placed individual achievements ahead of his responsibilities to his team and other players. He knows what players in the past have done for him, and he knows his responsibility to future players. It's never been an issue."

As the opening of spring training camps approached, Cal verified his agent's words. Cal told Claire Smith of the *New York Times* during Washington negotiations in the first week of February: "That notion [of playing by means of union dispensation to cross picket lines] is ridiculous to me. I feel proud of what I've been able to accomplish, but I know why I have the opportunity—because of what the players before me and the Players Association have accomplished."

How would he feel if his streak were ended by a replacement at shortstop? "Maybe at some point, I'll say that's unfair," he told Smith. "I've still accomplished what I wanted to accomplish. You don't need recognition from it. You don't need a record to prove it."

While the general atmosphere was gloomy, plans moved ahead: What if the strike ended. . . . Where would game 2,131 be played? The tentative 1995 schedule called for that game to be played in Oakland. However, the Birds were confident that the American League would accommodate a change to Oriole Park. The American League "made it very clear," said O's director of business affairs Walt Gutowski, "they want to work with us on making an adjustment at some point."

That was in December. As Angelos hardened in his stand, Oakland GM Sandy Alderson had other ideas. "You can be assured that we're not doing a hell of a lot to cooperate with Angelos and the Orioles," said Alderson. "I'd like nothing better than to see Ripken break the record at the Oakland Coliseum. It would be one of the highlights of my career."

Camps opened in February, and two managers offered their views on Cal and the Streak. Detroit skipper Sparky Anderson won cheers from many for stepping down because he wanted nothing to do with replacement players. But the plaudits, he insisted, belonged to "old Calvin," who would rather give up his pursuit of the record than play with replacements. "Just imagine what he's risking," said Anderson. "Is that character? You think I got character? I got to take a backseat to old Calvin. That is strong character you cannot buy. It's unassailable."

On the other hand, rookie O's manager Phil Regan chooses to think positively of the day Cal will pass Lou Gehrig. He told us from Orioles spring training in Sarasota at February's end of the "privilege" of being part of baseball history. "The record of Lou Gehrig is one that nobody thought would ever be broken," said Regan. "Just imagine playing 10 years without missing one game, which could come because of a broken finger, a hamstring, or countless other reasons. And Cal has gone beyond these 10 years.

"I feel fortunate that in my first year as manager of Baltimore I may have that 'privilege' of bringing out the lineup card with Cal Ripken, Jr., on it."

The "may" moved closer to a distinct possibility when the longest strike in pro sports history ended after 232 days. The 1995 season was set to open April 26.

16

NUMBER 8: HIS PLACE IN HISTORY

In his book on baseball's Hall of Famers, Lowell Reidenbaugh begins his article on the Flying Dutchman, Honus Wagner: "While discussions may rage about the greatest all-time players at other positions, a unanimity prevails on the foremost shortstop in the first century of baseball." Wagner won eight batting titles, amassed 3,430 hits, and compiled a .329 average. John McGraw insisted that Wagner was the greatest player he had seen in his 40 years as player and manager.

Where does number 8, Cal Ripken, Jr., rank in baseball history? While the data is not yet complete on the Orioles shortstop, 13 years and 2000+ games allow for proper evaluation.

Beyond pure statistics, Cal Ripken, Jr., must be assessed on his standing in the eyes of teammates, opponents, and baseball savants. Moreover, Cal Ripken, Jr., must be appraised beyond statistical achievements on the diamond.

It is impractical and unfair to compare Cal to diamond heroes of days gone by: Babe Ruth should not be compared to Ken Griffey, Jr.; Christy Mathewson should not be compared to Nolan Ryan; Cal Ripken, Jr., should not be compared to Honus Wagner. Players—and all other professionals—can only be evaluated by comparison with their contemporaries. That being said, we offer Cal's stats and those of former greats only for statistical reasons—not to rate the merits of Cal and others.

Through 1994 Cooperstown has enshrined 16 shortstops (Ernie Banks has been included although the Hall of Fame and Museum Yearbook lists the Cub as a first baseman). In addition to Wagner, Luke Appling, Joe Cronin, Hugh Jennings, Joe Sewell, and Arky Vaughn had career .300 averages. Lou Boudreau and Travis Jackson had .295 and .291 averages, respectively. It is reasonable to assume that in the years of his contract (through 1997) or even longer, Cal will not be able to raise his career average from .277 to those numbers.

However, the story is much different in terms of hits, RBIs, and homers, just to take three categories. In addition to Wagner, only Appling (2,749), Luis Aparicio (2,677), Rabbit Maranville (2,605), and Ernie Banks (2,583) had more than 2,500 hits. If Cal continues his present pace, he certainly will pass 2,500 and may even surpass Appling.

Only Wagner, Banks (1,636), and Cronin (1,423) have more RBIs than Cal. With more than 90 RBIs a year, Cal will come close to Cronin, perhaps even exceeding his total. Only Wagner (651), Cronin (514), Appling (440), and Sewell (436) had more two-baggers. Maintaining his present pace of 33 doubles a year, Cal could pass Cronin in 1997.

In 1993 Cal established himself as the greatest home-run hitting shortstop in Major League history, eclipsing Ernie Banks, whose 512 career wallops included more than 200 while he played first base.

Cal holds two other offensive records: In 1991 he made AL history for a shortstop with 368 total bases and crafted the only combination of .300+ batting average, 30+ homers, and 100+ RBIs.

Prior to 1994, Cal had amassed 710 extra base hits as a shortstop. According to the Orioles' Media Guide, it is very difficult to determine the numbers that Wagner and Cronin posted while playing only shortstop. However, during the years that they were primarily shortstops, Cronin and Wagner had 765 and 737 extra base hits, respectively.

Baseball fans are fortunate to have been treated to a few great shortstops in the 1980s and 1990s. Cal's contemporaries have included Robin Yount, Alan Trammell, and Ozzie Smith. During his 20-year career with Milwaukee, Yount registered more than 3,100 hits, 1,400+ RBIs, and a career average of .285, which brought him two MVP Awards. While he came up as a shortstop, his last 10 years were primarily as an outfielder.

Now in his 18th year, Trammell was the Tiger shortstop until he was briefly supplanted in the 1990s by Travis Fryman. He entered 1995 with over 2,200 hits, a .287 career average, with 964 RBIs. His manager, Sparky Anderson, whose Red Machine was anchored in the infield by shortstop Dave Concepcion, said, "I always thought Dave Concepcion was untouchable. But when you take everything into consideration, we may be seeing someone even better than him. . . . Taking into consideration his speed, power, defense, hitting, and instincts, right now he [Trammell] may be the best player in the game."

One year after Trammell arrived, the Wizard of Oz, Ozzie Smith, broke in with San Diego, where he played for four years until being traded to St. Louis in 1982. He has collected 2,265 hits, but only shows a .262 career batting average and 734 RBIs. However, when one speaks of Smith—and Yount, Trammell, and Cal Ripken—one has to factor in heavily the fielding of these shortstops.

Reflective of peer recognition of fielding supremacy is the awarding of the Gold Glove. Trammell has taken 4, Smith, 13, and Cal, 2. But Cal's fielding artistry obviously goes beyond prizes, for implausibly he has been passed over several times for this honor.

He holds or shares 11 Major League or American League fielding records for a shortstop, among them the M.L. records for fielding percentage in a season, fewest errors in a season, most consecutive errorless games, most consecutive chances without an error, and a record-tying mark for most years (six) leading the Majors in double plays. His .9782 lifetime fielding mark is fourth all-time in M.L. history, behind Tony Fernandez, Larry Bowa, and Ozzie Smith. But he holds the highest fielding percentage ever for a shortstop whose home games were played on grass.

Among active shortstops, Cal is second only to Smith in assists per game (3.07 to Smith's 3.36). When history rates Cal defensively, he ought to be compared to the shortstops of his day. Only Smith will rate—statistically—higher.

The five major defensive categories are: fielding percentage, assists, chances-per-game, putouts, double plays. Smith has rung up 28 defensive titles: percentage (7), assists (8), chances (6), putouts (2), double plays (5). Cal comes in second among active players, with 24 titles: percentage (2), assists (7), chances (3), putouts (6), double plays (6). Looking back 50 years, only Hall of Famer Luis Aparicio comes close, with 23 titles.

If one concedes that the acrobatic wizard Smith is the best defensive shortstop of his day, who can challenge the claim that Cal is "second best"? He is not flashy, nor is he a showman, but he positions himself well, is able to get to the ball, and knows what to do with it. Smith is the wondrous magician and Cal is the crafty scholar, the scientist of infield play. "Ripken studies hitters fanatically," said O's catcher Chris Hoiles. "Cal knows everything about everybody."

On his *Coast-to-Coast* radio show on August 15, 1994, Bob Costas repeated Cal's analogy of a dancer, whereby the Oriole compared himself to the Wizard.

Cal was the dancer who had to learn all the lefts and rights in baseball à la Arthur Murray; however, Ozzie was the "natural dancer," who trotted out to the ballroom with the grace of Fred Astaire.

Cal's peer Alan Trammell has been highly impressed by all facets of Cal's play. "To play as demanding a position as he does and to play as well as he does is unbelievable," raved the Tiger. "He has got to be as strong mentally as anybody who has ever played this game. There is no question in my mind."

Vincent Bagli called Cal "the best shortstop who's ever played." Then again, Bagli's remarks may be that of a "homer," whose sentiments are voiced on WBAL Radio. So let's leave this discussion with the thoughts of White Sox shortstop whiz Ozzie Guillen, "If I was a manager I want Cal Ripken to be my shortstop."

Any player analysis must include the "intangibles." Cal is not a leader, come the voices of the detractors. As Mark Maske wrote in a June 1991 *Washington Post* column, "Ripken, Jr., is privately criticized for his reluctance to accept a forceful leadership role." What does leadership mean? What does "forceful leadership" connote? Does it mean being a take-charge guy, having a locker room presence, and the like? Do we measure leadership by the number of times a player has "brought" his club into the postseason competition?

Looking at the last question, only the baseball myopic will reason that a team could win without an outstanding shortstop. So how does one account for only one Orioles postseason appearance during Cal's days (World Series champions, 1983)? Following this logic, among shortstops, the most plaudits go to Phil Rizzuto and Pee Wee Reese, who led the Yankees and Dodgers, respectively, to the promised postseason land ten and seven times. Wagner and Cronin were in only two and one postseasons, respectively. Luke Appling never made it.

True, teams without a superior shortstop will find it difficult to be of championship calibre; however, not all teams with such shortstops will win. Certainly, the Yankees won with Rizzuto, but they also had Hall of Famers Yogi Berra and Mickey Mantle and a Hill staff of Hall of Famer Whitey Ford, Vic Raschi, Allie Reynolds, and Ed Lopat, among other stars. And Pee Wee captained Dodger teams with Hall of Famers Jackie Robinson, Duke Snider, Roy Campanella. The Bums were also fortified with potent bats, outstanding fielders, and quality hurlers for a decade, beginning in 1947.

Define leadership as you choose, but leadership is not served best on the bench or in the clubhouse. It must be on the playing field. In the national Sunday night broadcast on April 17, 1994, of the Birds versus Texas at Arlington, commentator Jeff Torborg, former player and manager, remarked about the Baltimore shortstop, "He's a presence on the field. . . . The pitchers know he's there. . . . He's a force on the team . . . a special player."

Jimmie Reese was a teammate of Lou Gehrig's during 1930–31 and in recent years was a conditioning coach for the California Angels. Before he died in the summer of 1994 at age 90, he told us, "I can't say I know Cal Ripken well, but I have watched him on the field. He is a presence. I don't want to compare him to Lou. That's not fair. But Lou carried himself with a great deal of class. So does Cal Ripken."

Cal also has earned encomiums from Yankee principal owner George Steinbrenner, who called the Oriole "one of the most consummate athletes I've seen in all of sports."

Sportswriters have been convinced of Cal's value. He has won two MVP Awards; Ernie Banks is the only other shortstop with this distinction. Doesn't being most valuable involve being a leader?

But, continue his opponents, Cal Ripken, Jr., is boring and without the "pizzazz," let us say, of a Reggie Jackson. Perhaps this might explain a contradictory *Baseball Weekly* poll of March 1994, in which Cal ranked close to the top among the most underrated *and* most overrated players. Thomas Boswell had the right retort in the March 1992 *Washington Post Magazine:* "Tell Ripken he's dull, and it makes his day. He still thinks doggedness is his trump card in life. He's sure he can do some boring, self-improving thing more often than you can. And he's right. Fortunately, he doesn't think that makes him better than you."

Yes, he is wealthier and better known than most of us, but with apologies for the cliché, success hasn't changed Cal Ripken, Jr. Cal has often spoken of the playing part of baseball, the business side of baseball, and the off-the-field side of baseball. After game

2,000, we asked Cal in the locker room about his ever-growing reputation as a role model. "I will not say that all athletes have an obligation to their public in the way they lead their lives off the field," he responded. "But I feel I do. I know how I looked at baseball players when I was a youth. They were in a position of influence. I molded my behavior on the examples of Brooks Robinson, Ken Singleton, and Eddie Murray.

"Years later, I remember how these players influenced my life. I accept the responsibility and obligations of being perceived as a role model. . . . If my image is good, I will do my best to sustain it and improve it."

He certainly has. Along with his wife, Kelly, Cal has been in the forefront of community activities and programs. All this earned him the Roberto Clemente Award, which is symbolic of community service accomplishments. In Baltimore, Cal is an icon, not only for his many on-field achievements.

"Baltimore is especially appreciative of Cal's work ethic," said Oriole GM Roland Hemond. "They are hard-working, conscientious people who will always applaud those who give their best, who are there every day, and those who truly care for their city. That's why Cal is so special here."

The need to search for icons, for sports heroes, has invited much examination and reflection in an age where these idols are so scrutinized, worshipped, and sadly, too often found wanting and less than heroic. Long Island sports psychologist Frank Gardner is quoted on this subject in a June 1994 *New York Daily News* article by Wayne Coffey titled "Hard Time for Heroes." According to Gardner, athletic achievement has been compromised "by all the personal and business stuff. You just can't look at Michael Jordan. . . . Does he have a character flaw? Since we've opened up their financial and personal lives to such rigorous scrutiny, unless we find the perfect person, it becomes harder and harder to find heroes."

In 1993, Roberto Clemente, Jr., son of the caring Hall of Famer, recalled that his father had been concerned about the seriousness of athletes as role models. "He always felt that children were a very significant part of society and should be cared for and influenced in positive ways." The son was strong in his belief that the same rule applies in the 1990s: "Kids today are having such a hard time in society and . . . athletes make so much money and have so much exposure. They should take care of themselves and their images outside the lines of the game."

One must not deny the function of parents, teachers, and religious leaders as role models for children. However, the fact still remains that children will look up to sports heroes, learn from them, and remember them when they are no longer children. Beyond the 2,000+ games, beyond all the offensive records, beyond all the fielding statistics, beyond all the community-service contributions, and beyond eventual enshrinement in Cooperstown, each baseball follower will have his own memory of the tall Orioles shortstop.

But we will remember the words of Orioles coach Ray Miller in 1982 that go beyond the baseball diamond. Looking at the unproven rookie, he said, "I just wish he were my kid."

APPENDIX

PERSONAL

Born: Aug. 24, 1960
Height: 6'4"; **Weight:** 220
Bats, R; **Throws,** R
Position: Shortstop
Birthplace / Residence: Born in Havre de Grace, MD, but grew up in nearby Aberdeen . . . Resides in Reisterstown, MD
Contract Status: Signed thru '97
Tenure: 13 years, 16 days
Signed originally with: Orioles by Dick Bowie

CAREER RECORD

YEAR	CLUB	AVG	G	AB	R	H	2B	3B	HR	RBI	BB	SO	SB	CS	HP
1978	Bluefield-1	.264	63	239	27	63	7	1	0	24	24	48	1	1	2
1979	Miami	.303	105	393	51	119	28	1	5	54	31	64	4	3	1
	Charlotte	.180	17	61	6	11	0	1	3	8	3	13	1	0	0
1980	Charlotte	.276	+144	522	91	144	28	5	25	78	77	81	4	2	3
1981	Rochester	.288	114	437	74	126	31	4	23	75	66	85	0	2	2
	Baltimore	.128	23	39	1	5	0	0	0	0	1	8	0	0	0
1982	Baltimore	.264	160	598	90	158	32	5	28	93	46	95	3	3	3
1983	Baltimore	.318	+162	*663	*121	*211	*47	2	27	102	58	97	0	4	0
1984	Baltimore	.304	+162	641	103	195	37	7	27	86	71	89	2	1	2
1985	Baltimore	.282	161	642	116	181	32	5	26	110	67	68	2	3	1
1986	Baltimore	.282	162	627	98	177	35	1	25	81	70	60	4	2	4
1987	Baltimore	.252	*162	624	97	157	28	3	27	98	81	77	3	5	1
1988	Baltimore	.264	161	575	87	152	25	1	23	81	102	69	2	2	2
1989	Baltimore	.257	+162	646	80	168	30	0	21	93	57	72	3	2	3
1990	Baltimore	.250	161	600	78	150	28	4	21	84	82	66	3	1	5
1991	Baltimore	.323	+162	650	99	210	46	5	34	114	53	48	6	1	5
1992	Baltimore	.251	+162	637	73	160	29	1	14	72	64	50	4	3	7
1993	Baltimore	.257	*162	*641	87	165	26	3	24	90	65	58	1	4	6
1994	Baltimore	.315	112	444	71	140	19	3	13	75	32	41	1	0	4
ML Totals		.277	2074	8027	1201	2227	414	40	310	1179	849	896	34	31	43

ALCS		AVG	G	AB	R	H	2B	3B	HR	RBI	BB	SO	SB	CS	HP
1983	Bal vs. Chi	.400	4	15	5	6	2	0	0	1	2	3	0	0	1

WORLD SERIES		AVG	G	AB	R	H	2B	3B	HR	RBI	BB	SO	SB	CS	HP
1983	Bal vs. Phi	.167	5	18	2	3	0	0	0	1	3	4	0	0	0

ALL STAR		AVG	G	AB	R	H	2B	3B	HR	RBI	BB	SO	SB	CS	HP
1983	AL at Chi	.000	1	0	0	0	0	0	0	0	1	0	0	0	0
1984	AL at SF	.000	1	0	0	0	0	0	0	0	0	0	0	0	0
1985	AL at Min	.333	1	3	0	1	0	0	0	0	0	0	0	0	0
1986	AL at Hou	.000	1	4	0	0	0	0	0	0	0	0	0	0	0
1987	AL at Oak	.500	1	2	0	1	0	0	0	0	0	0	0	0	0
1988	AL at Cin	.000	1	3	0	0	0	0	0	0	1	0	0	0	0
1989	AL at Cal	.333	1	3	0	1	1	0	0	0	0	0	0	0	0
1990	AL at Chi	.000	1	2	0	0	0	0	0	0	0	0	0	0	0
1991	AL at Tor	.667	1	3	1	2	0	0	1	3	0	0	0	0	0

YEAR	CLUB	AVG	G	AB	R	H	2B	3B	HR	RBI	BB	SO	SB	CS	HP
1992	AL at SD	.333	1	3	0	1	0	0	0	1	0	0	0	0	0
1993	AL at Bal	.000	1	3	0	0	0	0	0	0	0	1	0	0	0
1994	AL at Pit	.200	1	5	0	1	1	0	0	0	0	2	0	0	0
ASG	Totals	.226	12	31	1	7	2	0	1	4	2	3	0	0	0

*Led league +Tied for lead
1–Selected by Orioles in June '78 free agent draft (2nd round Baltimore's 4th selection)

GAME HIGHS & STREAKS

Runs—3, 31 times .... (April 27, '94 at Cal)
Hits—5, 3 times .. (May 5,'85 at Min), (Sep 3,'83 at Min), & (Aug 22,'82 at Tex)
HR—2, 13 times .... (latest Aug 27,'93 at Tex)
RBI—7 .... (Apr 13,'91 at Tex)
Hitting streak—17, 3 times .... (latest June 12–29,'92)
Grand Slams—3 .. (July 13,'89 vs Oak), (Sep 14,'82 vs NY), & (July 3, '94 vs Cal)

		1994 Season					Lifetime				
		AVG	AB	H	HR	RBI	AVG	AB	H	HR	RBI
Totals		.315	444	140	13	75	.277	8027	2227	310	1179
Bal		.305	203	62	5	36	.266	3881	1033	153	585
Away		.324	241	78	8	39	.288	4146	1194	157	594
vs.	Bos	.348	23	8	1	6	.289	643	186	18	76
	Cal	.404	52	21	3	16	.277	617	171	25	105
	Chi	.174	23	4	0	1	.266	568	151	28	94
	Cle	.350	40	14	1	5	.277	638	177	27	102
	Det	.310	29	9	1	6	.292	631	184	27	95
	KC	.350	20	7	2	2	.289	574	166	25	87
	Mil	.282	39	11	2	9	.260	662	172	29	112
	Min	.250	36	9	1	5	.303	588	178	23	98
	NY	.381	42	16	0	3	.272	655	178	21	72
	Oak	.244	45	11	0	8	.244	630	154	27	72
	Sea	.324	37	12	0	4	.276	609	168	18	75
	Tex	.250	24	6	0	4	.295	586	173	20	97
	Tor	.353	34	12	2	6	.270	626	169	22	94
vs.	East	.352	128	45	4	21	.281	2555	717	88	337
	Central	.285	1158	45	6	22	.279	3030	844	132	493
	West	.316	158	50	3	32	.273	2442	666	90	349
Before ASG		.306	337	103	12	65	.279	4264	1189	169	643
After ASG		.346	107	37	1	10	.276	3763	1038	141	536
vs.	Left	.345	110	38	2	16	.288	2313	666	98	320
	Right	.305	334	102	11	59	.273	5714	1561	212	859
As	PH	–	–	–	–	–	.000	4	0	0	0
	DH	–	–	–	–	–	–	–	–	–	–

		1994 Season					Lifetime				
		AVG	AB	H	HR	RBI	AVG	AB	H	HR	RBI
In	Apr	.340	94	32	1	19	.278	1033	287	38	175
	May	.219	96	21	2	15	.264	1332	351	57	192
	June	.354	113	40	7	20	.298	1403	418	49	200
	July	.340	97	33	2	16	.282	1350	381	58	218
	Aug	.318	44	14	1	5	.273	1440	393	53	206
	Sep/Oct	–	–	–	–	–	.270	1469	397	55	188

CAL RIPKEN AT SHORTSTOP BY YEAR

Year	Pct	G	PO	A	E	TC	TC-E	DP
1981	.946	12	11	24	2	37	35	5
1982	.972	94	155	289	13	457	444	47
1983	.970	*162	272	*534	25	*831	*806	*113
1984	.971	*162	*297	+583	26	*906	*880	*122
1985	.967	161	*286	474	26	786	760	*123
1986	.982	162	240	*482	13	735	722	105
1987	.973	*162	240	*480	20	740	720	103
1988	.973	*161	*284	480	21	785	764	119
1989	.990	*162	*276	*531	8	*815	807	*119
1990	+.996	*161	242	435	+3	680	677	94
1991	*.986	*162	*267	*528	11	*806	*795	*114
1992	.984	*162	*287	445	12	744	732	*119
1993	.977	*162	226	*495	17	*738	*721	101
1994	.985	112	132	321	7	460	453	72
Totals	.979	1997	3215	6101	204	9520	9316	1356

*Led American League; +American League Record

500 CONSECUTIVE GAMES PLAYED (33)* AS OF THE END OF THE 1994 SEASON	
PLAYER	GAMES
H. LOUIS GEHRIG	2130
CALVIN E. RIPKEN	2009
L. EVERETT SCOTT	1307
STEVEN P. GARVEY	1207
BILLY L. WILLIAMS	1117
JOSEPH W. SEWELL	1103
STANLEY F. MUSIAL	895
EDWARD F. YOST	829
AUGUSTUS R. SUHR	822
J. NELSON FOX	798
*PETER E. ROSE	745
DALE A. MURPHY	740
RICHIE ASHBURN	730

*Only players with two streaks.

PLAYER	GAMES
ERNEST BANKS	717
*PETER E. ROSE	678
H. EARL AVERILL	673
FRANK A. MCCORMICK	652
SANTOS C. ALOMAR	648
EDWARD W. BROWN	618
ROY D. MCMILLAN	585
GEORGE B. PINCKNEY	577
WALTER S. BRODIE	574
AARON L. WARD	565
GEORGE J. LACHANCE	540
JOHN F. FREEMAN	535
FRED W. LUDERUS	533
J. CLYDE MILAN	511
*CHARLES L. GEHRINGER	511
VADA E. PINSON	508
JOSEPH CARTER	507
ANTHONY F. CUCCINELLO	504
*CHARLES L. GEHRINGER	504
OMAR R. MORENO	503

*Only players with two streaks.